THE RAVEN KING

MARCUS TANNER

THE

RAVEN KING

*Matthias Corvinus
and the Fate of his Lost Library*

YALE UNIVERSITY PRESS
NEW HAVEN AND LONDON

Copyright © 2008 Marcus Tanner

The right of Marcus Tanner to be identified as Proprietor of this work has been asserted by him in accordance with the Copyright, Designs and Patents Act 1988.

All rights reserved. This book may not be reproduced in whole or in part, in any form (beyond that copying permitted by Sections 107 and 108 of the U.S. Copyright Law and except by reviewers for the public press) without written permission from the publishers.

For information about this and other Yale University Press publications, please contact:

U.S. Office: sales.press@yale.edu www.yalebooks.com
Europe Office: sales@yaleup.co.uk www.yaleup.co.uk

Set in Sabon MT by SX Composing DTP, Rayleigh, Essex
Printed in Great Britain by St Edmundsbury Press Ltd, Bury St Edmunds

Library of Congress Cataloging-in-Publication Data

Tanner, Marcus
  The Raven king: matthias corvinus and the fate of his lost library/Marcus Tanner.
  p. cm.
  Includes bibliographical references and index.
  ISBN 978–0–300–12034–9 (alk.paper)
  1. Matthias I, King of Hungary, 1443–1490. 2. Matthias I, King of Hungary,
  1443–1490—Library. 3. Hungary—Kings and rulers—Biography.
  4. Hungary—History—Matthias I, 1458–1490. I. Title.
  DB931.T36 2008
  943.9'03092—de22
  [B]
                                                                        2007032188

10 9 8 7 6 5 4 3 2 1

Contents

Illustrations

Acknowledgements

I would like to acknowledge the help offered by all the libraries I visited in connection with this book, including the Rare Books and Manuscript Room staff at the British Library for showing me the two Corvinas in their collection, the staff of the Bibliothèque Royale de Belgique in Brussels who kindly allowed me to look at the Attavante missal even though I had forgotten to bring any of the right accreditation with me, Ed Steen for his help in Brussels, Lourdes Alonso de Viana of the manuscript section of the Biblioteca Nacional in Madrid who showed me the library's copy of the De Conchis manuscript, the staff of Chetham's Library in Manchester for showing me their copy of the *Noctes Atticae*, Susan Reynolds of Holkham Hall library in Norfolk for showing me the gospel lectionary, the *Evangelistarium secundum*, and for sharing information about its provenance, Angela Dillon Bussi for discussing her findings in the Biblioteca Medicea Laurenziana, and Orsolya Karsay of the National Library in Budapest, the Orszagos Szechenyi Konyvtar, in Budapest, for agreeing to see me at the start of my project. I would also like to thank Ugo Grazioli for his work in translating several Italian essays on the Corvinian library for me, Anna Meller for translating Hungarian newspapers and essays while I was in Budapest, Simon Jones for translating Naldi and Bonfini for me from Latin, Peter Sherwood for attempting to teach me some Hungarian in London, and Victoria Clark for reading through the manuscript and making useful suggestions and corrections. Finally I want to thank my agent, Natasha Fairweather, for first putting this idea into my head and Robert Baldock of Yale University Press for enabling me to bring it to fruition.

Preface

In the summer of 2006 I visited the Bibliothèque Royale de Belgique in search of a magnificent missal. It had once been the possession of Matthias Corvinus, the fifteenth-century King of Hungary so named after the raven that adorned his royal coat of arms and that he adopted as his chief emblem. Illuminated in Florence in 1485, the manuscript reached Brussels about half a century later in the baggage of Mary of Hungary, the last Queen of Hungary before the Ottoman invasion of 1526.

After her husband, Louis II, had perished at the hands of the Ottomans at the Battle of Mohacs on 29 August 1526, the Hungarian chronicler Gyorgy Szeremi wrote that Mary waited only hours after hearing the news before collecting some belongings and riding out of the Logod Gate on 1 September by torchlight.

Mary had had no time to pack up the magnificent library which Louis's predecessor-but-one, Matthias Corvinus, had assembled towards the end of the previous century and which had been the wonder of the age. But the beautiful missal, richly illuminated by the Florentine artist Attavanti degli Attavante was dear to her. Under chaotic conditions, she gathered the missal up with a handful of other volumes and took them into exile in the Low Countries. There the missal remains.

I had not truly expected to see this book because I had not written to the director beforehand, and I had brought no references. On discovering that, the librarian let out a Gallic-sounding 'oof', pulled a long face and rolled her eyes. But I was in luck. Within minutes, the manuscript was in front of me, larger than I had imagined, and I was left alone to luxuriate in the vivid illuminations of Matthias and his Italian queen, Beatrice of Naples. To my naked eye Attavante's work had a luminous quality and a texture that no photograph had ever conveyed.

Looking at these exquisite depictions of the King's ugly, powerful features alongside those of his pudgy, spoiled consort – Matthias dressed in the blue of an emperor and Queen Beatrice in the red of suffering and passion, one of the principal colours of the Virgin, both kneeling before the crucified Christ – I felt a sudden sense of the immediacy of the royal couple.

By the time I got to Brussels, I had pursued Matthias's legacy for more than two years. I had peered at some of the illuminated books from his once famous library, whose disappearance and mysterious fate after the Ottoman invasion had tantalised generations of scholars and treasure hunters. I had tacked back and forth between Hungary, Austria, Transylvania and Slovakia, hoping visits to the scenes of his birthplace, childhood and reign might offer up new clues about the character of the great potentate.

Matthias had stamped his image on his era. Extensive foreign conquests meant that by the end of his reign he ruled a European superpower – a state large enough, so it then seemed, to form a mighty dam against the expansionist designs of the Muslim Ottomans. His fame among his contemporaries rested on other achievements, too. In Buda Matthias had presided over an intellectually brilliant court. The arts, science and culture of Renaissance Italy, of Florence in particular, found a more appreciative audience in the Hungarian capital than anywhere else outside Italy. The royal library, perhaps numbering 2,500 Greek and Latin volumes and about 6,000 works (for volumes often contained several works), was one of the great libraries of the known world. Even if one included Italy, probably only the papal library in Rome outclassed it in size. Assembled at a tremendous speed in the 1480s, it was a monument to Matthias's inexhaustible appetite for knowledge, as well as to his magnificence. No wonder the humanists, as the devotees of the Renaissance subsequently became known, united in a chorus of praise, hailing the long-awaited successor to Hercules, or Caesar – the ultimate philosopher-king.

But revisiting the sites of his triumphs had evoked disappointingly little. I began my search in Romania, because it was there that Matyas Hunyadi, to give him his Hungarian name, was born and grew up, Transylvania, the land 'beyond the forest', having then formed a part of Hungary.

Hungary was not then the small, flat, landlocked state we know today. Approximately four times the size of the present republic, its northern frontier was the high ridge of the Tatra mountains of what is now Slovakia. To the south it stretched across what is now the flat and monotonous Serbian province of Vojvodina all the way to Belgrade. To the south-east, it embraced the undulating hills and forests of Transylvania, which the Hungarians call Erdely. The union of the crowns of Hungary and Croatia in the early 1100s,[1] meanwhile, drew in the Croat lands of Slavonia and Dalmatia, too, making the kings of Hungary lords of the Adriatic.

After the victors in the First World War broke up the Austro-Hungarian Empire, this thousand-year-old kingdom disappeared. After Romania assumed control of Transylvania, the new authorities in Bucharest aggressively promoted the region's exclusively Romanian identity, decrying or ignoring its ancient connection to Hungary. In Matthias's birthplace of Cluj, or Kolozsvar in Hungarian, although the old Hunyadi family house still stands in a side-street a short distance from the medieval parish church of St Michael, I found many Romanians still hostile to the memory of the town's greatest son.

This attitude of ambivalence, or dislike, centres on the monumental equestrian statue of Matthias dominating the main square. The work of the Hungarian sculptor Janos Fadrusz, it was unveiled amid popular rejoicing in 1902, when Cluj was very much Kolozsvar. But it became the object of a tussle in the 1990s, when the Romanian nationalist mayor of Cluj[2] virtually laid siege to the statue, surrounding the plinth with deep archaeological excavations that undermined its foundations and gave it a very forlorn appearance. In case anyone should miss the point that Cluj was now Romanian, the mayor had the nearby park benches and even pavements painted in the national colours of red, yellow and blue.

This hostility was – and is – inappropriate. Matthias belongs to the Romanians almost as much as to Hungarians. His ancestors were not ethnic Hungarians, or Magyars. They came from Wallachia, the land to the south of Transylvania which – along with Moldavia – formed the core of the modern state of Romania. Some Romanian historians acknowledge this freely and have even acclaimed Matthias as a Romanian hero. But this enlightened attitude has never won over the Romanian nationalists who remain suspicious of all monuments to Hungarian kings, viewing them as rallying points for Transylvania's discontented Hungarian minority.

At Hunedoara, Vajdahunyad in Hungarian, where Matthias grew up, the Romanian authorities have maintained the Hunyadi family castle less grudgingly. But the late communist dictator, Nicolae Ceausescu, took a none too subtle revenge on the memory of Matthias here as well. Perhaps to stop it from becoming a Hungarian shrine, he had the Gothic turrets and battlements – most of them, admittedly, the work of restorers in the 1860s[3]

– ringed with iron and steel factories. Most have long since closed and rusted away, their principal legacy being the layer of ash and dust that covers the roofs of the town, giving it its peculiarly grey pallor. But the view from the castle remains dismal and is enough to dissuade all but determined visitors. Moreover, Romania's wariness about Matthias's memory means that references to the great monarch inside the castle are surprisingly scant. While wandering the draughty halls, I found some rooms had been given over to sales of tourist tat and another to an exhibition of waxworks. In the latter, one model was a likeness of Osama Bin Laden and another was of the late Princess of Wales. It was interesting to chance on this reminder of 'Lady Di's' iconic status, even in Romania, but I wondered why her memory took precedence over that of Matthias in this of all places.

In Hungary, the hunt for relics of Matthias threw up different problems. There was no hostility there to his memory. On the contrary, the cult of the Hunyadis has always enjoyed official patronage. Even the Hungarian communist regime gave a nod to it. In Budapest, the words Corvin or Corvinus are casually attached to almost anything of cultural significance, from bookshops to publishing houses. Budapest's Corvin cinema was the site of some of the fiercest fighting in the 1956 uprising against the Soviet Union. Images of Matthias pepper the city, from the vast, bronze statue of Matthias out hunting, situated in Buda's castle district, to the copy of the enthroned image of the King sitting in the niche of the wall beside the Hilton hotel. Nearby, the so-called 'Matthias' church recalls the site of his two weddings. The National Gallery, also in Buda's castle district, contains numerous paintings of Matthias, mostly fanciful renditions by nineteenth-century artists. Over the river in Pest, there are fewer mementoes. But visitors ascending the grand staircase of the imposing National Museum can hardly fail to miss the portrait of Matthias surrounded by his scientists, which forms part of an epic frieze of Hungarian history running around the ceiling.

Yet the search for echoes of the 'real' Matthias was as hard in Hungary as it had been in Romania. Indeed, physical relics of the period are more plentiful in Romania, for the simple reason that the Ottomans occupied most of modern Hungary for a century and a half whereas they left Transylvania alone as a vassal state. That is why the Hunyadi home stands in Cluj, the castle remains in Hunedoara and why the tomb of Matthias's father, Janos Hunyadi, lies undisturbed in the cathedral of the former capital of Transylvania at Alba Iulia, or Gyulafehervar.

In Hungary, there is no trace of Matthias's own tomb at the coronation town of Szekesfehervar. The Ottomans destroyed it, along with virtually everything else that he built. In Budapest, the buildings that appear to predate the eighteenth century are imaginative reconstructions and exercises in make-believe. The Matthias church, outside which so many coach parties are deposited, is a piece of late nineteenth-century Gothic whimsy, the work of the architect Frigyes Schulek, who replaced virtually every single stone. The bronze statue of Matthias in Buda castle by Alajos Stobl and most of the paintings in the National Gallery are even purer inventions. Looking at the painting *Matthias Returning from the Hunt*, which showed the stout, dark-haired King as a blond Apollo, I sympathised with the desire of the nineteenth-century artist to conjure up a lost golden age by giving Matthias looks he never possessed. But I did not feel these representations brought me any closer to the historical personage. Nor did peering at the books from his library in Hungary's National Library. Neatly laid out under glass panels, these revered objects were hard to connect with the busy working library of Matthias's lifetime, when it was alive with the bustle of the King, the Queen, the librarians and a throng of Italian, German and Croatian scholars, architects and astronomers.

If I discerned Matthias with such difficulty in Hungary it was because no amount of devotion to his memory could make up for the simple fact that his physical legacy had been wiped out. The extent to which the Ottomans made a *tabula rasa* of their Hungarian fief is almost inconceivable to us in Western Europe. The landscape of England, for example, remains studded with architectural testimonies to the past glories of its monarchs. The reign of the first Tudor, Henry VII, partly overlapped with the reign of Matthias.[4] But while Henry built on a modest scale compared to Matthias, England still has the magnificent chapel he completed in Cambridge at King's College and the fan-vaulted Lady Chapel in Westminster Abbey.

No similar monuments survive in Hungary to bear witness to Matthias's much grander designs. Of the palaces and churches he built or reconstructed, only shards and fragments remain – a tile here, an arm of a statue or a broken fountain there.

The annihilation of his achievements occurred within years of his death from a stroke in Vienna in 1490. From being a great power, Hungary dwindled rapidly, becoming a bewildered pawn of the Habsburg emperors and the Ottoman sultans. Crushed with overwhelming force by Suleiman the Magnificent at Mohacs, most of the country was fully incorporated into the Ottoman Empire a few years later, in 1541. History affords very few examples of powerful states that have collapsed at quite such a speed.

Within months of his death, Matthias's conquests in Austria, Moravia and Silesia had been reversed. Within years, his domestic reforms, which aimed to check the predatory instincts of the nobles, had been pushed aside. Within decades, Hungary reaped the consequences at Mohacs, when the Ottomans overran a demoralised country with pathetic ease.

A century and a half after Mohacs, when the Habsburg Emperor, Leopold I, 'liberated' Hungary from Ottoman rule, the old kingdom was restored to life, albeit as a subordinate and often mutinous unit within the Austrian Empire. But Matthias's churches and palaces had been razed by then; they had burned to the ground, as in Buda, or crumbled as a result of continual fighting between the Austrians and Ottomans, as at the summer palace in Visegrad. The gap between what admiring visitors insisted they had seen in Matthias's lifetime and what remained was vast. It inspired incredulity. Had they dreamed it all?

To be sure, contemporary writers were not journalists. Eager to parade their knowledge of Greek and Roman culture, they harmonised their accounts to match the words of well-known classics. To a modern ear, their constant allegories, puns and mechanical praises are grating. We want to know facts. Why didn't any of the admiring visitors to Matthias's library count the books, rather than comparing the collection to 'the bosom of Jove'? The humanists praised people they had never met and places they had never seen. The Florentine Naldo Naldi eulogised Matthias's 'august' library in a poem in the mid-1480s without leaving Florence – the few details in his description probably drawn from what Matthias's librarian, Taddeo Ugoleto, confided to him during a mission to Italy.

Such blurred but intriguing accounts were partly to blame for the tropical jungle of legends that grew up around the library. In the centuries that followed Matthias's death, the royal library grew and grew. Figures of 30,000 or even 50,000 volumes were liberally bandied about – which, had they been remotely accurate, would have meant the collection dwarfed the huge papal library many times over.

The legends surrounding the Bibliotheca Corviniana, as it now came to be called, spurred kings, princes of the Church, aristocratic collectors and rich bankers on in a frantic hunt for items from the collection in the book markets of Constantinople and Venice. The surviving manuscripts were always sought after. Many were genuine works of art, fine creations of the workshops of quattrocento Florence. And many were easily identifiable, owing to the tiny blue raven perched on the royal coat of arms of the frontispieces.

The idea that such a massive and valuable collection of books was still 'out there' somewhere, hidden in the damp and smoky ruins of Matthias's castle in Buda, or locked away in the dark vaults of the palace of the Seraglio in Constantinople, teased and tortured the imaginations of collectors well into the seventeenth century. After the Austrian conquest of Buda in 1686, their interest switched once more to Constantinople. This became the destination of a new generation of book-hunters, this time mainly Hungarians, seized by the notion that the return of Matthias's library from Constantinople and its restoration in Budapest would almost mystically seal their country's resurrection.

The campaign to bring home the Corvinus manuscripts from Constantinople, which gripped Hungary in the 1860s and 1870s, had its madder aspects and the descriptions of the vast crowds and processions that attended the return in 1877 of a few dozen codices seem bizarre today.

In fact, their return dispelled much of the magic that had surrounded the myth of the lost library. Once even a portion of the manuscripts was back in Hungary, professional scholars could realistically assess the library's original dimensions, and to the shock and dismay of many, they broke the news that many of Matthias's books were not works of genius but poor, hastily executed copies, full of mistakes. This work of sober reassessment continued in the twentieth century, especially under Csaba Csapodi, whose *Corvinian Library, History and Stock* and *Bibliotheca Corviniana* became definitive studies.

There was a handful of losses in the twentieth century as a result of the Second World War, especially the tragic destruction of the Homilies of Chrysostom, in Warsaw in 1944,[5] and the virtual destruction of a copy of Cicero's letters as a result of the bombing of Dresden. At the same time, there have been new discoveries of forgotten 'Corvinas' in the Medicea Laurenziana library in Florence. In Britain, too, a single magnificent volume complete with a raven on the front, the *Noctes Atticae*, turned up in Manchester in the 1960s. The hunt for the library now seems well and truly over. It is just possible that another volume embellished with a tiny but eye-catching raven motif may turn up somewhere, having lain hidden in some private collection, but with every passing year it becomes less likely. Instead, scholastic interest has become absorbed in exploring the library's function within the context of Renaissance ideas of princely power and legitimacy.

While academics and art historians debate the library's role in its contemporary context, Matthias is remembered on a popular level in different terms. He is the star of numerous folk tales; the timeless 'just' king, rescuing distressed maidens from cads and delivering on-the-spot justice on behalf of aggrieved peasants at the expense of bad barons. This cult is still widespread, stretching far beyond modern Hungary and throughout old kingdoms in what are now Croatia, Slovenia and Slovakia.

In the English-speaking world, on the other hand, Matthias is little known. Csapodi's works on the library were translated in the 1960s and 1970s but little has ever appeared in English about the personalities of Matthias or his charismatic consort, Beatrice. English-language readers are only dimly aware of the titan who bestrode the map of fifteenth-century Europe. This gap and the lack of books in English that place the story of the library in the context of the King's private life is my main justification for attempting this work. I am not an art historian and cannot claim to reveal anything exceptional about the extant illuminated Corvinas. But by looking again at the contemporary Latin sources on the library and the life of the King, by comparing them to a wealth of more recent material in Italian, French, German and Hungarian, and by visiting the lands and sites associated with his reign, I have tried to bring to life to a contemporary audience the story of a great King and his inspiring cultural project.

If the tone of this book seems suffused with the message 'vive le roi' I plead guilty, in part. I do not deny that like Matthias's first pope, Calixtus III, I find the story of a teenage commoner who passed from prison cell to throne very compelling. Calixtus saw Matthias's progress as literally miraculous – as evidence that the hand of God was as active in fifteenth-century Europe as it had been in the Old and New Testament. Today we may not choose to see a divine hand in these events but the story retains an epic character. The fact that the boy who seized a crown then reigned in splendour for more than thirty years, transforming his country into a superpower and sponsoring a tremendous cultural awakening, adds to the story's appeal.

Matthias was no wooden hero. Though so much about his life has disappeared irrevocably from view, there is enough to reveal a rounded human being. Compared to the grim and miserly Henry VII, Matthias's sinister father-in-law, Ferdinand, or Ferrante, of Naples, or some of the other contemporary European monarchs, his humanity and sense of humour stand out. A loving father to his only son, John, he was a patient husband to his difficult second wife. In an age characterised by a climate of religious bigotry – the expulsion of the Jews from Spain took place a few years after his death – he stood out for religious tolerance. Brought up in the anti-Semitic culture of the friars, he became a benefactor of the Jews as an adult. It was another example of how he constantly exceeded and transcended his background.

He had his foibles. A man who appoints a seven-year-old foreigner as an archbishop cannot avoid the charge of displaying a cynical attitude to religion. His claim that he attacked Bohemia on behalf of the injured Catholics there was almost laughable. In both Bohemia and Austria, the conduct of his mercenary 'Black Army' was gruesome. The old-fashioned Hungarian historians were over-generous in their assessments of Matthias's motives in his expansionist wars. They insisted his great aim was to create a state large enough to withstand a future Ottoman attack. That was true enough, but he also waged war for his own glory and to make himself a power in Germany. It must also be acknowledged that his cultural and military projects bankrupted the country and so propelled Hungary towards the catastrophes that followed his death.

Then there are question marks over the Renaissance he planted in Hungary. It has often been pointed out that enthusiasm for the new learning never extended far beyond the famous bronze doors of Matthias's palatial castle in Buda. The nobility remained strangers not only to the glories of the ancient classic writings but to the skill of writing at all. When one recalls that even the great officers of state were unable to sign their own names to an international treaty, the Treaty of Pressburg, in 1491, it has to be conceded that the Renaissance in Hungary was an elite undertaking with a limited appeal. It is a melancholy fact that the brilliance of Matthias's court depended on the presence of a great number of foreigners. To an extent, native Hungarians became virtual spectators at their own court, and jealous ones at that.

Matthias failed to create the institutions that would carry on his work of scientific and literary renewal and creativity after he had left the stage. Where, after several decades on the throne, was the great university to rival the fourteenth-century foundations of Cracow and Prague? After the King's great helpmate and mentor, Archbishop Vitez, laboured to found a university in Bratislava, the Academia Istropolitana, Matthias allowed it to languish after the Archbishop's death in 1472.

Why this should have been so is, I have suggested, because Matthias was principally an enabler. His genius lay in his willingness to let others express *their* genius. In partnership with his amanuensis, Vitez, with Vitez's tortured but brilliant nephew, Ivan Cesmicki, alias Janus Pannonius, with his Italian librarian Taddeo Ugoleto and with a crowd of Italian artists he never met, great things happened. When he was left alone, matters tended to drift.

The Renaissance towards which each of them contributed never grew deep roots. But an abiding popular attachment throughout Central Europe to Matthias's memory is a sign that the King's Herculean efforts to make his mark on the world were not completely wasted. As for his bright jewel, the library, this, too, fulfilled some of its original promise. If one of its purposes was to guarantee its founder immortality in the form of perpetual fame, it succeeded in doing so. The huge crowds that attended the exhibition of his books held in Budapest on the 500th anniversary of his death in 1990 proved that. So does the great project to unite all the remaining codices around the world in digital form. Begun in 2001 by Hungary's National Szechenyi Library in 2001 and supported by Unesco, this attempt to reunite the scattered library under one roof in cyberspace, through the means of modern technology, is being followed with enormous interest. Matthias, who was fascinated by modern inventions, would be absolutely delighted.

Whether across the chasm of the centuries his reign has other lessons to teach us is an interesting question. Matthias wore a crown at a time when Europe was struggling, none too successfully, to reach an accommodation with, and an understanding of, the resurgent force of Islam as represented by the Ottoman Empire.

After abandoning his family's crusading tradition, Matthias came to the conclusion – to the distress of several consecutive popes – that there was no alternative to reaching a *détente* with the Ottoman Turks. The fall of Constantinople in 1453, which had occurred when he was ten, had permanently changed the balance of power in Europe and the Near East, and Matthias implicitly accepted that it was no longer practical, as it had been in his father's day, to dream of expelling the Turks from Europe altogether.

Instead, he was determined to contain the Ottomans to the Balkans and speak with the sultans from a position of strength. At the same time, he clearly believed Europe could only overcome the great strategic challenge it faced from the east if it was culturally as well as militarily confident. The battle of ideas interested him as much as the clash of arms. His faith in knowledge, incarnated in the creation of the royal library, informed his faith in a Europe without intellectual frontiers. It also made him an honorary Italian in an age when Italy stood for all that was most progressive and exciting in the arts and sciences. Uninterested in genealogy, ancient rituals and history for its own sake, he appreciated history primarily for what it could teach him about his own time. In an era of soul-searching about Europe's identity and the challenge of fundamentalist Islam, a time marked by fearful calls for a retreat into cultural and religious conservatism, the great adventure that was the life of the raven king – as well as the sad, subsequent fate of his achievements – provides thought-provoking parallels.

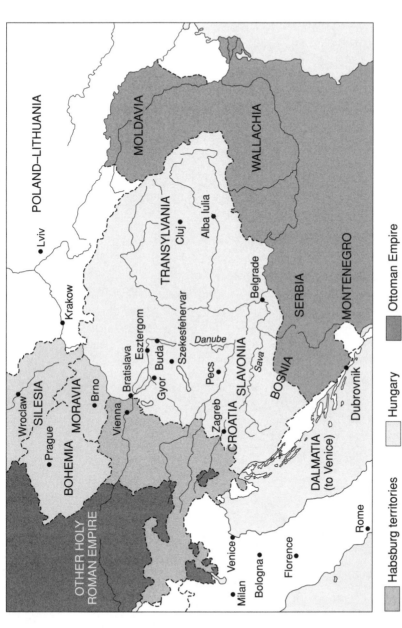

Hungary in the fifteenth century

Habsburg territories — Hungary — Ottoman Empire

CHAPTER ONE

'Deep inside the palace'

God who has appointed the sun in the heavens as king of the sky and stars also appointed under the sun Matthias alone.

Marsilio Ficino of Florence[1]

It was the fig that killed him. The ceremonies of Palm Sunday, 1490, had already exhausted him. Unable to walk the few yards from his palace to St Stephen's cathedral in the centre of Vienna, unable even to risk trying to get there on a litter, Matthias struggled no further than a purpose-built wooden chapel, which he had erected in the courtyard and where he knighted the Venetian ambassador.

Matthias knew he was almost finished and that at 47 his once muscular body, never a thing of beauty but strong and sturdy, had become a wreck, his health shattered by years spent in the saddle in all climates on the battlefields of Bosnia, Croatia, Moldavia, Transylvania, Bohemia, Silesia and finally Austria. That was not to mention the toll on his constitution taken by drinking and carousing.

Now, although at the peak of his power, having driven the Habsburg Emperor, Frederick III, from Vienna itself, as humanists and men of letters acclaimed the new Mars, Hercules or Attila, he felt death's hand on his shoulder.

It had only made him hurry faster. The negotiations aimed at securing the succession of his illegitimate son, John Corvin, had taken on a frantic aspect in recent months. Matthias had traversed the realm, assembling nobles and prelates and bullying them into swearing oaths of loyalty to the diffident teenager. He had arranged a suitable marriage for his son with Bianca Sforza, niece of the ruler of Milan, Lodovico Il Moro, 'the Moor'.[2] The need to settle John's succession before his health collapsed had even forced him to contemplate returning all his recent Austrian conquests to his Habsburg enemies, including Vienna. They would not go to Frederick, whom he despised, but to the Emperor's son, Maximilian.

Then there was the library, the King's trophy and sanctuary. Here, Naldo Naldi wrote, sunbeams poured through high, stained-glass windows, casting curious patterns on the vaulted ceilings. Beneath tall lancet windows, light fell on to the King's couch, a 'bed with golden coverings on which the royal hero is often wont to snatch some peaceful rest for his limbs'.[3] Here the King reclined, scrutinising a recently purchased illuminated manuscript, or chairing a debate between rival clerics or philosophers. Naldi continued:

> *Deep inside the palace stands a square hall*
> *Bold arches from the vaulted roof descend*
> *On walls of rock, hewn stones and tiles*
> *Two windows tall admit the noontide sun*
> *The gleaming, coloured glass with pictures strewn*
> *All marvel who behold their perfect art ...*[4]

In the library, light also fell on to jewel-encrusted veils, set in place to shield the most expensive and cherished items of the collection from the bleaching sunlight. These books did not lie stacked upon one another in heavy chests like the majority of volumes. They stood upright on snakeskin tripods, waiting for the hand of the King, Queen, or the librarians, to part the curtain and reveal the liquid colours beneath.

According to Naldi, the curious bookrests attracted particular interest 'because the spotted skin of a snake covered those tripods and a shining gold-covered cloth covered them, adorned with so many heavy gems and sparkling precious stones that you would think Matthias had accumulated whatever the kings of Persia are thought to have possessed'.[5] The Florentine likened the care lavished on these exotic tripods to Matthias's reverence for the goddess of wisdom, for it was the tripods that 'receive the greatest authors' and wisdom itself that 'opens the books that ought to be read, which the ancient ones composed, and which taught what wisdom was'.[6]

For five years, ever since Matthias, his Queen, Beatrice and his son, John, had entered Vienna in triumph, his passion to create the greatest library in

Europe had grown. It was to become a repository of all known knowledge, a lasting monument to his wisdom, liberality and magnificence, proof that he rivalled the emperors of Rome in stature. This was his passport to immortality.

The mania for collecting had set in quite slowly. Unlike his soldier father, Janos Matthias had been well educated in the family's remote castle in Transylvania. But for the first half of his reign, he was too preoccupied with wars and conquests to devote much time to collecting. In those years, he collected books simply by being on the receiving end of a stream of unsolicited works, which foreign, mainly Italian, humanists, dedicated to him. He did not need to seek dedications; the extraordinary circumstances of his early life – and an early reputation for financial generosity – had long ago seized the imaginations of ambitious Italian writers. They saw the position of King of Hungary as heroic in itself. Following the example of Enea Silvio Piccolomini, later Pope Pius II, they viewed Hungary as a shield defending their soft, vulnerable land from the blade of the advancing Ottomans.

The battles waged against the Ottoman Turks by Matthias's father had thrilled the Italians, who warmed to the theme of a noble barbarian race fighting far away to keep their own homeland safe. As the Ferrara humanist, Ludovico Carbone, recalled in the 1470s in a fawning 'dialogue' in praise of Matthias, 'When I was a boy there was nothing more famous than the name of Janos [Hunyadi] and his glorious victories over the Turks were frequently proclaimed.'[7]

Piccolomini, meanwhile, put Hungary on the mental map of educated Italians through his 1458 work, *De Europa*. He was passionately concerned with the strategic importance of Hungary, the lonely guardian of Europe's eastern marches. As he had once put it in 1443, he was 'concerned for the security of the Christian faith, which I know cannot be secured unless her rampart, Hungary, is unharmed'.[8] Poggio Bracciolini, the famous hunter for lost classical works, wrote to Hunyadi offering to write his biography, having been inspired by his Latin translation of Xenophon's life of the Persian general, Cyrus.[9]

Italy in the fifteenth century may have been divided into a multitude of quarrelsome tiny states but Italians rejoiced as one over the news of Hunyadi's great victory against the Ottomans at Belgrade in 1456. In Venice, the celebrations had been spectacular. In Bologna, the festivities lasted for three days and the heads of St Petronius and St Dominic and the hand of St Cecilia were borne in triumphant procession through the streets. In Rome, Calixtus III ordered bonfires and peals of bells. The Milanese ambassador reported that the Pope was 'so full of the great victory that he constantly reverted to it. He praised Hunyadi to the skies calling him the greatest man the world had seen for three hundred years'.[10]

Matthias inherited his father's fame and during his long reign from 1458 to 1490 exceeded the expectations Hunyadi had raised. From the start, the children of the Renaissance saw Matthias as a man who to a peculiar and unusual degree viewed the world through their eyes. He was their most important royal ally, and would deliver their dream of a great cultural reawakening in Europe that was to be achieved through the restoration of the peerless civilisations of Greece and Rome.

It helped, of course, that he rewarded writers who attracted his attention with their poems and eulogies. When the Florentine Bartolomeo Fonte wrote to Matthias to tell him that Florence was 'inflamed with an incredible love for Your Majesty', after Matthias's librarian, Taddeo Ugoleto, had addressed the city on the theme of his generosity, we can be sure this was the case. Fonte himself soon trod the well-worn path to Buda to see if the reports were true.

Economical princes who failed to reward writers and orators appropriately earned dismal reputations. As Sigismondo de Conti warned Sixtus IV, 'the wound of a dagger was less to be feared than a satirical pen'.[11] Sixtus hardly needed such advice; nor did Matthias, who well understood the significance of opinion-formers.

No wonder that writers competed to list and describe Matthias's virtues – at length. The Florentine, Marsilio Ficino, was among the most important Italian admirers. An intimate of Matthias's rival as collector and librarian, Lorenzo de Medici, Ficino showered praise on the sovereign of distant Hungary.[12]

Ficino was the great propagator of the cult of Plato in Florence, devoting his life to translating his works, and somehow combining near-worship for Plato with the orthodox Christian faith of a Catholic priest. In Ficino's eyes, Matthias embodied the Platonic ideal of the philosopher-king who united martial and moral excellence, displaying the virtues of justice, wisdom, temperance, fortitude and clemency. Delighted by the warm reception in Buda of his occasionally controversial translations, some of which offended traditional Christian thinking, Ficino praised Matthias over many years in his letters and book dedications. He was 'the invincible King of Hungary' and a 'victorious Hercules' whose 'lofty palace' in Buda had been transformed into 'the very temple of the graces'.[13] 'God who has appointed the sun in the heavens as king of the sky and stars also appointed under the sun Matthias alone who should set the oceans as the shores of his sway and the stars as the limits of his glory.'[14]

For the first two decades of his reign, Matthias simply collected these flattering dedications, which were dispatched to his realm or presented to his ambassadors on their visits to Italy.

The dynamics of his collection only changed later when, with the help of librarians, he began actively to commission works himself. Most came from Florence, the city at the heart of the Renaissance and by the 1460s the centre of the book trade. Only Florence possessed the resources to supply copiers, illuminators and bookbinders in one place, their work taking place in dozens of shops that crowded the narrow lanes lying between the cathedral and the old abbey, the Badia.

In the last five years of Matthias's reign, the steady trickle of books entering his library turned into a flood as Matthias felt time was running out to assemble all the knowledge of the ancient world under one roof. The list of works that needed to be bought, copied and accommodated grew constantly, for the boundaries of what constituted necessary knowledge were shifting. Where was he to stop? He had to find room in the high-vaulted chamber firstly for the Latin greats, meaning the comedies of Terence, the tragedies of Seneca, Caesar's war histories, the letters of Cicero, the epigrams of Martial – so inspirational to Matthias's protégé, Janus Pannonius – and the works of Livy, Aurus Gellius, Quintilian, Catullus and many others. But Matthias had grown increasingly interested in the more recently rediscovered Greek works, too. Indeed, it appears he set aside a separate chamber for the Greeks – Sophocles, Euripides, Aristotle, Ficino's beloved Plato and others.

Like most admirers of the Renaissance, Matthias believed the culture of Greece and Rome represented the pinnacle of human endeavour. But he could not shut out the best writings of the inferior centuries that followed the fall of Rome. He had to make room in the chests, if not on the snakeskin tripods, for the greatest Byzantine and Greek histories like Agathias's *De bello Gothorum*, 'On the Gothic War', and the *Ekklésiastiké historia*, the 'Ecclesiastical History', of Niképhoros Kallistos. There was an honoured place for the speculative theological works of the early Church Fathers, too, such as Origen, Tertullian, Ambrose, Jerome, Chrysostom, Cyril and Augustine.

There were occasional Arab works. Astrology was the King's obsession and it was Arab writers who had translated and so preserved the works of the great Greek astronomer and geographer Ptolemy of Alexandria,[15] whose writings formed the most important texts on the subject until Copernicus revolutionised people's understanding of the universe in the sixteenth century.

As well as more recent translations of Ptolemy's *Geographiae* and the *Almagest,* the tenth-century commentary by Ali Abu Hassan ibn Radwan on Ptolemy's astrological 'bible', the *Quadripartitum*[16] was a prized item in the collection. It was not only the magnificence of the manuscript which shows the King valued this work but its age, for Matthias rarely collected books that had been copied long ago, and the *Quadripartitum* had been copied and illuminated in Prague years before his birth, around 1400.

There was the question of what to do with works written in more recent centuries. Matthias did not want to ignore the seventh/eighth-century English churchman, Bede, whose *De natura rerum,* 'On the Nature of Things', found its niche in the library. More recent still were the works of the eleventh-century philosopher and Archbishop of Canterbury Anselm and those of the systematic theologians of the twelfth and thirteenth centuries, Peter Lombard and Thomas Aquinas. The fathers of the Italian Renaissance had to be included, starting with Dante and Petrarch.

Finally, the letters and works of the most admired poets, orators, geographers, astronomers, military strategists and natural historians of his own time had to be accommodated somewhere. This meant devoting more space in the chests and on the tripods to works like Ficino's *Epistolarum ad amicos,* the 'Letters to Friends', the astronomical tables and commentaries on Ptolemy written by Matthias's court astronomer, the German Johannes Müller 'Regiomontanus' and the theological works of the Greek scholar and Catholic convert, Cardinal Johannes Bessarion.

The selection of works from modern times was inevitably the most eclectic of all, reflecting the need to arbitrarily condense a choice of the prolific writings of recent years. It brought together a pot-pourri of histories of the Turks, Hungarians and Italians, such as Thomas Seneca's history of Bologna, the *Historia Bononiensis,* philosophical treatises, and hymns of praise to Matthias's genius, like Naldi's poem, the *Epistola de laudibus augustae bibliothecae,* and to his military feats, like Alexander Cortesius's *De Matthiae Corvini Ungariae regis laudibus bellicis carmen.* Eulogists had to be careful. Matthias was not like Borso d'Este who had his library filled with extravagant and absurd-sounding tributes to himself. The King enjoyed being praised by a man of Ficino's reputation but it was unwise to overstep the mark. He could be very cold to those who delivered idiotic or plainly inaccurate tributes. Ludovico Carbone's slobbering eulogy, for example, *Dialogus de Matthiae regis laudibus,* entered the library in silence. Clearly the tone of the work did not appeal to Matthias for he neither thanked Carbone nor invited him to Hungary.

He valued the celebrated treatise on architecture by Leon Battista Alberti, *De re aedificatoria,* on the other hand. Room was found also for the works of the translator and educational pioneer Guarino Veronese whose humanist academy in Ferrara moulded Janus Pannonius among many others. Guarino was represented in the library by his own work, the *Libellus,* and by the monumental *Geographia,* the work of the first-century BC Greek encyclopaedist Strabo, which he translated into Latin.

The surviving 216 volumes, containing more than 600 works, show that Matthias had the literary tastes of a classic 'alpha male'. It has often been noted that he had a marked preference for secular as opposed to religious works. Indeed, once one subtracts liturgical aids such as bibles, gospels, psalters, missals and breviaries, which in any case belonged in the separate palace chapel library, there are not many books like the *Hours of the Blessed Virgin Mary,* now kept in Melk Abbey, Austria, which can be categorised as devotional works. Even within the broad category of secular works from the library it is easy to spot Matthias's particular enthusiasms: war stories, lives of great rulers, and books about inventions, geography, medicine, natural wonders and the stars.

Hence two surviving copies of the deeds of Alexander the Great by Curtius Rufus, Flavius Arrianus's work on Alexander's expeditions and Silius Italicus's *De secundo bello Punico,* 'On the Second Punic War', a work we know Matthias read and enjoyed, because in a surviving letter of 1471 he thanks the Roman humanist Pomponio Leto for having sent it. Hence also Herodianos's work on the Roman emperors, Appianus's 'Civil Wars of the Romans' and the biography of Cyrus the Great of Persia by the fifth-century BC Greek writer Xenophon, which was translated into Latin as *De institutione Cyri.*

Finally, one should not forget the *De re militari,* 'On the Arts of War', a work by Matthias's Paduan contemporary, Roberto Valturio, two copies of which survive from the library in Jena and Modena. This work dealt with one of Matthias's favourite subjects, recent military inventions, and came complete with descriptions and drawings of such novelties as revolving gun turrets, diving suits and even prototype tanks, as well as advice on the best way to use a pontoon bridge or a siege ladder. The content of Valturio's book, and many others, so obviously dovetailed with the King's known interests that it would be wrong to think of the library purely or even principally as an ornament or demonstration. It was designed to impress outsiders but it was the King's own house of learning, too.

As Matthias's health declined and he became less mobile, he commissioned with mounting speed, as if racing towards a goal that was continuing to elude him. Alas, we cannot know exactly how far he got because no inventory of the stock survives, if it was ever made. On the basis of the 216 volumes usually identified as items from the royal library, experts like Csapodi estimated that these represented about a tenth of the original stock, which is how the figure of 2,000 or 2,500 has been reached. But there is no certainty in this field whatever; it remains an educated guess and some historians have put the probable total well below that figure.

If one does assume that Matthias had collected about 2,200–2,500 Latin and Greek works by 1490, it is clear why the collection was hailed as a behemoth and as a wonder of the age, and why the Latinist Naldi made the 'august library' the keynote and title of his poem in praise of Matthias.

Both royal and university libraries in the mid-fifteenth century were usually modest in size before the invention of printing revolutionised matters in the last decades of the century. As for the great monastic libraries of the early Middle Ages, they were mostly in an advanced state of decay. The library of Matthias's French contemporary, Charles VIII, numbered 130 books. Even the papal library was small until the humanist Tommaso Parentucelli, as Pope Nicholas V, expanded it in the late 1440s. An inventory compiled in 1443 under his predecessor Eugenius IV revealed only 340 volumes.

Most university libraries at the time were unimpressive. The library of Cambridge University was tiny well into the fifteenth century although some of the individual colleges were richly endowed with books. Merton library in Oxford possessed about 500 by 1372,[17] because 'every fellow was expected to leave his books to the college at death or if he entered a monastic order'.[18] Bishop Wayneflete created a great library in Magdalen almost overnight by making a present of 800 books in 1480. But there were far fewer books in most colleges. The libraries of England's ancient cathedrals and monasteries were often meagre. St Paul's cathedral in London had 171 books listed in the 'nova libraria' in 1458. The small size and feeble quality of the stock at Salisbury shocked Bishop Richard Jewel in the 1560s. He told the Archbishop of Canterbury he had 'ransacked our poor Librarie of Sarisburie' and had 'found nothing worthy the findinge saving only one booke'.[19]

There is not much point in judging libraries solely on the basis of size, of course. Contemporaries agreed that Matthias's library merited paeans as much for the quality of the books as the number. Among his contemporaries who were rival collectors, only the popes, Alfonso of Naples and his son Ferrante, Lorenzo de Medici, the Sforza and Visconti dukes of Milan and Federigo de Montefeltro, Duke of Urbino, were thought to have assembled comparable collections.

The Milanese ducal library at Pavia, for example, numbered 988 volumes as early as 1426, though an inventory for the 1450s listed fewer works. After the reign of Nicholas V, the papal collection grew exponentially, numbering more than 3,600 books by the 1480s. Evidently this library was bigger than Matthias's. But it was also a very different library to the King of Hungary's, dominated by ecclesiastical works and patristic literature. Old and New Testaments alone made up 59 volumes while glosses on the scriptures made up another 98.[20]

The Medici libraries and the ducal library in Urbino were more obviously similar in intention to Matthias's collection. The fine quality of the books in Federigo's library, which numbered 700 to 1,100 books, drew especially high praise from the Florentine bookseller Vespasiano da Bisticci, no doubt because he was responsible for supplying half or even two-thirds of them. Like Matthias, the Duke of Urbino was a sensitive and educated man of war. Both men scorned the printed books suddenly coming into fashion as vulgar innovations, greatly preferring manuscripts copied by hand.

Vespasiano played an important role also in the formation or embellishment of the several Medici libraries in Florence, the family's private library, a second library at the Medici villa at Fiesole on the outskirts of Florence and the public library established in the Dominican house of San Marco in the city.

The collections of Matthias and Lorenzo so often duplicated each other as to beg the question of who inspired whom. Given Matthias's love of Florentine work, it was inevitable that two patrons would end up drawing on the same copyists and illuminators. The same Latinists scribbled eulogies to both families, Naldi penning 'in praise of' poems to Matthias, and to Lorenzo's grandfather, Cosimo.

Did Matthias create the greatest library of its time in the whole of Europe, excluding the popes' collection? This is impossible to say, as so many rival collections, as well as his own, were dispersed or altered out of recognition. Matthias's library disappeared into the Sultan's maw in the 1520s. Alfonso and Ferrante's library at Naples was plundered in the 1490s by Charles VIII whose army removed about 1,100 books, which gives a rough idea of its size. The Visconti–Sforza library at Pavia was carried off to Paris a few years later by Charles's successor, Louis XII. Federigo's library in Urbino survived for much longer, until the 1630s, but there is nothing left of it now in the original library building, which has survived.

The speed with which Matthias collected manuscripts in the late 1480s, evidenced by the fact that one-third of all surviving manuscripts date from this period, means it is possible that within a few years he might have outrun his secular rivals and even started gaining on the Pope.

As it was, to assemble a library that *might* have been the greatest of its time, so far from the civilised heart of Europe, was an astonishing feat. This is what set him apart from the dukes of Milan and Urbino, the popes and the Medicis. The Medicis had only to walk yards to view the works of the illuminator Attavante or consult with the book merchant Vespasiano. Matthias faced a different task. Communications between Hungary and Italy took weeks or months. Matthias's wife, Beatrice, spent three months travelling to Buda from Naples in 1476, a hellish-sounding journey from mid-September to early December. The court historian and translator, Antonio Bonfini, said her party never began a day's ride 'unless scouts sent out the previous day had informed them that they could proceed' and while they crossed Croatia 'they saw frequent traces of fires and devastation and . . . even came across the bodies of the slain lying about everywhere, not yet decomposed'.[21] Apart from Turks, highwaymen infested the land route from Italy to Hungary, especially the wooded, hilly region around Zagreb. 'All the roads of this region are the prey of bandits,'[22] one Italian noted as he passed through. When Ficino sent a package of books to Matthias, much to their embarrassment robbers intercepted them.

It was an act of willpower on the part of Matthias to keep up a flow of commissions to writers and artists in Florence and have their expensive and laboriously produced works transported item by item or batch by batch on horseback from Tuscany up to northern Italy, across the northern Adriatic to the port of Senj in Croatia, from there to Zagreb, then to southern

Hungary and finally to Buda. The creation of a great library in Buda in such circumstances was almost a miracle.

The fateful plate of figs consumed in Vienna at Easter 1490 brought all this activity to a halt. Beatrice was to blame. Matthias's headstrong wife had gone out and delayed his lunch. By 1490, Beatrice was no longer the blushing teenager 'to recall in every way Venus in beauty and deportment', as the court historian Antonio Bonfini claimed in his great history of Hungary, *Rerum Ungaricarum decades*.[23] She was now a heavy-set, double-chinned matron with an unfortunate profile, features captured in the white marble relief portrait of her carved in the late 1480s, probably by the Dalmatian sculptor, Ivan Duknovic, also known as Giovanni Dalmata.

If Beatrice was out and about in Vienna it was not surprising. Quick witted and pleasure loving, the Queen probably preferred her sojourns there to life in Buda, let alone to visits to other towns in Hungary, where her indifference to all things Hungarian, starting with the language, had made her disliked. No doubt a princess hailing from the great metropolis of Naples and a granddaughter of Alfonso 'the Magnanimous' saw Buda as a hardship post. The constant flow of letters to her sister, Leonora, Duchess of Ferrara, and her insistence on surrounding herself with Italians reflected her loneliness and yearning for Italy. It was all very well admiring 'the rampart of Christendom' from afar, as Pius II had done. Living there – and getting there – was another matter.

Vienna, a few hours up the Danube by boat, was a very different place. 'The city within, when you enter, seems not to be a city but a palace,' marvelled Bonfini. 'The whole city tries to please its guests and every house attempts to vie in grandeur of building, to delight the beholders more . . . You might say they were all palaces of nobles.'[24] The houses of the wealthier burghers of Vienna were grander than those of their counterparts in Buda, with 'spacious dining rooms covered with wood panelling . . . [and] windows all full of glass', not to mention the charming cages that the Viennese hung in their windows, which they 'fill with singing and chattering birds, so that as you walk about the city you seem to be walking in melodious pleasant woods; everything, squares, streets and crossroads, pleases. One can see churches built at extraordinary expense.'[25]

The Viennese had early on gained a reputation for frivolous delight in pleasure and a sensual relationship with food, characteristics bound to interest Matthias's moody, frustrated wife. A later English chronicler noted the 'abundance of all provision', especially of corn, beer and wine. 'They eat much wild Boar, whereof the Fat is delicious ... they want not Hares, Rabbits, Partridges, Pheasants ... [as well as] some odd dishes at their Tables; as Guiny-Pigs, divers sorts of Snails and Tortoises,'[26] he wrote. 'The Danube ... afford[s] them plenty of Fish, extraordinary Carps, Trouts, Tenches, Pikes, Eels, several sorts of Lampreys, and many fishes, finely coloured ... [and they] are supplied with Oysters, with salt Sturgeon and ... also with Oranges, Limons and other Fruits'.[27]

The Hungary that lay beyond the gilded cage of Matthias's castle could not compare. Buda, seat of the Hungarian court since the early 1400s, was home to about 10–12,000 people. A woodcut of the city from Hartmann Schedel's *World Chronicle* of 1493[28] shows a homely town of two-storey stone houses, overshadowed by the ramparts and battlements of the royal castle. The spires of only two significant churches are visible, one the church of Our Lady, the 'Matthias' church, and the other St Mary Magdalene, the principal church of the city's Hungarians. The attractions of Buda, with its divided community of Germans, Hungarians and Jews, three gates and weekly market, did not detain Beatrice for long.

Even contemporary chroniclers found it difficult to work up much enthusiasm in describing Buda once they had finished eulogies to the royal residence, the library and the town's setting on the Danube. Miklos Olah, born in 1493, who was among the last chroniclers to recall life in the city before the Ottoman conquest, struggled to say much about it in his book *Hungaria*, once he had finished describing the King's books, 'bound in coloured and embroidered silk'.[29] Olah wrote tersely: 'Its splendid buildings ... are magnificent enough to provoke admiration'. Without elaboration, he continued: 'Apart from its site and the royal palace, Buda was notable for the relic of St John the Almsgiver.'[30]

It was in the imposing churches of Vienna, the great Gothic cathedral, the church of Our Lady, or in the many cloisters of nuns and colleges of priests, that Beatrice spent the last, fateful Sunday of her husband's life.

Her prolonged absence from the dinner table had forced Matthias's hand. According to Bonfini, 'While the Queen, who in several churches of the town was performing her devotions had set the meal for later, he helped himself to some figs ... [and] tasting the first and finding it rotten, he flew into a temper'.[31]

After a howl of anger broke from his lips, other, far more terrible, sensations followed. Soon Matthias lay helpless on his bed. He lost consciousness at dusk but was still breathing and was probably well aware that around his prostrate figure circled the plotting figures of his courtiers, doctors, clergymen and close advisers, among them the ambitious and unscrupulous figure of Bishop Tamas Bakocz. The anxious Queen, returned from her pilgrimage, flitted beside the sickbed, as did Matthias's 17-year-old son, John. Perhaps Beatrice's over-indulged nephew, Ippolito d'Este, was also in the throng, the face of this spoiled and disagreeable infant twisted into a grimace because for once he was not the centre of events. After receiving the archbishopric of Esztergom at seven – to the horror of Pope Innocent VIII, who judged such nepotism blatant even by the standards of the Church – Ippolito had got used to getting his own way. That same morning he had been present on the dais, watching his uncle invest new knights. Now the child-archbishop was temporarily displaced in the mêlée as the Queen took charge, shouting into the King's ears and, according to Bonfini, pulling open his eyelids and remonstrating with doctors.

Bonfini recalled that disastrous afternoon: 'The Queen, who had meanwhile returned, sought to calm him and ordered various dishes. But he rejected them all. After complaining that he was dizzy and could not see, he let himself be taken to his bedchamber. Here at around 6 p.m. he became paralysed.'[32] He continued: 'The cries "ach", "ach" and "Jesus" broke from his convulsed, closed lips . . . [but] the doctors stood idly around as if they had lost their heads. Only the Queen made desperate attempts to help her husband, opening his mouth to put in medicines, his eyes, calling in his ears and beseeching the doctors to bring help.'[33]

The following day, Monday, he lost all power of speech. 'The whole day he spent in a half slumber. At times awakening, he would fasten his gaze on the bystanders. He strained to speak. Beatrice asked him with imploring words if he would declare his will and she overwhelmed him with questions but his lips never opened again.'[34]

The struggle ended on Tuesday, 6 April between 7 and 8 a.m. The aftermath was anticlimactic. It was as if, now that the terrifyingly vital presence of Matthias was no longer there, the pieces on the chessboard could quickly and freely rearrange themselves. Even as the King's body was brought back by barge to Buda for burial in the cathedral of Szekesfehervar, where he had been crowned, the muttering began. There had been too many foreigners at court, it was said in the first parliament held in Buda after his death. Too much money had been spent on luxuries.

Later, most Hungarians would regret their complaints and wish Matthias were back among them. Some would call for his relics to be dug up and paraded round the country. By the second decade of the 1500s it had become apparent that dismantling Matthias's legacy would not restore an imagined, easygoing *status quo ante*. It had merely brought about a dramatic loss of confidence and power, tempting an Ottoman invasion that resulted in the brutal division of the kingdom between the Habsburg and the Ottoman spheres. It meant the liquidation of everything Matthias had constructed.

In Matthias's lifetime, his two palaces with their grand entrances, audience chambers, bronze statues, marble fountains and hanging gardens had impressed foreign diplomats and scholars with their apparent permanence. There was so much 'gold, pearls and precious stones' in Buda, the papal legate reported to Sixtus IV in 1483. He wrote of 'so many woven tapestries, so many carefully wrought golden and silver vessels that I believe fifty men would not be able to carry them away'. There were 'more than 590 great bowls, 300 golden tankards', he continued, and 'basins without number. It can all scarcely be estimated. I have seen ... so many ... costly vessels and such brilliant chambers that I do not believe Solomon in his glory can have been greater.'[35]

Bonfini described the palace, or castle, in Buda in similar terms. 'There were spacious dining rooms, very grand chambers [and] everywhere diverse gilded ceilings adorned with a great variety of emblems,' he wrote. 'One treads everywhere on chequered and vermiculated floors and many are tiled; all about are hot and cold bathrooms.'[36] In the courtyard, he went on, stood large statues of Matthias, his warrior father, Janos, and his brother, Laszlo, 'Matthias in a helmet, leaning on his spear and shield, thoughtful, on his right his father and, somewhat sad, on his left Laszlo'.[37]

Bonfini recalled other emblems of Matthias's magnificence like the bronze fountain placed within a marble pool over which Pallas Athena in helmet and girdle towered. He described the great twin staircase of purple marble that led visitors from the main courtyard to the chamber of audience, at the foot of which stood a pair of vast bronze candlesticks. At the top of the stairs visitors passed through great bronze doors whose panels were decorated with the Labours of Hercules. The rooms of the upper storeys, Bonfini went on, were decorated with paintings of the stars. In the dining rooms, he wrote, 'one looks up not without astonishment at its decoration with the twelve constellations of the sign-bearing sphere [i.e., the zodiac].'[38]

There seem to have been at least two such astrological ceilings in Buda, one of which was painted to match the precise conjunction of the stars and planets at the time of Matthias's coronation as King of Bohemia in 1469.

Matthias respected the stars and their 'influences'. Recalling his preparations for war in Austria, Bonfini wrote that he 'consulted the stars and took
auspices for the expedition, for it seemed he never did anything without
consulting the stars'.[39] Galeotto Marzio, another long-term Italian fixture at
Matthias's court, described him as 'rex et astrologus'.

Astronomy or astrology – there was no real difference at the time – was
the obsession of the age. The King's ally and fellow collector, the Duke of
Urbino, maintained two court astrologers in the later 1470s and 1480s,
named in a list of his courtiers as 'Maestro Paolo Astrologo' and 'Maestro
Iacomo Astrologo', namely Paul of Middelburg and James of Spiers.
Interestingly, the latter was a priest while the former eventually became a
bishop.[40]

Matthias's Habsburg foe, the Emperor Frederick, was just as susceptible.
According to one biographer, 'with astrologers and alchemists he penetrated into the hidden and mysterious majesty of nature. Instructed by them,
he ... learnt the combination and influence of fortuneate [sic] stars.'[41] His
son, Maximilian, was the same. So was another of Matthias's contemporaries, Borso d'Este,[42] Duke of Ferrara during the first years of Matthias's
reign. When Pope Pius II summoned Borso in 1459 to attend the Council of
Mantua, where the Pontiff hoped to rally the European powers against the
Ottomans, the Duke refused to attend because, so he claimed, 'the stars
foretold his death if he went to Mantua'.[43] Pius – who never liked Borso,
claiming he 'wanted to appear generous and magnificent – rather than
genuinely to be so'[44] – accused Borso of hiding behind his astrological fears
in order to have a plausible excuse to stay home and go hunting. As for
Borso's successor and half-brother, Ercole – husband to Beatrice's sister –
one contemporary complained that he 'fills up his time with astrology and
necromancy, giving very small audience to his people'.[45]

Not everyone succumbed to the attraction. Long ago in the 1360s,
Petrarch had written of 'swindling astrologers and lying prophets who
empty the coffers of the credulous'[46] and Ficino's friend, Giovanni Pico della
Mirandola, was inclined to agree. But Ficino himself was more typical of his
generation, happily absorbing the Platonic concept of the universe as a vast,
harmonious organism linked by seen and unseen influences, correspondences and radiations. Notwithstanding his vocation as a cleric, Ficino was
fascinated by ideas of white magic and by the notion that there existed
guardian spirits, known as daemons, which mediated between the vibrating
sources of power.

Matthias enthusiastically shared Ficino's belief that astrology allowed man to unlock the divine cosmic patterns and map out the sequences, correspondences and reflections. In that way, one might determine the likely course of events. A man's life, character and prospects could be gauged by establishing the precise conjunction of the heavens at the moment of his birth, or at certain key points in his life. Hence the mania for horoscopes, and Matthias's decision to have the position of the stars at the exact moment of his Bohemian coronation painted on the palace ceiling.

Ficino felt that the relationship of the planets to his own birth horoscope had been responsible for his mood swings and depressions and like Matthias would undertake no important journey without examining the heavens. To travel when the more malicious planets were in the ascendant was to invite disaster, as he told Miklos Bathory, the Bishop of Vac, in 1487 when politely declining his invitation to Hungary. 'You write that Matthias, the invincible King of Hungary, desires our presence ... to unfold the mind of Plato', he wrote. '[But] It would be a wonder for me to leave the home of my birth, for either the move will be prevented by Saturn rising upon us in Aquarius ... or perhaps my feeble body, unfit for hardships, will prevent the journey.'

Ficino's work *De vita*, the third book of which he dedicated to Matthias in July 1489, dealt in detail with their favourite topic. 'The safest way will be to do nothing without the favour of the Moon since she conveys heavenly things generally frequently and easily to things below',[47] he stated. 'Observe the Moon when she aspects with the Sun and is coming together with Jupiter ... if necessity or business should force you to have recourse to only one out of the great ones, have recourse to Jupiter or preferably to both the Moon and Jupiter. For no star supports and strengthens the natural forces in us ... more than does Jupiter ... for Jupiter is always beneficial, the Sun often seems to harm.'[48]

Ficino's predictions were sadly inaccurate. In the prologue to *De vita*, he had assured Matthias: 'Your lucky stars have decreed for you a life among mortals which is prosperous and fairly long.' By paying attention to astrologers, he went on, you 'can so arrange things that the stars ... even extend it further'.[49] Those words were dated 10 July 1489 and Matthias was dead nine months later – probably before he had a chance to read Ficino's advice.

The King's summer palace at Visegrad, a short journey upstream from Buda on the Danube, did not contain ceilings painted with astrological sequences. In all other important respects it was as luxurious and showy as the palace in Buda. Olah recalled a vast complex of 350 rooms arranged around a court of honour dotted with fountains and antique sculptures. It had 'enough room in it for four kings and all their retinues', he said. Olah said the courtyard was 'like a hanging garden, situated over vaults of extensive and magnificent wine cellars'. It had been planted up with lime trees, too, that 'breathe forth a sweet perfume'. The courtyard contained an especially magnificent red marble fountain, embellished with reliefs of the Muses and topped with a figure of Cupid, from which red and white wine flowed at times of celebration, the wine being 'cleverly introduced into pipes at the foot of the hill higher up'.

There was an imposing chapel decorated inside with white alabaster and containing an organ and a fine monstrance. Olah said the Visegrad palace had been so impressive that when an Ottoman emissary was escorted into the courtyard 'he was lost in amazement at the glittering splendour . . . [and] all this made him forget what he had come to say'.[50]

At Visegrad, the worlds of the Renaissance and the Balkans sometimes collided rather uncomfortably. Seated beside the red marble splashing fountain, or strolling beneath the scented limes, unwary visitors in the 1470s might chance on an unusual figure with huge, luminous eyes. It was Vlad Tepes, 'the Impaler', known also as Dracula. A fellow Transylvanian – though of a different stamp to Matthias – he spent several years in Visegrad from 1462 to 1475 during his enforced exile from neighbouring Wallachia as Matthias's guest and prisoner.

Matthias's and Dracula's lives were intertwined. Matthias's father, Janos, had been a patron to the promising young Walachian prince in 1452, taking him to court in Buda that Christmas. After Dracula lost power in Wallachia to his brother, Radu, Matthias confined him in Visegrad, before attempting to restore him to the Walachian throne in 1475 – a vain business because one of Dracula's many enemies murdered him within months of his return home.

Matthias never shared his guest's morbid interest in perfecting strange tortures, though Dracula's ghoulish reputation did not worry him. If it had, he would not have allowed Dracula to marry his own cousin, Ilona Szilagy, during his Visegrad stay. On the contrary, Dracula's sadistic eccentricities appealed to Matthias's morbid sense of humour and the King enjoyed showing off his notorious guest to bookish visitors. In 1462, he horrified the papal legate, a scholastic Croat known as Nikola Modruski, assuring him, no doubt with deliberate exaggeration, that Dracula had butchered 'forty thousand people of both sexes and various ages', adding that some had been 'crushed under cartwheels, [while] others were stripped naked and skinned alive until their entrails showed and others were impaled and roasted'.[51] Matthias mused to his fellow book collector that Dracula also thrust stakes into the rectums of his victims and sometimes even impaled babies on their mothers' breasts.

It must have been after a visit to Visegrad that the Croat penned some lines on Dracula's appearance for the benefit of a curious Pius II. Dracula was 'not very tall but very stocky and strong, with a cold and terrible appearance, a strong and aquiline nose, swollen nostrils, a thin and reddish face ... [and] large, wide-open green eyes', Nikola wrote. In Rome, Pius perused the Croat Bishop's words with fascination. 'Such is sometimes the discrepancy between a man's appearance and his soul!' he noted.[52]

After the Ottomans conquered Hungary, they stripped the pleasure gardens and halls of the palace in Visegrad. But whereas they occupied the palace in Buda and kept it going after a fashion, in Visegrad they built nothing in place of the ruin they had made. When a fire broke out in the adjacent town in 1543, the area returned to nature. A German traveller at the end of the sixteenth century found that 'goats were grazing among the walls'.[53] Not even the walls survived for much longer. When the Emperor Leopold captured Hungary in the 1680s, he sent German settlers to repopulate Visegrad. The industrious Bavarian incomers stripped away whatever had been left of the palace, using the rubble to build houses and churches. In the 1890s, a block of limestone decorated with Matthias's shield was found in a nearby parish church at Kisoroszi.[54]

Until Hungarian excavators chanced on parts of the palace walls in the 1930s, only mounds of earth, covered in dense vegetation, remained. By then it had become commonplace to write off Olah's description of Visegrad, written in the 1530s in Brussels at the court of the exiled Queen Mary, as an exile's fantasy. But when the diggers chanced on some tantalising fragments, they were able to refute the claim that Olah simply invented his account. The greatest discovery, in 1941, was of the broken but recognisable pieces of a magnificent red octagonal marble fountain. Executed in classic quattrocento style, possibly by Duknovic, the extant panels were decorated with the lion of Bohemia, the arms of the town of Beszterce in Transylvania, the arms of Bohemia and Hungary and the familiar raven. They also found a headless figure of Hercules, which had crowned the fountain. Unusually, this Hercules was shown as an infant, wrestling with the nine-headed Hydra.

The discovery of the Hercules fountain, so quintessentially Florentine in inspiration, served as a reminder that while some subsequent accounts of Matthias's court may have been rose-tinted, they were not fabrications. Sadly, the fountain was almost a solitary find. A marble Madonna, the work of an Italian artist from around 1480, was the only other discovery of significance. The fountain that Olah had described, topped not by Hercules but Cupid, whose panels were decorated with representations of the Muses, has never been found. Whether the Ottomans smashed it to pieces, hauled it away, or whether it still lies somewhere deep in the earth is a mystery.

Hungarian officialdom has tried too hard to breathe life into the ruins of Visegrad. In a heavy-handed way, they rebuilt part of the structure but their work fails to convey any impression of the palace Olah described. Constructed largely of brick and concrete, parts of which have been painted in stark white while others are salmon pink, it looks more like an abandoned nineteenth-century hospital, asylum or boarding-school than the 'paradise on earth' one papal nuncio remembered.

In the palace of Buda, the epigram running above the bronze doors, and which Bonfini composed, read: 'The halls with statues cast from bronze and doors proclaim the genius of the Prince Corvinus. That Matthias should perish, after gaining so many triumphs over the enemy, his virtue, bronze, marble and writings, forbid.'[55]

It seemed inconceivable that all that 'bronze and marble' could ever decay, let alone disappear. Yet vanish it did. There is no trace of those bronze doors today. That was the great irony. Both Matthias and his contemporaries would have been most surprised to discover that the only items that would remain to proclaim the 'triumphs' of the reign were the most delicate and perishable treasures of them all, the books.

CHAPTER TWO

Beyond the forest

Matthias was born in your midst and under your household gods he attained his manhood.

Matthias's uncle, Mihaly Szilagy, to the Estates of Transylvania, 1458[1]

The train from Budapest to Cluj takes the best part of a day, crossing the border with Romania before Oradea after a couple of hours. As it dawdled at the frontier, a Transylvanian German woman in her seventies, returning to claim property nationalised after the Second World War, chattered away nervously. 'Gypsies come on to the trains and rob people,' she said in German, looking relieved that she was not going to have to face this outrage alone in the carriage for the three remaining hours of travel to Cluj.

Just before the train pulled out of the Keleti station in Budapest, I had watched her out of the corner of my eye, observing her equally elderly Hungarian friend help her into her seat, lavishing goodbye kisses on her plump cheeks. The sight of those fervent kisses, accompanied by much stroking of the cheek, clasping of hands to breasts and loud, emotional sighs, startled me, used as I was to the stilted adieus of Britain. The German woman just sat there, smiling back at her friend, her china-blue eyes wide open, receiving this almost sensual homage as her due. She was, I felt, a woman who was used to endearments and to being helped.

As the train moved, I told her I was going to Cluj to see the birthplace of Matthias Corvinus and to meet some local Hungarians who apparently knew about the Hunyadi family. The woman nodded but did not echo my use of the Romanian word, Cluj, or the Hungarian, Kolozsvar. 'Ja, ja,

Klausenburg,' she said with a sigh and a smile, recalling the old German name that is now increasingly confined to history books. The Germans of Transylvania, widely – and inaccurately – known as 'Saxons', though they never came from Saxony, have almost vanished from the land they named Siebenburgen, the seven boroughs, or fortresses. Almost a million strong at the turn of the last century, the fortified churches they built to withstand Ottoman raids dot the landscape around Sibiu, which they called Hermannstadt. But the community that built those fine churches is now a tiny remnant, the villages largely given over to Romanians, or to Roma.

Cluj finally loomed into view, a decayed, shabby-looking town, ringed by the usual grim housing developments that the Ceausescu regime built all over Romania, but especially in Transylvania, in order to build up the ethnic Romanian element. Magyars are now a minority in Cluj. However, a crowd of them leapt into the carriage when we arrived and escorted the old woman off with yet more fervent kisses and shrieks of welcome. No longer needing me, she left without a backward glance.

The Romanianisation of Kolozsvar and its transformation into Cluj began long before the communists took power in Bucharest in 1947. It started immediately after the First World War, as soon as the Treaty of Trianon had formally transferred Transylvania from Hungarian to Romanian rule. When Walter Starkie,[2] the Irish scholar, translator and fiddler, visited the town a few years later, he was struck by the state of apartheid that reigned between the resurgent Romanians and the older Hungarian inhabitants who were not reconciled to their loss of status. 'The city possesses two distinct societies, one Hungarian and the other Romanian, and hardly a member of one knows a member of the opposite faction', Starkie wrote. 'The Magyar noble families live in sad retirement . . . and cry out against the sad change that has come over their lives'.[3]

The changes Starkie described in Cluj in the 1920s were nothing compared to the social engineering that Ceausescu oversaw during his long rule from 1965 to 1989, when thousands of Romanians were brought in to alter Cluj's demography. The poisonous atmosphere Ceausescu encouraged did not disappear with his fall in 1989, either. A Romanian ultra-nationalist, George Funar, then took over as mayor, bent on making life for Cluj's diminishing Hungarian community difficult. Gimcrack monuments to Romanian heroes were placed on every street corner and the park benches were painted in Romania's national colours to remind the Magyars who was boss. It was then that the statue of Matthias lost its inscription 'Rex

Hungariae', though even Funar balked at demolishing it, contenting himself with surrounding the monument with unsightly holes.

My two Hungarian acquaintances greeted me at the railway station and escorted me to the statue, complaining angrily all the way about the excavations, made in search of relics of the ancient Dacians, the Roman tribe from whom Romanians claim descent.

At the town museum we viewed an exhibition mostly devoted to these Dacians – row upon row of bits of broken pottery, knives and axes in glass cases, all supposedly harking back to the Romans and proving that the Romanians settled Transylvania long before the Magyars arrived in the 990s. There was next to nothing in the museum about the centuries that stretched between the fall of the Roman Empire and Transylvania's transfer to Romanian rule in 1918–20. I found nothing about Matthias, his father, or the Saxon colonists who had built the medieval town and the great pitched-roofed church of St Michael in which Matthias was probably baptised. There was almost nothing but axe heads and piles of crockery.

The two young Hungarians I had been put in touch with turned out to be poor guides as far as Matthias was concerned. They had no real interest in Matthias or the Hunyadi family and wanted only to repeat horrific stories about the lives of ethnic Hungarians in the area. The boy had been beaten up in a bar. His girlfriend's father had been forced to surrender his shop in a nearby town to a jealous, less successful, Romanian rival. So it went on, a long and depressing tale of mutual mistrust and loathing that transported me back to the grimmest era in Northern Ireland, or to Kosovo where similarly embattled and embittered Serbs had plied me with accounts of spiteful acts and favours not returned, of houses pelted, old women intimidated, youths beaten and newspapers closed.

It was clear there was no point in asking these two any more about Corvinus, whom they saw only as a reference point. They were not really engaged with the past; fixation with the baleful present consumed their energies and sympathies.

Back in the 1920s, while Walter Starkie had observed the fall of the Hungarians of Cluj with some sympathy, the bustle and energy of the Romanians had attracted him. Like his Irish fellow countrymen, the Romanians had been serfs and underdogs for centuries, as well as adherents of a despised religion. He felt optimistic about their future. 'In a few years a city like Cluj will be one of the intellectual centres of Eastern Europe . . . the Oxford of the East', he predicted.[4]

Walking around the decayed landscape of twenty-first-century Cluj, one could only note the inaccuracy of that prediction and hope European Union membership for Romania might do something to lift the wintry atmosphere. I felt sorry for Cluj, Kolozsvar, or Klausenburg, both for the Romanians' attempts to manipulate and erase the town's history and for the Hungarians' inability to stop mourning a past that was not going to return. Kolozsvar, like Klausenburg before it, had gone. That fact was brought home on the following Sunday morning. After observing the small and rather elderly crowd of Magyars leaving morning service in St Michael's, I watched a huge crowd spilling out of the much newer Romanian Orthodox cathedral. The latter outnumbered the former by about ten to one.

Matthias was born on 23 February 1443[5] in the era of Klausenburg, when German 'Saxon' merchants dominated urban Transylvania. The two-storey Hunyadi townhouse, where his mother, Erzsebet, lay while going into labour, is comfortable enough in appearance but far from palatial. No one then imagined a Hunyadi would sit on a throne.

By the 1440s the Hunyadis were wealthy, thanks partly to Erzsebet Szilagyi's own large fortune. But they were still a parvenu family, recent descendants of immigrants who had crossed over the Carpathian mountains from Walachia in the 1390s and climbed the greasy pole of preferment during the long reign in Hungary of Sigismund of Luxembourg, from 1387 to 1433. There were only two normal routes for such people to realise their ambitions, the Church or the army, and the Hunyadis were a military family who profited from Hungary's vulnerability on the border with the Ottoman Empire.

Matthias left no record of his earliest impressions. Had he done so, he would probably not have lingered for long on the family house in Klausenburg. He would have reminisced far more about the castle that Sigismund presented to his grandfather, Voicu, or Voyk, in 1408 at Vajdahunyad, one year after the birth of Matthias's father.

In spite of the necklace of industrial clutter ringing Hunedoara, this remains one of the most significant and evocative sites in connection with Matthias's life. Although Gabor Bethlen, Prince of Transylvania, modernised the castle in the seventeenth century and it was reconstructed vigorously after being damaged by fire in the 1860s, enough remains to recall the time when this castle was Matthias's home.

It is still possible to imagine Matthias as a lad strolling across the inner courtyard after stepping out from one of the Gothic doorways, or saddling up for the ride to the nearby Hunyadi fortress of Deva, with its commanding views of the surrounding hills. In Matthias's youth, the castle stood alone in the landscape. Standing on the parapets, he would have glimpsed only church spires or the chimneys of peasant huts. But he did not gaze out over a rural idyll. The land surrounding the castle was not at peace. Six years before Matthias's birth, a peasant revolt had shaken Transylvania. As Matthias rode through the villages around the Hunyadi castle, he might have noticed the sullen and angry stares of the peasants, smarting at the oppression they endured from their landlords. It may have sowed the seeds of a conviction that a strong society rested on a basic degree of justice. As king, he worked to shield the peasants and townsmen from the worst forms of exploitation by the magnates and to strengthen the independence of judges.

As Matthias scanned the horizon from the parapets he would have become aware of other threats. Throughout the 1440s, the Ottomans were pressing hard against Transylvania, having overrun much of Serbia, to the south. Transylvania was the next target. In 1441, the Ottomans launched a major attack on the Hunyadis' ancestral homeland of Wallachia. The following year they attacked Transylvania, by March reaching Sibiu. Their progress looked unstoppable until Hunyadi checked them at Alba Iulia.

In spite of that setback, the Ottomans launched another invasion of Transylvania in August 1442. Months before Matthias was due to be born, Hunyadi had to take to the field once more. Only the crushing victory he pulled off that September cleared the Ottomans from Transylvania for the duration of Matthias's childhood.

The castle had changed its appearance a good deal during the years preceding Matthias's birth. Hunyadi was illiterate but cultivated, fully alive to the significance of the great cultural changes taking place in Italy. After marrying Erzsebet Szilagyi, a woman well above his social station, in the early 1430s, he travelled widely, seeking his fortune in Italy as a *condottiere*, or soldier of fortune, at the Visconti court in Milan. A few years later, following the birth of his first son, Laszlo, in 1433, he rejoined the family's benefactor, King Sigismund, at the Church council in Basle, in Switzerland. After that, he accompanied the King to his other kingdom of Bohemia, fighting the Czech Hussite heretics who were barring Catholic Sigismund's entry into Prague. The châteaux and castles he saw on his journeys inspired him to remodel his home in Transylvania. Its continental appearance reflected Hunyadi's determination to drag his own rustic corner into the European mainstream.

The worn images of ravens now visible above the doorways are mostly the work of later restorers. But they are a reminder of the bird that the family, unusually, adopted as its emblem. The Hunyadis became particularly fond of their raven motif, for the nickname 'Corvinus' or 'Corvus' was used also by Janos Hunyadi and by Matthias's brother, Laszlo. Matthias used it more and more as he got older and by the 1480s it was appearing on his books and fountains and had become an alternative surname. Naldi's poem in praise of the library was dedicated to 'Matthias Corvinus', for example, and the beautiful missal that Attavante illuminated for him in Florence in 1485 featured a medallion of the King under the inscription 'Matthias Corvinus'.

It was most probably under his librarian, Taddeo Ugoleto, who systematised the books and their bindings in the 1480s, that the image of the raven took on a standardised form, perching on a branch with a ring in its beak. Most books from that decade featured a royal coat of arms on the frontispiece, in the centre of which a raven always appears. The raven appears far less frequently in the decoration of the King's books. Of the King's favourite Italian artists only the prolific Attavante routinely incorporated ravens into the illuminated borders of pages.

Matthias's court historian and translator, Antonio Bonfini, also helped popularise the term 'Corvinus' in the world through his magisterial history of Hungary, the *Rerum Ungaricarum decades*. Written shortly after Matthias's death, it was widely read in the sixteenth century and its translation into German gained it a broad audience. The term spread, and by the seventeenth century Matthias was known even in distant England as Corvinus. In 1667, when the English travel writer Edward Browne wrote an account of the Habsburg library in Vienna, he added: 'The choicest Books in the famous Library of Buda, of King Matthias Corvinus, Son unto Huniades, are now in it.'[6]

It was the seventeenth-century Habsburg court librarian, Peter Lambeck, who began using the word Corvinus in connection with the library, as a result of which the term 'Bibliotheca Corviniana', the Corvinian library, gained currency. It had never been used in Matthias's own lifetime, when the library had been lauded in terms of its attributes. It had been the 'famous' library, or, as Naldi put it, the 'august' library. Now the Corvinian library took over and the books were increasingly referred to as 'Corvinas'. The persona of the raven had truly been conflated with that of the King.

Matthias would be surprised by the extent to which the world now identifies him entirely with the raven, for it was not the only emblem that appealed to him. Others included Hercules and images of lions and other beasts. When the Signoria of Florence sent two lions to Matthias in 1469, they did so knowing the King would appreciate the gift both as a reference to his own courage and military prowess and as a symbol of Florentine liberty. There is also an intriguing reference to Matthias's appearance at court in Buda dressed in a long gown decorated with a striking pearl-embroidered image of a bat.[7] A one-off? The discovery in the 1950s of an image of a metal bat in the ruins of Buda castle suggests the iconography of the *Fledermaus* appealed to Matthias.

What was the significance of the ring in the raven's beak? Then, as now, the unbroken circle was a symbol of eternity. However, more exotic explanations attached themselves to the raven's ring. One popular story held that Matthias's father was an illegitimate child of King Sigismund. The King had presented Janos Hunyadi's mother with a ring as a token of his love and the young Hunyadi had then returned it to an astonished Sigismund years later, when he first appeared at court. The story looks like another attempt to suggest that royal blood flowed through Hunyadi veins.

In his *Rerum Ungaricarum decades*, Bonfini spread an entertaining and equally implausible legend concerning the origin of the name of Corvinus, concocting a direct link between Matthias Corvinus and Valerius Corvinus, the heroic Roman general, consul and dictator who lived in the fourth century BC. In reality, the use of the raven motif is unlikely to have predated the early 1400s, when the family gained their castle from the King in Transylvania and adopted a coat of arms.

Bonfini was not the only writer to let his imagination take wings when it came to ravens. More recent Romanian historians have come up with equally far-fetched theories, suggesting the bird is a deliberate play on the arms of Wallachia – a conscious tribute to the family's Romanian origins. The theory has little weight, because the Hunyadi raven bears scant resemblance to the Walachian eagle.

Whatever the significance of the ring, the choice of the raven as an emblem was not as odd as it now appears. Seen through the prism of Edgar Allan Poe's horror stories and countless films as a symbol of darkness and evil, its image was then more nuanced. The Bible had invested the raven with mysterious and enigmatic qualities. In Genesis, Noah granted the raven the privilege of being the first bird to be sent from the Ark after the flood to see whether the waters had receded. (The raven has a similar role in the flood narrative of the much older Mesopotamian epic, *Gilgamesh*.) Later in the Old Testament, the raven reappears. He is a divine messenger in Kings, sent by God to feed the Prophet Elijah, and an instrument of divine vengeance in Proverbs, plucking out the eyes of the wicked. He possesses a sensual kind of beauty. In the Song of Solomon, the hair of the Beloved is 'black as a raven'.

The Church drew on this contradictory image, seeing the raven as a bird of special significance in the divine order. Several Lives of Saints feature ravens sent to feed holy men in wildernesses, such as St Antony and St Paul the Hermit, while the raven is a divine intercessor in the life of St Benedict, preventing the saint from consuming poison. The raven possessed charisma. He was a shapeshifter and a prophet, mysterious and ominous. Whether those qualities are what appealed to grandfather Voyk when he first chose a coat of arms after receiving his castle from Sigismund in 1408 we cannot know. But the symbolism of the raven evidently appealed to his grandson.

Matthias never saw his Wallachian grandfather who died around 1419, a quarter of a century before he was born. But he would have been aware that his family had only recently joined the Hungarian 'nation', which then implied the noble class rather than the ethnic Magyar community. As king, he neither belonged to, nor sought the favour of, the caste-conscious magnates, remaining a stranger to their xenophobic instincts as well as to their philistine indifference to letters.

That does not mean he lacked patriotic pride. When he told Beatrice's brother, Alfonso, that he 'knew the Hungarians better than anyone' he meant it. But it is unlikely Matthias ever felt a more specific and exclusive Magyar loyalty. As an adult he was not content with the society of Magyars, let alone of Transylvanians. Instead, he sought the company of foreigners, marrying first a Czech and then an Italian and filling his court with Italians, Germans and Poles, his army with Romanians, Germans and Czechs and bestowing the most important archbishopric firstly on a Croat, secondly on a German and finally on an Italian. We do not even know for certain what his favourite language was. As Beatrice did not master Hungarian, the royal couple must have conversed much of the time in Italian. The language of international diplomacy was naturally Latin.

It is also unlikely that Matthias felt much nostalgia about Transylvania. When he was crowned in 1458, his uncle, Mihaly Szilagyi, wrote an ecstatic letter to the Transylvanian Estates. 'Matthias was born in your midst and under your household gods he attained his manhood,'⁸ he declared. 'You may rejoice in a higher measure than others ... so open up the springs of general joy ... and may the great good God be thanked for such a glorification of your homeland.'⁹

The letter appealed to an assumed sense of pride in a local hero. But there is not much sign that the Transylvanians or Matthias regarded each other with any great sympathy. Matthias returned 'home' as king in autumn 1462, ostensibly to aid Dracula in his battles but in fact to arrest him. He returned in 1467, even less willingly, when the Magyar nobles of Transylvania revolted against his tax reforms. After marrying Beatrice in 1476, he never took her to Cluj or to Hunedoara, though that may have reflected the Queen's resistance to wasting time in what she saw as the sticks. The effect of Matthias's Transylvanian childhood was in fact largely negative. Its chief legacy was a robust, almost militant, cosmopolitanism and contempt for all that was traditional, stuffy and provincial.

Matthias's early facility in foreign languages stimulated his cosmopolitan tastes. The courtier Galeotto Marzio claimed that a Polish embassy addressed the King for two hours at Visegrad in their own language, 'for Matthias alone in that great assembly of men understood the Slavonic language [and] ... when their speech was finished King Matthias asked them whether they wished him to reply in Latin or Polish.'¹⁰

Bonfini agreed about the King's linguistic skills: 'He knew many languages. Apart from Turkish and Greek, he was versed in all the tongues of Europe.'¹¹ We need not take that too literally but he could clearly get by in several tongues.

His childhood in Transylvania had, of course, acclimatised him to the sound of languages other than Hungarian. After the devastating Mongol invasion of Hungary in the 1240s, Slavs and Romanians had resettled the border areas of the kingdom, while Germans and Walloons came from the Moselle, the Rhineland and Luxembourg to revive the ruined towns. 'The whole of Hungary these days includes people of various kinds', wrote Olah, whose own surname suggested a Vlach, or Romanian, origin. 'There being, apart from the Hungarians, Germans, Czechs, Slavs, Croats, Saxons, Szekelys, Romanians, Serbs, Cumanians, Jazygians, Ruthenians ... all of whom speak different languages.'¹²

Matthias would have heard some of these languages while growing up in Hunedoara. To the south and east of Hunedoara lay the lands of the German settlers. In Matthias's time, Brasov, Sibiu and Sighisoara, then known as

Schässburg, were all enclaves of German thought and speech, as was his birthplace of Cluj, further north. Sprinkled between the German towns and the villages of Magyars were transient Vlach communities. The richer among them took the path of the Hunyadis, assimilating themselves into the Hungarian mainstream. The poor and landless majority, many of them shepherds, remained apart. Shunned by the Saxons, Magyars and the closely related Szeklers, the Vlachs remained faithful to their Latin-based language and Orthodox faith. With their Romanian roots, home in Cluj/Klausenburg, and recent ties to the Magyar nobles, it seems likely that Janos Hunyadi and his two sons knew all three languages.

Matthias's father combined a life spent in the saddle, fighting the Turks, with a fascination with the new learning in Europe. The routine of life at the Hunyadi homes in Cluj and Hunedoara and on his wife's Szilagyi estates in Timisoara was regularly punctuated by visits of the warrior's intellectual friends. Matthias must have developed his taste for speculative discussions in childhood, listening to these animated discussions. One of the first and most interesting of his father's intellectual companions was the Polish humanist Grzegorz z Sanoka, Gregory of Sanok. The future Archbishop of Lviv, then in Poland, now in Ukraine, was a passionate bibliophile who as archbishop slept in a filthy, disordered bedroom with tomes of the classics strewn around amongst bits of food and weapons,[13] according to his biographer, Filippo Buonaccorsi. He also said Hunyadi committed the care and discipline of his sons to him on account of his extraordinary mind.[14]

Gregory was the kind of oddball intellectual that Hunyadi liked to rescue from a scrape, dust down and present as a novelty to his family. After leaving home aged 12, Gregory had pursued the wandering, lonely existence of the Renaissance scholar, lecturing on the classics in Poland before drifting south to Hungary. He nearly perished for his pains, after accompanying Hunyadi into the disastrous Battle of Varna in Bulgaria against the Ottomans in 1444. Not only was the Hungarian army virtually wiped out but the defeat had wider consequences, sealing the doom of the encircled Byzantine capital Constantinople and ensuring that the Ottomans would not be driven from the European mainland for generations. Hunyadi was lucky to escape from Varna with his life and so was the Pole, possibly wondering why he had ever given up a comfortable life at the Polish court for such an expedition. Hunyadi then transported him to Transylvania and gave him a new role as tutor to his children.

Gregory passed out of Matthias's life early on after accepting his
archbishopric, a decision he later regretted 'with tears in his eyes', according
to his biographer, 'deploring his fate . . . and from the beginning he thought
of abandoning everything and returning to his friends in Hungary'.[15]

The sound of their eccentric Polish schoolmaster declaiming Virgil was
heard no more in the classroom at the Hunyadi castle. But now a new
learned guest frequented it. This was Janos, or Johannes, de Sredna, so
named after the town in Croatian Slavonia from which his family came.
Later, he became universally known as Janos Vitez, though this was not a
name he used in his lifetime.

Now in his mid-forties, Hunyadi was still a vigorous man, far more so than
Matthias would be at the same age. Paradoxically, the disaster at Varna in
1444 had made him more indispensable to Hungary than ever. Among the
casualties of the battle was the then king, Sigismund's successor, Ladislas.
This left a power vacuum in Hungary because the late king's son, known as
Ladislas the Posthumous, was still in his mother's womb. In 1446, therefore,
the Hungarian parliament appointed Hunyadi as 'gubernator', or governor,
making him the effective ruler of Hungary.

He did not hold this post for more than a few years. Another military
débâcle, at Kosovo in Serbia in 1448, dented Hunyadi's prestige and in 1453
he prudently withdrew from his post, taking the lesser title of captain of the
army. The Hunyadis were not really stepping down, however. By now they
were the single most powerful family in the country, having made good use
of the preceding years to amass vast landholdings.

The Hungarian nobles remained hostile. The meteoric rise of the
Hunyadis from obscurity in Transylvania generated enormous jealousy
among the old noble families, though there was not much they could do
about it. The combined wealth of the Hunyadis and Szilagyis had enabled
them to build up and maintain a great faction in the country. Uniting all
those who resented the overweening ambitions of the nobles, the family's
core supporters came from the lower gentry and the towns. Hunyadi's
courtship of men of letters, meanwhile, ensured him the loyalty of people
like Vitez, whose bishopric of Oradea, Nagyvarad in Hungarian, had been
a direct gift of Hunyadi's. He had secured his friend's elevation to the
wealthiest see in eastern Hungary after the previous incumbent, an Italian
named De Dominis, perished at Varna.

In 1553, Hunyadi helped to push Vitez further up the ladder. That year,
the bishop was appointed chancellor. Thus, in the year that Hunyadi

appeared to retreat from power, he in fact left behind his devoted servant at the heart of government. Vitez was never just a client. He was a friend, counsellor and family troubleshooter. A passionate bibliophile who combined the instincts of the politician and the intellectual, he exercised enormous influence on the young Matthias.

Vitez was never able to journey to Italy himself. But he made up for it by networking with Italian humanists and using his diplomatic trips to Cracow, Prague and Vienna to seek out men of letters. A visit to Vienna in 1452 introduced him to the future Pius II, then working as secretary to the Emperor Frederick III. The two men swapped books and ideas concerning the need for Europe to unite against the Turks. Vitez also lured foreign scholars to his court, including Sanoka the Cypriot, Filippo Podocatharo, and the Polish astronomer Marcin Krol.

His most important intellectual catch was Pier Paolo Vergerio, an Italian humanist whom King Sigismund had encountered at the Church council in Constance in 1414–15 and brought back. He remained in Hungary until his death in 1444, passing the final years at Vitez's court in Oradea.

Vergerio was an important guest. Knowledge of Greek was increasingly seen as vital to a rounded education and Vergerio had studied under the Greek teacher, Manuel Chrysoloras, who had spread the knowledge of what was then a little-known language in Florence in the 1390s. Vergerio may have taught some Greek to Vitez, as the Bishop became an enthusiastic collector of Greek manuscripts and the notes he wrote in the margins of some of them suggest that he at least understood Greek.

Vergerio provided Vitez with other useful contacts. He was the link between Vitez and Guarino Veronese, master of the school in Ferrara, which was admired for the modern spirit with which it grounded pupils in the *studia humanitatis*, the liberal arts or 'humanities', from which the term humanist eventually sprang. This was crucial for the course of the Renaissance that would flower in Matthias's Hungary because after Vergerio introduced Vitez to Guarino, the Bishop entrusted his brilliant nephew, Ivan Cesmicki, to Guarino's care. In Italy, the boy cast off his old name and adopted that of Janus Pannonius, Pannonia being the old Roman province that encompassed his native Slavonia. It was indicative of his total conversion to ancient Roman culture that he did not merely add a Latin suffix 'us' to his existing surname as most contemporaries did, Naldi becoming Naldius, Bonfini, Bonfinius, and so on. He was not content with such a symbolic break. After the sojourn in Italy from 1447 to 1458, the name Cesmicki disappeared.

As Pannonius, the young man mastered grammar, rhetoric, history and poetry. Indeed, he was possibly the brightest student the school in Ferrara had ever encountered. As Guarino's son, Battista, recalled: 'He would ask us to come up with subjects on which we wanted him to compose [epigrams] ... But we would scarcely have started writing them down before he was dictating the verses in a single jet.'[16] The outlines of a genius, therefore, were clear. At the same time this *wunderkind* scoured the bookshops of Italy, on a mission to assist his uncle the Bishop in building up the finest classical library in Hungary. It was here in Italy that the work of assembling Matthias's future collection began.

CHAPTER THREE

'I delight in everything that's new'

*One of his first acts was to gather a magnificent library, for which he gathered
books from Italy and all the other countries, and many which he failed to find
he caused to be transcribed in Florence, regardless of cost.*

Vespasiano da Bisticci, on Janos Vitez[1]

In the centre of Florence, where the flagstones echo to the tramp of armies
of tourists performing their cultural pilgrimages, I made my way down the
Via del Proconsolo. Passing a crowd that was walking towards the Uffizi,
I headed instead towards the medieval Benedictine abbey, the Badia
Fiorentina. Holding a rough map sketched by the Florentine art expert,
Angela Dillon Bussi, I found the junction of the vias Proconsolo and
Ghibellina, where some believe the fifteenth-century bookseller, Vespasiano
da Bisticci, once had his bookshop, or *cartolaio*.

Nothing now marks the site as the place where the 'princeps omnium
librariorum Florentinorum' held court. Today, a pizza-and-cocktail bar
stands on the premises. But the area's old connections to the book trade
linger on in such names as Via dei Librai – 'street of the books'.

Florence has changed drastically since Pannonius walked these streets.
The area around the Badia, which then hummed with the activity of
countless artisans' workshops, is less diverse now. One would have to go
to Marrakesh or the other great markets of Morocco, or to a souk in
Syria or Egypt, to recapture something of the flavour. Recent guidebooks
proclaim as a fact that many old family trades still operate in the area, just
as they have done for centuries. But central Florence looks like one big

restaurant and hotel. Hospitality is the only serious business in town, and the only real traders I saw were North Africans – tall men, standing impassively and with inscrutable expressions in front of spread-out rugs laden with leather goods, sunglasses, imitation Rolex watches and umbrellas. At night, this disciplined army packs up its wares and heads for the sites on the edge of the city, where the men camp for the duration of the summer season.

The lanes around the Badia are much darker, too, than they were in Pannonius's time. Most of the modern city dates from the nineteenth century. It was massively rebuilt in the middle decades, especially the 1860s, when Florence briefly served as the capital of the new kingdom of Italy. Buildings four or five storeys high became the norm, transforming narrow streets into virtual tunnels. Those streets would have been airier and lighter when Pannonius strolled down them in his long Hungarian cloak.

Still, Pannonius would spot certain landmarks, which he would certainly not be able to do in Buda, or Budapest, as the united city became in 1873. There, he would find little familiar except the curve of the Danube. In Florence, on the other hand, he would surely smile at the sight of the recently completed cathedral, the Duomo, and at the bronze Baptistery doors that Ghiberti finished only a few years before Pannonius's arrival in Ferrara. He would know the foundling hospital, the work of Brunelleschi in the 1420s, and the great churches of Santa Croce and Santa Maria Novella, though the latter's black-and-white façade would be new to him, as Alberti finished it in the 1470s, long after Pannonius had returned to Hungary.

In his memoirs the Florentine bookseller Vespasiano da Bisticci recorded Pannonius's first visit to the city, which must have occurred towards the end of his eleven-year sojourn in Italy around 1458. 'After his arrival in Florence with horses and servants the first person he wished to address was myself,' Vespasiano wrote with evident pleasure, 'because through me he would have introductions to the learned men of the city. He wore a purple mantle and as soon as I saw him I said "Are you indeed the Hungarian?" . . . He then embraced me and addressed me with the most gracious and apt words I have ever heard.'[2] Vespasiano said Pannonius made an excellent impression on Cosimo de Medici – the grandfather of Lorenzo – and had shown his verses to Poggio Bracciolini. He also bought a great many books, though Vespasiano did not list their titles. 'He visited all the libraries of the city and having bought many books . . . left with the good wishes . . . of all who had seen him', he wrote.[3]

The bookseller and the book-lover were reunited in 1465. Seven years after Pannonius had gone back to Hungary to reluctantly don the robes of the Bishop of Pecs, the main see in southern Hungary, he returned in grander state as head of an embassy travelling to Rome on Matthias's behalf. His goal was to obtain money from the Pope for a campaign against the Ottomans, and to obtain a papal foundation bull for the university that his uncle planned to erect in Bratislava.

According to Vespasiano, book purchases again consumed a great deal of Pannonius's time in Florence and on each leg of the embassy's journey in Rome, Ferrara and Venice. 'He determined to collect a fine library, therefore he bought at Rome all the books in Greek and Latin he could find, in every faculty', Vespasiano wrote. 'When he came to Florence he made further large purchases and was most liberal in his payments. When he departed he left several hundred florins for the transcription of those Greek and Latin books which he still lacked.'[4]

Vespasiano was struck again by what a true connoisseur the young man was. 'Even when he was journeying ... he would always be found with a book in his hand, reading diligently', he observed. On one occasion, after dining with Vespasiano, the bookseller recalled that Pannonius had spent three hours absorbed in a work by Plotinus – without stirring: 'When he had shaken off his abstraction, he turned to me and said, "If you want to know how the Bishop of Pecs occupies himself, say that he does nothing besides translating Plotinus and attending to his bishopric." '[5]

That wasn't quite true. Besides translating Plotinus and 'attending to his bishopric', which did not interest him in the slightest, he spent a lot of time arranging for the transport of manuscripts to Hungary. Indeed, Pannonius vented a jokey feeling of exasperation about having to buy so many books in such a short time and for different people. 'By Jove, it is lucky that none of you can understand Greek', he complained in a letter. 'If it were not for that, I would not have a single Greek work with me. When you have learned Greek, I shall learn Hebrew, so that I may collect Hebrew books. I ask you, is the love of books so insatiable a desire?' He went on to publicise the merits of Italy, and of Vespasiano's shop in particular. 'Italy is full of such treasure,' he wrote. 'You may order books there to your satisfaction; send money to Florence and Vespasiano alone will supply you.'[6]

The bookshops that Pannonius haunted off the Via del Cartolai in the 1450s and 1460s were then at their height. He may have been familiar with at least a dozen, for between 17 and 20 such firms operated from premises

that they rented from the Badia in the mid- to late fifteenth century.[7] This
elite trade mainly served the rich. The most magnificently illuminated books
were dizzyingly expensive. When a thief stole part of the *Book of Hours* that
Giovan Pietro Birago had illuminated for Bona Sforza, Duchess of Milan, in
the 1490s, the outraged artist complained that the complete work had been
worth 500 ducats.[8]

Even more ordinary books were out of the reach of the broad mass of
people. According to Curt Buhler, 'A typical vellum manuscript of the
fifteenth century, in finished form and bound, cost between seven and ten
ducats; this equalled a month's wages for the average official at the
Neapolitan court.'[9]

The British art expert, Albinia de la Mare, suggested that books in the
period 'were probably on a par in expense with fine clothes'.[10] When the
luggage of Angelo Decembrio was stolen in France, for example, she noted,
his 26 lost books were valued at 300 florins, or a little more than ten florins
each. By way of comparison, she said Vespasiano and his brothers paid 18
florins a year for the maintenance of their nephew in 1480–81, while the
annual rent for their shop was 15 florins. A domestic servant at an Italian
court might expect to receive seven ducats a year above and beyond his
board and lodging[11] – considerably less than the average price of one of
Decembrio's books.

A scholar whose services as Latin orator and composer of elegies were in
demand might compile a small library, on the other hand. Lorenzo
Francesco, one of the most successful, wrote to Lorenzo de Medici in 1475
to boast that he had secured an annual salary of 600 florins at the papal
court.[12] Such stars could easily purchase books. So of course might the
wealthier bishops and cardinals, who enjoyed 20,000 ducats a year or more.
They were not that far in income from the rulers of small Italian courts. The
Duke of Urbino, for example, drew in 50,000 ducats a year.

Overall, the cost of books and their status as a luxury items dictated the
small size of most contemporary libraries until the mid- to late fifteenth
century and the invention of printing in the 1460s.

To describe a *cartolaio* as a bookshop does not quite convey the nature of
the place, which resembled a publisher's, art studio, bindery and bookshop
combined. Vespasiano's shop and the other *cartolai* that Pannonius visited
would have been more like small factories than shops. While no description
survives of Vespasiano's premises, De la Mare imagined 'baths for soaking
leather and parchment, frames for stretching it, presses for binding and

some sort of flat table for ruling. The shop's stock would include quantities of new paper and parchment, loose or in reams and quires, [five sheets, folded into two] both for sale and for use in preparing Vespasiano's own manuscripts.'[13]

The parchment used for the highest-quality manuscripts was of goatskin and the Florentines were acknowledged experts in preparing the finest skins, first soaking and then shaving them before scraping and whitening them for use. An entire goat might supply only enough skin for a single leaf of the largest types of books. Large leaves were required for bibles, missals and other liturgical works. Before the quires were sent off to the copyist, the sheets had also to be ruled with needles.

The pricked, blank book was then fit for the attention of the copyist, or scribe. Mistakes were hard to correct and even the best copyists often made them, prompting discerning patrons to kick up a fuss. When Ludovico Gonzaga of Mantua ordered a bible from Vespasiano in 1461, for example, he complained on receiving it that it was badly copied.[14] Booksellers with reputations to protect had to compete for the services of the copyists who were deemed most reliable. They might offer such men good rates, perhaps a florin per quire, according to De la Mare. Serious bibliophiles like Alfonso of Naples, Beatrice's grandfather, kept the cost of copyists down by paying monthly retainers of 10 to 20 ducats (a florin and a ducat were of similar value) to a team of full-time scribes.[15]

Copying was a gentlemanly occupation and the kind of work that city priests with humanist leanings, or even nobles, went in for. As the old, densely packed Gothic script gave way to the new, rounder, more legible 'classical' style that Bracciolini pioneered in Florence, known as *lettera antica*, copying gained in prestige and popularity. The best practitioners now began to advertise their services on the works they had copied. It was a sign of the new egoism of artists in the Renaissance, and of an assumption that books were now intended for an audience – a public – rather than a single patron.

The Florentine priest Pietro Cennini, who styled himself Petrus Cenninius, and who was highly regarded for his accuracy, was fond of signing off works with personal flourishes. 'Ecripsit Florentiae Petrus Cenninius Anno Domini 1467', he wrote at the end of Curtius Rufus's history of Alexander the Great.[16] 'Hoc opus, o lector, descripsit Petrus', he wrote in the same year, when he had finished copying the *Strategemata* of Frontinus.[17] The inquisitive and sociable Pannonius clearly knew the Cennini family, which was well known in Florence, Pietro's father, Bernardo, having helped Ghiberti work on the Baptistery doors. Pietro Cennini copied at least half a dozen works for Pannonius, including the history of Alexander that ended up in Matthias's library.[18] He copied most of these works in the year 1467, which suggests that he received his commission in person from Pannonius when as Bishop of Pecs he visited Italy in 1465.

After the copyist had finished his work, the expenses mounted; the highest-paying clients were not interested simply in the words of the ancients. They wanted beautiful illustrations, too. As the century progressed, a form of artistic inflation encouraged the *cartolai* to compete in offering ever more elaborate and luxurious designs on the frontispieces of their books. The illustrated title-pages became more extravagant as artists experimented with the use of three-dimensional effects and more convincing trompe-l'oeil. Architectural motifs became popular in the 1480s. Great doorways and triumphal arches made their appearance as frames for the page, surmounting pedestals on which reliefs depicted episodes from the classics.

The emphasis on realism and the move away from simple decoration meant that lifelike human figures now also appeared. With fluid movements and gestures these were far removed from the stiff, stylised and almost unidentifiable figures of the Gothic era. The inside pages of the manuscripts changed, too. Simple borders of *bianchi girari*, literally white vine stems, interlaced with plant life, animals and birds, gave way to crowded, elaborate, three-dimensional borders replete with foliage, or tall candelabra, and painted in a multitude of colours. The thick and luxurious borders were now punctuated by swirling medallions. These might contain portraits in profile, such as Matthias depicted as a Roman emperor, imperious-looking with a crown of laurel leaves, opposite another medallion containing a portrait of his wife.

More ambitious miniature scenes also appeared within the huge initial letters at the top of pages at the start of a new chapter or section. These might house a scene of a scholarly saint, sitting in a *studiolo*, the small private study that became the rage in the Italian courts in the 1450s. Behind him one might pick out an entire landscape or the skyline of a city like Florence. The emphasis on three-dimensional effects and on the depiction of motion encouraged illuminators to try their hand at portraying new symbolic objects or angelic beings in the dense flow of the foliage on the page border. Flying cherubs, or putti, made their appearance, often holding up the royal coat of arms that was normally found at the bottom of the frontispiece. So did jewels, mechanical and astronomical devices and new beasts and fishes.

While the general trend was towards greater sophistication, the illuminators all had their very different styles, reflecting the artistic trends and fashions of Florence, Naples, Lombardy or elsewhere. Attavante showed off his proficiency at depicting perspective through the use of architectural frontispieces with deep recesses. He loved dense crowded borders, and certain symbols such as barrels, beehives, hourglasses, wells, globes and ravens.

The brothers Monte and Gherardo di Giovanni used many of the same devices, though with even greater delicacy and finesse. Their illuminated frontispiece for Didymus of Alexandria's *De Spiritu Sancto* is among the finest extant works in Matthias's library. It displays all the advances made by the artists of the 1470s and 1480s, showing Matthias and Beatrice kneeling within an architectural frame at the centre of which opens a large round window, in which St Jerome is working in his *studiolo*, with a lion snoozing at his feet.

A mass of symbols climbs up the columns that rise above the King and Queen, including helmets, shields, clocks, wheels and other devices, while the plinth on which they kneel is decorated with reliefs of Apollo and classical scenes. Most intriguingly, four other figures peep out from behind the columns behind the royal couple, among them a long-haired youth that may well be Matthias's son, John, and an old woman that may be his mother, Erzsebet.

Not all Matthias's illuminators went in for the same profusion of detail as the brothers Di Giovanni or Attavante. Francesco del Cherico chose lighter, airier, more floral and generally less overpowering designs for his frontispieces. He was not so interested in impressing an audience with a virtuoso display of his skill in triumphal arches, swirling medallions, candelabra and human portraits. As for the illuminators from Naples and Lombardy, they chose different colours and designs altogether. The Neapolitan artists were not in quite the same league as their top Florentine counterparts and their designs can look formulaic, flat and coarse by comparison. It is not surprising that Matthias greatly preferred Florentine work.

These artistic creations of the latter part of his reign of course required more money than the older illustrations. Lapis lazuli, the base for ultramarine, the most expensive colour, cost around three ducats per ounce in the fifteenth century according to De la Mare, though it was possible to use other shades of blue that cost far less. The overall cost of a lavishly decorated frontispiece might run to 25 ducats,[19] especially if it came from the hands of an artist like Attavante whose services were in demand. The work of such stars was not always subcontracted by booksellers: popes and kings jostled for their attention directly.

No contracts survive for Attavante's work for Matthias. However, the contract he signed with King Manuel of Portugal to illustrate a bible in April 1494 sheds light on what these agreements usually contained. It laid down tight conditions concerning payment, offering the artist 25 gold ducats for the title-page of each of the seven volumes of the bible. It also included a penalty of up to 200 ducats in the event of delays. There were no strict conditions concerning the choice of illustrations. This was left to Attavante. The contract merely suggested that the work should be as good as possible, 'nella perfectione delle figure et adornamente'.[20] An illuminator of Attavante's standing dealt directly only with the most significant illustrations. The rest was left to minor members of the studio, the apprentices, or *garzoni*, whose inferior style is easy to detect.

Even now, once the front page had been decorated and gleamed with newly applied blues, reds, whites and golds, the bookseller's task was not complete. Once the manuscript was returned to the *cartolaio*, it had to be bound. The cheapest bindings of plain wood or glued paper cost little, but more important clients would expect the kind of bindings that Matthias, or his librarians, chose for the collection in the 1480s. These were boards of wood covered in dyed calfskin or leather and finished with geometrical patterns of studs and the King's armorial bearings in the middle. Only about half a dozen of these survive. According to Olah this was because when the Ottomans seized Buda in 1526 they tore off the bindings to get hold of the silver clasps. None of the clasps from Matthias's books, assuming they existed, has come down to us, though the beautiful clasps preserved on Beatrice's psalter, now in Wolfenbüttel, give us some idea of what they looked like.

At the top end of the range some wildly extravagant bindings were available. The binding prepared for Borso d'Este's sumptuous bible by the Ferrarese *cartolaio* Gregorio Gasparino, now sadly lost, was made of cloth-of-gold, lapis lazuli and silver. Lorenzo de Medici's missal, a gift at his wedding, was bound in solid silver and crystal, which alone cost 200 florins.

The books that Pannonius sought for his uncle and for himself in Italy in 1465 would not have been so extravagant. They were probably much like the books in the collection of Lorenzo de Medici's father Piero. His inventory, also dating from 1465, shows many valued at between 30 and 50 florins.[21]

It is tempting to imagine Pannonius's delicate fingers turning the pages of the most exquisitely illuminated books of the day, his intelligent eye lighting up at the sight of those glinting liquid hues, knowingly spotting the tell-tale signature device of the artist. Tempting, but wrong. The great age of illuminators like Attavante and the brothers Di Giovanni lay in the 1480s and 1490s, long after Pannonius's premature death. These impresarios appeared at the tail end of Vespasiano's working life in Florence, when he was completing his last great commission, a bible for the Duke of Urbino.

It is also very questionable whether Pannonius much appreciated master-pieces of illumination. The more expensive the illuminations, the worse the copy, some historians assert. That would have irritated a man with a keen eye for grammatical and textual errors. Elaborate illuminations were also the hallmark of Latin works and Latin translations. Artists rarely took the same pains for works written in Greek. And as Vespasiano suggested, Pannonius had long moved on from the Latin of his college years to Greek.

Pannonius's feelings about books, as reflected in his writings, were also unpredictable. Much as he loved the world of men like Vespasiano and Pietro Cennini, his spirit revolted against a cult of antiquity for its own sake. 'Farewell to you great library, so filled with books from ancient times', he wrote nostalgically of his uncle the Bishop's library in Oradea. But in the poem, De amatore librorum veterum, he vented different feelings:

A thousand books they've written through the years,
Learned perhaps, but not great works of art.
Now, I delight in everything that's new
Not ancient and decayed, Bartholomew . . .[22]

Knowledge of Greek was indeed 'new', in Western Europe. In the late 1450s, when Pannonius first met Vespasiano and Cosimo de Medici, the Greek revival was only half a century old. For the previous millennium, it had been virtually unknown outside a few enclaves in southern Italy. Fragments of Greek learning had survived the Church's hostile attitude to 'pagan' learning, while portions of the Greek classics had also reached the new universities of the west from Muslim southern Spain. But this knowledge was partial, limited to science and logic rather than literature. It was also based on second- or even third-hand translations of Greek into Arabic and then into Latin, a process that inevitably led to corruptions. According to Deano Geanokoplos, Byzantine visitors to fifteenth-century Italy 'were amazed and horrified by the corruption of the Greek (and Latin) manuscripts of Greek works used by the Scholastics . . . so bad were most of these texts that not only was the text often inaccurate but the meaning was often distorted.'[23]

The Europeans needed to learn Greek to recover the original sense of the texts. Many of their teachers were Greek intellectuals fleeing the doomed city of Constantinople in the years before the Ottoman conquest. The great apostle of Greek studies in Italy was Manuel Chrysoloras whose appointment in 1397 to the chair of Greek studies in Florence, revived in 1361, marked a milestone. Not only was he brilliant, but he was also the first Greek from the Byzantine Empire to hold the post, his predecessor Leontius Pilatus, or Pilato, having come from a Greek enclave in Calabria in southern Italy. It was Chrysoloras who took Greek studies forward in Florence. According to Geanokoplos, 'the desire to learn the long-neglected Greek language and literature was, through Chrysoloras's inspired teaching, transformed into a veritable mania that spread rapidly from Florence through much of Italy'.[24]

The Pope's decision to hold a Church council in Florence in the 1430s gave the Greek revival a further lift. The aim was to try – again – to end the schism between the western and eastern branches of the Church and so stave off the imminent Ottoman conquest of the 'second Rome'.

Although the Byzantine 'empire' now comprised little more than the city of Constantinople, a faded glamour still attached itself to the forlorn figure of the Emperor John Palaeologus VII and Italy braced itself to welcome the 700-strong deputation from the city, which left for Italy in November 1437, headed by the Emperor and the Patriarch. Humanist scholars headed to Florence to catch a glimpse of this extraordinary and exotic embassy. The young Vespasiano, then a teenage apprentice, was probably among the crowds who lined the streets of Florence to watch the entry of this fabulous and tragic delegation. On the Greek side, the star was not the ultra-conservative Patriarch, who busied himself with disputes over precedence with the Pope, chiefly concerning who should kiss whose shoe, but Gemistus Pletho. An eccentric member of the Patriarch's clerical team (he was later to be accused of outright paganism), his lectures on Plato created a terrific stir, encouraging the cult of Plato that Ficino inherited and sustained.

Another member of the Byzantine delegation, Johannes Bessarion, made a permanent home in Italy. After staying on following the closure of the council in 1439 he was rewarded with a cardinal's hat, becoming the most important patron of Hellenic learning in Italy, an expert in Latin as well as Greek – 'inter Graecos, Latinissimus, inter Latinos, Graecissimus',[25] as one admirer put it. He was also an important book collector.

Pannonius reached Italy a few years after the exciting but inconclusive events of the Council of Florence. His transformation from rustic youth to urban intellectual took place in the late 1440s, after the Emperor had returned home empty-handed, the reunion of the Churches agreed at Florence having failed to win over most Greeks or generate significant western military aid.

The academy he attended in Ferrara during those years was a magnet for youths from all over Europe. As Pannonius himself recalled:

From every corner of the world they come to learn from you,
To you they sail from far Dalmatia's shore
To you they speed from Cyprus, Crete and Rhodes . . .
For you the youths of France desert their masters
And Germans leave the scholars of Vienna
The Spanish come from far Gibraltar's rock
The Poles from distant northern lands
And Britons who wander here . . .[26]

Two of those Britons were William Grey, the future Bishop of Ely who studied under Guarino in 1445–46, at the start of Pannonius's sojourn, and Robert Flemmyng, a future Dean of Lincoln.[27]

By the standards of the era, Guarino was ancient by the time Pannonius reached Ferrara in 1447. Born in 1374, he had spent five years in the dying capital of the Byzantine empire studying Greek at the feet of Chrysoloras; in 1409 he returned to Italy to teach in Florence, Venice and Verona before accepting the invitation of Borso d'Este's father, Niccolò III, in 1429 to come to Ferrara.

When Vitez selected Ferrara as the right place for his nephew, as we saw in Chapter Two, he did so because Vergerio had probably recommended Guarino as the ideal pedagogue. Another former pupil of Chrysoloras, he was enthusiastic about the new ideas on education based on the *studia humanitatis*. Indeed, Vergerio had committed his own ideas on the subject to paper in 1402 in *De ingenius moribus*, perhaps the first humanist treatise on education.

If the hallmarks of the humanist were also a spirit of inquiry, a feeling of optimism about the future and boundless confidence in man's potential, those sentiments were exemplified in Pannonius. As he put it in a panegyric that he composed to Guarino in 1456:

> *A new knowledge is developing, the old world is reborn.*
> *The times of Alexander the Great and of the glorious Caesar you can experience today.*
> *The present is gleaming, and can serenely rival the past.*
> *Knowledge beams out light and summons the spirit of man.*[28]

Guarino and other modern educationists believed education was the key to forging a more enlightened generation, invested with a new perception of man's dignity. Abandoning the traditions of the medieval Scholastics, who emphasised logic and metaphysics, Guarino made literature, rhetoric and grammar the centre of the curriculum. The grammar syllabus comprised the writings of Cicero and Quintilian, the dialogues of Plato that Pletho had popularised in Florence and the translations of Hermogones of Tarsus, the principal Byzantine author on rhetoric.

These had recently reached the west through another Byzantine refugee, George of Trebizond, who in fact came from Crete. Trebizond reached Italy aged 20 in 1415 and spent the rest of his life there. A quarrelsome man, who got into a violent brawl with Bracciolini, his reputation for violence was passed on to his sons, who were suspected of poisoning Matthias's astronomer, Johannes Müller 'Regiomontanus'.[29]

Though difficult to work with, George of Trebizond was unquestionably brilliant. His compendium of the Byzantine rhetorical tradition, *Rhetoricorum libri V*, was described as 'the greatest Latin summa of rhetoric since Antiquity'.[30] He must have come across Pannonius personally because he dedicated his translation of St Basil, *De Spiritu Sancto*, jointly to Vitez and Pannonius, writing in the preface, 'I know you have always felt real love for me and my family'.[31]

Apart from rhetoric, Guarino's school emphasised mastery of a 'pure' written Latin that had to be indistinguishable from that of Cicero. Next came history, which, as Vergerio said, was valued mainly because it 'gives us concrete examples of the precepts inculcated by philosophy'.[32] Then came poetry, especially Virgil, along with science and astronomy. Although Ptolemy had been known in the west since the Middle Ages from the Arabic translations, the quality of these works was poor and it was not until 1451 that George of Trebizond finished his new translation of Ptolemy's *Almagest*, dedicating a sumptuous copy of this work to Matthias in 1467.

Finally there was the study of Greek itself. The pupil 'must study on his own the great encyclopaedic works of the empire: the *Noctes Atticae* of Aulus Gellius, the elder Pliny's *Natural History*, and Augustine's *City of God*. Those with stamina could also tackle Strabo's *Geography*, which Guarino himself had translated.'[33]

Guarino's academy transformed Pannonius into a cosmopolitan Italian. He was the star of the academy, thanks to his precocious brilliance in composing Latin epigrams, and he bought into the worldview of the most advanced humanists. They already mocked the excesses of medieval Catholicism, jeering to each other in their perfect Latin about the misplaced confidence of the unwashed masses in relics and shrines. Pannonius shed not only the 'superstitions' that all humanists now laughed at but every vestige of conventional religion. He poured scorn on his school friend in Ferrara, Galeotto Marzio, for going on a pilgrimage, insisting religion *per se* was incompatible with the calling of a poet:

> Leave this to simpletons from foreign lands,
> Or mobs afraid of spirits of the dead . . .
> Then bid farewell for ever to the Muses,
> And smash the sacred lyre.[34]

The enthusiasts for the new humanist syllabus insisted it was eminently practical. History, especially that of Rome, was considered essential to rulers, with its precedents, lessons and salutary examples of greatness and decline. Rhetoric was seen not as an isolated skill but as the handmaiden of effective government, for displays of rhetoric accompanied every important state occasion.

But whether Guarino's education was equally useful to all its students is questionable. Guarino's syllabus was designed to turn out young men with superb skills in speaking extempore classical Latin. Such youths had no problems in finding employment in Italy because the various city-states 'regaled them with administrative, secretarial, advisory, academic and tutorial posts'. There were a lot of jobs to fill. Italy was honeycombed with courts, varying in size from Milan, Naples and the papal court, with thousands of salaried staff each, to small courts like that of Urbino, which employed 350 to 500.[35] The question was whether the rhetorical skills that were such a marketable commodity in Italy had much of a role in fifteenth-century Hungary. As one historian put it, the study of the liberal arts 'made no sense outside the context of cities, of municipal eminence and rewards, of importance vouchsafed to oratory'.[36]

It is also clear that Pannonius learned more than excellent Greek and Latin in Ferrara. There was an undercurrent of sexual licence, ambiguity and adventure at the school that the aged master, now in his seventies, was possibly not aware of. Perhaps he knew all about it and was not bothered. About twenty years before Pannonius reached Ferrara, Guarino had been one of the few humanists to publicly praise Antonio Beccadelli's infamous work, the *Hermaphroditus*, which broke every conceivable taboo with its graphic descriptions of homosexual sex. Whether or not Guarino knew what was happening, when Pannonius reached Ferrara he plunged willingly into a world of homosexual intrigue that he eagerly recorded in his epigrams. As he wrote in *In Pindolam*:

> *Now I see Pindola why you were often so nice to me,*
> *The shame of it! You're obviously buggering my friend.*
> *That's the word my teacher uses when an old guy sticks his*
> *Prick into the bum of a straight-backed youth*
> *His ugly buttocks quivering all the while . . .*

In *In Leonem Cineadum*, he wrote:

> *Sometimes Leo plays the man and sometimes the girl*
> *But his hind parts always seem to do the job.*

Pannonius's erotic verse contained numerous references to such homosexual encounters. He also wrote poems on sexual intercourse with women, but of a more routine, pedestrian quality. The same-sex works on the other hand drew on what sounds like personal experience. Pannonius's contemporaries clearly regarded him as a homosexual. As Vespasiano put it: 'By common opinion he had never known women.'[37]

An acknowledgement of Pannonius's sexual make-up is important, as it was one of the factors that contributed to his deep discontent when he returned to conservative, martial Hungary and that led to his eventual destruction. This mattered, because much of the intellectual ferment in Hungary during the first decade of Matthias's reign depended on this brilliant Latinist's talents. His dramatic defection was an event of cultural as well as political significance.

When Vespasiano first met Pannonius in 1458, all this lay in the future. Then he appeared a rising star and a man with everything to look forward to. He was heading back to Hungary at an exciting time. When he had arrived in Italy in 1447 he had probably never heard of Janos Hunyadi's obscure second son, Matthias. Now, a strange twist of fate was about to bring this unknown boy to the throne.

During Pannonius's last two years in Italy, tremendous changes had taken place in Hungary and among the Hunyadi family. The trouble began in 1456, when reports reached Hungary of a great Ottoman army heading northwards through the Balkans towards Hungary. It was not an unexpected development, as strategists had long predicted that the fall of Constantinople in 1453 would free up a huge reserve of Ottoman man-power. Vitez's friend in Vienna, Piccolomini, had recognised its significance at once. 'Mahomet now reigns among us', he had wailed to Pope Nicholas V. 'The Wallachians must obey the infidel. Soon the Hungarians and Germans must share their fate.'[38]

Four months after the fall of Constantinople, on 30 September 1453, the Pope proclaimed a crusade. But there was a deafening silence among the German princes of the Holy Roman Empire, even after a charismatic Franciscan friar, Giovanni da Capistrano, appeared at the Imperial Diet in Regensburg to summon them all to arms. When Nicholas V died in spring 1555, talk of a crusade lapsed and Hungary was left alone to face the onslaught from Mehmed the Conqueror, although the indefatigable Capistrano rounded up a raggle-taggle volunteer army to head east towards Hungary.

By June 1456, Mehmed's army was in sight of Belgrade, whose position at the confluence of the Sava and the Danube commanded the flat plains of southern Hungary. When the Ottoman siege began on 4 July, few gave Janos Hunyadi, then captain of the Hungarian army, or the aged Capistrano, now 71, much chance. Certainly not the Hungarian court, for the teenage King, Ladislas the Posthumous, had already fled from Buda back to Vienna.

But Hunyadi gloriously vindicated the two defeats he was associated with at Varna and Kosovo. On 22 July, the Ottoman assault on Belgrade was smashed and the army slaughtered as it retreated. The débâcle was so shattering that Hungary was spared a serious invasion for three-quarters of a century. Tragically, Hunyadi was unable to savour his triumph. An epidemic swept through the Christian camp and on 11 August the great warrior succumbed to fever. His body was brought back to Transylvania for burial in the cathedral in Alba Iulia.

One blow after another now fell on his widow, Erzsebet, then staying on her estates in Timisoara. The epic victory at Belgrade made hearts beat for the Hunyadis among Hungarian patriots and the hero-worshipping humanists of Italy. But the Hungarian magnates and their young King did not share those sentiments. Instead, the Hunyadis' aristocratic enemies decided the hour had come to cut this over-ambitious family of Transylvanian *arrivistes* down to size.

Once Hunyadi was safely dead, the King journeyed south to Belgrade to take the credit for a victory he had done nothing to bring about. With him came his former guardian, Count Ulrich of Cillei (now Celje in Slovenia), a bitter enemy of the Hunyadis who was determined to supplant that dynasty with his own. Cillei had an extra reason to loathe the Hunyadis. In an ill-fated attempt to heal the breach between the two families, he had agreed to betroth his daughter, Erzsebet, to Matthias, only for the girl to fall ill and die in September 1455 while staying in the Hunyadi castle at Hunedoara. She had hardly died of neglect. When the girl fell ill, Erzsebet Szilagyi had been distraught, begging Friar Capistrano to come to Transylvania. 'I am convinced that even if you found her dead you would bring her back to life,'[39] she wrote, movingly. But the little girl remained dead, and became an additional bone of contention between the clans.

A poisonous triangular meeting, seething with mistrust, took place in Belgrade on 8 November 1456 between Cillei, the King and Matthias's older brother, Laszlo. The new head of the Hunyadi family was nervous, was fully aware of Cillei's enmity and was determined to take pre-emptive action. The day after the meeting he murdered his rival.

The King showed remarkable presence of mind. Affecting indifference to this outrage he smoothly confirmed Hunyadi in his father's post as captain of the army before journeying back towards Buda. Even now he did not lose his cool, lulling the Hunyadis into a false sense of complacency by halting for weeks in Timisoara and taking part in the elaborate ceremonies of welcome that Erzsebet laid on.[40] The King did not leave Timisoara until the following spring, by which time he felt ready to lay a trap for the Hunyadis. From Buda, he sent an innocuous invitation to Timisoara, summoning both Hunyadi boys to court.

Notwithstanding their father's axiom that 'both boys should never be at court at the same time'[41] – words that still weighed on his widow – they accepted. No doubt Matthias, now in his teens and shedding boyhood, hankered for brighter lights than those on offer in rustic Timisoara or Hunedoara and an escape from the suffocating piety of Erzsebet's household. The two brothers reached Buda at the beginning of March, their fears over their security allayed by a retinue of some 1,200 men, including many of Erzsebet's Szilagyi relatives and hangers-on.

The court put its plans into rapid execution. On the afternoon of 14 March 1457 the gates of Buda castle suddenly closed and the drawbridges were pulled up. The two brothers found themselves trapped inside while their men were on the other side of the Danube in Pest. The King and his magnate advisers acted with great thoroughness. Not only were both Hunyadis caught but Bishop Vitez, the manager of the Hunyadi faction, was also flung in jail.

The papal legate, Cardinal Juan Carjaval, was outraged by this assault on a family almost as famous in Italy as it was in Hungary, and sent word to Rome. But the King moved faster. Laszlo Hunyadi was accused of treason and of plotting against the King's life, 'led by an ambition for the throne that originated in the heart of the father'.[42] He was dead within 48 hours of his arrest, executed in the palace courtyard of Buda on 16 March.

The judicial murder of the son of the hero of the siege of Belgrade sent a thrill of horror through the courts of Europe. It was also a tactical disaster. In Rome, Nicholas V's successor, Calixtus III, roused himself on behalf of the jailed Vitez, ordering the King to release the Bishop. Meanwhile, the Hunyadi party prepared a counterattack from Erzsebet's headquarters in Timisoara, to which her brother, Mihaly, now headed. Too late, the King sent peace envoys to Timisoara. As a mood of revulsion rippled through Hungary, power visibly drained from his bloodstained hands. 'The King has been abandoned by most of his party', the Venetian ambassador reported on 13 June.[43] By then, the question of what to do with Matthias was rearing its head. So far, he had been virtually forgotten. But with Laszlo dead, the other Hunyadi boy suddenly became an important player – or pawn. The King was taking no chances and may have been planning to kill him. In the meantime, he removed Matthias from his temporary jail in Buda, in a little house by the keep at the south end of the royal castle,[44] and took him to Vienna.

Matthias had now been in prison for three months. He must have expected every turn of the lock in his cell to be followed by the entry of an executioner. But once again, the wheel of fortune turned in dramatic fashion. The King had decided to marry. As he was King of Bohemia as well as Hungary, he moved to Prague, having decided to meet his French bride there. Matthias unwillingly accompanied him. What followed is a mystery. The court reached Prague in September. But in the third week of November, the King suddenly complained of feeling ill, and on 23 November 1457 he died.

Hungary was shocked and delighted at the same time. So were many Italians who had followed the confusing sequence of events with interest. As Giovanni Pontano of Naples recalled in the 1490s, in his work *De fortuna*, Matthias's sudden liberation from jail made a terrific impression. 'As a mere stripling he languished long in prison, in chains, in fear of the executioner's axe and the wrath of the King', he wrote. 'But he was swiftly and quite unexpectedly released from that foul and abominable place and elevated to the royal palace.'[45] Vespasiano put it more concisely: 'One brother had his head cut off, the other, in prison, was made King.'[46]

In his apartments in Rome, Calixtus III felt deeply moved, seeing the will of God in the strange events. Surely, he reasoned, this all came to pass so that this mysterious child could lead the longed-for crusade against the Ottoman Turks. The thought that Matthias might follow his brother to the scaffold had made the old Catalan tremble. Matthias must be released from Prague at once, he wrote to Cardinal Carjaval, 'for we have often heard that the young Count will follow in the footsteps of his father'.[47] While the Pope scribbled away, the recently released Vitez was riding towards Prague. In fact, now the King was dead, Matthias was no longer in any danger. Power in Bohemia had passed swiftly into the hands of the country's Czech governor, George (in Czech, Jiri) Podebrad. And Podebrad had no intention of killing Matthias. On the contrary, looking at Matthias, and looking at his teenage daughter Katarina, he was already planning a marriage. As Vitez negotiated the boy's release in Prague, he found himself coming under pressure to agree that Matthias should wed Podebrad's daughter.

Suddenly, the way was open for Matthias not only to be released from jail but to become King, the first commoner to wear the crown in centuries.

Indeed, his election by the parliament looked a foregone conclusion even before the bishops and nobles assembled in Buda towards the end of January 1458. To exclude all doubt, Matthias's uncle, Mihaly Szilagyi, rode into the city at the head of 15,000 armed men who set up their camp in the Fields of Rakosi, just outside the castle where the magnates had gathered. The crowd grew impatient as the speeches stretched out over several days but on 24 January, so the Venetian ambassador wrote, a crowd of tens of thousands burst into cheers when the news broke of Matthias's election.

The Pope was thrilled. 'The news of your election has filled our heart with such joy and satisfaction that we long hesitated over what words we might bestow on our emotions', Calixtus wrote excitedly to Matthias. 'In the elevation of Your Highness we glimpse the fruit of our own prayers and tears', he continued. 'We recognise the man whom God has sent not only for the Kingdom of Hungary but for the whole Christian world . . . [so that] he may consecrate his strength to the glorious struggle to stamp out Mohammedanism'.[48]

What of the teenager on whose shoulders so many expectations were being laid? The experience of the previous months shaped his character for life, reinforcing an element of cynicism that lay just below the surface affability. It is tempting to attribute King Matthias's ruthless instinct for self-preservation to those nine months that followed his arrest in spring 1457. He never forgot the older brother, cut down in his prime. Laszlo's image in bronze, alongside that of his father, Janos, greeted him every time he crossed the palace courtyard in Buda. On his return to Buda in triumph, his first act was to visit his brother's body to pay his last respects before it was transported to Alba Iulia cathedral.

No lifelike portrait survives of Matthias from this time. There are only seals and wooden representations of the King from a couple of books in his collection. A missal from 1469, copied in Vienna by 'Georgius Cathedralis' – George of the cathedral – now in Rome, contains one of a handful of illustrations of the King in the first decade of his reign. It shows a crowned and regally robed Matthias kneeling before the pale figure of a crucified Christ, his shield with its raven motif resting in front of him. It sheds no real light on the King's appearance, or personality, whatever. There is no evidence from this work that 'George of the cathedral' had seen Matthias in the flesh, or if he had done, that this was an attempt at realistic portraiture. This was a conventional image of a monarch with a crown, as was the portrait of Matthias in another early work, the *Libellus de regiis virtutibus* – 'Account of the Virtues of Kings' – presented to Matthias around 1467 by a Hungarian monk living in Italy, Andreas Pannonius.

The Corvinian expert, Ilona Berkovits, cited the Vienna missal as evidence that even in the 1460s Matthias was 'striving to amass an extensive library'.[49] It does no such thing. As the inscription inside the missal indicates,[50] Matthias did not even keep the book, donating it to a Hungarian monk named Thomas. This would have been an odd gesture on the part of a collector. Moreover, the quality of the painting is crude. It is hard to imagine this humble volume taking its place beside the magnificent volumes of the Di Giovanni brothers, Attavante or Cherico. The trail that superficially appears to link it to the Bibliotheca Corviniana thus goes cold.

Though there is little that can be said about a royal library in this era, Matthias's enthusiasm for the art, sculpture and architecture of Italy was already evident. The Italianophile Vitez, now in the ascendant as chancellor and in 1465 Archbishop of Esztergom, following the death of Cardinal Denes Szechy,[51] encouraged it.

In the early 1460s, Italian artists and engineers began descending on Buda, where the new King planned to radically remodel Sigismund's palace. Pannonius's school friend from Ferrara, Galeotto Marzio, had certainly arrived by 1467. The architect Aristotele Fioravanti was also present by 1468, after Matthias lured him from Italy to work on the palace and on defensive fortifications in southern Hungary. Fioravanti later moved unwisely to Moscow where the Tsar, Ivan III, imprisoned him when he tried to leave. By the time 'George of the cathedral' had finished copying the missal for Matthias, Vitez's new university in Bratislava had also been working for two years, Pannonius having brought a papal bull of foundation back with him from Rome.

Vitez probably chose Bratislava as the site of the academy over Buda because it lay further to the west and was thus more accessible to scholars coming from Vienna and Germany. His great triumph was to lure the services of a celebrated young astronomer, Johannes Müller of Königsberg, who rejoiced in the Latin alias 'Regiomontanus' (Königsberg, or king's mountain, in Latin). Regiomontanus was a dynamic character who attracted a following; he must have been a real showman because after his premature death aged 40 in 1476 the most extraordinary feats were attached to his name, including the invention of printing and 'the construction of a mechanical fly that would flutter about a banqueting hall and then return to the host's hand'.[52] Along with Regiomontanus came Marcin Bylica, a former student in Cracow of the great Polish astronomer, Marcin Krol. Given the passion for astrology at Matthias's court, it is not surprising that one of the two men's first tasks was to 'select a horoscope for the university, which would assure it a splendid future'.[53]

If Vitez was the driving force behind the university, Matthias was behind the decision to bring Fioravanti to Hungary. In 1465, he had written to the authorities in Bologna, requesting the services of 'magister Aristotele, architectus singularis', explaining that 'because my main occupation is war against the infidel I very much need such a man'.[54] Warfare was the King's own department. But most of the cultural projects of the first 15 years of the reign, like the university and the recruitment of Regiomontanus, Marzio and the astronomer Bylica, can be traced to Vitez or Pannonius. Significantly, Regiomontanus dedicated his astronomical tables, the *Tabulae directionum*, to Archbishop Vitez, not King Matthias.

The King was corresponding independently with foreign humanists by the 1470s, as his letter of 1471 to Pomponio Leto of Rome indicates. In it, he not only thanked the Roman academician for the gift of a copy of Silius Italicus but described the safe return from Rome of an agent named Blandius who had been sent to acquire books for Matthias. This is the only significant reference to a royal library in these years. As has been noted, the only library Pannonius described in verse was his uncle's. George of Trebizond's words of dedication in the *Almagest* were also indicative, addressing Vitez and Pannonius directly and referring to Matthias only as a third party. The assumption was that Vitez and Pannonius were the patrons of culture, while the King was described as a warrior.

The course of Matthias's life during those early years suggests he had precious little time to dedicate to libraries. He was almost continually at war for more than a quarter of a century; indeed, until the conquest of Vienna in 1485. The fighting started the moment the cheers subsided at his election in January 1458, after the magnates, temporarily thrown into confusion, once more closed ranks against the teenage upstart. Powerful forces outside the country supported these rebels. The rulers of Austria and Poland both believed they had the right to wear the Holy Crown of St Stephen, Frederick III especially, as the Habsburgs had already supplied Hungary with kings in the form of Ladislas the Posthumous and his father, Albert.

Frederick was determined to assert what he saw as his right. He was also in physical possession of the actual Hungarian crown, which Helena Kottaner, lady-in-waiting to Albert's widow, had spirited into Austria in

1441 after Albert's death. It was a powerful bargaining counter, because the Hungarians attached great reverence to this object. 'There are three laws in the kingdom', Helena Kottaner wrote in 1441. 'The first law is that which says that the king of Hungary has to be crowned with the holy crown. The second is that he must be crowned by the Archbishop of Esztergom. The third is that the coronation must be held in Szekesfehervar.'[55]

With the crown in his keeping, Frederick took the advice of a deputation of Hungarian magnates who told him the teenage Matthias would probably back off if Frederick proclaimed himself king, which he did on 27 February 1459. To his surprise, this announcement did not intimidate Matthias, so the Emperor decided to invade. But his army never got far. Frederick was no general.

Calixtus's successor, Pius II, Vitez's old friend, fired off messages to the Emperor through the papal legate, urging him to leave Matthias alone. It was uncomfortable work for Frederick's former secretary but he did not mince his words. Hungary, he told Frederick from Mantua, where he was vainly trying to assemble a crusade, 'is the shield of all Christendom under cover of which we have hitherto been safe'. He went on: 'If the road is thus opened to the barbarians, destruction will break in over all and the consequences of such a disaster will be imputed by God to its authors.'[56]

By May 1459, the military threat from the Habsburgs in Austria was over. But a new danger loomed from the south as the Sultan moved north to Sofia, sending a large army further north to wipe out the last Serbian redoubt at Smederevo, a little way downstream on the Danube from Belgrade. Matthias could do nothing to save the last fragment of the once mighty Serbian state. But he had to lead an army down to southern Hungary to stage a show of force, holding a parliament in the southern town of Szeged.

There was no time to consolidate matters after the Ottomans had been warned off. After realising that he would not be able to control his nephew as he had imagined, Mihaly Szilagyi himself became mutinous. Moreover, his actions gave fresh encouragement to those magnates who still looked to Frederick. Matthias had to hurry back from Szeged to Buda to avert an open revolt on the part of his uncle, promising to make him King of Serbia if he would repel the Ottomans from Smederevo. There was still no peace even after Szilagyi had been dispatched to the south. Once again, Matthias had to set out from the capital, this time to go north-west to deal with the disturbances caused by a Czech warlord, Jan Jiskra, which Frederick was encouraging.

Desperate to obtain relief from the almost continual turmoil, Matthias became anxious to secure the return of the Holy Crown so that his right to the throne could be confirmed once and for all. With the aid of Vitez and a new papal legate – the unflappable Carjaval having been recalled – he hammered out a deal. However, the Emperor struck a hard bargain. Firstly he wanted money: 80,000 ducats in all. More crucially, he wanted to be designated Matthias's heir should he die without issue.

Matthias probably gave little thought to this clause of the Treaty of Wiener Neustadt. He had just married his Bohemian princess in the spring of 1461 and Frederick, born in 1415, was easily old enough to be his father. He little suspected that the treaty, ratified on 19 July 1463, would come back to haunt him.

Treaty signed, Matthias had only weeks to catch his breath before yet another eruption. This time, the trouble came from Bosnia, the land that lay directly south of Croatia on the south side of the River Sava. The status of this mountainous, obscure and sparsely populated land was disputed. Claimed by the Croats as part of their domains, Bosnia had fallen into the orbit of the Hungarian crown following the union of the Hungarian and Croatian kingdoms. Hungary had never seriously tried to impose itself on Bosnia. Indeed, Bosnia functioned as an independent entity in the medieval era. Whether it considered itself independent was of little interest to Hungary, as long as no one else interfered. This, however, is precisely what Mehmed II did once he had dealt with the Serbs.

In 1463, an Ottoman army of 150,000 men, so it was claimed, advanced north through Skopje in Macedonia to Vucitrn in Kosovo and Sjenica in south-west Serbia before heading west into Bosnia. They met no resistance, surrounding Stjepan Tomasevic, King of Bosnia since 1460, in Jajce, in the north. Jajce fell within days, after which the Turks executed the King.

Matthias recognised this as a mortal challenge. With the ink barely dry on his treaty with Frederick, he hurried south in the summer of 1463, travelling through Virovitica in Slavonia and charging across the Sava into northern Bosnia. He soon took Jajce from the Ottomans and in the bitter winter months that followed, forced them from one town after another in northern Bosnia, securing Croatia's southern flank and Hungary's, too. Wearing his victor's laurels he returned in January 1464 to find Buda *en fête*. The joy of victory was marred by the sudden death of the young Queen. But even this tragedy did not stop Matthias from proceeding with the overdue coronation in Szekesfehervar, now he had finally prised the Hungarian crown from Frederick's custody.

Once again, the King had to mount his horse. The loss of Jajce outraged Mehmed, who decided to accompany a fresh conquest of Bosnia himself. Matthias again rode south across the Sava towards Jajce, successfully seeing off an Ottoman siege. The humiliated Ottomans retreated. However, the Hungarian army was also exhausted. Over the summer and autumn of 1464, Matthias made a last attempt to drive the Ottomans from their crucial fortress in eastern Bosnia at Zvornik, on the west bank of the River Drina. But the Ottoman garrison in Zvornik held out and this time it was Matthias who retreated, heading back to Szeged in December 1464. Matthias made one last expedition to Bosnia the following year but the results were inconclusive.

By 1465, it dawned on Matthias that he had been in one battle after another with scarcely a break for the seven years that had passed since his election as king. He had been hailed as Christ's Athlete and as the appointed redeemer of Christendom. But as he ruefully noted to Pius II, shortly before the Pope's death in August 1464, allies in this sacred undertaking had been in short supply. As he told Pius, who shared his disappointment, Hungary could not roll back the Ottoman Empire unaided.

He had, in fact, reached a crossroads and was about to make two crucial decisions. One was to dispense with his traditional feudal army, which was dependent on the nobles, and create a new, mercenary force responsible to him alone. That required the complete overhaul of the crown's finances and the imposition of new and more efficient tax mechanisms.

The other decision was to abandon the whole idea of leading a great crusade against Ottoman rule in Europe. This was a real revolution in terms of his family history. Janos Hunyadi had sacrificed his life to holy war against the Infidel. It was this cause that had made the Hunyadis wildly popular at home and abroad. Two popes, Calixtus and Pius, had supported Matthias's right to wear the crown mainly because they believed he would resume the struggle interrupted in 1456 by Hunyadi's death.

Matthias talked to the end of his life about crusades, especially to popes. Months before his death, he assured Innocent VIII that he was about to take up his cross. But after 1465 this was just talk. Frustrated with the hopelessness of leading solitary campaigns in the Balkans, Matthias was shifting his gaze towards the north and west. To the north lay Bohemia whose heretical king was no longer his father-in-law. To the west was Frederick, whose imperial title was threadbare and who only really governed a patchwork of Habsburg lands in Austria. They were both tempting targets. The problem was that this change of policy appalled such crucial supporters of the Hunyadi family as Vitez and his nephew Pannonius. To them, it smacked of utter betrayal.

CHAPTER FOUR

'Ceaselessly entangled in warfare'

Thus, in a short space of time, both archbishop and bishop died miserably.

Vespasiano on the deaths of Vitez and Pannonius[1]

In Esztergom, I took a narrow set of stone steps leading from the riverside Vizivaros, or 'water town', to the high rock on which the cathedral perches. A winding road runs up towards this grey classical pile but I followed a group of tourists ascending by the more direct route, pausing as they stopped to pant and catch their breath, before we all finally emerged at the summit, among swallows wheeling and screaming on the air currents.

The view from the top was magnificent, allowing me to scan far beyond the Danube on to the plains of what is now Slovakia. It is a favourite spot for lovers and newly-weds to pose beside a rather ugly white statue. Centuries ago, however, it was Esztergom's strategic location rather than the romantic atmosphere that appealed to Hungary's first rulers. It is why they chose this site as their capital after their conquest of the great plain.

In 1933, a teenage Briton, Patrick Leigh Fermor, began his account of a journey from Hungary to Transylvania at Esztergom. During a visit on Easter Saturday, Fermor caught a last glimpse of the aristocratic pre-war regime, observing the regal figure of the Archbishop descending from his carriage amid lighted torches before disappearing into the cathedral with an escort of colourfully dressed relics of the feudal era. That social order has vanished along with the piety that went with it. The Hungarians I followed into the gloom of the cathedral crypt neither bowed nor crossed themselves as they strolled past grandiose tombs and effigies of former archbishops. They merely stared, or took the odd photograph.

Most walked straight past the older tombs, heading for the shrine-tomb of Cardinal Mindszenty, whose defiance of the post-war communist order and self-imposed isolation in the American embassy in Budapest made him a hero to anti-communists. Ribbons decorated with the Hungarian tricolour lie strewn over his tomb, which still attracts crowds of visitors. Even here, however, I detected a slight awkwardness, for the communist Hungary that Mindszenty detested and despised has left its stamp. There is little left of the fierce nationalism, the social deference or the piety that Fermor observed. His world of wandering geese, portly innkeepers, village fiddlers, virgin brides, peasants dressed in peculiar costumes and gentry rotting quietly in crumbling castles has gone. The relationship of the homogenised, westernised, classless and secular modern Hungarians to their glamorous past is not always easy to dissect. Between Mindszenty's world and that of the day-trippers in Esztergom cathedral I sensed a great gulf.

I left the Hungarian day-trippers staring at the tomb of Mindszenty and returned to a spot none of them had shown any interest in – the tomb of Archbishop Vitez. The effigy of Matthias's great counsellor lay in semi-darkness, an imposing sight in red marble, dressed in episcopal robes with mitre and crozier. There was no hint here of the catastrophic note on which his life had ended, nor any reference to the equally dismal end of his nephew. But it was here in Esztergom that the drama of his final months was played out.

It is hard today to imagine how the palace of Esztergom must have looked in Vitez's lifetime. As in Buda and Visegrad, time has effaced all. Apart from the tombs in the cathedral crypt, only the marble chapel that Tamas Bakocz constructed as archbishop in the 1500s, which was dismantled during the Ottoman occupation and later reconstructed, recalls the lost world of the Hungarian Renaissance.

Engravings in the local museum recapture the likeness of the Esztergom that Vitez knew, however. These depict a walled and gated town, towering above riverside suburbs. The twin towers of the cathedral of St Adalbert can be seen in the middle, while the roof of a palace and, a short distance away, the spire of the church of St Istvan, or Stephen, are visible. Another wood-cut, dating from 1595 when Habsburg armies briefly recaptured Esztergom, shows the walls of the palace or castle still standing but roofless and in obvious decay.

Imprecise as they are, the woodcuts convey just enough of the flavour of the place that Vitez inhabited from 1465, when he received the arch-bishopric, until 1472. His elevation would have seemed a great vindication of his long connection to the Hunyadi family, first to the heroic father, now to the astonishing son. With his nephew now a fellow bishop in Pecs, one of the wealthiest sees in the country, the triangular partnership between the three men looked invincible.

Yet 1465, this year of triumph, when Vitez became Primate and Pannonius was entrusted with leading the embassy to Italy, was the beginning of the end. Gradually, the two humanists were coming to the conclusion that their royal prodigy was swerving from the path they had mapped out for him; that he was leading the country to disaster.

When Vitez had escorted the teenage Matthias back from Prague, he appeared grateful to his father's friend and adviser. Years later, as Vitez brooded over the course of events in his apartments at Esztergom, he prob-ably reflected that worrying signs of Matthias's wilful, dictatorial, tempera-ment had been there all along. First, there had been the unfilial way he had dismissed his troublesome uncle, Mihaly Szilagyi, from the court. Within months of Matthias's return from Bohemia, the young King had banished him to the front line in Serbia to fight the Ottomans. Conveniently for Matthias, the Turks had captured and decapitated him. We have no record of the reaction of his sister, Erzsebet, to this loss but she must have been devastated at this new blow to her shrinking family. Having lost her husband to fever at Belgrade and her elder son to an executioner's axe in Buda, she now lost her brother to an Ottoman scimitar.

There is no evidence that Vitez had opposed this particular manoeuvre, startlingly brutal in one so young and inexperienced. But when Matthias turned the tables on the Archbishop and his nephew, he may have wondered at his earlier failure to notice the ruthlessness of his young protégé.

Then came the great volte-face in foreign policy, after the failure to capture Zvornik in Bosnia in the winter of 1464. This was the bigger shock to Vitez. As a policy reversal, it was as challenging as the attempt to recast Hungary after the Second World War as an ally of Russia's, when the whole thrust of Hungary's history since 1849, when Russian armies crushed Hungary's war of independence against Austria, had been anti-Russian. Men like Vitez had great difficulty in accepting that the natural order of affairs was *détente* with the detested Ottomans and warfare with the Christian Czechs.

Perhaps Erzsebet Szilagyi also felt confused by her son's rejection of the values for which her husband had died. But she was a loyal figure and revolt against her only living son was inconceivable. Vitez was made of different material.

It was the Pope who inadvertently offered Matthias cover to make a discreet exit from the business of warfare against the Ottomans and divert his attentions to Bohemia. The kings of Bohemia and Hungary resembled each other in several respects. Podebrad was also a strong man who had risen to the top through his own efforts and who had defied the principle of dynasticism in doing so. 'He had much in common with his contemporaries Matthias Corvinus of Hungary, Casimir IV, Louis XI and Edward IV', one recent historian said. 'He was not a member of any of the great dynastic families of his day; he had not a drop of Luxembourg, Habsburg, Jagiello, or even Premyslid blood in his veins; he was a native Czech, merely the most successful of the newly enriched landed nobility who by his eminent ability . . . outlived or outdid his fellow oligarchs . . . making the whole realm his estate.'[2]

Matthias viewed his royal neighbour to the north with no particular fellow feeling, however. He saw his former father-in-law simply as a weak link in the surrounding chain of sovereigns and as the ruler of a country whose anomalous, schismatic Church rendered it a convenient and legitimate target.

The affairs of the Bohemian Church were complex. In essence, it had been out of communion with Rome for years by the time Matthias and George of Podebrad took their respective thrones. After the popular reformist Czech preacher, Jan Huss, answered a summons to the Diet of Constance in 1415, only to be burned for heresy, Bohemia had rebelled in a patriotic fury against Rome and its own sovereign, Sigismund, King of Hungary and Bohemia. As a result, Sigismund had not been able to enter Prague until a year before his death in 1436. By then, the most radical elements in the Bohemian Church had been defeated and the more socially and ecclesiastically conservative gentry had gained the upper hand in Prague under Podebrad and his ecclesiastical ally, Jan Rokycana.

After a couple of botched German invasions failed to subdue the newly assertive Czechs, the papacy – which was then under enormous internal pressure to surrender much of its autocratic powers to Church councils – had no option but to reach a deal with the Czechs. A compromise was hammered out at the Council of Basle in 1432. Known as the Compacts of

Basle, the terms did not solve the Czech crisis but contained it, permitting the Bohemians their minimum demands: a vernacular liturgy and use of the communion cup by the laity, privileges generally forbidden by the Catholic Church elsewhere.

Only the most naïve contemporaries imagined this was anything more than a holding solution. It was clearly unlikely that the Catholic Church would permit the permanent existence in the heart of Europe of a national church that answered to nobody and took an à la carte approach to theology and practice.

Vitez's future friend, Piccolomini, now Pius II, was not among them. The once easygoing and rather libidinous humanist had hardened in middle age into a militant Catholic. His loathing of the Hussites had grown accordingly. The decision of the Bohemian parliament to select Rokycana as Archbishop of Prague in 1435, ignoring the Pope in the matter, outraged his sense of Catholic discipline. In 1448, he had described him to Nicholas V as that 'pestilent Rokycana, son of darkness, confessor of the devil and prophet of Antichrist'. It was 'unheard of, horrid, detestable [that] Rokycana, who was neither called to the see [of Prague] nor sent to it, names himself archbishop and rules the metropolis . . . Oh, that Your Holiness would not let such a crime go unpunished!'[3] As Pope from 1458, he was as determined to challenge this monstrosity in Central Europe, and the arrival in Rome of a Bohemian delegation in March 1462 did nothing to reassure him. On the contrary, he revoked the Compacts of Basle on 31 March.

Annulling the Compacts was one thing. Finding a suitable Athlete of Christ to execute his words was another. Pius II never achieved his aim of humbling Bohemia. His former master, the Emperor Frederick, was little help; he had his grand title but – as Pius knew only too well – little else. Moreover, Podebrad had wisely ingratiated himself with the Emperor, sending him military aid when his brother was besieging him. The Pope's second choice, Casimir of Poland, was not interested in warring with the Czechs, either. That left one other candidate: the King of Hungary, who began discovering scruples about the Hussites that he had not been aware of when he married a Hussite princess.

Shortly after Pius summoned the Czech King to Rome, he died in 1464 at Ancona. But Pius's death only increased the pressure on Bohemia, for his successor, the Venetian Pietro Barbo, who reigned as Paul II, turned out to be equally hard line. On 28 June 1465, the new Pope appealed to Bohemia's neighbours to cease all communications with Podebrad and on 8 December he issued a papal bull, branding him a heretic and 'the son of perdition' and nullifying the Bohemians' allegiance to their ruler. A second bull in December 1466 deposed Podebrad altogether as an 'obstinate heretic and protector of heretics'. Now he was 'deprived and divested of all dignity, dominion and possession, also of all the rights of a king, margrave, duke and all other such rank'.[4] The post of Bohemian king was now vacant in Rome's eyes, though the current occupant showed no sign of withdrawing.

Podebrad's weak spot was not Bohemia, where patriotic sentiment rallied the Czechs to their native-born King, but Moravia, where Czech nationalism was weaker, and Silesia, where the urban population was mainly German. These townsmen looked on the Czech heretics with especial loathing, compounded by feelings of deep racial rivalry with the Slavs. As the Czech struggle with Rome intensified, the town of Wroclaw, or Breslau in German, became the headquarters of the enemies of the Czech King.

Over the course of 1467, the rebels – an unlikely consortium of German merchants from Wroclaw, traditionalist Czech magnates from Bohemia and the Catholic Bishop of Olomouc in Moravia – looked around for a champion. They found him in Buda, where Matthias had been touting his services as potential leader of a crusade against the Hussites and as next King of Bohemia for some time. Shortly after the death of his first wife Katarina, he had told Paul II in October 1465 that he fervently supported the Pope's 'apostolic proceedings' against the 'so-called King of Bohemia', adding: 'I have, most Holy Father, dedicated myself and my realm for all times to the service of the Holy Roman Church and of Your Holiness . . . nor shall old treaties constrain me . . . thus whether the call to war is against the Czechs or against the Turks, Matthias and his Hungarians will be ready.'[5]

Immediate action was not practical, however. In the mid-1460s, with the help of his treasurer, Janos Ernuszt, a Viennese convert from Judaism,[6] Matthias was busy pushing through comprehensive tax reforms, abolishing the various exemptions that the nobles had squeezed out of earlier kings and introducing a new tax on the basis of the *porta*, or gate, collected on an annual basis, or more often if necessary.

The reforms transformed Matthias's income from around 250,000 florins a year at the start of the reign to around 700,000 or even 800,000 florins. The tax on the *porta* accounted for around half that sum, the rest coming from monopolies, mints, towns and other sources.[7] Among other things it enabled him to dispense with the feudal levy and establish his long-planned mercenary army. Parliament went along with the reforms, but they offended the nobles in Transylvania who mustered a surprisingly large rebel army that briefly converged on Matthias's home town of Cluj, setting up its headquarters in a Benedictine convent. There, the rebel leaders drew up a protocol complaining of 'all the oppressions to which they and all the inhabitants of Hungary are now subjected'.[8] The revolt in Transylvania fully occupied Matthias until Christmas 1467, when the rebel army melted away following the King's startlingly rapid arrival in Cluj.

Once Transylvania had been pacified – and the remnants of the rebel army pursued over the border into neighbouring Moldavia – and after Matthias had received a high-ranking Ottoman delegation in Oradea offering a lasting truce, he felt freer to put his Bohemian plans into effect. In March 1468, therefore, he advertised his plans to parliament, painting the Czech peril in vivid colours. Penning an aggressively worded missive to Podebrad's son, Viktorin, he admitted he now sided with Podebrad's opponents, claiming that he was taking up arms on behalf of the Emperor – the same man Podebrad had saved from defeat at the hands of his brother only a few years before. To give his actions a veneer of theological respectability, Matthias further claimed that his injured religious sensibilities also impelled him to act. 'We will take into protection the Catholic inhabitants of your lands with regard to your unjust proceedings, as befits a Catholic ruler at the special invitation of the Holy Apostolic See', he wrote. 'May the Lord of Hosts, the shield of justice, stand by us.'[9]

Podebrad answered this sanctimonious hot air with dignity. 'When you had already resolved to engulf us in war, you could have spared us accusations that will definitely not bring victory but only complicate reconciliation,' he wrote back.[10] Matthias was unmoved, churning out more religious grievances in the manifesto he released from Bratislava in April. The forthcoming campaign in Bohemia, he declared, was a war 'no less holy than those we have long waged with the Turks . . . what alone spurs us is our sympathy for the oppressed . . . the only reward we anticipate is peace'.[11] It was an unattractive half-truth, for it seems clear that opportunism – not sympathy for the oppressed Catholics of Bohemia – was the main spur to Matthias's decision to take up arms.

Victory by the newly proclaimed protector of Bohemia ought to have been a walkover because Matthias's tax increases had made him a rich man. His 700,000–800,000 ducats a year did not make him the richest ruler in Europe; at its late fifteenth-century zenith, the annual income of Venice was estimated at over a million ducats.[12] As for the Ottoman Sultan, he could muster many times that amount. But the King of Hungary was now in the premier league. Bohemia was far poorer and smaller than its southern neighbour, and its ailing 48-year-old King could not afford to keep an army in the field for very long when a single mounted soldier cost about a ducat a week.

Matthias, according to observers, dispatched at least 16,000 men into the first Bohemian campaign, including 8,000 cavalry and 50 heavy guns. The Emperor, not wanting to be left out, lent about 3,000 infantry.[13] To contribute to the air of magnificence, Matthias dragged half the court off with him to Bohemia, setting out with Vitez, Pannonius, the Archbishop of Kalocsa and an ambitious young Silesian, Johannes Beckensloer, the Bishop of Eger. A large company of Hungarian and rebel Bohemian grandees brought up the rear.

However, Matthias was denied the victory he expected. While Wroclaw and the Catholics of Moravia hailed Matthias as a saviour, Hussite Bohemia rallied to its popular leader. It soon became clear Matthias would not be making a triumphal entry into Prague, the city he had last seen in chains.

Nor was the Hungarian generalissimo a particularly great military tactician, it turned out. By the summer of 1468, Matthias had brought Silesia and most of Moravia under his control but Podebrad, as Oliver Cromwell was to remark of Charles I, had only to remain in the field to triumph and by September, when Matthias retreated to Hungary, Podebrad had not been dislodged.

The second season of fighting that began in the New Year of 1469 confirmed that Podebrad and Viktorin were the better captains. After Matthias marched north in February from his camp at Brno towards the Czech stronghold of Kutna Hora, the Czechs surrounded him at Vilemov. It looked as if Matthias might once again revisit his old prison cell in Prague. His quick wit and a talent for dissimulation saved him, however, as Matthias convinced Podebrad that he would mediate on his behalf with Pope Paul in return for his liberty.

It was a major tactical error on Podebrad's part. The moment Matthias escaped from the Czechs he reneged. He received Podebrad in high style in his tent in Olomouc in April, only to present the Czech King with a list of insulting demands, including Podebrad's public submission to Rome, the appointment of a papalist archbishop to Prague, and the nomination of himself as heir to the Bohemian throne. After Podebrad unsurprisingly declined to sign this political suicide note, Matthias repaid Podebrad's earlier generosity to him by having himself declared King of Bohemia in the cathedral at Olomouc on 3 May 1469. Matthias recalled it as one of the highlights of his life, ordering the horoscope for that auspicious day to be recorded in paint on the ceiling of his palace in Buda. The Czechs recorded the event differently. As one historian wrote: 'There are in history not many examples of the chivalrous spirit manifested by George on the one hand, and of the perfidy which directed Matthias's steps soon afterwards.'[14]

No actual coronation was possible in Olomouc, as the Bohemian crown remained in Podebrad's possession in Prague. But Archbishop Vitez was on hand to lend respectability to this dubious ceremony, tendering the oath to Matthias in the cathedral before the rebel Catholic lords of Bohemia and the papal legate. A sumptuous banquet followed for 400 guests with the usual wine fountains set up in the streets to slake the thirst of the crowds. In May, Matthias moved to Wroclaw to display his Catholic devotion at that year's Corpus Christi procession, at which four bishops, the papal legate and several German princes, including Frederick of Brandenburg, took part, defying the extraordinarily heavy rain.

The celebrations at Olomouc and Wroclaw, remarkable for their pomp and expense, revealed a new side to Matthias's character. Hitherto his reign had evinced a martial, almost spartan, quality and the court had been known for its simple lifestyle and lack of ritual. Now those characteristics receded as a new culture of conspicuous expense took its place and as Matthias revealed his determination to buy his way into the front row of Europe's monarchs. It would have been fascinating to observe the expression on Vitez's face as he tendered the oath to Matthias in the alien and incongruous setting of Olomouc cathedral. Did he look uncomfortable in his heavy archiepiscopal robes? Vitez did not appear in the Corpus Christi procession in Wroclaw, allegedly detained by state business. If he looked outwardly unperturbed, it was a mask. Underneath, he was a shaken and disillusioned man.

The fact that Matthias had abandoned warfare against the Ottomans caused him deep misgivings. Vitez was no religious zealot, so making a parade of Catholic purity against the Czech heretics would not have engaged him. More to the point, the war with the Hussites was unwinnable – a 'quagmire', in modern military parlance. It was consuming more and more money, having swallowed an estimated 400,000 ducats by 1469. We know the King's growing contempt for his authority deeply offended Vitez. It was wounding for a man who had practically dandled Matthias on his knee to see him disregarding his advice in private and humiliating him in public, as he did very notoriously, striking him on the face at a fraught session of the royal council.

No record survives of the exact nature of their argument. However, one may imagine the Archbishop's voice, now tremulous with old age, for he was about 60, listing the King's follies one by one: the absurdity of waging war against Christians in the west; the failure to confront the Turkish menace in the east; the immense cost of the campaigns; the alienation of the Magyar nobility; the insult to the memory of the King's own father. We can also imagine the effect these words had on their quick-tempered hearer: the King's purple face; a clenched fist banging the table; a goblet of wine skittering on to the stone floor; and then the King rising to grab the Archbishop by his cloak and slap his face.

There must have been several red faces among the other royal counsellors as they tried to gauge what was happening. But one was less abashed. Bishop Beckensloer of Eger, one of the clique of Silesian Germans who had attached themselves to Matthias, knew his star was in the ascendant.

The Silesian party at court had no interest in Ottoman campaigns. The Turks were nowhere near Wroclaw. The Czechs were, however, and the Silesian Germans lobbied constantly for the continuation of Hungary's war in and against Bohemia. Beckensloer was by all accounts a deeply unattractive man – belligerent, greedy and devoid of piety. Pannonius also lacked piety, but he was a genius by way of compensation. Beckensloer was little more than a thug. But he could be ingratiating when he had to be. He had happily accompanied the King to the battlefields of Bohemia in 1468 and had stood beside Archbishop Vitez at Matthias's improvised coronation in Olomouc the following year. Now he stood ready to stick the knife into Vitez's back and profit from a fortuitous rupture between Matthias and his chief adviser. Biding his time, he waited for a far more important post than the bishopric of Eger to fall into his lap.

Vitez felt increasingly isolated in the months following Matthias's coronation in Moravia, and still more as the fruitless war in Bohemia dragged on into 1470. His most important foreign ally, Pius II, was long dead and Vitez was not close to his successor, Paul II. The Hunyadi party had dissolved. Mihaly Szilagyi had been killed. Matthias's mother, Erzsebet, had withdrawn to the shadows. Of the Archbishop's *grands projets*, only his university in Bratislava and his library remained.

The Primate was not alone in his bitter disappointment. His nephew shared his growing antipathy to Matthias. Pannonius was a lonely man in Hungary for reasons that have been discussed. He was also ill with tuberculosis, and sliding steadily out of favour with the King following the relatively meagre results of his trip to Italy in 1465. He had never fully adjusted to life as a Hungarian prelate after the over-long sojourn in Italy. Equipped by Guarino for a career as a diplomat, orator, or member of one of those 'academies' that Italian humanists loved to found in fifteenth-century Rome, Florence or Naples, he was almost redundant in warlike Hungary.

Hungary had not been right for him. As the editor of Pannonius's *Epigrams*, A. Barrett, noted: 'The cities were few and small, their burghers mostly German craftsmen and traders, the nobility pretty poor and the great lords, with few exceptions, unlettered ... The affairs of state were too numerous to permit leisure even for the best. It is characteristic that even Janus, poet, bishop and royal orator, had to join the King on campaigns or even take part in the command of the southern defences, while in the west by the mid-fifteenth century a man of his qualities would have little to do with military matters.'[15]

In his last years, he confided to verse a conviction that his return home had destroyed his health. 'Blood is seeping from my sagging bowels,' he lamented. 'And a fever has raged for three days. If this was the wretched welcome my native soil had for me, I ought never to have returned.'[16] He also confided his growing loathing of the martial atmosphere at court, writing a pointed diatribe against warfare in 1470, 'Pleading with Mars for Peace':

> *Waster of plough lands, destroyer of towns,*
> *World's depopulator, filler of hell,*
> *Eater of corpses, drunk on human blood,*
> *Man's horrible plague, cursed by all women.*[17]

Pannonius complained that the return to Hungary had destroyed his creativity as well:

> *In Latin soil I wrote perhaps in a style more Latin*
> *But now in a barbaric land, I babble out barbaric lines ...*
> *Put Virgil here and Virgil's lyre will grate*
> *Let Cicero come here and Cicero will be mute.*[18]

As Pannonius's biographer, Mirjana Birnbaum, wrote, Pannonius combined hostile thoughts about the wastefulness of warfare with public panegyrics to the King's military exploits. One was penned in 1469, at the height of the Bohemian campaign. But Birnbaum has described these outpourings as lifeless, 'cranked out as a token of the poet's loyalty, displaying above all [their] author's lack of genuine enthusiasm toward his subject'.[19]

Did Matthias also detect insincerity in the Bishop of Pecs's mechanical praises? The year 1469 marked the last time that he promoted either Vitez or Pannonius. That year he appointed the Bishop of Pecs as ban, or viceroy, of his native Slavonia, alongside Johannes, or Ivan, Thuz, a close relative of Osvald Thuz, the Bishop of Zagreb. It was a dispiriting experience. Pannonius was not much of a general and there was little he could do to stem the frequent Ottoman raids from Bosnia while the main army was far away in Bohemia. He was soon relieved of his command.

Back in Slavonia, Pannonius must have been deluged with complaints from his fellow countrymen about the price they were paying for the King's new foreign policy. Living close to the front line with the Ottomans, it was Croat towns and defences that were being neglected while the King struggled to subdue the Czechs. Whatever treasonous thoughts floated around Pannonius at this time were clearly shared by other Croat magnates, including Bishop Thuz, a key figure in the emerging conspiracy.

Podebrad's death, aged 50, on 22 March 1471 brought the conspiracy to a head, as it became clear that the Bohemian war would go on and on. In the months before Podebrad died, Matthias was no nearer to delivering a knock-out blow than he had been at the start. Indeed, the Czechs were gaining the upper hand; their defeat of the Hungarians in the field on 2 November 1470 had prompted Podebrad to boast to the Margrave of Brandenburg that 'as the King of Hungary had drunk with us Bohemian beer, so shall we with God's help all the more certainly drink with him Hungarian wine'.[20]

Podebrad's death robbed him of the chance to take the war to Hungary as he had hoped. But he had acted to ensure Matthias would never profit from his death to obtain the Bohemian crown.

Prudently calculating that his sons would not be able to hold on to the throne in such adverse international conditions, Podebrad made separate provisions for them. In the summer of 1469 he bequeathed Bohemia's crown to Casimir IV of Poland's eldest son, Wladislas. Matthias had to watch in impotent rage from his Moravian redoubt as a parliament in Prague confirmed the Polish candidate as the new King of Bohemia on 25 May 1471, after which three Polish bishops travelled to Prague to crown him on 22 August.

Unbeknownst to Matthias, the younger brother of the Polish prince, called Casimir like his father, was by now on the receiving end of regular communications from Matthias's disillusioned subjects, led by Archbishop Vitez and the bishops of Pecs and Zagreb. Despairing that the war in Bohemia would ever end, they sent a stream of encouraging messages to the 13-year-old prince's father. As he was still a boy, the plotters probably envisaged a joint regency, lasting for four or five years.

The Polish court was receptive to the plot maturing in Esztergom, Pecs and Zagreb. Like Frederick III of Austria, they had never quite swallowed the idea that an upstart commoner like Matthias should wear the Holy Crown of Hungary and had shown their true feelings on the matter by dismissing Matthias's request in 1468 to marry King Casimir's daughter. The Poles were persuaded – as Frederick had been a decade earlier – that an invasion would trigger a general revolt.

An unknown cleric in Esztergom probably overheard the Archbishop's talk and betrayed Vitez's plan to Matthias in Moravia. With his instinct for survival honed in the prisons of Buda and Prague, Matthias knew when he faced mortal danger and hurried back to Hungary with his army. Surprised before their plot had reached fruition, the rebels were thrown into disarray as the King marched into Buda, again displaying those arts of dissimulation for which he was well known. Matthias was an expert in delivering the soft answer that turned away wrath and he soon had the rebels at odds with one another, graciously promising to right all wrongs and unexpectedly handing out favours to many who might well have expected terrible retribution. At the parliament he called in September he won round the assembly by promising never again to rule without their counsel, to summon the assembly annually and to honour all its former rights and privileges. (Not surprisingly, he did the opposite, summoning fewer and fewer parliaments after the mid-1470s.)[21] He even handled the head of the conspiracy with kid gloves – at first. There were no Dracula-style impalings and boilings: Matthias simply arrested the Archbishop and confined him to Esztergom under armed guard.

The result was total confusion when a Polish force of 12,000, assembled by King Casimir on behalf of his second son, crossed the Hungarian border in the first week of October only to meet absolute silence instead of applauding crowds. Pannonius, deciding his life was finished anyway, recklessly opened the gates of the northern town of Nyitra to the Poles. But this was not enough to breathe life into the botched invasion, which rapidly dissolved after Christmas as the soldiers fled helter skelter back to Poland.

The King now dealt with the rebel chiefs at his leisure. He moved Vitez from Esztergom to a jail in his own palace in Visegrad. His nephew fled into the arms of his fellow conspirator, Bishop Thuz of Zagreb, hoping to stop there for a while before dragging his dying body back to his beloved Italy. Thuz was probably embarrassed by the arrival of this dangerous and undesirable guest. Perhaps he had already received some intimation from Buda that the King might consider him for parole if he played his cards right. However, Thuz did not have to play host for long. Pannonius never made it to Italy but died a fortnight after he reached the Bishop of Zagreb's castle at Medvedgrad, on 27 March 1472. He was buried in the Pauline church at Remete, near Zagreb, and reburied in Pecs. Vitez followed him a few months later, on 9 August, shattered by the knowledge that his prodigal nephew was dead and that a lifetime's work had turned to ashes.

The news of the deaths of the two great humanist scholars soon reached Italy, and it grieved Vespasiano. He had only heard of Vitez from others but he had known Pannonius personally, when the world had been the youngster's oyster. 'Thus, in a short space of time, both archbishop and bishop died miserably', he noted in his memoirs. 'These two had been the chief ornaments of the kingdom and had drawn thither many men illustrious in every branch of learning, who now that they were dead, took their departure.'[22]

That was a slight exaggeration. As has been noted, Matthias was not like his house guest, Dracula – then kicking his heels in Visegrad, pulling the wings off birds and crucifying mice to pass the time. Matthias could be duplicitous, as his conduct towards Podebrad had shown. But inflicting vile punishments on defeated enemies was beneath him. Throughout his life he let off plotters remarkably lightly, often promoting them to put them out of harm's way. This time, the Thuz family was left untouched. The Bishop remained at his post in Zagreb for another quarter-century, his treason long forgotten. He kept himself busy erecting stout fortifications against the Turks around Zagreb cathedral and died in 1499, long after Matthias's death. Miklos Ujlaki, another key conspirator, was also kicked 'upstairs', Matthias granting him the fine-sounding, if empty, title of King of Bosnia.

It was not true, as Vespasiano claimed, that an exodus of humanists from Hungary took place after 1471. Pannonius's friend Galeotto Marzio tactfully absented himself for a while in Bologna. But he cannot have been that scared of the atmosphere at court in Buda because he returned, cap in hand, having brushed with the Inquisition in Italy. Matthias was as bluff and as hail-fellow-well-met towards the returnee as ever. He probably found the business of Marzio's scrapes in Italy hugely amusing. He kept Marzio beside him in Buda for the rest of his reign.

The astronomer Regiomontanus left the court in 1471. But he left Hungary for Nuremberg between mid-March and the end of April,[23] some months before the revolt erupted and it is unlikely he was aware of it or understood what it was about. He had already shifted his operations from Bratislava and Esztergom to the royal palace in Buda, working with the King on the creation of an observatory. (Matthias had clamoured for his attention.)[24] Matthias did not regard the German astrologer as linked in any way to the rebellion and when Regiomontanus died in 1476, he sent Hans Dorn, Regiomontanus's old colleague from the Buda observatory, to Germany to try and recover his books and instruments. He also moved Regiomontanus's book of astronomical tables, the *Tabulae directionum*,[25] dedicated to Vitez, to his own library.

Significantly, Regiomontanus's colleague, the Pole Marcin Bylica, stayed put in Buda after 1471. Like many of Vitez's allies and protégés, he coolly switched from the Archbishop's service to the King's. Like Marzio, Bylica also remained at court in Buda until Matthias's death.

Matthias was generous to the memories of his disgraced former advisers. Vitez got his splendid tomb in Esztergom and Pannonius may have got the same. Admittedly we have only Bonfini to rely on for this information, and it may be only a charming legend, but the Italian historian claimed Matthias was taken aback on seeing the humble nature of Pannonius's tomb in Pecs and ordered his reburial in grander style under the inscription: 'Here lies Janus, with whom came first to Danube's shore the laurelled goddess of Helicon. This triumph, envy leave unto the dead; malice, spare at least his remaining dust.'[26]

According to Bonfini, the King ensured Pannonius's lasting fame by entrusting Archbishop Varadi of Kalocsa with collecting up his Latin epigrams. Again, the claim cannot be proved one way or the other. The oldest extant published work of Pannonius's, his panegyric to his beloved teacher Guarino, postdates Matthias's death by almost a quarter of a century and was printed first in Vienna in 1512 and then in Basle in 1518. What books or accounts these versions drew on is unknown. As for Varadi, he had only a certain number of years to complete his compilation of Pannonius's works because in 1484 he also fell foul of the King for obscure reasons and was arrested. He remained in jail until the King's death. As he was released in 1490 and lived until 1501, it is quite conceivable that Bonfini knew what he was talking about when he said Varadi was Pannonius's royally appointed literary executor. But we cannot be certain.

There is one telling incident that might be said to shed some light on Matthias's attitude to the conspirators, however. Shortly after Pannonius's death, his former fellow student in Ferrara, Lodovico Carbone, composed his obsequious eulogy to the King. The author obviously hoped the *Dialogus de Matthiae regis laudibus*[27] would prompt an invitation to Buda to join the throng of pampered foreigners ensconced there. The manuscript was sent to Buda, entered the library and survives. Yet Carbone received a royal snub. There was no response to his honeyed words and no invitation to court. This may have been on account of the prose, or, as has been said, because Matthias disliked the character of the flattery. Perhaps Carbone was unwise to write: 'None who comes to court to see and greet you leaves empty-handed. You grant money . . . to all learned men.'[28] ('No, I do not,' Matthias may have thought.)

But the snub may also have been because Matthias had read the work and bristled at the author's clumsy attempt to ingratiate himself with the King by making hostile references to Pannonius.

Even if the outcome of the plot was less damaging to the cause of the humanists in Hungary than Vespasiano suggested, the downfall of Vitez and Pannonius had consequences. These two had been the active agents of the Renaissance in Hungary. As one historian put it, 'Without Vergerio, no Johannes Vitez, without Vitez, no Janus Pannonius, without both, no humanist court of Matthias's, and no Quattrocento in Hungary.'[29]

Without them, the ideas they represented stagnated. The new man striding confidently down the palace corridors, Bishop – now Archbishop – Beckensloer, was no substitute for Vitez or Pannonius. The humanist public abroad greeted his rise to eminence with icy silence, declining to dedicate their books and treatises to him as they had to his great predecessor.

While the fall of Vitez was the beginning of the end for the university in Bratislava, it marked a whole new beginning for the King's library. Matthias did not help himself to the whole of Vitez's collection because Beckensloer deposited some of his predecessor's books in Salzburg in the mid-1470s, when he defected to the Emperor Frederick. But he did not take all of them to Salzburg. Vitez had been building up his library for years and it may have numbered 500 volumes by his death.[30] If so, it was not much smaller than the famous collections of Cardinal Bessarion in Venice, the Duke's library in Urbino or Niccolo Niccoli's library in Florence; his collection of 700 or 800 works was seen as prodigious for a private individual, as opposed to a king or a pope.

Vespasiano and Pannonius were not the only contemporaries to insist on the significance of Vitez's library. 'Scholars from all parts flocked to him, the father of scholarship who magically transformed Hungary into the home of the Muses of the New Age', Marzio wrote in *De homini libri duo* – the work that got him into trouble with the Inquisition in Italy.[31] He referred to it as the 'famous library in which all disciplines are gathered'.[32]

The bibliophile Croatian Bishop and papal legate, Nikola Modruski,[33] also recalled Vitez's library in lyrical tones. 'We often sat together with many scholars in your magnificent library,' he wrote with nostalgia, 'and spent a pleasant and happy time amid the innumerable volumes.'[34] The Viennese astronomer George Peuerbach, Regiomontanus and Filippo Buonaccorsi wrote likewise.

It is hard to imagine a man as acquisitive and curious as Matthias resisting the temptation to acquire at least a portion of a collection that had attracted such international attention. Archbishop Beckensloer – more interested in women than books – would not have stopped him.

Matthias may have taken the same course of action with the library of Vitez's nephew. We know far less about Pannonius's collection, but Vespasiano's descriptions and Pannonius's own letters leave no doubt that he was a serious collector. Again, it seems unlikely that his books were simply left for the next bishop of Pecs to flip through and for provincial canons to dust and clean, when the King knew that a better future awaited them.

It seems very likely, therefore, that large portions of these two humanist libraries joined the royal collection. As has been noted, there are few references before the mid-1470s to the existence of a royal library, apart from the King's letter of 1471 to the Roman, Pomponio Leto. The letter proves Matthias had purchased some books from Italy by the early 1470s but little else. No description whatever survives of a royal collection from this time. The fact that about a third of the surviving Corvinian works date from the first 15 years of the King's reign does not mean Matthias commissioned these works. It makes more sense to see them as stock seized from the libraries of Pannonius and Vitez, which only joined Matthias's collection after 1472.

It is significant also that books which we know were part of Vitez's collection turned up centuries later among Matthias's books in Constantinople.[35] Csapodi suggested that this was because when the Ottomans captured Buda in 1526 they raided the stock of Matthias's and Vitez's separate libraries, merging the two collections back in the Ottoman capital. It is more likely that Vitez's library disappeared decades before 1526 and the books had long ago disappeared into the Bibliotheca Corviniana. There is no certainty Vitez even had a library in Buda as opposed to Esztergom. If it ever existed, no one referred to it.

If it is accepted that much of the older stock of Matthias's library came from the libraries of Vitez and Pannonius, many things become clear, among them the presence of notes in the margins of several older works by Vitez but not by Matthias, and the lack of the decoration of most of these earlier manuscripts.

Several works of the 1460s associated with the Corvinian library contain brief comments and remarks by Vitez, usually noting that he had corrected or approved the text. In the commentary on Cicero by Victorinus, for example, he scribbled the date '27 September 1462' and in Tertullian's *Adversus Marcionem*, 'Against Marcion', he dated finishing reading the text on 2 June 1468, in Nyitra, in northern Hungary, now Slovakia. There are similar notes in the Pseudo-Clement of the early 1470s, in Tacitus's annals, and in the *Scala paradisi*, the 'Steps to Paradise' of Iohannes Scholasticum, in which Vitez wrote that he had finished reading this work on 26 September 1470. In other works, like that by Chalcidius on the immortality of the soul, Csapodi noted that Matthias's arms appear to have been painted over another set.

These early works are sparsely decorated compared with the luxurious books commissioned by the King in the 1480s. Either Matthias radically changed his taste over the years, or, more likely, these earlier books were not commissioned by Matthias in the first place, but by two men who were not particularly interested in art work.

There is another reason for believing that Vitez and Pannonius, and not Matthias, were the active book collectors in Hungary in the 1460s. As has been noted cultural life in Hungary stalled in their absence. The university closed, as we have seen, and so did the country's first printing press, under Andras Hess. It is true that Matthias despised printed works and did not think they deserved inclusion in his library. But it is still curious that an ardent bibliophile should have let the country's only printer go under after he had published just two works.

Matthias always needed helpers and advisers for his cultural projects, and in 1471 Vitez and Pannonius filled that important role. After their deaths, a space opened up. However, it was not filled for five years, until the arrival of Beatrice of Aragon and Naples. When she became Matthias's next wife, a new chapter began in the story of the King's life and of his library.

CHAPTER FIVE

Beatrice

I assure Your Majesty that until she has learned the language of the Hungarians she will have many disagreements.

Diomede Carafa's advice to Beatrice in 1476[1]

Bonfini said she looked like Venus, Diana and Pallas all rolled into one.[2] 'She would have been able to inflame the very heart of Socrates', he declared. Perhaps. However, those words came in a book that he dedicated to the Queen. And the white marble bust that the Dalmatian sculptor Francesco Laurana[3] executed between 1474 and 1475 on the eve of her marriage tells another story. It shows a woman named 'Diva Beatrix Aragonia' in the first flush of youth. Her neck is bare and her chest partly exposed by an exquisite bordered tunic cut low in the permissive style of the Renaissance.[4] The downward-glancing eyes suggest modesty and piety.

But few would claim that the life-size image is that of a beautiful woman. She 'possesses the large head, the short abrupt features and the rounded chin of her elder brother [Alfonso of Calabria]', one art critic noted.[5] Later, she looked still less attractive. The white marble profile of Beatrice, now 'Regina Hungariae', executed around 1489, probably by Duknovic,[6] shows a woman with a jowly face, a small double chin and piggy eyes. She had clearly inherited the family's unappealing physical traits. Guido Mazzini's bronze bust of her brother, Alfonso, created a little later than Beatrice's portrait, reveals an exaggerated, male version of the former. It shows a rather ugly man, round faced and with bulging eyes.

By the time Duknovic made his relief portrait, Beatrice and Matthias were a dozen years into a marriage that had proved somewhat disappointing to both partners, for it was childless. What looks like a sulky expression on the part of the Queen may just have been despair.

Matthias's first wife, that forgotten Bohemian princess, had been dead for almost 13 years by the time the King wed again. In the meantime, war in Bohemia had consumed his energies and his finances – Matthias extracting an empty title as King of Bohemia while his younger Polish rival actually ruled Prague. Matthias probably knew he would never now ride into the Bohemian capital as monarch. But he continued fighting, albeit in a fairly desultory fashion, now concerned only to find an honourable exit.

Middle age had crept up on him, filling him with foreboding for the future of his line. While the Italian and Dalmatian architects tastefully remodelled his palaces in Buda and Visegrad, erecting those red marble fountains in the courtyards, along with bronze statues of Matthias's father and brother, he must have wondered whether those statues would ever be accompanied by newer images of younger additions to the Hunyadi family. His mother, Erzsebet, was still alive. She who had lost so many immediate members of her family – brother, husband, son – must also have prayed hard for fresh signs of life: a male grandchild above all.

But finding the right consort had not been easy. Matthias had sought the hand of Casimir of Poland's daughter but the Poles had turned up their noses. After Casimir then tried to dislodge Matthias from his throne in 1471 there was no more talk of a Polish princess becoming queen.

Then there was Archduchess Kunigunde, the blonde and chubby daughter of Frederick III. The Emperor appeared to entertain the idea of a Hungarian marriage, although his daughter was only five years old. The omens looked so good that Vitez had led an impressive embassy to Vienna in the autumn of 1469 at the height of the Bohemian war in order to get the Emperor's agreement in writing. Frederick was at his evasive best – agreeable but noncommittal. Matthias came to Vienna himself in February 1470 with Bishops Pannonius and Beckensloer in his train and at the head of a concourse of several thousand knights. Matthias brought his two new lions along – a gift from the previous year of the Florentine Signoria. He even performed a dance in front of the Emperor, though, sadly, there is no precise description of its steps.[7] The Emperor seemed delighted. Perhaps Kunigunde would be suitable once she reached 15, he exclaimed. 'Now he was with the Emperor body and soul',[8] Matthias joyfully told the Milanese ambassador. Alas, the wily Emperor deceived Matthias just as Matthias himself had deceived Podebrad months before. Frederick prevaricated and dawdled and somehow the ratification of the promised marriage treaty never took place. Matthias returned to Hungary by boat, empty-handed. He was so angry that he refused even to take formal leave of his host.

By the time Matthias returned in a sulk to Buda, thoughts of the chubby-cheeked Kunigunde receding from his mind, the woman who was to become his queen was growing up motherless, quick-witted and precocious under the blue skies of Naples. How differently Matthias's life would have turned out had his wife been the docile daughter of the pious and phlegmatic Emperor. Instead, the position went to the daughter of a royal household run on very different lines from that of the Emperor's dull, threadbare establishment – a household known for sexual athleticism, debauchery, staggering luxury and eyebrow-raising intellectual tastes. Both Beatrice's father and eldest brother had a sadistic streak in them, too. Beatrice did not share that family trait, fortunately, unless constant nagging counts as evidence of sadism. Nor was she sexually voracious. But she certainly brought her family's high-spending ways with her to Hungary, along with their advanced intellectual tastes. The package gained her mixed reviews in her new homeland, though no one could deny it also made her an unusual consort.

Her famous grandfather, Alfonso 'the Magnanimous' and her future husband had much in common, even though Alfonso was born into a royal house while Matthias was not. Both were essentially adventurers and outsiders who had impressed themselves on their domains by force and compensated for a certain lack of legitimacy by showmanship. Both were enthusiastic patrons of the Renaissance for its own sake as well as because they saw the vindication of their rule in a classical culture that exalted virtue, military prowess and magnificence over the hereditary principle. For Alfonso as well as for Matthias, the Renaissance was more than an attractive literary, artistic and aesthetic movement. It provided an ideological framework for their kingship, with admiring humanists 'supplying psychological and propaganda support for Alfonso's caesarian concept of his role in the world'.[9]

When Flavio Biondi told Alfonso in 1443 that 'only those adorned by letters deserve to be called true kings', this was music to the King's ears. As if anticipating Matthias's boast to Pomponio Leto in 1471, when he had claimed to spend hours each day, even in battle, reading classics, Alfonso claimed he also set aside time each day even in battle to pore over the works of Caesar and Livy. While Matthias took the raven as his emblem, Alfonso took as his an open book; paraphrasing Plato, he held that 'kings ought to be learned men themselves, or at least lovers of learned men'.[10]

Alfonso's right to rule Naples was questioned because he was not Italian. He was Aragonese, and indeed partly Castilian, a cadet branch of the royal house of Castile having assumed the Aragonese crown in 1412. His candidacy to rule the great kingdom of Naples arose only in 1421, when he was about 25 and the eccentric and libidinous Queen of Naples, Giovanna, or Joanna, harassed by the papacy, invited Alfonso to Naples and settled the succession on him, only to change her mind before her death in 1435 and give it to René of Anjou.

Alfonso was not deterred by being forced abruptly to quit Naples. Neighbouring Sicily was already his, as the island had been united to Aragon back in the 1280s. Alfonso pursued his claim to the southern Italian mainland for seven years after Giovanna's death and finally conquered Naples in 1443, the year Matthias was born. But the Neapolitans never quite accepted their new Spanish ruler. As the sixteenth-century historian Camillo Porzio wrote, the kings of Naples were so despised that 'even their own barons plotted against them'.[11]

This tense and brittle atmosphere explains why Alfonso was so eager for humanists to proclaim the benefits of his rule over Naples and why, like Matthias, he spared no expense in winning their favour.

Beatrice never knew her illustrious grandfather. He died in 1458, shortly after her birth on 14 November 1457. But she grew up in his long shadow. As a child she gazed at the magnificent triumphal arch that Alfonso had erected in 1453 in the royal palace, the Castello Nuovo, in what he thought of as true Roman style. Depicting Alfonso as a classical emperor, it showed him riding in a triumphant procession in his chariot beneath an arcade featuring the Four Virtues.

She must have wandered countless times as a child through the great library on which Vespasiano said he spent 20,000 ducats in the last year of his life.[12] Alfonso used it, as Matthias would do, as an arena for literary seances and debates. According to Adamo di Montaldo, most evenings after dinner Alfonso retired to his library 'where he took great delight listening to learned men discuss literary and historical issues'.[13] Sometimes these occasions were heated. The library may have been the stage for the spectacular rows that erupted periodically between Alfonso's prize humanists, Lorenzo Valla and Antonio Beccadelli 'Panormita', over who wrote the best Latin verse. Alfonso also used his library as a mini-university, paying one of his librarians, Juan Torries, 50 ducats a year to maintain several students there, three of whom were later sent to Paris at the King's expense to study theology.[14]

His library was the pride of the court and his illegitimate son and heir Ferrante, or Ferdinand, Beatrice's father, built up the stock, employing about 30 scribes as copyists and translators. One of them, Joan Marco Cinico, ranked Ferdinand above all the contemporary princes of Europe on account of his efforts to conserve great works of literature.[15]

Alfonso's pet humanists were not known for Catholic piety. Valla, though brought up in papal circles in Rome, enthusiastically bit the hand that had once fed him. His dialogue on pleasure *De voluptate*, written in 1431 before he went to Naples, was a provocative epicurean assault on the Christian idea of virtue. In 1440, after he had moved to Naples, he delivered a more infamous blow to the Church. Applying all the new techniques of historical criticism, he demolished the claims to authenticity of the 'Donation of Constantine', the document on which the Church had based much of its claim to temporal authority in the early medieval era.

The relevance by this stage of the Donation, which was probably forged in the eighth century, should not be exaggerated. 'It was already out of date by the 11th century',[16] one historian wrote. By Valla's time, popes had distanced themselves from the potentially dangerous idea that their predecessors received their powers on earth from mere emperors. Received thinking now was that popes derived their authority from Christ alone. Nevertheless, Valla's work confirmed his reputation as an intellectual gadfly, and Alfonso's, too, as a patron of daring and unorthodox thinkers.

Francesco Filelfo was another brilliant ornament to Alfonso's circle. Born in Ancona, he had studied in Byzantium from 1419 to 1427, bringing back a haul of Greek works to Venice. Like many members of the first generation of humanists, he was extraordinarily conceited. 'All men love and honour me,' he boasted from Florence. 'My name is on every lip. Not only the leaders of the city but women of the noblest birth make way for me.'[17] When he descended on Alfonso's Naples in 1453, his journey across Italy resembled 'a triumphal progress'.[18] Alfonso promptly dubbed him a knight before – in the new Renaissance fashion – crowning him with a poet's laurels. It was not the end of this turbulent man's peregrinations. By the time he died in 1481, aged 83, he had again moved to Rome, and then moved on again to Milan, and again to Florence.

Beccadelli was another fascinating but equally disruptive character who found a congenial hideout in permissive Naples. Born in Palermo, from which he took the Latin nom de plume 'Panormita', he studied in Florence in the 1420s before writing his explosive two-volume collection of porno-graphic epigrams in 1425, audaciously dedicating them to Cosimo de Medici. As a recent biographer remarked, 'one has to admire his courage in dedicating the book to Cosimo'.[19]

The *Hermaphroditus* was a long string of graphically described sexual encounters, many concerning anal sex. If that was not disturbing enough, it was clear from the contents that many of these forensically detailed encounters were based on the author's personal experience. One, a plea from beyond the grave by one Pegaso, urged visitors to perform sexual acts on his tombstone:

> *Passer-by, if you want to know . . . what I desire most, Listen!*
> *And incidentally you may satisfy your own urges as well.*
> *When you happen to bugger some accommodating youth,*
> *I beg you, passer-by, to do it on this tomb,*
> *And so appease my spirit, not with incense but with sex.*[20]

The rest continued in much the same jocular and teasing vein. 'Why is it that someone who has once indulged in fellatio or pederasty can never forget the experience?' one epigram asked. 'Anyone who has ever got a boy to bend over for him will never be able to rid himself of the habit.'[21]

'The one thing you can't call your own is your bottom', read the epigram entitled 'Against the effeminate Lentulo, a man of the highest rank and the lowest morals'.[22] 'Be off with you Quinzio, you loathsome and shameful slut,' it continued. In 'To Coridone who burns for Quinzio, a repellent and deformed youth', he asked: 'Could anyone calculate how many pricks your gaping arse has swallowed?'[23] And so it went on, all, of course, in the most exquisite Latin.

Pannonius's teacher Guarino prematurely rhapsodised about *Her-maphroditus*. Panormita 'had shown himself the equal of Catullus and Ovid',[24] he sighed. This turned out to be the equivalent of one of those 'first night' reviews that goes wholly against the grain, for Catholic Europe soon made it clear it would not be mocked so flagrantly.

Of course, Panormita was not the first humanist to blaze a trail in his writings about sex. But the overt and enthusiastic portrayal of homosexual acts in *Hermaphroditus* caused real offence, which was only magnified by the author's unwise attempt to popularise his work by sending review copies all around Italy.

Not even the most avant-garde humanists spoke up on behalf of Panormita as the anathemas began to rain down and as the authorities in Bologna, Ferrara and Milan publicly burned his book. They kept quiet, or even criticised him, worried that he was endangering them all. Even Guarino was forced into making a public retraction. The attack launched by the Milanese Franciscan, Anton de Rho, in 1431, was typical. 'This wretched little book along with its author ... should be deported, as are the worst criminals, to the most remote islands and distant territories,' he wrote. 'He should be buried for eternity in the lowest hell. That would be better than having him seduce youngsters into his Sicilian cesspool.' Accusing Panormita of attempting 'to blanket the gleaming and unsullied city of Milan with this filth',[25] the friar went on: 'That wretched little book will never be read without declaring your indecency, how filthily, recklessly lustfully and barbarously you have lived your life.'[26]

Panormita was, therefore, a hot potato in the early 1430s, especially after the puritanical Eugenius IV became Pope and as the campaign against him led by the friars took off. Significantly, however, Alfonso felt no misgivings about taking Panormita into his service in Palermo in 1435. Indeed, he rode by Alfonso's side when the King staged his triumphal entry into Naples in 1443 in his gilded chariot, followed by an innumerable cavalcade of dukes, counts and bishops. There he remained, comfortably remunerated and entrusted with important court and diplomatic posts. Alfonso clearly delighted in Panormita's company and, when he fell ill in Capua, asked him to sit beside his sickbed, reading extracts of one of his favourite books, Curtius Rufus's life of Alexander. (It was one of Matthias's favourites, too.)[27] Panormita's own work of 1455, *De dictis et factis Alfonsi*, based on Xenophon, provided a model for Marzio's subsequent work on the deeds and words of Matthias.

Alfonso's death in June 1458 did not end Panormita's career in Naples, where he continued to serve Beatrice's father. He may have been familiar to the young princess, as she was 14 when he died in Naples in 1471, at a grand old 76.

Beatrice's father was widely seen as a poorer version of his father – fatter, less noble, more sadistic – though his adverse reputation reflected the bad press he got from contemporary humanists on account of his relative economy as a patron.

Alfonso spent money like water, throwing vast sums at books, humanists, processions, tournaments and court hunts at which thousands of beaters were employed to chase the game. His jewel collection was stunning, outdoing even the famous jewels of the duc de Berry. The royal church services were a spectacle in themselves. According to Giovanni Pontano, 'In his day, King Alfonso outstripped all the kings of that age both in acquiring and exhibiting the things used in the Mass and for the adornment of the priests.'[28] His favourite humanists were lavishly rewarded, George of Trebizond securing a munificent 600 ducats a year in the mid-1450s.

Ferdinand's struggles with his rebellious barons at the start of his reign meant that some of these expenses had to be curtailed. But when peace returned to Naples in the mid-1460s the court resumed its luxurious ways. Alfonso's library also maintained its role as an important department in the royal household. By then it contained many valuable and expensive works, for when Ferdinand reluctantly pawned 199 of his important manuscripts and 46 books to raise military funds in 1481, his Pandolfini lenders gave him 38,000 ducats, which was well over 100 ducats per item. Ferdinand was obviously devoted to the stock, because he insisted on redeeming the books within a year.[29]

Beatrice, therefore, was brought up on modern lines and in a household that put a premium on the acquisition of knowledge as well as material goods. Her schooling reflected the progressive conviction of the humanist writers and pedagogues that princesses as well as princes ought to be both learned and pious. She may have exaggerated a little when she recalled the rigours of her childhood regime for the benefit of Bonfini, but her recollection was that she rose at dawn, consecrated the first part of the day to prayer and then headed to the schoolroom along with her siblings until the first break at 9 a.m. More lessons followed, after which the children listened to the Lives of Saints. After that there was usually 'a little walk under the portico, or in the fresh, delicious, charming garden', where religious images had been scattered among the shrubbery to prompt spiritual reflections. 'Evening came and the sacred and unceasing task of devotion called us anew. After supper we always had a moral lecture and an instructive talk, and I had no need to summon sleep, it descended on me without waiting . . .'[30]

It was a charming picture, though touched up, for it contains no real clue to how the product of such an austere and nun-like environment can have evolved into a foot-stamping, selfish and very materialistic adult. Of course, Beatrice's conversations with Bonfini in Buda about her childhood contained not one word about the less delightful and educative side of her father's court. There was, for example, Ferdinand's ghoulish penchant for maintaining a museum full of the stuffed bodies of his enemies in the palace. It was 'a frightful sight', according to the historian, Paolo Giovio, for the 'dried cadavers were displayed pickled with herbs . . . in the dress they wore when alive'.[31] Perhaps little Beatrice kept her eyes firmly averted from this reminder of the more sinister side of her family's character. She preferred to dwell on memories of the charming garden.

She was without doubt very well read. Had she not been, her father would not have presented her with two works of Cicero for her fifteenth birthday.[32] Beatrice was also musical, like her father and grandfather, both of whom scoured Spain, France and even England for suitable musicians for their court. Beatrice's own Flemish musical tutor, Iohannes Tinctoris, was well known – 'one of the most important music theorists of the entire Renaissance period'[33] – and the fact that he dedicated three theoretical treatises to her suggests he had high regard for his young pupil.

Beatrice retained her strong appreciation of music to the end. Organs were fashionable during the Renaissance: Lorenzo de Medici had at least five. From 1484, there is a report of Beatrice ordering her own organ to be transported from Bratislava to Hainburg, in Austria, which suggests she was able to play that most royal of instruments.[34] In a letter from the same year, Beatrice begged Lorenzo de Medici to pay the famous Florentine 'maestro d'organi' Stefano del Paone da Salerno, to build her another organ, promising to reimburse the Medicis in full, later.[35] Beatrice's musical tastes were not restricted to organs. Lutes and harps were much favoured by royal women at the time, as trumpets were by princes. Beatrice's sister, Leonora, played the harp, so it seems likely her younger sister did as well.

She did not have to start from scratch in Buda when it came to music; Matthias had for years cultivated a taste for French, Burgundian and Flemish singers in his royal chapel. The splendid organ, decorated with silver, that Matthias installed in his palace in Visegrad, which Olah much admired, was almost certainly his idea, not hers. The Saxon ambassador who was present at his wedding to Beatrice in Szekesfehervar in 1476 wrote admiringly concerning the 'frantzosisch' (French) singing that the King had arranged for the ceremony.

Nevertheless, growing international praise in the 1480s for the quality of the music heard at the Hungarian court reflected Beatrice's influence.[36] The decade saw a swelling crowd of foreign musicians at court, including Johannes Stokem, one of the King's choir masters, who came from Liège, Jacques Barbireau of Antwerp and the Polish-German, Heinrich Finck. As one French musical historian put it, 'Il n'y a aucun doute que l'arrivée de Béatrice en Hongrie ait donné une impulsion à la culture musicale de Bude.'[37]

Along with erudition and an ear for music, the splendour of Neapolitan court life left an indelible mark on Beatrice. Naples itself formed a splendid backdrop to the public tournaments and processions for which the city was famous. It was the largest in Italy and one of the biggest in Europe, with around 125,000 inhabitants in the mid- to late fifteenth century, more than twice the size of Rome or Florence and larger even than Milan or Venice, which had around 100,000 inhabitants each. Then, as now, it was a city of staggering inequality, its size stemming partly from a lack of urban rivals in southern Italy. Year by year, country people drifted in and the struggle began for a precarious living serving the magnificent few. Beatrice grew up among vast, surging crowds and remained a city girl at heart.

The lack of a mother was another important ingredient in the formation of her character, Isabella having died in 1465, when Beatrice was only seven. The little girl transferred all her love to her sister Leonora, seven years her senior. Leonora's marriage in 1473 to Ercole d'Este, Duke of Ferrara, therefore, was a milestone in Beatrice's early life. It marked the end of childhood and the final break-up of the nursery. After that, the 16-year-old obtained her own court along with an annual allowance of 1,000 ducats.[38]

Her sister's splendid marriage ceremonies lasted for more than a month. The progress of the bridal train up through Italy from Naples to Ferrara was, as one historian wrote, 'one continuous triumph'.[39] Sixtus IV received them with 'stupendissimo onore' and the Neapolitans made their entry into Rome preceded by trumpeters, pipers and drummers. A temporary palace was erected whose opulent furnishings were 'held to mark the culminating point of extravagant display of the century'.[40] The grandest of the many banquets prepared in the party's honour on 7 June lasted for six hours and involved an endless succession of fantastical culinary creations, including sculptures of sugar as well as 'cranes, pheasants and even a bear, which were served whole and in their original skins'.[41] At the high point of the evening's entertainment, a man jumped out of a mountain of sweet confectionery. A later writer declared, with disgust, that it 'recalled the heathen days of imperial Rome'.[42] But the jamboree turned Beatrice's head – much more than devout and serious Leonora's. It helped confirm in her a lifelong taste for conspicuous consumption. Her new homeland was less equipped than Italy to satisfy it, however.

Beatrice's pathway to Hungary was circuitous. After Matthias had cast around for Austrian and Polish brides without success, he turned to Italy. It was Ferdinand who then took the initiative, at first suggesting Leonora as a possible candidate. Her little sister only came into view later on, after Leonora's marriage to the Duke of Ferrara put her out of the running. By then, Ferdinand had lined up a couple of suitors for Beatrice, including the Dauphin, later Charles VIII of France. But they dropped out or became unsuitable for one reason or another.

It was only in the spring of 1474 that Matthias settled on Beatrice as his future bride, dispatching two ambassadors to Naples to seek Ferdinand's permission, which he granted on 5 September. By the time the Hungarian ambassadors returned Matthias was in Silesia, where he showed his delight at the news by having the bells of Wroclaw rung in celebration on 30 October. The distance between Hungary and Naples meant that nothing could move ahead with any great speed. It was not until the Feast of the Purification in February 1475 that the ambassadors of Naples reached Buda to present their King's formal reply to the proposal, after which another Hungarian embassy left for Naples to conduct the Princess on her journey east. The team included the Bishop of Veszprem and Bishop Thuz of Zagreb, Pannonius's old accomplice in the plot against Matthias. His inclusion was another signal that the Thuz family had been fully forgiven for its important role in the plot of 1471.

For Beatrice, the proposal was both exciting and daunting. Hungary was far away – a cold and barbarian land in Italian eyes, though not unknown, thanks to the cult of the Hunyadis encouraged by Pius II and the Italian humanists. Hungarian students had been studying in Italy, especially at the University of Bologna, for centuries. At the same time, Italians had also been drifting to Hungary, especially after Vergerio settled there in 1418. 'Many men of my race live in your kingdom and have acquired great wealth and honour',[43] Piccolomini had written to Vitez's predecessor, Archbishop Szechy of Esztergom, in 1445. A little colony of Italians had made their home in Oradea in eastern Hungary long before Vergerio arrived there. A fragment of a fourteenth-century fresco from the Catholic cathedral reveals a strong Italian influence,[44] and it is known that Andrea Scolari, the cultured Bishop of Oradea from 1409 to 1426, imported other fellow Italians to work as artists in the diocese. One of his successors, Giovanni de Dominis, Vitez's immediate predecessor as bishop from 1440 to 1444, was another Italian. It was these Italian bishops of eastern Hungary who probably laid the foundations of Vitez's own library there.

We can safely assume that Beatrice, now 17 and at the height of her brief beauty, felt equal to the task of undertaking the long journey to this far-off country. Whether ordinary Neapolitans shared her enthusiasm is less certain. They were taxed to the hilt to provide her with an enormous dowry of 200,000 gold pieces – almost three times the dowry her sister took to Ferrara.[45] The collection of that huge sum is unlikely to have weighed on the conscience of the young Beatrice. It was only towards the end of her life, when she was back in Naples, shaken and disillusioned by the course of events, that she reinvented herself as a saintly queen, devoting herself to good works and helping the poor. In her prime, humanitarian work was not her forte.

In 1476, Beatrice was probably salivating at the prospect of the money and status that were about to be hers. She was not only marrying a military hero but a rich one with an annual income of about 700,000 or 800,000 ducats – 700 times her present allowance! The thought of becoming a queen must have been deeply satisfying. After the marriage to the son of Louis XI of France never came off for various reasons, she might well have ended up a humble duchess. Instead, she was to be raised above Leonora, enabling her to become her beloved older sister's patron and benefactor.

Matthias's marriage party, 756 strong and including – a typical Matthias touch – 20 captured Turkish soldiers – reached the Castello Nuovo in September, where the Cardinal Archbishop of Naples, Oliviero Carafa, celebrated Beatrice's marriage and coronation in the church of the Incoronata, Matthias being represented at the ceremony by Janos Pongracz, the 'Voivode', or royal governor, of Transylvania.

At the banquet that followed, the diplomat-turned-humanist Diomede Carafa presented Beatrice with a richly decorated memorial, *De institutione vivendi*, now in Parma, which she brought with her to Hungary. It is often counted among the surviving 216 works of Matthias's library, although it most probably remained in the Queen's own separate collection. Decorated with the arms of Aragon and the symbol of the open book, it contains an illustration of the young Beatrice receiving the work from the author, who is on his knees. Inside, Carafa urges her to live a virtuous life and to learn Hungarian.

'I assure Your Majesty that until she has learned the language of the Hungarians she will have many disagreements', Carafa wrote. 'With regard to her husband, but also to be able to speak with the people and especially with the women who come and present their homage, she will have to learn it as soon as possible. She can start ... during the voyage itself.'[46] It was a nice thought. Carafa also suggested she live in an economical fashion in her new land, on the sensible grounds that subjects tended to admire thrifty sovereigns. Some hope! Beatrice kept the book but took no notice of the contents. The 'disagreements' that the humanist warned about were to loom large in her life in Hungary.

Beatrice set off on 18 September 1476 with her large Hungarian retinue and three of her brothers, one of whom, Francesco, aged 15, accompanied her all the way to Hungary. She set sail from the port of Manfredonia on 2 October, travelling up the coast to Chioggia, and then proceeding on land to her sister's new home in Ferrara, into which she made her solemn entry on 16 October. When she left the Este domains on the 21st she cannot have guessed that this was the last time she was ever to set eyes on her sister.

After first passing the pilgrimage town of Loreto, where she was impressed by the address delivered by a middle-aged teacher of Greek and Latin named Antonio Bonfini, she embarked for Venice. Following a meeting with the Doge, she resumed the journey north by land on 29 October, heading next for Villach in Austria. Now she was not far from her destination. At Ptuj, a reception party headed by that ghost from the past, Erzsebet Szilagyi, awaited her. In the company of her mother-in-law, a woman whose character could hardly have been more dissimilar to her own, she journeyed into Hungary towards the coronation town of Szekesfehervar. There Matthias was waiting in a state of high excitement.

Poor Erzsebet. She may have struggled to counter an instinctive feeling of dismay on her first encounter with the actressy, spendthrift chatterbox that was about to become her daughter-in-law. She could hardly have had the faintest idea about the moral and religious climate of Naples, let alone have come across the notions contained in such works as the *Hermaphroditus*. But she may well have detected something too knowing and confident in the gaze of the chubby Italian, a look that made this pious and austere daughter of Transylvania want to retreat further towards the silence of the cloister. Whatever it was, after this encounter with Beatrice, Erzsebet made her final exit from the public stage. She must have attended her son's wedding and the showy ceremonies that followed in Szekesfehervar. But she did not become a live-in queen mother in Buda. Instead, the woman described as 'sanctissime et sapientissime mulier',[47] who was recalled, in 1490, long after her death, simply as the heroic woman – *mulier heroica* – slipped away to die quietly in Hunedoara. The exact date of her death in the 1480s is unknown.[48]

If Erzsebet felt one way about Beatrice, Matthias definitely felt another. For him it was love at first sight. Everything that probably appalled Erzsebet about her daughter-in-law delighted her son, starting with Beatrice's sophistication, wit and expensive, cosmopolitan tastes. Entranced from day one – 'he couldn't bear to be apart from her for an hour',[49] the German banker Fugger reported – he remained loyal in his fashion to the end.

The excitement had been building in Buda since the first week of December. At the Feast of the Conception on 8 December, the King left Buda for Szekesfehervar with an enormous retinue, reaching the town the following day. With only one day to spare before the Queen was expected to arrive, workmen rushed to complete huge, ornate tents for the King and new Queen and their foreign guests, though these were somewhat thin on the ground, Casimir of Poland and the Emperor Frederick having both failed to appear.

Bonfini, as has been said, insisted she looked like a goddess. However, as he did not reappear in Beatrice's life until the late 1480s, his flattery can be dismissed as a humanist's conventional platitudes. And yet it is possible that neither the image of the Queen by Francesco Laurana nor the much later relief portrait quite did her justice, for Matthias was undoubtedly smitten.

Her own reaction on catching sight of her new husband can only be guessed at, however. Beatrice must be forgiven for having possibly felt slightly disappointed. The heroic tales of the Hunyadis that she must have come across in Italy would have furnished her active imagination with images of a tall, clean-looking warrior. Matthias did not look like that at all. As later portraits of the King in his books in the 1480s make clear, he was powerful, squat, with ruddy, fleshy features, and with a round face framed by lank curly hair. He may have been a pin-up compared to Beatrice's atrocious-looking brother Alfonso, but he was not handsome by conventional standards. Nor was he a sexually charismatic womaniser like her own father, Ferdinand, whose numerous liaisons had generated a large brood of children, both legitimate and illegitimate, all of whom peopled the same nursery.

Matthias had been linked to only a few women since the death of his Bohemian queen years before and only one, Barbara Edelpock, a dalliance from his Silesian campaigns, presented him with a child, named John, or Janos, in 1473. Three years old by the time Beatrice reached Buda, he was a factor that the new teenage Queen initially felt able to ignore. Her family was fertile; her sister, the Duchess of Ferrara, offered ample proof of that. By the time Beatrice visited her in Ferrara in 1476 she had already given birth to three children, Alfonso, Isabella and Beatrice, the last named after her aunt. Beatrice could look forward to many sons. So she and her husband thought.

After their first meeting in a tent on the frozen fields of Szekesfehervar the couple rode into the town under a canopy, Beatrice on a white steed and Matthias on a brown one. At the gate of the town bishops and priests marshalling an array of holy relics waited to receive them and escort the procession past the gawping crowds to the cathedral for the service of Te Deum. A coronation service followed two days later, on 12 December, at which Beatrice was arrayed in a superb mantle of scarlet and gold, her hair sparkling with pearls. When the crown was placed on her head, the trumpets sounded so loudly that not a word of that part of the service could be heard.[50]

The following day, the royal pair set off for Buda for more receptions, banquets and tournaments on a yet grander scale. At the gate of the city a deputation of richly dressed Jews under their prefect, Jacob Mendel, some wearing hats of ostrich feathers and chanting loud songs of welcome, waited to present to the royal couple gifts including two huge stags and a bag of ten pounds of silver, suspended from the tip of Mendel's sword.[51] There was a moment of muddle when the Jews also tendered a scrolled Torah for Beatrice to kiss. The King and Mendel were old companions. He had probably been present at Matthias's coronation in 1464 and Matthias formally bestowed the new title of 'prefect' on him around the time of his wedding to Beatrice. The King was clearly interested in Hebrew because in 1481 he invited the Dominican scholar, Peter Schwartz, to Buda from Ingolstadt where he was well known for his knowledge of Hebrew and the Talmud, although his stance, as a friar, was predictably hostile. But we can assume that Matthias had a fair idea of what was happening when the Jews lifted up their scrolls. Beatrice on the other hand was confused, and refused to kiss them.[52] Mounted on white steeds and heading a procession of eight golden chariots, each drawn by six white horses, the royal couple then headed into the city.

At a great banquet, the foreign ambassadors presented their own gifts. After a feast served on gold and silver plate, at which a star turn was a silver barrel suspended from the ceiling from which wine flowed through pipes,[53] the tables were cleared for dancing. The new Queen made a great impression, dancing for a full hour with her younger brother, Francesco.[54]

The following Sunday, the Queen went through a second marriage ceremony, this time with her husband beside her, after which the royal free boroughs presented their gifts, such as gold standing cups, falcons and stallions. One ominous event blighted the celebrations. Pongracz, the Voivode of Transylvania, and the man who had stood beside Beatrice at the wedding ceremony in Naples, suddenly and quite literally dropped dead. As a result, the court had to go into mourning.

Another important person was missing from the ceremonies in Szekesfehervar and Buda – for less understandable reasons than the late Voivode of Transylvania. Beckensloer, the Primate of Hungary, had defected. As he was not available to preside over the nuptials of the King and Queen, the task had to be deputed to a junior archbishop from Veszprem. The significance of this omission probably had no impact on the Queen. But Matthias inwardly seethed. Archbishop Beckensloer had chosen the worst moment possible to embarrass the King who had showered him with favours.

Quite why the once ingratiating Silesian who had climbed with such agility over Vitez's corpse into the archbishopric now slipped off to Frederick's camp is a mystery. It is possible that he left before suffering a public loss of favour, having suspected the King now regarded him as a philistine boor. He was certainly loved no more in his new role as Archbishop of Salzburg than he had been in Esztergom. However, demotion or disgrace was one thing. Flight was another. Apart from the public slight to the King's reputation, he took with him the treasury of Hungary's wealthiest see, containing about 300,000 ducats, money he deposited with the Emperor, enabling the cash-strapped Frederick to pay off his domestic enemies. He also took some of Vitez's books to Austria, including a copy of Tertullian's *Apologeticum*.[55] It was a public humiliation of the first order for Matthias, and the enraged King blamed the Emperor Frederick for it. Coming after the Emperor's failure to support the 'crusade' in Bohemia, it awoke in Matthias thoughts of revenge.

There was more bad news to come from Austria. In the same month that Matthias married Beatrice, news reached him that Frederick had concluded a public alliance with the new Polish King of Bohemia. It infuriated Matthias further. He had now been fighting in Bohemia for the best part of a decade, and the struggle had drained his treasury. A coronation in Prague would have justified all these losses, establishing Matthias as the dominant power in Eastern and Central Europe and improving his chances of one day succeeding Frederick as Holy Roman Emperor, for the King of Bohemia was one of those who elected the emperor.

Now that the Emperor had shattered any lingering dreams of taking Prague, Matthias began to ponder whether he might not conquer Vienna instead. He had seen the city as a captive in 1457 and as Frederick's guest in 1470. Now he laid plans to see Vienna as a conqueror. Matthias waited a few months after his wedding before taking action, but on 12 June 1477 he suddenly declared war on the man he had once seen as a potential father-in-law. Beatrice got her first taste of life near the front line as the court moved westwards to Gyor and Bratislava. While Beatrice stayed there, her husband moved off to conduct his army of 17,000, comprising 10,000 infantry and 7,000 on horseback, into a series of battles around Vienna, capturing the outlying positions of Bruck, Trautmannsdorf and Klosterneuburg and reaching as far as the outskirts of Linz, where Frederick had retreated. It was a walkover: the tiny feudal levy of the Emperor stood little chance against Matthias's mercenary 'Black Army'. 'He conquered the greater part of Lower Austria with more than a hundred castles', one Hungarian reported back admiringly in October.[56]

It was the first round in a longer skirmish, which finished when the Emperor agreed to withdraw recognition of Wladislas as King of Bohemia and recognise Matthias's exclusive claim to the title instead. There was also the question of an indemnity. Matthias – who had had to pay to recover his own crown from Frederick in the early 1460s – now enjoyed presenting Frederick with a ridiculous demand for 800,000 ducats. In the end he settled on 100,000 ducats.

The next year was one of family reunions for Beatrice. In the absence of the Primate, who was skulking with the Emperor, Matthias resolved to give the archbishopric of Esztergom to his wife's older brother, Giovanni, whom she had last seen at Manfredonia and who was now 25. Giovanni had been earmarked for promotion in the Church since childhood. When he was presented with the illustrious abbey of Monte Cassino in 1472, Sixtus IV had loaded more honours on to the lad, adding a cardinal's hat five years later.

The summer of 1479 was taken up in Buda with plans to receive the young Neapolitan who reached the city in December. Nothing could blight the Queen's happiness. Except for one thing. Whereas Leonora had conceived immediately after her marriage, the palace in Buda did not echo to the sound of crying babies. Instead, lurking in the background of the Queen stood Barbara Edelpock and her little boy. The Queen was only 22 but a faint shadow had passed over a once cloudless horizon and the failure to produce an heir was soon attracting attention. The longer this situation continued, the more John Corvin, as he was called, was brought into the frame, literally. Within a few years of the marriage the miniaturists of Florence, alert to the desires of their royal patron, incorporated the boy's image into their designs.

First as a small boy, and then as a teenager, he began advancing across the illuminated frontispieces of the King's books. He can be seen walking in a blue and gold cloak behind Matthias and Charles VIII of France in the third volume of the bible illuminated at the end of the King's reign by the brothers Di Giovanni (if this isn't a case of mistaken identity and is in fact a French princess). It also appears to be John who is standing on a triumphal chariot, a coronet on his head and the royal shield in his left hand, entering the conquered city of Vienna in the copy of Philostratus's *Codex Heroica*. A particularly magnificent work, it was prepared specially to mark the conquest of Vienna in 1485 – translated into Latin by Bonfini and illuminated by Boccardino il Vecchio.

There is a lack of certainty on the part of Matthias's Italian artists about John Corvin. As we saw earlier, in the luxurious copy of Didymus's *De Spiritu Sancto*, John is not at the forefront of the scene beside the crowned and kneeling figures of Matthias and Beatrice: he peeps from the rear of the stage and from behind a pillar. It is as if the brothers Di Giovanni felt he needed to be included somewhere – but they were not entirely certain where he fitted in the hierarchy of things. The illuminations of the prince befitted his somewhat indeterminate status as the King's illegitimate, but only, heir.

CHAPTER SIX

'The Emperor has fled'

The King is of a tireless spirit, absolutely martial, thinking of nothing but war.

The papal legate to Sixtus IV, 1483[1]

The oval plaque that marks the spot where Matthias once resided and from where he ruled over Vienna is hard to find, for the Backergasse is a narrow lane, so passers-by have to crane their heads to read the faded lettering, or stand on the far pavement. Tucked away behind a small square a few minutes' walk from the cathedral, this discreet memorial above the entrance to an office building attracts no attention. None of the office staff I saw strolling in and out, lighting cigarettes or with mobiles pinned to their ears, so much as glanced at the lettering, which records that the building stands on the site of the house of a Viennese merchant named Niklas Teschler, which Matthias purloined in the 1480s.

Vienna has a great ability to shrug off uncomfortable memories of former dictators, returning with a sigh and a smile to its pleasure-loving ways. At the city museum, the maps and stucco models concentrate on another siege, the Ottoman siege of 1683, whose relief marked the end of the centuries-long struggle against the Turks. That was a defining experience for Austria and Vienna. It explains why the Viennese treasure the Ottoman cannonballs that lodged in the solid walls of the cathedral as if they were relics. It also sheds some light on why Turkey's proposed entry into the European Union touches a raw nerve.

The Hungarian siege two centuries earlier, though no less savage, has no equivalent claim on the national consciousness. There are no maps or reconstructions of this event in the city museum and it is mentioned only briefly even in the heftier histories of Austria and the Habsburgs. There is no trace of Matthias's Viennese residence to jog people's memories. Like his palaces in Hungary, it has gone for good. Books alone survive to tell the tale and, in Vienna, a humble plaque.

By 1480 a decisive clash between Matthias and the Emperor had become inevitable. As has been shown, the roots of the conflict date back to the first year of Matthias's reign, when Frederick invaded on the invitation of the Hungarian magnates. Then followed the wrangle over the custody of the Holy Crown, which ended with the Treaty of Wiener Neustadt, and the return of the crown in exchange for an agreement that Matthias would leave the throne to Frederick should he die without an heir. When Matthias was a healthy teenager, that possibility appeared remote. But the longer he remained without an heir, the more that clause in the treaty came between the two rulers, demanding either a revision of the agreement, which was out of the question for Frederick, or a fresh settling of accounts.

While Matthias was at war in Bohemia, the confrontation had to be put on one side. At the same time, the Emperor's duplicity over Bohemia – at first encouraging Matthias to invade and then recognising his Polish rival as king – confirmed Matthias in his determination to strike at some point. The defection of Archbishop Beckensloer to Frederick in 1476 provided a *casus belli*, triggering Matthias's first campaign against Austria in 1477. But for a couple of years afterwards, until 1480, the deteriorating position of the southern border with the Ottoman Empire dictated its own priorities.

The plight of large parts of Croatia, Dalmatia and Transylvania had been increasingly dire for some years. In the summer of 1475 a huge Ottoman force crossed the River Maros, reaching north as far as Vitez's old episcopal see of Oradea. Matthias had responded with a campaign in northern Serbia and the seizure of the fortress of Sabacs, near the Serbian border with Bosnia. The King then returned to Buda for his marriage at the end of 1476. But the loss of Sabacs did not deter the Ottomans. For the rest of the decade they continued to probe the weak points in the kingdom's defences, especially the flat plain of Slavonia. In those years, the almost annual invasions from Bosnia obliged Matthias to concentrate anew on shoring up his southern defences, and he employed Italian architects to build a chain of manned fortresses across the south-east, visiting Zagreb in person to inspect the state of the south-west.

It was fortunate for the King, and still more for the inhabitants of these battered frontier lands, that Mehmed II 'The Conqueror' died in 1480. It was still more fortunate that neither of his sons was cut from the same material and that a fratricidal struggle between the brothers Bayezid and Djem consumed the Ottoman Empire's energies for years, especially after Djem unwisely defected to the west in the hope of gaining foreign support for his bid to take the throne. While Bayezid remained Sultan until 1512, Europe enjoyed over 30 years of respite from Ottoman aggression.

In the meantime, the struggle between Djem and Bayezid left Hungary looking far stronger. The rulers of the city-state of Dubrovnik were fascinated by the change in fortunes, and by the impact it would have on their little Christian outpost on the Adriatic, Europe's listening post for events in Ottoman-ruled Bosnia. 'Of the Turkish magnates, some stand by the older brother and some by the younger brother', the city council wrote to Beatrice's father in Naples in 1481. 'How matters will finish between them is not clear to us ... [but] everything is in Matthias's grasp; to Matthias all eyes are turned.'[2]

In fact it was not that simple, and Matthias was deeply frustrated by the apparent failure of his plans to gain custody of the fugitive Prince Djem. But the effective end of hostilities with the Ottomans meant Matthias could switch his attention back to the west. By then, he no longer thought of dislodging Wladislas from Prague. With his ambitions turned towards Vienna, his only strategy regarding Bohemia was to make a graceful exit and be confirmed in possession of his existing gains in Silesia and Moravia. The Poles were open to a deal on such terms and Wladislas and his father Casimir sealed the agreement by descending on Matthias's headquarters in Olomouc in Moravia in the first week of February 1479. The meeting of three kings was one of those gaudy pageants that Matthias enjoyed arranging. He put on a similar junket for Wladislas's exclusive benefit that July, when Olomouc again became a stage for three weeks of tournaments, plays and gold-plated banquets in the central square.

According to the *Chronica Hungarorum* of Janos Thuroczy, 'In the palaces and streets, the lord King displayed ... so many novelties in gems and precious stones and in gold and silver ... in an astonishing and hitherto unseen multitude that Xerxes, former king of the Persians and of Babylon is scarcely believed to have displayed so many splendid possessions at that memorable banquet of his for the princes of his realm.'[3] While the writers struggled to find new superlatives, descriptions of Matthias as 'above

Alexander the great and all other kings of the world',[4] having become routine, the young Queen Beatrice danced with the languid, loose-limbed Wladislas, a man 17 years younger than Matthias but her senior by only one year. The experience planted the seeds of a certain interest in Beatrice towards the younger man, who was already married to Barbara of Brandenburg. This interest would have embarrassing consequences for Beatrice a decade later, when she attempted to pursue it.

By the time Wladislas left Olomouc for Prague on 30 July – his luggage train laden with gifts and a present of 20,000 ducats towards the renovation of his palace – the Bohemian war that had overshadowed much of Matthias's reign was over and the Peace of Olomouc had granted each of them what they wanted. Wladislas had been left with the heart of the kingdom, while Matthias retained Silesia and Moravia. The men had agreed to recognise each other's title as King of Bohemia, an unusual and imaginative solution to what had once seemed an insoluble problem. Matthias had in fact cut his losses with grace and, by neutralising Poland, freed his hand for a second round in Austria.

Frederick felt the hot breath of the Hungarian King on his back almost the moment Matthias and Beatrice left Olomouc for Buda. Hungary's preparations for war started immediately. In February 1480 an army lumbered across the Austrian frontier, Matthias justifying his action on the grounds that Frederick had failed to pay the 100,000 ducats promised as reparations for the earlier conflict in 1477. Frederick's decision in the meantime to exacerbate the conflict over Archbishop Beckensloer by elevating the refugee to the see of Salzburg, even though this meant shunting aside a sitting archbishop, provided Matthias with an additional excuse; the injured prelate, Bernhard von Rohr, archbishop since 1466, unsurprisingly appealed to Matthias over the case.

It was only a preliminary probe. At the end of the campaigning season in autumn 1480, Matthias went through the rigmarole of pretending to heed the anti-war protests of Sixtus IV, then vainly trying to piece together another crusade against the Turks.

The Emperor's allies among the German princes also played their part in trying to cool the dispute. George of Bavaria, for example, waylaid Beatrice in Bratislava in August and encouraged her to mediate between the two men. He had no success. Whatever difficulties Beatrice had with her husband – and they were many – she supported his military campaigns to the hilt.

The two rulers who now confronted each other for a final showdown were as different from one another as could be. Their only interest in common was astrology: on the importance of this they were as one. Indeed, Frederick was reported to have delayed consummating his marriage to Leonora of Portugal for several weeks after the wedding in order to wait for the perfect astrological sequence. But that was about it. Where Frederick was slow, ponderous and indecisive, Matthias was the opposite. And whereas Matthias came from an obscure Transylvanian family that had been virtually unknown before the 1430s, Frederick's family had supplied the Holy Roman Empire with an emperor back in the 1270s and was by now ancient. Frederick delighted in genealogy and the practice of ancient rituals. He was, wrote one historian, 'probably more aware of the legendary and mystical antecedents of his house than any of his predecessors'.[5] Obsessed with coronation ceremonies and the significance of the regalia, he made sure his own imperial coronation in Aachen was magnificent, ordering a new crown from Nuremberg goldsmiths in 1442 and new reliquaries for such treasured items as the Holy Tablecloth, the Holy Apron and the Holy Lance.

Matthias was not devoid of interest in conventional religious curios and practices. He organised a grandiose reception in Buda in 1489 for some relics of St John, which he then deposited in the palace chapel. He liked to keep abreast of religious disputes, chairing a debate on the doctrine of the Immaculate Conception – quite possibly in the library – between his wife's Italian confessor, Anthony of Zara and one of his own pet theologians, the Paulist, Michael the Hungarian (the King's man won).[6] He was punctilious in his observances, if the papal nuncio of Sixtus IV is to be believed. Maraschi told the Pope he was 'moved and shamed' when watching how 'this temporal prince surpasses us with regard to religious observance'.[7]

But it was not hard to exceed Sixtus IV in religious devotion, and in any case, neither Matthias's heart nor his mind was genuinely occupied, or occupied for long, with such matters. He was more truly at home in the observatory that Regiomontanus and Marcin Bylica had installed for him in Buda than in the chapel.[8] For every minute spent on relics, he would have happily spent an hour toying delightedly with the astrolabes and the celestial globes[9] – another great Renaissance craze – that the two men had built for him. Aside from Regiomontanus and Bylica, Matthias could draw on the services of Regiomontanus's former colleague in Vienna, Hans Dorn, a brilliant instrument maker who moved to Buda a few years after Regiomontanus left in 1471 and stayed there until the King's death.[10] Another member of the observatory was Johann Tolhopf, a former rector of Leipzig

University installed at Matthias's court from about 1480 and whose book on the movement of the stars in Matthias's library, *Stellarium*, survives in Wolfenbüttel. If the royal library had a pronounced Italian flavour to it, the observatory was a mainly German concern. Sadly, none of the instruments that the King commissioned for own observatory has survived; his feeble successor, Wladislas gave them away and they were lost.[11] But we have only to look at the superb globe that Dorn built for Bylica's own use in 1480, engraved with meridians, zodiacal signs and 36 named constellations and bright stars, to get an idea of the appearance of the King's own instruments. As Bylica's globe has been described as 'the most elaborate of all the metal globes constructed in Christian Europe before 1500',[12] one wonders what the King's presumably more elaborate and expensive globe looked like.

A deep interest in the mysterious significance of coronation rituals was not for Matthias. He had fought to recover the Holy Crown from Frederick for practical reasons, because he knew the Hungarians would never fully recognise him as a legitimate ruler until they saw this object on his head. But after his coronation in Szekesfehervar, the imagery of Christian monarchy sat fairly lightly on Matthias. Among surviving images of the King, those that portray him in a traditional manner, crowned and seated under a canopy of state, belong mainly to the early years of the reign. The Vienna *missale* of 1469 and *Libellus* of Andrea Pannonius of 1467 were typical. There is a handful of such images from later years. The *Epithoma rerum Hungararum,* a history of Hungary, written in the 1490s by the Sicilian Dominican diplomat Pietro Ransano, or Petrus Ransanus,[13] portrayed Matthias and Beatrice in an entirely traditional fashion, crowned and enthroned under a canopy and listening to the discourse of a mitred bishop standing before them, presumably Ransano.

But by the standards of Matthias's later commissions, this was an old-fashioned-looking portrait. In the 1480s the Italian illuminators of the King's books usually opted for a classical look, portraying Matthias as a new Caesar or Alexander and wearing a classical laurel wreath rather than a crown on his head.[14]

The most important difference between Matthias and Frederick, however, was not their respective attitudes to the Renaissance but their financial status. Matthias was wealthy even after years of military campaigns, as he was able to tax his domains relentlessly. The Emperor had fewer people to tax, with only the small Habsburg hereditary territories, embracing Vienna, Wiener Neustadt, Graz and Linz. Hence his reputation for stewarding whatever he had in a meticulous, somewhat miserly fashion. When Frederick had journeyed to Rome in 1453 to receive his crown from the Pope personally – a historical extravaganza that appealed to his sense of history – he was unable to cover the cost of his expedition and the Pope had to foot much of the bill. While the cities of Padua, Ferrara, Bologna, Florence and Siena fêted him on his way south, delighted to take part in an anachronistic pageant, sharp observers noted his financial predicament.

It was typical of Frederick that he should have been the last Holy Roman Emperor to try and breathe life into this ritual. In reality, no emperor since Frederick II in the 1250s had attempted to assert his right to rule Italy. Since then there had only been ghosts and feints: the make-believe factional party politics of imperial Guelphs versus papal Ghibellines, and the pleasing, deceptive memory of a universal empire that had never really existed – and which Frederick III was not about to resurrect.

When the Emperor returned to Italy in 1469, the note of farce was even more evident. Again unable to pay his way, he was 'reduced to pouring out a profusion of diplomas [and] creating counts, knights, poets-laureate and doctors, literally by the score ... [as] it was a highly profitable business concern and the amounts that he got back in fees refunded his royal and imperial Majesty for the costs of his journey'.[15]

Against Matthias, Frederick had a couple of advantages, however. One was his health. Perhaps it was his ponderous gait and the way he kept his elephantine body motionless for hours as he communed with the plants in his herbarium. Though old enough to be Matthias's father, by the early 1480s it was clear that he was ageing at a different, slower pace. The Emperor's other advantages were a legitimate heir in the shape of his son Maximilian and his sheer obstinacy. Those hours spent poring over the ancient lore of his house and the inner meaning of hidebound rituals had strengthened his faith in the mission of the Habsburgs. Every setback had to be set against his beloved but mysterious acronym, AEIOU, whose meaning he revealed to the world shortly before his death as 'Austria Est Imperare Orbi Universo' – 'Austria is to rule the world'.

Against the pledges of heaven, Matthias could be dismissed as a temporary interruption which fate would deal with in time. Frederick believed he had only to endure, and 'to forget what cannot be recovered',[16] as his own axiom put it.

In the event, the Hungarians did not have it all their own way. When the King resumed the campaign in March 1482, it proved less of a walkover than the campaign of 1477. Although the German princes, who in theory were the Emperor's lieges, more or less abandoned Frederick, he was able to draw on the outraged pride of the Austrians and of the Viennese. They had experienced enough of the King of Hungary's bullying, and rallied to their unappetising-looking monarch.

As he had done in 1477, Matthias relied on brute force and on what a later, conquering army would describe as the tactics of 'shock and awe'. One of his siege guns was so heavy that it required 80 horses to transport it. But there was no quick march to Vienna, only a painful, slow advance through eastern Austria, where the King's mercenary force, the Black Army, distinguished itself, as it had done in Bohemia, with indiscriminate violence. The army set off in two prongs, one heading west from Gyor towards Merkenstein while the other moved west from Bratislava towards Hainburg and Lower Austria. After a long struggle, Hainburg surrendered on 30 September.

The army had not achieved a great deal by the time it retreated in winter 1482 to Gyor, but no amount of protests from Rome was going to deter Matthias from making his grand entry into Vienna, however long it took. When Sixtus IV sent a bishop to reopen truce talks he found Matthias uninterested. The envoy tried to persuade him that the struggle was absurd by appealing to his vanity, suggesting it was like a lion attacking a mouse. Matthias was unmoved. 'He knew the Emperor better and he knew how little one could trust him', the envoy reported back to Rome, citing Matthias's response. 'If what he lost in war was returned to him [Frederick], he would immediately forget to fulfil his obligations.'[17]

The Bishop warned Matthias, presciently as it turned out, that notwithstanding the amount of humiliation he dished out, Matthias 'would not succeed in breaking the Emperor's obstinacy'.[18]

In his communications with Rome, the Bishop also complained about the conduct of the Black Army mercenaries. The soldiers had burned the village of Fürstenfeld's 800 houses to the ground, he said. In the charred ruins, the corpses of about a thousand people had been found. Priests were routinely killed and their goods seized. 'The King is of a tireless spirit, absolutely martial, thinking of nothing but war',[19] he wrote.

When the campaign resumed in 1483, the Emperor had to shift from his old bases in Vienna and Wiener Neustadt to the relative safety of Salzburg, Graz and the Tyrol. Matthias was in his element, plotting strategy and leafing through his favourite classical accounts of wars, quite possibly one of the (at least) two copies he possessed of Roberto Valturio's *De re militari*, with its fascinating line drawings of siege engines and the like. Perhaps he was already pondering the dedication to his library of a particularly sumptuous work in honour of the conquest of Vienna. This was to be the *Codex Heroica* of Philostratus – an appropriate work, taking the form of a conversation about the heroes of the Trojan War.

The enthusiastic scientist in him was always busily calculating the perfect mathematical formula for a cost-effective victory.

'Our army is divided into three orders,' he had informed the Venetian ambassador in 1481. 'The heavy cavalry who cannot be hired for less than 15 ducats a quarter per mount . . . the light cavalry, or hussars; they demand ten . . . [and] the infantry, also divided into various orders. Some are light foot soldiers, others are heavily armed; some are shield bearers. In addition there are gun masters . . .' The King explained that he used the heavy infantry as a defensive outer wall around the rest of the troops, enabling the light foot to dash out on command and make sorties. When they showed signs of losing momentum, they had orders to retire behind the testudo of the heavy infantry. 'The big shields around them give the impression of a fort, within which the light infantry are protected, and fight as though behind fortifications, attacking when the opportunity is ripe,' he said.

As military historians have noted, it was not a recipe for a blitzkrieg but for slow, steady progress. It was why Matthias's campaigns and sieges took years rather than months to achieve their goals, and why the towns he besieged usually surrendered only when the garrison inside was starving. It was an expensive affair. An invasion force of 15,000, which was probably the size of the core force he sent into Austria in 1477, might cost 400,000 ducats if kept in the field for a year. The army that the King sent into the field in 1482 may have been smaller than that of 1477, which could explain the slower pace of the advance. But it was kept in the field for longer, so the total cost must have been prohibitive.

Progress remained miserably slow in 1483 and 1484, considering that Vienna lay a short way west of the Hungarian frontier, exposed and unprotected by significant natural features. The gateway town of Bruck did not fall until March 1484, and it was not until December, when Korneuberg surrendered, that Vienna was surrounded.

By Christmas the anxious burghers of Vienna were praying for a miraculous deliverance at the hands of a relieving army assembled by the Emperor's son, Maximilian, or the German princes. After the fall of Klosterneuburg, Francesco Altovini, the Venetian ambassador, described the city's position as hopeless. 'The Emperor has lost almost the whole of the duchy around Vienna', he wrote. 'In Vienna, struggles rage, thousands of the [Hungarian] King's men have already occupied most of the towns and villages, and the Emperor has left and fled towards Salzburg.'[20]

The siege of the city started on 28 January 1485 and the first bombardment was at noon. Three Hungarian armies were now camping outside the walls at Hundsmuhle, St Bartholomaus and beside the Danube. If the Viennese entertained any last hopes of an Ottoman invasion providing a diversion, these were dashed in February when an Ottoman delegation turned up to congratulate Matthias on the outskirts of the city. Meeting the King and a large party of several hundred of his knights at Korneuberg they presented him with a pack of camels – a thoughtful gift from Sultan Bayezid, who no doubt knew of Matthias's fondness for exotic beasts to put in his menageries.

Still the city endured. But by April 1485 time was running out. The Viennese no longer believed in the possibility of relief by Maximilian or the princes. By the first week of May food supplies were gone and the city was split between die-hard Habsburg loyalists and a majority ready to throw in the towel.

The latter now sent a letter to Matthias's camp. Talks on the modalities of surrender, and whether the city or the university should take the key role in drawing up the terms, lasted from 15 to 19 May. Two days later a Viennese delegation took the surrender terms to the King's camp. On the following day, the 22nd, they sent a meek and apologetic note to the Emperor, informing him that if no relieving army reached them before the end of May the city would surrender to the King of Hungary the following day. It was formal adieu. On Friday, 27 May the last imperial officials left the city.

The following day, several days before the official surrender to the King was due to take place, Matthias's son, John, entered Vienna, heading first towards the cathedral and then to the Rathaus with his party. The frontispiece of the *Codex Heroica*, the volume that Matthias commissioned around the time of the fall of Vienna, probably refers to this event. Boccardino il Vecchio depicts a young boy with long hair in armour, standing on a chariot and surrounded by attendants and outriders. The backdrop is of a walled city with several spires peeping over the top. Might this be a rendition of Vienna? The small boy certainly looks the right age; John was 12 at this time.

His father waited until the time appointed by the treaty of surrender before entering Vienna on 1 June at the head of one of those fabulous processions. Comprising 8,000 men arranged in three formations, it was headed by 32 chariots filled with food for the starving citizens, 2,000 cavalry, the 24 camels recently sent by the Sultan, all loaded with royal treasures, 24 bishops arrayed in full ecclesiastical dress, another thousand or so cavalry, the King, another thousand cavalry, the infantry and – right at the end – about a thousand oxen.

The fact that the earth trembled on the day of the vast procession, not from the weight of the oxen, cavalry and camels but from a mild earthquake, gave rise to much speculation as to whether God favoured the proceedings or not.[21]

Beatrice was not to be outdone. She had her moment – albeit in the rain – when she made her own entrance on 5 June, and it was to the Queen, not the King, that the university presented itself to seek confirmation of its traditional privileges.

The new Duke of Austria, as Matthias styled himself from 24 June, soon dispelled any fears among the Viennese that they might suffer some frightful retribution on account of their steadfast loyalty to the Habsburgs. After the City Fathers made their homage to Matthias on 6 June, he confirmed them in all their rights. There was no punishment and no plunder – a remarkable achievement. Matthias was his usual magnanimous self in victory. In fact, he had already decided to make Vienna his joint capital.

The long struggle against Frederick – against all those who had opposed Matthias's legitimacy since he was a teenager – was virtually over. It was almost the end of Matthias's many wars, although a few mopping-up operations lay ahead. The Emperor's other redoubt, Wiener Neustadt, did not fall until 1487, allowing Matthias to make his state entry on 14 August. Matthias even confronted a small, footling invasion on behalf of the humiliated Emperor led by the Duke of Saxony. It did not get far.

Matthias was sated. The ceaseless warring with the Ottomans in the east and south, with the Czechs in the north and with the Austrians in the west was finished. Even though he had not obtained the coveted title of emperor, Matthias had made his country the centre of an empire. If the vassal states of the Romanians were included, it could be said to stretch from the Black Sea to Austria and from Moravia and Silesia to Dalmatia and Bosnia.

The time had come for consolidation. Throughout his adult life he had communicated with humanists in Italy and Germany, receiving the works they dedicated to him. But it was only now, as the sound of battle finally faded, that acquiring books became a mania. It was only after the fall of Vienna that men began to talk of Matthias as a great collector and that books of growing splendour began to stream out of the workshops in Florence to the vaulted chamber in Buda. It was only now, too, that the existing books began to be bound with luxurious leather covers and silver or gold studs and clasps. This sudden change of tempo was not the work of the King alone. He did not have the wherewithal or the time to select from long lists of translations and new works. If the King's was not the only guiding spirit in the enterprise, it begs the question of who else was involved. Extravagant claims have been made on behalf of Beatrice's cultural influence. On her death, it was said that she shone the torch of civilisation into the dark recesses of a rude and ignorant land, building 'a new Athens'[22] almost single-handedly. At Ferrara, the poet Celio Calcagnini, who delivered her elegy, made equally sweeping claims. 'Raised among her brothers in the traditions of an illustrious house, she would fulfil with dignity her vocation as queen when she became the spouse of a powerful sovereign; with infinite wisdom, she softened the ways of this prince raised among barbarians,'[23] he wrote.

Matthias would have taken issue with the idea that he was 'raised among barbarians' – a term that hardly matches what is known of Janos Hunyadi and Erzsebet Szilagyi. Significantly, these assertions came mostly from Beatrice's former courtiers like Bonfini, or from friends of her wider family. Calcagnini was a tutor to the Estes and to Beatrice's niece, also Beatrice.

Beatrice was certainly important in the Buda court. A lesser queen might have retired to the sidelines, humiliated by her failure to produce an heir. Beatrice simply became louder and more intransigent. Humanists felt it worth dedicating intellectually demanding books to her, which the authors clearly assumed she would read. Bonfini dedicated two works to her, one of which, the *Symposion trimeron,* treated so freely the theme of conjugal relations that it was placed on the papal index of forbidden books.

In the late 1490s, the Ferrarese Augustinian monk, Jacopo Filippo Foresti,[24] or Jacobus Filippus Bergomensis, dedicated another interesting work to Beatrice. *De claris et selectis mulieribus,* 'Concerning Famous and Select Women', was an updated version of an earlier work by Boccaccio containing biographies of famous women from classical goddesses to Roman prostitutes and Pope Joan. Foresti evidently anticipated that this theme would appeal to Beatrice. Just as Diomede Carafa had done in his memorial to Beatrice, he included an illustration of her seated and receiving his book from his hand. Several of the extant Corvinian works, dating from the last years of Matthias's reign, bear the arms of both Hungary and Aragon, suggesting these were joint dedications. The gesture makes no sense unless the Queen is seen as a significant patron in her own right.

Finally, it is worth recording that Bonfini was her protégé, not Matthias's. It is Beatrice who appears to have spotted his talents during her journey from Italy to Hungary in 1476, although it was not until 1485 that Bonfini, then almost 50, asked for leave from his duties as a professor in Recanati to present his works to Matthias, 'from which', he said, 'the whole town will get honour and glory'.[25] The council gave him three months' leave and money to cover travel expenses, and he never returned. After selling his services to the King as a translator among other things, Bonfini settled in Buda as Beatrice's 'reader'.

Historians have pointed out the errors in Bonfini's history of Hungary but he remains the outstanding chronicler of the reign and his close connection to Beatrice confirms her reputation as a refined, sophisticated woman. So does the handful of extant books from her library.[26] She was unusual even in the Italy of the Renaissance, where, as one historian has noted, 'Even noblewomen who acquired personal libraries owned mainly breviaries, Books of Hours, saints' lives and the like.'[27] That was not enough for Beatrice whose reading was as wide as her husband's, unlike her sister, Leonora, whose library consisted almost entirely of devotional books.[28]

Nevertheless, the sudden expansion of Matthias's library after 1485 cannot be ascribed directly to Beatrice. Instead, it stemmed from her determination to surround herself with Italians in Buda. This was crucial to the future of the library, for Matthias and Beatrice did not do the donkey work of poring over lists of potential texts that they wanted to acquire, let alone arrange their bindings. Beatrice was, in any case, a Neapolitan and would not have been familiar with Florence, which is where most new manuscripts came from. The hard work of creating a library appropriate to the magnificence of the conqueror of Vienna was the work of the Italians who streamed into Hungary in Beatrice's wake. Among them, one man, Taddeo Ugoleto, stood out.

CHAPTER SEVEN

The librarian Ugoleto

*They all passed through the hands of the librarian Ugoleto who carefully
placed them in their rightful place.*

I. Affo, *Memorie di Taddeo Ugoleto*, 1781

Bonfini always maintained that Matthias preferred war to peace, and life in
the saddle to the sedentary pleasures of life at court. But now the great
battles were over, there was more time for conspicuous expenditure at
home. In the absence of the longed-for child, there were banquets, parades
and receptions.

According to Bonfini, people observed a marked change in court culture
in the last years of the King's reign. He attributed the change to Beatrice and
her Italian retinue. 'Hungarian kings had been used to living on terms of
familiarity with the chief men and nobility', he wrote, 'keeping open house,
admitting beggars as petitioners, giving alms, ready to listen to everyone,
allowing everyone, even the most unfortunate, to enter the King's presence.'

It is easy to imagine Beatrice's disapproval at the sight of wandering
beggars and messy, informal Magyar meals, with everyone poking sloppily
into the same platter. Under Beatrice's careful stewardship, beggars found
their way into the royal palace stoutly barred, while free-for-all banquets
gave way to sedate affairs at which a stronger sense of hierarchy was
maintained. 'After the Queen came,' Bonfini wrote, Matthias 'improved his
board and manner of life, introduced sumptuous banquets, disdaining
humility at home and beautified the dining rooms.' He added: 'The King
removed himself from popular access, appointed strict doorkeepers, forbade

easy access and restored the royal majesty so as to keep its glory far more ostentatiously . . . he grafted Italian manners on to Scythian ones.'[1]

The Italians in Buda shared Beatrice's contempt for traditional Hungarian manners. 'They don't eat like us, each one with a plate,' Galeotto Marzio said of the Magyars, 'but all from the same plate, and to take the pieces they do not serve themselves with forks, as is done with us in Italy . . . but with their fingers and a slab of bread.'[2]

The Duchess of Ferrara played her part in 'improving' the quality of the dining at her sister's distant court, sending Beatrice packages of Italian comfort food and delicacies such as cheeses, olives, cumin and onions preserved in vinegar.[3] Beatrice introduced dining 'al fresco' to the palace in Buda, which was a novelty in Hungary, where most Magyars ate as they slept – indoors and in heated rooms wherever possible. She also encouraged men to shave, which was equally puzzling in a society that had traditionally prized a manly mass of facial hair and a luxuriant moustache.

Her husband continued to rebuild his palaces, relying especially on craftsmen like Duknovic. The Dalmatian had worked earlier in Rome for the Barbo family on such prestigious projects as the tomb of Pietro Barbo, Pope Paul II, before moving to Hungary in the early 1480s to help recon-struct and refurbish the palaces in Buda and Visegrad. He probably oversaw the construction of the Hercules fountain in Visegrad and other marble fountains that attracted many admiring comments. These were larger models of Medici fountains, another example of the fruitful rivalry between the courts of the Medici and Matthias Corvinus.

Duknovic had plenty of company among fellow Dalmatians in Hungary in the 1480s. While the sound of Italian echoed in the Queen's chambers and dominated the library, the harsher and less musical sound of Croatian was audible in the builders' yards. Duknovic was part of a large Croatian and Dalmatian mafia in Buda and Visegrad that included sculptors, masons and even the King's favourite barber, Stefanus de Ragusio – Stephen of Dubrovnik.[4] 'The few sources show a surprisingly high proportion of Dalmatians among the artists who played a prominent role in the Hungarian renaissance',[5] as one historian has noted. Three of the sculptors who worked on the royal palace in Buda, listed only as Johannes, Jacob and Petrus, came from Duknovic's home town of Trogir. With their help, Matthias's palaces, country retreats and churches were elevated to a new standard. 'He began to improve the citadel of Buda, where apart from Sigismund's buildings there was nothing worth looking at', Bonfini wrote.

'He greatly adorned the modest palace in which he set up a pavilion on the side facing the Danube and embellished it with a double fountain of marble and silver; he built a most honourable college of priests. Besides this he built a library, filled with a wonderful abundance of both languages.'

Bonfini listed these developments in his *Rerum Ungaricarum decades* in a section dated 1486. It is possible that this was indeed the year when the King's growing collection of books was moved into the vaulted chamber with the stained-glass windows that Naldi described in *De laudibus augustae bibliothecae*. The historian Jolan Balogh believes Naldi probably wrote the poem between 1484 and 1486.[6] The date fits, because the library began to draw international attention at about this time.

Bonfini was probably right to link the construction of new premises for the library to the period when Duknovic and the other Dalmatian sculptors and builders were refurbishing the two main palaces 'differing little in sumptuousness with those of Rome with spacious dining rooms, grand chambers and everywhere diverse gilded ceilings adorned with a great variety of emblems'. According to Bonfini, the masons worked on other projects too at this time, including another villa with a portico surrounded by gardens, a maze, aviaries, covered walkways and fishponds, a second lodge on the other side of the river in Pest, and a third residence 'at the third milestone where well stocked enclosures of wild forest animals were to be seen'.

The masons and sculptors hammered away in the coronation town of Szekesfehervar, restoring to glory the cathedral where Matthias had been crowned. Bonfini writes that Matthias 'began to extend the high altar so as to be far broader than the old one and to set up a mausoleum here for his father. Also he most dutifully brought here the body of his mother, Erzsebet, who had departed this life not long before, to dedicate a shrine here for his parents, his brother and himself, a work begun skilfully with an arch of tortoiseshell and made most loftily of hewn stone, which ... was built up with many arches around it'.

The previously run-down palace at Visegrad was rebuilt with gardens, enclosures of wild animals, fishponds and covered walkways, while the builders embellished the fortress at Tata with dining rooms and extra defences. They built another lodge for the King on an island in the Danube, near Komarom. Plans were also laid for a bridge to be built over the Danube there. Nor were the King's architectural schemes confined to royal residences and chapels. He was the patron of a number of ecclesiastical projects around the country that included a new Franciscan church in his birthplace of Cluj and Paulite monasteries at Szent-Lorincz and Feheregyhaza ('White Church'), near Buda.[7]

Some of the grandest schemes remained on paper. The last years of the King's life saw plans drawn up for another university, not this time in Bratislava but in Buda itself, based around the Dominican monastery. It was to have comprised college buildings erected around courtyards, housing a very substantial body of students.[8]

The drastic upgrading of the King's library was another of these expensive *grands projets*. The money was the King's and the guiding spirits were his and the Queen's. But the sudden change in the speed and character of this endeavour also involved another Italian, Taddeo Ugoleto, of Parma.

Ugoleto was not the first or only librarian at court. Galeotto Marzio may also have held an official post in connection with the King's books before the fall of his friend Pannonius in 1471, or even after he returned from Italy in the 1480s, following his unsuccessful sojourn in Bologna. Marzio certainly saw himself as the King's librarian; he referred to himself in a later work, dedicated to Lorenzo de Medici, *De doctrina promiscua*, as 'Bibliothecae Budensis Praefectus' – Prefect of the Buda Library.

In spite of this claim, however, there is no evidence that Marzio presided over the extensive remodelling of the royal collection in the late 1480s.[9] Although he was certainly no fool – the Inquisition would never have been alerted to the possibly heretical contents of his writings if he had been – it does not appear that he was regarded as an intellectual heavyweight in Buda. Ugoleto's biographer, Affo, maintained that Marzio was never officially made tutor to the King's son because he was not viewed seriously. His Florentine contemporary, Bartolomeo Fonte, he said, had once described Marzio 'as a light-hearted, humorous, epicurean scholar . . . so it is not to be believed that the most knowledgeable King, despite loving Marzio, wanted him to be his son's teacher'.[10] The image of Marzio as the King's companion rather than his mentor is confirmed by Marzio's own account of court life, *De egregie, sapienter, jocose dictis ac factis regis Mathiae* (Concerning the Wise and Humorous Deeds and Sayings of King Matthias), which he dedicated to the King's son.

This short and entertaining account of the King's wit and earthy table talk as well as the plentiful descriptions of his calorific and ultra-high-cholesterol meals makes it clear he had spent many a happy hour at the King's table. (It also explains why Marzio became so obese: his profile on a medallion shows he became exceedingly overweight.)

Ugoleto supplied many of the qualifications that Marzio may have lacked. Born in Parma in the mid-1440s, he was perfectly suited to a life among the bookshelves. Books were his life, as his own medallion, featured in Affo's biography, shows. Depicting Ugoleto's face in profile on one side, it showed a pile of books and an hourglass on the other. Ugoleto grew up in a milieu of collectors, printers, illuminators and copyists. Etienne Coralle, a lodger in the family home, would later become one of the first printers in Lyons. Ugoleto's brother, Angelo, managed a printer's workshop, a business to which Ugoleto returned as a partner after Matthias died.

He appears to have reached Hungary in the typical fashion of a wandering humanist, making his way there after travels through Switzerland, Germany and France, mostly spent collecting manuscripts. Lured by Matthias's reputation for liberality he continued to Buda because, as Affo reflected, 'Corvinus was always eager to meet scholars and cultivated men'.[11]

Once there, he rapidly gained the King's favour, though initially it was his skills in rhetoric that most interested Matthias. His first posts at court were diplomatic. He went to Vienna as an ambassador to Frederick and then to Rome just before start of the war in Bohemia, remaining in Rome almost until Paul II's death in 1471, after which Matthias ordered him back to Hungary, 'since Matthias admired Ugoleto very much'.[12]

Ugoleto, therefore, was ensconced in Buda well before Beatrice arrived. He must have continued to impress Matthias, for it was he and not Marzio who was placed in charge of John Corvin's education, though as John was not born until 1473, the post cannot have meant much until the 1480s. By then he was also the King's chief librarian, buying, sorting and rebinding the growing collection. Affo described the library as a kind of general resource and workshop for the foreign humanists in Buda as well as for the King and Queen. 'It would have been no use gathering so many scholars in Buda and not providing them with books,' he wrote. 'The wise King knew about the existence of the libraries in Alexandria under Ptolemy, as well as those of Athens under Pisistratos and Rome under Augustus ... [and] to feed all those scholars, he thought of setting in his palace a superb library.'

Affo added that Matthias gave Ugoleto prime responsibility for this project. 'He gave Taddeo the task of gathering codices from everywhere, written in any language and on any subject. He also spent a conspicuous sum of money to pay copyists, proof-readers [and] miniaturists to manufacture a large amount of elegant books, which were put into place by the expert hands of his librarian, Ugoleto.'

Affo suggested the occupation suited a man of Ugoleto's scholastic leanings. 'The new job gave Taddeo the rare opportunity to pursue his studies', he wrote. 'Like many other scholars, he had started collecting a series of notes . . . in which he described the process of returning to classical works their lost integrity through corrections to the texts, and through explaining the obscurities in the prose and discerning genuine works from apocrypha. 'Through the journeys Taddeo made on the King's account to find books in various provinces and kingdoms, he learned more and more, enhancing his knowledge.' These voyages took him to 'all the libraries known in his time and, as he himself claimed, all the libraries of Europe'.

According to Affo, the most significant literary and diplomatic expedition to Florence took place in 1487. This matches claims that the King's collection grew spectacularly following the conquest of Vienna in 1485. On this expedition, Affo continued, 'Ugoleto must have been introduced to Lorenzo [de Medici]'. He noted also that Ugoleto now held 'the title of Royal Buyer'. He quoted two letters from the humanist Bartolommeo Fonte to Matthias, recalling the deep impression that Ugoleto's visit made on Florence.

'Taddeo Ugoleto came to this city to enlarge your library', he quoted Fonte as saying:

> Every time the city of Florence heard him talk about your benevolence to men of letters and your immortal desire to revive the arts, all of Florence burned with an incredible love for Your Majesty.
>
> In spite of the weight of great affairs, your thoughts are on saving the monuments of the ancient writers from destruction and you animate the intelligence of your contemporaries with great promises of remuneration and of honours.
>
> For this you deserve the praise of the whole world and, besides, assure yourself a glory more eternal still in posterity than all those who placed famous libraries at the disposition of the public, such as Pisistratos in Athens, Ptolemy in Alexandria, Eumenes at Pergamon, Caesar at one time in Rome, and recently the Pontiff, Nicholas V.[13]

A second letter from Fonte, dated January 1488, again praised Ugoleto's success in fulfilling the King's literary and diplomatic business in Florence.

Ugoleto had been to numerous public and private libraries in Florence, Fonte said. 'He bought many of the oldest books and many others were offered him by those to whom rewards from King Matthias were promised.'[14] Affo mentioned three books that Ugoleto had taken back to Hungary, including Ficino's *De vita coelitus comparanda* and Verini's verses. Fonte said he now felt encouraged to go to Hungary himself, a goal he would indeed soon realise.

As well as advertising Matthias's generosity and magnificence to the Florentines in 1487, Ugoleto made use of the visit to purchase part of the library of the Medici banker, Francesco Sassetti. The business affairs of the bank had taken a disastrous turn in the mid- to late 1480s, which had had a direct effect on Sassetti, the bank's general manager from 1463. As his personal fortune was bound up with investments in the bank, he had endured substantial losses. He was forced to sell much of his valuable collection[15] before setting out for Lyons in February 1488 to try and save the branch there from liquidation.

While the Medicis snapped up most of Sassetti's books, Ugoleto bought several for Matthias, including Gellius's *Noctes Atticae*, now in Manchester, which had been copied for Sassetti around 1472. It was probably Ugoleto who arranged for the book to be rebound in red leather with a raven in the middle and who had the arms of the Sassetti family effaced. Albinia de la Mare, who located this lost Corvinian work in Manchester, believed it was not the only book Sassetti sold to Ugoleto. He 'may have sold other manuscripts, now lost, to Matthias Corvinus, and perhaps to other collectors as well',[16] she wrote.

As Fonte noted, Ugoleto used the expedition to Florence to attract more 'names' to come to Buda with promises of pensions and honours, after which Fonte himself had gone.

Ficino, as we have seen, did not take up the offer. There was never a realistic chance that a man so bound up with the Medicis would abandon either Lorenzo or the Platonic circle in Florence that he had founded. 'He was always content with his present circumstances,' one biographer wrote, 'and was not to be enticed by any reasons, prayers, gifts to accept any other situations, however fine and rewarding, at the cost of abandoning the Medici.'[17]

Ficino was bombarded with requests to come to Hungary from several quarters in these years. After turning down the invitation of the Bishop of Vac, Miklos Bathory, he wrote separately to Matthias in October 1487, taking the opportunity to congratulate him on his latest conquests in Austria. After taking Vienna two years earlier, the King had just taken Wiener Neustadt. 'Your momentous victory', Ficino called it.[18]

Ficino compensated for his failure to come to Buda by tracking down important books for Matthias's collection as well as dedicating some of his own works to the library, including his letters and Book III of De vita. He thus served Matthias from a distance, once sending a cousin of his to Buda in his place, though the young man was unfortunately robbed en route. It was just as well he never attempted the journey in the late 1480s, for he had not many years ahead of him, dying in October 1490, only a few months after Matthias.

Ugoleto returned from Italy laden with booty and having handed out numerous commissions. 'All these volumes were dedicated to His Majesty and with them, as well as many other codices and . . . such things as medals, statues, and antiques, Taddeo left Florence for Hungary', Affo wrote. 'The King was very pleased with all those books and delighted to hear that the Florentine men of letters loved him.'[19]

Though Ugoleto was unquestionably Matthias's chief 'royal buyer' in the late 1480s, no accounts survive of his day-to-day management of the library. We have only the results – a trend throughout the decade towards standardised bindings and more lavish and elaborate illuminations. Accounts of contemporary princely libraries shed light on how Matthias's library functioned and looked, however. This was the era of the first public libraries in Europe, the idea having by then gained currency that a library should be more than a prince's private resource. It ought also to benefit the res publica. It was partly a response to the emphasis the humanist writers placed on the benefits of sound education. This was what motivated the Florentine scholar, Niccolo Niccoli, to leave his impressive collection to the people of Florence in the 1440s. It was also what prompted the people of Carpentras in France in 1452 to create a public library out of their late Bishop's collection 'for men of every estate, degree and condition'.[20]

Cardinal Bessarion was prompted to the same course of action by the fall of Constantinople to the Ottomans in 1453. Bessarion had been determined to make sure his collection would be preserved so that the wider public would never forget the Greek culture of 'the city that once was ours'.[21] Using his Greek contacts in Athens, Thessaloniki and Constantinople to buy up books, he first revealed his intention to found a public library out of the stock in Venice in a will dated nine years before his death, in 1463.

Borso d'Este, Duke of Modena and later of Ferrara, had started the fashion of putting princely libraries at the service of learned men and distinguished visitors. Borso was not particularly intellectual and knew no Latin, which, as one biographer recalled, 'does not seem to have caused him a moment's anguish'.[22] His library was quite modest in size; a list from 1467 numbered 148 works.[23] But it contained the magnificent illuminated bible which had taken eight years to copy and illustrate and which he took with him to Rome in 1471, just before his death. Borso's exhibitionist tendencies were also revealed in the number of works in his library listed as *Laude del Duca Borso*, or even as *Deificatio de Duca Borso*.[24] From 1467 to the end of the century, under his half-brother, Beatrice's brother-in-law Ercole, the Este library tripled in size. The birth of the public library, or the princely library that was open to the public, brought about the rise of the professional librarian. He was now expected to liaise not only with the Prince but with a host of visitors. Ercole d'Este appointed what one historian called 'the first real librarian', Pellegrino Prisciano, to manage a collection that by the 1490s totalled some 700 volumes.[25]

To gain some appreciation of Ugoleto's likely obligations to Matthias, one must turn to the household regulations of Guidobaldo of Urbino, the heir to his father, Federigo, a kindred spirit to Matthias. Like his father, Federigo had been a *condottiere*, though unlike Hunyadi – or Borso d'Este, for that matter – he did not simply admire learned men but became one himself, thanks to several years spent at the humanist school run by Guarino's friend, Vittorino da Feltre, at the Gonzaga court in Mantua. Like Matthias (and Beatrice's famous grandfather, Alfonso), he saw himself as an intellectual soldier, and had himself painted in 1477, probably by the Flemish artist Justus of Ghent, in full armour, poring over a scarlet-bound manuscript, little Guidobaldo by his side.

Federigo was also a close friend of Bessarion, who was godfather to his son.[26] It was indicative of the relationship between the two men that when the Cardinal left Italy for France in 1472, he entrusted Federigo with his library in his absence.

Like Matthias, Federigo expressed his active commitment to the Renaissance through architecture. In his *studiolo* in Urbino, probably built in the mid-1470s, the 28 panels on the walls contained only a handful of images of saints – and most of those were Church Fathers such as Jerome. There were more pictures of the intellectual heroes of the classical world: Plato, Aristotle, Cicero, Seneca, Homer, Virgil and Ptolemy. Interestingly, the *studiolo* also contained portraits of contemporary humanist heroes like Bessarion and Pius II.[27]

Again like Matthias, Federigo had had problems fathering an heir. His first wife was childless and his second, Battista Sforza, gave birth to eight daughters before presenting Federigo with the longed-for Guidobaldo in 1472, a year before Matthias's son, John, was born. For both men the issue of the succession was never solved entirely satisfactorily. While John Corvin was illegitimate, Guidobaldo was sickly, dying childless in his twenties.

Federigo's library would appear to have been smaller than Matthias's, housing from 700 to 1,100 volumes, depending on which inventory is used. However, Vespasiano admired it enormously, though as he supplied between half and three-quarters of the books[28] it was in a sense his creation as much as the Duke's. We need to bear that in mind when recalling his claim that it contained almost 'every known work of that [Latin] or the Greek tongue, as well as the orators of the latter';[29] he mentioned works by Aristotle, Plato, Homer, Sophocles, Pindar, Menander, Plutarch, Ptolemy, Herodotus, Pausanias, Thucydides, Polybius, Demosthenes, Aeschines, Plotinus, Theophrastus, Hippocrates, Galen and Xenophon. It also housed one book that Matthias would have enjoyed, 'a very curious volume', according to Vespasiano, 'with every ancient or modern military engine'.[30]

Vespasiano said the Duke had spent about 30,000 ducats on collecting and binding his books, each work having been covered in scarlet leather ornamented with silverwork. 'It is thus truly a rich display to see all these books so adorned, all being manuscripts on vellum with illuminations and each a perfect copy – perfections not found in any other library.'[31]

The household regulations of Federigo's son made it clear that the post of librarian now involved a precise set of duties. It was his responsibility to keep up to date

an inventory of the books and keep them arranged, and easily accessible … [and] maintain also the room in good condition.

He must preserve the books from damp and vermin, as well as from the hands of trifling, ignorant, dirty and tasteless persons. To those of authority and learning, he ought himself to exhibit them with all facility, courteously explaining their beauty and remarkable characteristics, the handwriting and miniatures … when ignorant or merely curious persons wish to see them, a glance is sufficient.

He must let no book be taken away but by the Duke's orders and if lent

must get a written receipt and see to its being returned. When a number
of visitors come he must be especially watchful that none be stolen.[32]

The physical appearance of Federigo's library, which was completed in
1482 and remains *in situ*, is an important guide to the probable appearance
– or at least the atmosphere – of Matthias's library. According to one
description:

> The main door to the library . . . was from the courtyard and on entering
> one saw to the right works of sacred writing, law, philosophy and mathe-
> matics while on the left were works of geography, poetry and history.
> Above the shelves against the walls were paintings of the seven liberal arts .
> . . . on the floor were carpets and in the centre of the room tables and
> benches for scholars . . .
>   The manuscripts were bound in coloured velvet or leather and some of
> the bindings were decorated with filigree silver work. So it is unlikely that
> those latter were shelved with their spines only exposed, instead the orna-
> mental front would have been on view with their backs resting on sloping
> supports, perhaps. The lighting from the high windows is subdued, and
> one can imagine how colourful and at the same time how mysterious and
> yet restful the room looked when furnished.[33]

Keeping a keen eye on wandering hands and issuing borrowers' tickets
was not enough to stop thieves or, as was more often the case, prevent
borrowers from forgetting what they had taken. Borso d'Este spent a fair
amount of time during his last years trying to trace a copy of Pliny that had
been lent from his library in 1467 and never returned. Indeed, if the Este
library in Ferrara had similar regulations to those in Urbino, they were not
honoured, for the library was in chaos in the late 1480s. One imaginative
account describes how the librarian, Prisciano, tried to sort out matters for
Ercole and Leonora.
   'Prisciano was reduced to despair over the chaos which he found in the
library – a disorder, he says, which would have aroused compassion in the
devil . . . A Quintilian is lent to someone and passed onto a second person
. . . someone is detaining a Chronicle of Ferrara, the works of Villani seem
to have passed permanently into the hands of the Strozzi, the Pliny has
disappeared and among the number of borrowed books which cannot be
traced, no one knows what has become of Alberti's *De re aedificatoria*'.[34]

Vespasiano was another culprit, at the expense not of the Este library but of the Medici library in Florence. The fact that he had played a leading role in helping Cosimo de Medici to set up his new library at Fiesole, engaging a team of copyists and illuminators to work at high speed on the collection, did not turn him into a responsible borrower. After taking two Latin translations by Aristotle, *De generatione* and *De philosophia*, from the collection at San Marco on 13 March and 6 September 1480 respectively, he did not return them until July 1491.[35]

Many people borrowed books for years from the San Marco library, which the Medicis had formed out of Niccolo Niccoli's library. They were encouraged in their bad habits by the fact that while librarianship was still in its infancy, the business of issuing receipts was vague. One copy of a borrower's ticket from San Marco, dated 13 January 1489, read: 'I, Demetrius, the Greek, received from the library of Master Lorenzo [de Medici] the following books: Plato, Aristotle and a translation of Aristotle's ethics by Leonardo.' Miraculously, these books eventually reappeared, though after an absence of almost three years.[36]

Most princely libraries in Matthias's lifetime suffered from the same blight – often a consequence of the egotism and arrogance of many humanists. Books disappeared from the Visconti library in Pavia for years at a stretch. Pier Candido Decembrio borrowed three works of Homer from the collection in August 1439 but did not return them until 1446.

The library that Bessarion founded in Venice but which the authorities neglected to manage after his death, failing to find suitable premises, was another paradise for light-fingered borrowers. The 'Bibliotheca Marciana' remained an anomaly for years. Without a proper home until the 1520s, this valuable collection of 'nine hundred excellent and beautiful volumes in Greek and Latin'[37] languished in boxes – a tempting target for pilferers. Of seven books loaned to a visitor from Rome in 1478, only one had been returned as late as 1494. A commentary on Aristotle's logic, borrowed in 1501, was not recovered for 30 years. Not surprisingly, the authorities in Venice prohibited all further borrowing from the collection in 1506.

Vespasiano notoriously urged Lorenzo de Medici to appropriate one of the late Cardinal's prize commissions. When Bessarion died in 1472, Vespasiano was still at work on the 10-volume edition of the works of Augustine that he had ordered. Vespasiano unscrupulously suggested Lorenzo might want to take the volumes himself, as 'they were the most worthy objects in Italy' whose reproduction 'would not only be difficult but

impossible'. Lorenzo spurned this suggestion and made sure the books were
sent on from Florence to Venice.

In his own lifetime, Bessarion had been a thoughtless borrower. In Rome,
Calixtus III lent Bessarion many books. But of 11 Greek works that he
borrowed from the Vatican library, three were not returned until the latter's
death.[38]

The era of real growth in the papal collection, as has been said, followed
under Sixtus IV from 1471 to 1484. From around 1,209 works at the end of
the pontificate of Nicholas V, the stock had grown to 2,527 items in 1475
and 3,650 by 1486, two years after Sixtus's death. Bartolomeo Sacchi
'Platina', Sixtus's librarian from 1475 to 1481, played a role similar to
Ugoleto's in Buda, transforming this growing collection into an organised
institution. In Platina's case, the librarian was certainly the driving force
behind the changes. As one historian noted: 'At almost every step in the
completion and expansion of these facilities, the documents reveal the
guidance and immediate supervision of Platina ... It remains largely
Platina's merit that within a very few years after the decision was taken to
expand the library, Sixtus could boast one of the richest collections of books
anywhere in Europe.'[39]

Sixtus's principal role in Rome was like that of Matthias in Buda. He
supplied the funds, the goodwill and the commitment. Sixtus's interest in
many of the works in his library may have been scant, for the former
Franciscan Minorite was not a humanist scholar, even though he had once
been part of Bessarion's circle. He read little except Church history, canon
law and theology and had no interest in poetry. Yet he took more pride in
creating his library than in any other single achievement, and the inscription
on his tomb dwells at greater length on the opening of the collection to the
public than on the historic defeat of the Ottomans at the Battle of Otranto,
for which Sixtus took credit. It is a sign of how important the library became
to the Pope that a fresco in the hospital of San Spirito, which Sixtus rebuilt
from 1471 to 1482, records his visit to the reading room. The Pope is shown
standing there, surrounded by a mass of books laid flat on reading desks,
while a couple of scholars leaf through some of them.[40]

As the papal library grew in size and status, the librarian emerged as a
prominent court official. Platina's appointment as librarian in 1475 was
recorded in a celebrated fresco placed opposite the entrance to the hall of the
Latin manuscripts, the handsome Platina shown kneeling before the seated
Pope, who is surrounded by his nephews.

The obligations of Platina's successor, Manfredi, included such humdrum tasks as obtaining candles for readers, foxtails, brooms and juniper for dusting and cleaning and enough fuel 'pro usu bibliothecae propter frigidatem loci'. The regulations for users in Rome anticipated those of many modern municipal libraries. There was to be no chatting, scraping chairs on floors or climbing over benches. Platina was a generous lender, and some 400 books were borrowed between 1475 and 1485,[41] mostly by ecclesiastics. As one historian put it, 'Platina's register of loans reads like a Who's Who of the Roman intelligentsia. In addition to serious scholars, the Pope himself and his nephews, cardinals, bishops and abbots, secretaries, dataries and penitentiaries, theologians and rhetoricians, lawyers and printers, foreign ambassadors and merchants took advantage of the liberality of the papal library.'[42]

Possibly they took too much advantage of Platina's good will. In 1480, after at least 20 manuscripts from Nicholas V's collection disappeared,[43] the rules were tightened. It was no longer enough for borrowers to leave their names and the titles of the books they borrowed in a little book kept by Platina. From now on they had to leave a deposit as well.[44]

The decoration of the papal library, with its rich wood panelling, elaborate trompe-l'oeil frescos, stained-glass windows and the copious use of gold – like the library in Urbino – carries echoes of the descriptions of Matthias's library in Buda. It is quite possible that Matthias's own library was inspired by reports of either collection. Like Matthias's library, the papal library was divided into Greek and Latin sections. The libraries in Rome and Buda were both reference libraries for scholars and also made a statement about their illustrious patrons. Francesco della Rovere, Sixtus IV, like Matthias, was an outsider who never quite penetrated the noble and aristocratic society around him. Both men compensated for this by relying on showmanship to impress a sceptical world: and in this the possession of a magnificent library was an important tool.

We do not know whether Ugoleto's duties in Buda ever included such mundane tasks as buying candles and foxtail dusters, or whether this was left to minions. But we do know that he enjoyed a close, collaborative relationship with the King when it came to deciding on acquisitions. In one letter of 1485, Ugoleto discussed his progress in tracking down works in terms that make it clear he spoke as one equal to another. 'I'll take good care, great King, that all the works you ordered to be copied here will be sent in a short time', he wrote, listing the works in question: orations of

Aeschynus, the tragedies of Aeschylus, Arrian's *De expeditione Alexandri* (Alexander's Campaigns), Cicero's *Brutus* and the panegyric of Pliny. 'Scriptura elegans est, scriptores ipsos non ignaros censeo', he added.[45]

By the time Ugoleto visited Florence in 1487, Vespasiano was long gone from the scene, having retired to Antella in 1478 to write his memoirs. He sold his shop in 1485. His last great commission had been an illuminated bible for the Duke of Urbino. Federigo himself died in 1482, aged 60. During the last years of Matthias's reign, therefore, Ugoleto, Fonte and the King's other brokers and negotiators dealt with other *cartolai*.

At the same time, it seems as if the work of copying and illuminating a large quantity of manuscripts at once had become too much for the circle of trusted Florentine painters and copyists to handle, and that some of these tasks were now deputed to a workshop in Buda. There is no absolute proof, admittedly, that this Buda workshop existed. It is notable, for example, that while many of Matthias's books contained inscriptions noting that so-and-so had copied this work in Florence in such-and-such a year, there is not a single reference to Buda in any of them. And while there are distinct Florentine, Lombard and Neapolitan styles of illumination, it is questionable whether a Buda 'style' can be identified. Nor is there any certainty about whether the workshop – if it existed – concerned itself with copying, illuminating, binding, or all three.

It also seems unlikely that a workshop existed in Buda before the early 1480s. When the King's Hebraist, the German Dominican, Peter Schwarz, or Petrus Nigri, came to Buda in 1481 and wrote his defence of Thomist philosophy, the *Clypeus Thomistarum*, the work, dedicated to 'the invincible Matthias', was not copied in Buda. Instead, it was sent to Venice to be printed. If the workshop did exist, therefore, it was probably established in the mid- to late 1480s, after the conquest of Vienna. On the other hand, Miklos Olah, writing in the 1530s, insisted that there had been a workshop in Buda. In *Hungaria*, he said it had operated under the supervision of the Dalmatian polymath Felix Ragusinus – Felix of Dubrovnik.

'I heard from old people that while the King lived he always had around him 30 scribes, experts in painting, of whom I knew several after his death', Olah wrote. As for Felix Ragusinus, 'whom I knew in his old age, [he] knew not only Greek and Latin but Chaldean and Arabic. An expert equally in art and painting, he worked carefully that no error should occur in the transcription of the books.'[46]

Was this the same man as Feliks Petancic, who took the Latin name Felix

Petancius Ragusinus? The latter wrote several works on the Ottoman Empire after Matthias's death,[47] journeying to Constantinople, France and Spain on behalf of his successor, Wladislas. All that can be said is that it is possible that the two men were one and the same though some insist the master of Matthias's workshop and Wladislas's roving diplomat must have been different people. And some dismiss Olah's claim out of hand, saying it is far more likely that Matthias relied solely on the established workshops of Florence to build up his collection, and would never have attempted to recreate all their facilities in Buda.[48]

Olah's claim that Ragusinus knew Greek, however, does match what is known of Feliks Petancic. Born in Dubrovnik around 1455, he grew up in a city where the study of Greek had become well established as a result of the influx of refugees from Constantinople.[49] Olah's description of his Ragusinus as a master linguist also fits what is known of Petancic from his own works on the Ottoman Empire.

Apart from the question of Felix's identity, there are other clues in support of the existence of a workshop in Buda. One comes from the writings of the Sicilian diplomat Pietro Ransano, author of a history of Hungary, the *Epithoma rerum Hungararum*. He came to Buda in 1488 and maintained that Matthias employed illuminators there.[50] As he was present at Matthias's court, he was presumably in a position to know.

If there are question marks over whether Matthias's books were illuminated in Buda, it seems more than likely that some of the books were at least bound there. The binding of Gellius's *Noctes Atticae*, one of the few Corvinus manuscripts to retain its original binding, has been described by one writer as following geometrical patterns that were Central European, Hungarian or even Transylvanian in inspiration, rather than Italian.[51] Another intriguing work in this respect is the *Evangelistarium secundum*, now at Holkham Hall, Norfolk. This bears the Polish white eagle of Matthias's successor, Wladislas, or Ladislas, and the letters LA, on the principal illumination. It has been suggested that Wladislas's Polish eagle was painted over the arms of Matthias. But it is by no means clear that the work was doctored in this way. Moreover, it is thought that the Milanese illuminator Francesco da Castello went to Hungary in person. In that case, it would appear that the manuscript may have been copied and 'finished' in Hungary just after Matthias's death. If so, the workshop did not fold immediately in 1490 but survived into the first few years of Wladislas's reign.

There are also practical reasons for believing some kind of workshop existed by the late 1480s, connected to the library. By then, both Matthias and Ugoleto were in a terrific hurry. In fact, both Matthias and Lorenzo de Medici were collecting books at the same frantic pace in these years. Before his death in 1494, four years after Matthias, Lorenzo had added 350 books to his private library and, like Matthias, he now made collecting Greek works his priority. At the time of his grandfather Piero's death in 1469, none of the Medici collections had contained a single Greek work. By the time of Lorenzo's death, especially after buying the collection of the humanist Francesco Filelfo in 1481, he possessed one of the greatest collections of Greek works in Italy. Only the Vatican library and Bessarion's collection in Venice surpassed it.

Like Matthias, Lorenzo was a gifted amateur intellectual who felt comfortable in a humanist environment. He, too, wanted a library that would perpetuate his fame. Battles would be forgotten, paintings decay and palaces collapse. But a library was a stepping-stone to divinity as well as a refuge against what Bracciolini had dismissed as the 'stammering age' in which they lived.[52] As Angelo Poliziano told Lorenzo in 1477, in the *Raccolta Aragonese*, immortality was the reward of the greatest librarians. As custodians of the classics, future generations would honour their memories. 'Achilles would be nobody without Homer,' Poliziano wrote, 'and Pisistratos, the wise prince of Athens, nobody, had he not preserved Homer's poem for mankind.'[53]

Matthias, Borso d'Este, Federigo de Montefeltro and Lorenzo de Medici were all propelled by the same hunger for immortality. Matthias felt this pressure more than Lorenzo, who at least had sons. Matthias had no well-stocked nursery, not even a couple of nephews. There was only John.

Matthias adored his bastard son. 'I delight in your presence in all times, my son', the Florentine Aurelio Brandolini quoted Matthias as telling John in *De comparatione reipublicae et regni*, a dialogue written in the 1490s comparing monarchies to republics.[54] Whether Brandolini ever heard those words from the King's mouth we cannot tell, but they were true enough. However, John alone was not much of a defence against the forces conspiring against the Hunyadis. One son just was not enough.

CHAPTER EIGHT

'A glutton for books'

It is the King's aim to surpass all other monarchs in this matter, as he did with other things.

Bartolomeo Fonte, 16 September 1489[1]

Attavante degli Attavanti began work on a richly illuminated missal for Matthias in that year of victories, 1485. It would stand out for its grandeur, its obvious expense and for several portraits of a now very imperial-looking Matthias and Beatrice.

Large, lavishly illuminated bibles and missals were in vogue among Matthias's contemporaries, such as Borso d'Este and Federigo de Montefeltro. Attavante had illuminated Federigo's work, too. He was the contemporary equivalent of the pop star. Some judge his work formulaic and unspontaneous in comparison to that of the brothers Di Giovanni. There was 'a certain uniformity of presentation', one critic said.[2] His human figures are certainly flatter and more wooden than those wonderful saints in their *studiolos* that the Di Giovannis specialised in.

But technically he was brilliant. It is striking to compare the missal that he illuminated for Matthias in the mid-1480s with some of the books associated with the earlier years of the King's reign, such as the Vienna missal of 1469 and Andreas Pannonius's *Libellus de regiis virtutibus* of 1467. It is as if they belong not only to different libraries but to different civilisations. The latter are part of a provincial, Gothic world. Attavante's work is instantly recognisable as a sophisticated product of the Renaissance.

George of the Cathedral copied the Vienna missal in old-fashioned Gothic script, using spiked letters packed densely together, so that the words appear to run into one another, whereas Attavante's missal was copied in the new 'antique' humanist style, with visible gaps introduced between the words for greater legibility. The invention of the Florentine humanist Niccolo Niccoli in the 1420s, the use of *littera antiqua*, as it was not quite accurately called, spread rapidly in the following decades, hailed by humanists as the script of the 'never to be enough admired' ancients.

The difference in the type of script between the older and newer works tells only part of the story. The Vienna missal was painted simply and crudely, the artist's faint grasp of perspective lending the illustration of the robed King a medieval air. Attavante's missal is a riot of colour and imagery, designed to dazzle and demonstrate the artist's mastery of perspective. It was unusually rich in detail and appearance, and part of a trend among the books produced for Matthias in the last years of his reign, when magnificence had become the rule in the library, as in so many other aspects of court life.

Attavante was born in 1452 at Castelfiorentino, southwest of Florence, and when the demand for illustrated manuscripts in Buda reached its peak he was in his early thirties and at the height of his powers. It was a happy combination of circumstances, for he was very prolific. About thirty of his works survive, many of which were commissions for Matthias. They include a magnificent breviary, now in Rome, the sermons of Ambrose, the letters of Augustine,[3] a second work of Augustine,[4] Gregory's homilies on Ezekiel,[5] Hieronymus's commentaries on Ezekiel,[6] Philostratus's *Heroica*,[7] Marcian's *De nuptiis philologiae et Mercurii*, a work of St Ambrose,[8] Chrysostom's commentaries on St Paul, Origen's homilies, Hieronymus on the Psalms of David, Livy's history of the Romans,[9] a collection of miscellanea of the Church Fathers and other works by Ficino and Fonte. He was by far the most important artist working on Matthias's library.

With the arrival of this new generation of Florentine illuminators in the 1480s, a veil was lifted on pictorial representations of the King and Queen as they entered on middle age. If hitherto our image of them was blurred, the royal pair now come into sharp focus. Attavante included three portraits of Matthias and two of Beatrice in the missal, apart from the representation referred to earlier of the King and Queen in a crucifixion scene. There is very little to link the lifelike portraits of Beatrice in the late 1480s and Laurana's much earlier sculpture of 'Diva Beatrix Aragonia' in the mid-1470s. There is a single portrait from the early 1480s – a 'head shot' of a crowned Beatrice at the top of the frontispiece of Christoforo Persona's translation of a book on the Gothic wars by the Byzantine historian Agathias. A Neapolitan artist illuminated *De bello Gothorum* in 1483–84.[10] Coming from Naples, he presumably had some idea of the appearance of the former Neapolitan princess. For all that, it still looks like a standard royal bust. It is only with Attavante's début that the royal couple are depicted with some regard to personality and character as opposed to function and role.

The features that Attavante portrayed in the missal recur in Didymus of Alexandria's *De Spiritu Sancto*, illuminated by the Di Giovannis, and in the white marble relief portrait. Indeed, the representations of the King and Queen are so similar in all of them that they probably drew their inspiration from a single model. As all these works date from roughly within a few years of each other, it is impossible to tell who borrowed from whom. They probably all owe their inspiration to a medallion or portrait that Ugoleto or another agent of Matthias's brought to Italy.

The royal portraits from the late 1480s depict Matthias in profile as a jowly, round-faced man with a highly coloured face, long, curly, matted dark hair, and a prominent, slightly upturned, squat nose. They usually place an imperial wreath on his head. Beatrice is also shown only in profile, with a double chin, her curly hair tied simply and loosely at the back in the Italian fashion.

One can imagine Ugoleto, or Fonte, hurrying through Florence to the studio of Attavante or the Di Giovannis near the Badia, a copy of a contract or an image of the King under his arm. Attavante would have received his guest graciously but not exactly submissively, for he was a star in his own right and knew it. As the commissions flowed in from Matthias in distant Hungary, other patrons were clamouring for his attention. In the mid- to late 1480s, Attavante worked for two other important clients, the Medici Pope, Leo X, for whom he illuminated the letters of St Gregory, and Thomas James, Bishop of Dol, in Brittany, for whom he illuminated a missal. No wonder Attavante's contemporaries abandoned the discreet and self-effacing habits of the anonymous medieval artists and boldly advertised their contributions on the frontispieces.

This determination to sign and date works was not limited to artists. Not all copyists advertised their role in the production of Matthias's works, but some also said 'look at me!' It makes sense that some copyists worked anonymously if one accepts that the task was being increasingly farmed out to a workshop in Buda. The Habsburg diplomat and humanist, Johannes Köll 'Brassicanus', said Matthias also maintained a four-man team of copyists in Florence, working exclusively on his library. Their 'sole and unique work was copying all the best known works of Greek and Latin authors'[11] for Matthias, he wrote in his work *De vero iudicio et providentia dei,* published in 1530. These men are not likely to have signed their works.

But copyists working individually had no need to be so humble. Copying was a respectable occupation that combined happily with writing. Fonte was both author and copyist, for example, and it was Attavante who illuminated his copy of Juvenal's commentary. The elite copyists tended to be men of learning with a little time on their hands, such as priests of fashionable city churches, notaries or even nobles. Following the fashion of the age, they composed grandiloquent Latin names for themselves. Didymus's *De Spiritu Sancto,* for example, was copied by the wonderfully named Count Palatine Sigismundo de Sigismundi from Ferrara.

The Florentine priest Bonagius de Cantinis was one of Matthias's clerical copyists. When he worked on the sermons of Ambrose in 1488, which Attavante illuminated, he informed his reading public (the assumption of an audience was now clear) of his name and position in life. 'Manu Bonagiy de Cantinis, clerici Sanctae Mariae Floris de Florentia', he wrote. The priest who copied the breviary now in Rome, which Attavante also illuminated, signed himself as 'Martinus Antonius presbyter'. The Florentine notary, Carolus Hilarius de Fatariis, left a more personalised signature. 'Escriptum est hoc opus per me', he wrote, lest anyone should overlook the fact: 'Ad laudem et gloriam Regis Ungariae'. He must have finished copying and signing the work before the news reached him of Matthias's death in 1490, for he added some lines, reading: 'to the praise and glory of the King of Hungary of most happy memory who has recently died . . . in the year of our Lord Jesus Christ 26 June 1490.'[12]

The Florentine humanist Pietro Cennini, or Petrus Cenninius, as we have seen, was among the most prolific of the library's copyists, though his heyday had been years earlier. At least 25 of his manuscripts are extant, seven of which belonged eventually to Matthias's collection.

Not all copyists were Florentines, even if we exclude the men of the shadowy Buda scriptorium. Many constructed Latin pen-names around other places of origin, like Henricus Amstelredammis who copied some works of Aquinas in 1468 in Bologna. His surname and others like De Middelburgh or simply Hispanus are a reminder that while artists and copyists from Florence played the key role in the formation of Matthias's library, talented men of many countries also had a part.

The rapid growth of the library in the late 1480s devoured artists and copyists like a machine. Did standards drop as a result of the haste to pile Greek on Latin and stack Byzantine histories on manuals on medicine, wildlife, architecture and fortifications? Did the whole enterprise start to exhaust both Matthias and Ugoleto? Brassicanus remembered Matthias as a collector 'whom one should call truly a glutton for books',[13] a slightly backhanded compliment that hinted, even if unintentionally, at a lack of discrimination. More recently, many of the princely collectors of the late fifteenth century have been criticised for preferring quantity to quality and for collecting the Renaissance equivalent of coffee-table books. He was 'more interested in acquiring beautiful books than ancient ones',[14] one historian remarked waspishly of Federigo de Montefeltro. One writer in the 1950s attacked the claim that Vespasiano was a serious book salesman, too, claiming that most of the translations he oversaw were pretty abysmal. 'Whole lines are left out, mistakes abound, repetitions are left uncorrected rather than spoil the beautiful page. Vespasiano's manuscripts are written for people who wanted to possess these books not to read them,' he wrote.[15]

Inevitably, errors crept into what was often an excruciatingly monotonous job. Copyists were human, and translations were difficult to monitor in terms of quality. The process of checking was weak because hardly anyone – other than the translator – was in a position to check the translation against the original text. Archbishop Vitez did so, as the many annotations he left in the margins of his books show. Bonfini claimed Matthias understood Greek (and Turkish for that matter).[16] Even if that was true, it is still hard to imagine him, or Ugoleto, sitting on the famous couch in the library comparing a Greek original text to its Latin translation.

None of this means that Matthias and Beatrice were ignorant collectors, staring vacantly at the attractive illuminations of works they did not understand. A granddaughter of Alfonso the Magnanimous, brought up on Virgil and Ovid,[17] Beatrice could only be well read. When not creating a scene, shedding bitter tears, or plotting, she probably had her nose deep in a book. The woodcut illustration of her on the frontispiece of Foresti's *De mulieribus*, which showed her accepting a book from the author, was true to life in that respect. When Galeotto Marzio's account of court life described the Queen joining in a discussion about a female courtier and murmuring a Latin line on the theme of female inconstancy, it captured a brief, rather tantalising, image of a woman who could wear her learning lightly.

The presence in the library of some unique works also points to the creative spirit of its patrons. It shows that the King and his librarian were not simply obsessed with obtaining costly-looking works. At least two extant books are unique: the Byzantine Emperor Constantine Porphyrogenitus's work on court ceremonies and the *Ekklésiastiké historia* of Niképhoros Kallistos. If we assume extant works make up about 10 per cent of the original stock, the library at one point housed about 20 rare or unique works.

The lavish illustrations in the Brussels missal and Rome breviary of Attavante, in the Didymus of the Di Giovannis, in the Philostratus of Boccardino il Vecchio and the other works of the late 1480s represented Matthias to the world as invincible. However, the appearance of pomp and imperial serenity was an illusion. In fact, there was a terrible emptiness at the heart of all this triumphal imagery. There was no longed-for legitimate heir, or a clutch of sons, legitimate or otherwise, to accompany the portraits of the King and Queen. Matthias had only the one son – a poor guarantee of dynastic continuity in an age when death and warfare routinely wiped out children and youngsters long before their prime. No one knew this better than Beatrice, whose siblings began to die off in the 1480s in their twenties and thirties. Her talented brother, Giovanni, a discerning collector to whom Matthias had presented the archbishopric of Esztergom in 1480, died in 1485, while Attavante was illuminating the missal. He was only 29, a year older than Beatrice. Her younger brother, Francesco, died a year later, aged just 25. Had Beatrice herself conceived, the shadows might not have frightened her, but there was nothing, not even a pregnancy.

The representations of victory portrayed with such apparent conviction in the manuscripts of the library, therefore, had something of a sham quality. Matthias's court, marriage and dynasty were in crisis as the lack of heirs threatened to jeopardise all his achievements. Somehow, John was never an entirely convincing successor to the great Matthias. Even the artists in Florence picked up on feelings of ambivalence about his destiny.

While Attavante, Cherico and the Di Giovannis stirred the colours on their palettes and prepared to apply the paints to their exquisite creations – while they or their minions applied a last dab to a crown of laurels on the King's head – the real King fought off despair as his increasingly disordered spouse ranted and plotted, absurd dreams of ruling Hungary in her own right clouding her confused imagination. Chivalrous to the end about his difficult consort, Matthias was driven to such distraction by her behaviour that in 1489 he sent a letter to her brother, Alfonso, Prince of Calabria and heir to the throne of Naples. In it, he urged him to check his sister's behaviour, warning that if matters continued, the enraged populace might end up killing her.

There is something touching in the fact that by this time both of them were becoming ill. Beatrice had not aged well even by the standards of the time. At 28 she was in poor health and was prone to rheumatism and fevers. When her nephew, Ippolito d'Este, first saw her in 1487, typically she was too ill from fever to get out of bed to greet him. As for her husband, his health was ruined by his mid-forties, when he was almost unable to walk and was probably suffering, among a host of other things, from dangerously high blood pressure.

The decision to summon the infant Ippolito to Buda amid a great fanfare was a confession of defeat on both their parts. It was an admission that hope had died of a child of their own romping through the corridors of the magnificent palaces of Buda or Visegrad with their painted ceilings, ceremonial staircases, the library with its stained glass and the observatory full of curious inventions. Matthias had accepted that no child born of a union between him and Beatrice would run through the courtyards, splash the waters of the red marble fountains, tease the pompous-looking, many-chinned Marzio by tugging his cloak from behind, or race round the classical statues of gods, goddesses, grandfather Janos and uncle Laszlo.

In public, the Queen maintained a courageous front, at least until the autumn of 1486, when she assured her sister Leonora that she still hoped to conceive. Her assiduous patronage of shrines was probably linked to a lingering fancy that continual entreaties to heaven might still result in a conception. But the frantic interest she now showed in gaining custody of one of her nephews, and Matthias's indulgence of her whim, pointed in another direction. Had either of them believed they might yet have a child, they would never have put on such a show for a nephew.

Beatrice concentrated her energies on extracting Ippolito out of a some-what reluctant Ercole and Leonora as quickly as possible, using her brother Giovanni's death as a bargaining tool. 'In the midst of the desolation that the death of our brother of sacred memory has plunged us, we have remembered Your Highness's son', she wrote in March 1486. 'We have recommended him to the goodwill of our august husband, begging him to give Ippolito the archiepiscopal see made vacant by our brother's death.'[18]

The arrival of a set of two portraits, one of Ippolito and another of his brother, Alfonso, in the bag of the ambassador from Ferrara put Beatrice into a jubilant mood. Significantly, perhaps ominously, she began from this point to talk of Ippolito as her 'son', as an ambassador recalled in a dispatch. When he produced the likenesses of Ippolito and Alfonso d'Este, he wrote: 'She burst into rejoicing . . . saying . . . her son, that is to say, Ippolito, was much more handsome and likeable than the other . . . Her Majesty admired the portraits for a whole hour, and then sent them to her august husband.' Matthias played his part in this uncomfortable charade with characteristic chivalry, kissing the pictures of the new favourite fervently, 'which the other great men and nobles did also, and the portrait was passed from hand to hand throughout the court'.[19]

Beatrice made a quick pilgrimage to Pecs that summer, followed by expeditions to Bratislava and Vienna, before returning to the capital to prepare for the boy's reception. The moment Christmas was over Beatrice was back at her writing desk, piling pressure on Leonora and Ercole to expedite matters and telling her sister that 'tears came to her eyes' at the thought of her nephew's arrival. She urged her not to delay sending him off to Hungary beyond Easter 1487.

In fact, the child's anxious parents dithered until June 1487, when he was finally packed off with a large retinue and – a bizarre parting touch – no fewer than fifty-six masks and costumes for the carnivals and balls that his parents assumed he would attend in Buda.[20] The party crossed the Adriatic and landed at Senj in Croatia before being escorted across land by Matthias's loyal ally, the Croatian magnate, Bernardin Frankopan. Beatrice was almost beside herself with excitement, hurrying back from the outskirts of Wiener Neustadt in Austria, which her husband was besieging, to meet the boy in Sopron. As usual, too much excitement put her into a high fever. She took to her sickbed instead.

There was no question of cutting corners when it came to arranging Ippolito's *joyeuse entrée* into Buda. A reigning monarch could hardly have expected a greater fanfare. A convoy of 28 carriages and a body of cavalry was sent to escort the child from Zagreb to Sopron and then towards Buda, where the King waited on the outskirts of the city in his tent. Ippolito himself arrived with a large suite of about 150 men from Ferrara, including a group of musicians. He reported on the proceedings to his mother and father. 'About four leagues from the camp we were met by a numerous, brilliant troupe, and immediately after we noticed the King coming to greet me', he wrote. 'I bowed my head and saluted in the name of Your Highnesses. He received me with a kindness and an affability that I cannot describe and would on no account let me dismount from my horse. At last, His Majesty led me to a castle ... where Her Majesty was suffering from a fever. Her Highness my mother can imagine with what joy she received me!'[21]

Beatrice had her 'son' at last, but she had waited too long. Under her disastrously over-indulgent tutelage he matured into a disagreeable and ungrateful young man. Beatrice got little in return for a lavish display of needy love. The presence of this obnoxious and spoiled Italian at the same time fuelled Hungarian resentment against what was starting to resemble an Italian takeover. On Ippolito's arrival, the Italian contingent in Buda ballooned further in size, as the large Florentine camp was augmented by dozens of Ferrarese attendants. The roar of Italian chatter in the corridors delighted Beatrice. As her biographer Berzeviczy put it, flamboyantly, 'It was only with them that she could be familiar and amuse herself without fear of betrayal, from them alone she could take advice and it was to them that she confided the cares of her body and the salvation of her soul.'[22]

But the endless sound of Italians discussing the latest cultural fashions set the Hungarians' teeth on edge. The great Magyar families prided themselves on their military prowess, not on their table manners or their appreciation of Ficino's *Letters*. With the exception of a few clerics, the Magyars did not prize literacy and remained strangers to the King's library. For the moment, they watched, waited and muttered. As soon as the King was dead, they would make their true feelings known and Beatrice would feel the chilly blast of their stored-up resentment.

Matthias's profession of genuine enthusiasm about Ippolito's presence was not entirely contrived. He speedily accepted the boy as a fixture at court, allowing him to accompany him and the Queen on their expeditions and join them on the royal barge to Vienna. The King also robustly supported his wife's demand that the boy be granted the same high status that Giovanni had once enjoyed as archbishop and primate. So it was that another Italian who neither spoke Hungarian nor knew anything of the country became its chief pastor. Matthias was unabashed about that. The youthful champion of Calixtus III and Pius II now took a cooler and more distant line with popes. Any attempt by Sixtus's successor, Innocent VIII, to thwart his wife's determination to give Ippolito the primatial see would be crushed, he said. When Innocent continued to complain that it was unseemly to entrust one of the greatest posts in the Church to a child, Matthias responded grimly that if the Pope appointed another candidate to Esztergom, he would make sure that Ippolito drew the whole revenue of the archbishopric. 'He would show that he was King of Hungary and not the Pope', he declared – words that anticipated those of Henry VIII of England a few decades later.[23] Innocent gave way on 27 May 1487 and the child was able to occupy Vitez's old apartments in Esztergom. Not to be outdone, Lorenzo de Medici demanded that the Pope make his 13-year-old son, Giovanni, a cardinal.[24] Again, Innocent gave way.

The cold tone that Matthias adopted with Rome over the business of the archbishopric reflected his disappointment with the papacy since the 1460s, when he and Pius II had planned new crusades against the Turks. Those dreams had long since been stored away, as the Ottoman Empire and Hungary settled instead for *détente*, liberating Matthias to indulge his passion for conquests in the west. Matthias now felt he had nothing for which to apologise to Rome. His grudge against Rome was heightened especially by the strange affair of the Sultan's son, Prince Djem.

The younger son of Mehmed II, Conqueror of Constantinople, and a Serbian mother, Djem had fled to Europe after his father's death in 1481. Naïvely hoping the European powers would help him against his brother, Bayezid II, he spent the rest of his life a prisoner. Matthias had to be diplomatic in public with Bayezid, because a lasting truce between the Ottoman Empire and Hungary was crucial to his plans to conquer Vienna. But the King was desperate to take Djem into his own custody, believing he could help the young man gain the throne in Constantinople, a development that had the potential to transform the balance of power in Europe and end the threat of Ottoman invasion for generations.

Matthias viewed Djem's incarceration by the Knights Templar in Rhodes and then by Charles VIII in France as a shabby little scandal. He suspected – rightly – that the real reason why Djem was being locked up in this fashion was because Bayezid was paying enormous bribes to his jailers. In fact, an Ottoman delegation had offered a long-term alliance with France in 1489 on precisely those terms,

> if the [French] King would consent to keep Djem on his estates for the duration of the prince's life.
> Besides a large sum to be paid annually, they spoke of giving [Charles] all the relics that were then in Constantinople and in the other towns conquered by Mehmed II.[25]

There was even extraordinary talk of surrendering Jerusalem to French custody.

Matthias suspected that Innocent was working hand in glove with the French in this muddy business, especially when the Pope succeeded in prising Djem out of France in 1489 only to keep him under even tighter surveillance in Rome. Indeed, the Pope now enjoyed the annual subsidy of 45,000 ducats that Bayezid had formerly been paying the Knights of Rhodes and the French.[26] It confirmed a suspicion in Matthias that popes lavished praise on Hungary when they wanted something; but when the King of Hungary desired a favour in return there was silence.

Matthias never abandoned his great plan to gain custody of Djem and – finally – turn his attention eastwards. He moved mountains on Djem's behalf, packing a magnificent embassy off to France via Milan under Bishop Filipecz of Oradea. As ever, he aimed to impress. The Bishop reached the French court with an escort of gentlemen on horseback dressed in purple, some in pearl-encrusted coronets.[27] The luggage train included a clutch of fabulous gold- and pearl-encrusted vases for Charles VIII and a dress of pure gold for his famously venial sister, Anne. The outlay was totally wasted. So, too, was the lavishly illuminated three-volume bible that Matthias commissioned from Florence to consummate an alliance that never became airborne. The frontispiece of the third volume, one of the most beautifully illuminated works from the library, shows King David imploring the heavens while in the background can be seen Matthias, Charles VIII of France and a third figure dressed in blue, which might be either John Corvin or an unknown woman – possibly Charles's sister.[28]

The Hungarian embassy loitered for months in Laval, Angers and then Paris, frittering away money and 'maintaining the most splendid table in town'[29] to awe the not easily impressed Parisians. The episcopal ambassador was furious, complaining to his Venetian counterpart that he had intended to stay a fortnight in France and had instead wasted four months at a cost of 50 ducats a day. 'Believed this last assertion,' the Venetian diplomat noted, 'as the Hungarian ambassador entered Laval with 15 sumpter horses and ten mules carrying his baggage, covered with scarlet – and had 136 youths, well mounted.'[30] Finally, the embassy slipped away in October 1487, heading back towards Milan where the Bishop of Oradea had other business to conclude on Matthias's behalf in connection with John's forthcoming marriage. Djem never got his liberty. After he passed into the custody of Innocent following seven years in France he died in

1495, aged only 35. Most people thought he either pined to death or had been poisoned.

Matthias, meanwhile, continued to indulge his wife's passionate attachment to her nephew, partly to divert her attention from his plans to marry John into a suitably prestigious foreign house and complete the arrangements for his succession. Ippolito received his semi-royal welcome to Hungary but the King's books make no pictorial reference to his existence. When Matthias's illustrators portrayed Matthias and Beatrice *en famille* in the late 1480s, the third personage was John. As has been said, the frontispiece for the Philostratus, showing a boy standing on a triumphal chariot, may have been a rare representation of John alone, without his father. No humanists at Matthias's court dedicated books to Ippolito, either, whereas Marzio gallantly dedicated his own work, *De egregie, sapienter, jocose dictis ac factis regis Mathiae*, to John. Beatrice called Ippolito her 'son' but Matthias, as far as we know, never followed suit. He reserved that title and the emoluments that went with it to John.

Matthias's decision to let John make his triumphal entry into Vienna in 1485, when he was 12, was a mark of the favour he now enjoyed. Within a few years of his marriage to Beatrice, when there was no sign of her pregnancy, Matthias had begun drawing up contingency plans for John's reign. He began to load towns, lands and titles on to him, making him Duke of Lipto (now Liptov in Slovakia) and Count of Hunyadi. His doting grandmother Erzsebet had already dramatically altered his financial situation in the early 1480s when she left him her rich Szilagyi estates. John began to rise in meteoric fashion, as Matthias felt his time running out. Much to Beatrice's distress, it was clear that he planned to make the illegitimate son of Barbara Edelpock the next king. Matthias might fob her off by holding grand receptions for her nephew but he kept the arrangements for the succession in his own hands.

As the King had contracted a great marriage with one of the ruling houses of Italy, it was not surprising that he should seek an Italian bride for his son. His eye soon settled on the Sforzas of Milan, rulers of the most powerful state in northern Italy, apart from Venice. Moreover, the Hunyadis had maintained friendly links with Milan since the 1430s, when Matthias's father had served at the Milanese court as a *condottiere*. The Milanese were amenable, increasingly convinced that Beatrice would not conceive and that John would succeed his father as King of Hungary. On 25 November 1487, John married Bianca Maria Sforza, daughter of the late Duke, Galeazzo, and niece of the current ruler, Lodovico 'the Moor'. The marriage was conducted by proxy, with the Bishop of Oradea, freshly returned from the ruinously expensive and ill-fated visit to France, standing in for John.

Beatrice opposed the liaison with the Sforzas with all her might, and vainly tried to push Matthias in the direction of a daughter of her own house of Naples. The Queen's elderly father attempted to aid his daughter's cause, dispatching Pietro Ransano to Buda as his ambassador in 1488. Nominally a diplomat, Ransano's real task was to bolster Beatrice in her mission to dissuade Matthias from making John his heir in favour of making Beatrice Queen Regent instead. Hungary obviously fascinated Ransano because he soon devoted himself to writing his own account of the country, the *Epithoma Hungararum*.

The now almost constant tension cast a shadow over the last months of the King's life. The stress may have contributed to his final stroke. Diplomats at court were well aware that the issue of the succession had severely strained relations both between the King and Queen and between the Queen and John. In September 1489, the ambassador of Modena recorded that 'a violent argument occurred on this subject in the presence of the King between the Queen and the Prince John'.[31] At the same time, it seemed that the sheer number of Italians at court, many clustered around the Queen, was finally getting on the nerves of even the patient Matthias. An envoy from Ferrara reported that the King was saying he would give no more church benefices to Italians and 'no longer wants to see so many Italians around him'.[32]

It was then that Matthias, now thoroughly distrustful of Beatrice's father, wrote to the Queen's brother, begging him to try to dissuade Beatrice from her suicidal course. 'The Queen wishes after our death ... to succeed us on the throne and take into her hands the reins of government, which we would not be able to promise her even if she wished it', Matthias began. He warned that even if he backed Beatrice in such a course, it would only excite among the general population 'an eternal hatred against us and against the Queen'.[33]

He continued:

The Hungarian people are capable of killing up unto the last man rather than submit to the government of a woman ... We must add with all frankness that the Queen is scarcely loved by our subjects, which we realise with grief, but the Queen does not try to gain their affections. This is in particular why we may not do what she wishes, but she will not resign herself and importunes us night and day not only with her demands but with her continual complaints, recriminations and tears ... it is evident that the best counsels, when in opposition to her views, have no other effect than making her persist in her opinionated resistance and exciting her discontent.

Matthias closed this bleak and frank résumé of the last years of his marriage with an even starker warning about the penalties that the Queen might face after he was gone. He reminded Alfonso that the Hungarians clung to their right to elect their own rulers and might well use it to elect the Emperor Frederick or one of Frederick's heirs, rather than install John, let alone Beatrice.

'The right to elect its king belongs to the nation and it may make a choice contrary to our desires', he wrote. 'It may be that the nation ... elects he who is at this hour precisely the worst enemy of our person ... and who [is] no sooner seated on the throne [than he] will chase out the Queen and our son ignominiously ... it is even possible that the Queen may be put to death, for as we have said she is not loved and no one knows the character of the Hungarians better than us.'[34]

Whether it was worth appealing to Alfonso over a good cause was debatable. As one historian noted, 'at scarcely 20 he already equalled his father in terms of cruelty and perfidy if he did not surpass him'.[35] Alfonso had little time to digest this letter before events in Hungary took their course. Since March 1489, Matthias had not been able to walk unaided, so bad had the gout in his legs become. When he returned from Vienna that spring the envoy of Ferrara reported that four men had to carry him off the royal barge in a litter.[36] The warmer summer weather revived him a little and he used the respite to tour the country, visit castles and press the nobles to swear loyalty to his son. Such was his desperation to secure this great matter that he now made overtures to the Habsburgs – not to the irreconcilable Frederick, but to his son, Maximilian. Matthias was ready to return all the Austrian lands he had acquired in return for Maximilian's recognition of his son's rights in Hungary. The only bone of contention was money, because Matthias sought a hefty payment for evacuating the occupied territories while Maximilian was prepared to offer a derisory 50,000 florins.

The King no longer felt any interest in propping up Beatrice's annoying family in their various designs. In September 1489, when the Pope dangled

1 The Hunyadi castle near Deva, which Matthias's grandfather received from King Sigismund in the 1400s and where Matthias spent part of his youth.

2 Raven corbels in the Hunyadi castle. The origins of the Hunyadi emblem remain obscure and have generated numerous, often improbable, legends.

3 A typically fanciful image of Matthias's father, Janos Hunyadi, the victor of the Battle of Belgrade in 1456. In fact, no contemporary representation of Janos survives.

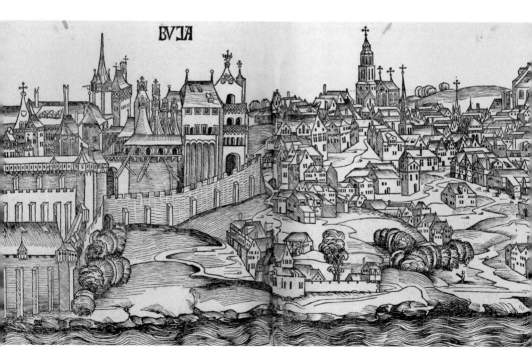

4 A highly stylised representation of fifteenth-century Buda from Schedel's *Liber Chronicarum* of 1493. The palace clearly dominates the city.

5 The tomb of Archbishop Janos Vitez, Matthias's chief counsellor during the early years of his reign. His pioneering library formed the basis of Matthias's own collection.

6 The triumphal arch at Castel Nuovo in Naples built by Alfonso the Magnanimous. Matthias's wife, Beatrice, inherited her grandfather's enthusiasm for Renaissance culture.

7 Francesco Laurana's sculpture of Beatrice just before her marriage in 1476 captured the fleeting beauty that soon disappeared under rolls of fat.

8 This marble relief of Matthias and Beatrice from the 1480s hints at their disappointment in middle age, after marriage had failed to produce the desired heir.

9 A copy in the Buda Castle District of the only known contemporary statue of Matthias, erected in Wroclaw following his conquest of Silesia.

10 Matthias and Beatrice portrayed in the Brussels Missal illuminated by Attavante (*c.* 1485–7). The artist probably copied the images from a medallion.

11 This sensuous depiction of Matthias as a Roman emperor comes from a work commissioned to mark the engagement of his bastard son, John.

12 The Neapolitan diplomat, Pietro Ransano, shown discoursing before the King and Queen, in an illuminated page from his own history of Hungary, the *Epithoma rerum Hungararum.*

13 Matthias's illegitimate son, John, may be the boy shown on a triumphal chariot in Philostratus's *Heroica*, commissioned to mark Matthias's conquest of Vienna in 1485.

14 The royal couple are shown kneeling on the frontispiece to *De Spiritu Sancto* by Didymus the Blind. Illuminated by the brothers Di Giovanni, it is one of Matthias's library's finest works.

15 The style of the Holkham Hall lectionary, which differs from that of the Florentine artists, has been attributed to a royal workshop in Hungary. The existence of this workshop has never been proven.

16 The *Noctes Atticae* is one of the few books from Matthias's library still in its original binding. Archbishop Miklos Olah claimed the Turks tore off the bindings when they captured Buda in 1526.

17 Sixtus IV investing Bartolomeo Platina as his librarian. The growth of collections in the Renaissance led to the emergence of the librarian as a public figure.

18 Like Matthias, his contemporary, Federigo da Montefeltro, Duke of Urbino, was both a military man and a man of letters. He is shown here reading beside his son, Guidobaldo.

19 Federigo da Montefeltro, kneeling in the Brera altarpiece. A close ally to Matthias, the two men built up their libraries at much the same time.

20 Lorenzo the Magnificent, by Giorgio Vasari. Lorenzo de Medici and Matthias both collected furiously in their last years. 'Matthias is dead, there will be a glut of copyists', Lorenzo gloated on hearing of Matthias's demise.

21 Life at the bibulous court took its toll on the profile of Galeotto Marzio who styled himself the King's librarian. That task in reality fell to Taddeo Ugoleto.

22 The charismatic German astrologer Regiomontanus helped to satisfy Matthias's typically Renaissance fascination with astrology during his stay in Buda.

23 Mary, the last queen of independent Hungary, rescued Attavante's missal from the library and took it to Brussels before the Ottomans reached Buda in 1526.

24 The Habsburg librarian Peter Lambeck was a seventeenth-century bibliophile obsessed with Matthias's library. What he found in Buda disappointed him.

25 Luigi Ferdinando Marsigli seemed unaware of Lambeck's earlier expedition; he still dreamt of finding the library in 1686, following the recapture of Buda.

26 After the recapture of Buda from the Turks and the torching of Matthias's palace, the dream that the library might be found hidden in the recesses died.

27 After 1686, Corvinus hunters fixed their hopes on the Seraglio in Constantinople, where Suleiman the Magnificent originally deposited the collection in 1526.

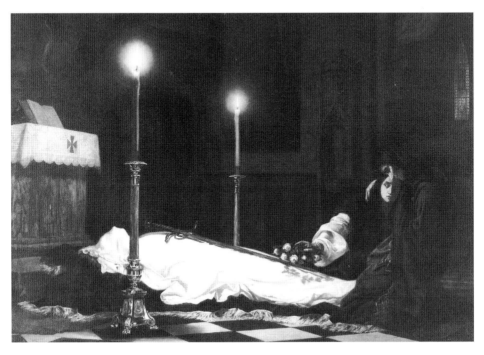

28 Madarasz's painting of Matthias's martyred brother Laszlo appealed to the patriotism of nineteenth-century Hungarians who clamoured for Matthias's library to be restored or recreated.

29 Sultan Abdul Hamid II's move to return Corvinian manuscripts to Hungary on the eve of war between Russia and Turkey led to scenes of wild rejoicing in Budapest.

30 The Matthias Fountain in Buda's Castle District, showing the young king out hunting, reflected the romantic invention of Matthias as a fairy-tale figure.

the possibility of transferring Prince Djem to Hungary, Matthias dispatched an excited letter to Rome. Referring to the worsening conflict between Naples and the papacy, he assured Innocent VIII that Ferdinand would not be able to count on the support of Hungary if push came to shove. (Typically, Matthias's instinctive generosity asserted itself, for in the same letter he urged the Pope not to attack Ferdinand on the grounds that he was 'an old man'.) For the last time, he pledged himself ready to take up the dusty crusading cross of the Hunyadis and – with Djem, he hoped, by his side – lead a war to the death against the Ottomans. 'At my own cost I will draw up such an army as the Christian world has never seen', he boasted.[37]

It was classic Matthias. But the portraits of the King in his most recent works, showing a remote and mighty Caesar, no longer corresponded even remotely to reality. The moment the cold weather returned, the King's condition declined precipitously. There was no more talk of crusades. By November, fevers and swellings held him in their grip while the Queen became increasingly unwell herself. With the all-important approval of the court astrologers, Bylica and Tolhopf,[38] Matthias, Beatrice and John departed for Vienna for the last time on 8 January 1490. The first stop was Visegrad, where they spent a week, most of it given over to meetings with bishops and magnates who were again urged to swear loyalty to John. The next halt was Esztergom. Then it was on to Vienna to meet one of Maximilian's emissaries and spend a last birthday, on 23 February.

Matthias loaded more treasures on to his affectionate son in the form of Wiener Neustadt, Retz, Wolfersdorf and lands in Carinthia and Carniola – all somewhat worthless, now that talks on returning the former Habsburg territories to Maximilian were in train. But there were other gifts of lands and towns in Silesia and even a plan to have John proclaimed King of Bohemia as a test run for the more important crown. Beatrice bore these humiliations stoically, her anger mollified by the rich gifts she also received in Vienna and which the Milanese ambassador said included jewels and a diamond cross.[39] The talks with Maximilian drifted on.

In Italy the copyists and illuminators worked on, each stroke of the pen or brush adding incrementally to the magnificent library that was the King's bequest to the world. In Florence, Attavante was working on the breviary that was to be the companion volume to the missal he had finished earlier. Elsewhere, Boccardino il Vecchio worked on the three-volume bible that Matthias intended as a gift for Charles VIII of France. There were many other artists at work. Perhaps a hundred books, or more, were in various stages of production for Matthias in Florence in 1490.

The writers continued to work on volumes that they intended to dedicate to Matthias, filled with laudatory accounts of his achievements. In Buda, Bonfini's quill worked slowly and methodically over the pages of his great historical account, the *Rerum Ungaricarum decades*. Beatrice's diplomatic ally Ransano was busy with his own shorter history, the *Epithoma rerum Hungararum*. Aurelio Brandolini was scribbling away at his dialogue on monarchy-versus-republic, *De comparatione reipublicae et regni*,[40] which took the form of a three-way debate between Matthias 'Corvus', John and a Florentine, Dominic, and whose frontispiece depicted John and his father seated and in conversation with a third party.

Hair grows for some time after a person's death. In the same way, the King of Hungary's copyists and illuminators continued to copy and paint in spring 1490, unaware that seismic events were taking place elsewhere. While they dipped their pens quietly into ink, while the artists or their *garzoni* ground the lapis lazuli into powder, while the illuminators paused for a second to add the last stroke of blue to an image of a blue raven with a diamond ring, while the vellum was being stretched and pricked, far away in Vienna a bowl of figs lay smashed on the ground.

If it is true that a person's life flashes before their eyes in the last moments of existence, a kaleidoscope of images must have arranged themselves before Matthias as Beatrice fussed around the sickbed with her potions and elixirs, lifting up his eyelids, as John wept and the ambassadors and courtiers glanced furtively at one another. His curious Polish tutor declaiming lines of Virgil in the schoolroom in Hunedoara, perhaps; his mother deep in prayer in their Transylvanian castle chapel; his father, recently returned from some battlefield in Bulgaria and leaning against a fireplace, talking with Vitez; his brother, giving him a last backward glance just after his arrest in Buda; his own jail cell in Prague; the faces of the Hungarian courtiers coming to escort him to Buda and the throne; Beatrice, radiant on her white horse, riding into Szekesfehervar; Barbara Edelpock, holding up a baby boy; Beatrice, dancing with the Prince of Poland at Olomouc; the burghers of Vienna on their knees; the sight and smell of a freshly illuminated manuscript and then – nothing.

Suddenly it was all over. Hungary had lost a tremendous, never-to-be surpassed ruler. Matthias was dead.

CHAPTER NINE

Collapse

Rest at Mohacs; twenty thousand Hungarian infantry and four thousand of their cavalry are buried.

War diary of Suleiman the Magnificent[1]

'Matthias is dead, justice has fled.' So went a saying of the peasants he taxed remorselessly in his lifetime. 'Matthias is dead. There will be a glut of copyists.'[2] So wrote Matthias's rival, Lorenzo de Medici, to his son, obviously unaware that his own life was drawing to a close. Both the Hungarian peasants and the ruler of Florence were correct. There was indeed a glut of copyists as the King's library suddenly ceased to expand. And justice did flee, or rather crumbled, along with the rest of Matthias's achievements.

The first pillar to crumble away was John's succession, the cause for which Matthias had sacrificed so much energy in his last years, bargaining away his Austrian conquests. The bishops and nobles who had sworn to uphold John's right to the throne went back on their word within days of the King's death. By the time his body had lain in state in St Stephen's cathedral in Vienna and returned to Buda on a barge on 20 April, the old Hunyadi party was in pieces.

The legacy of the late king was assailed almost immediately. According to Bonfini, the nobles who assembled in the first parliament held after his death devoted much time to carping at his 'senseless spending . . . day after day on vanities, and of wasting the taxes that had been levied for more useful purposes. He had not kept to the thrift and frugality of earlier kings.'[3]

Churchmen led the way in disparaging Matthias's memory. This attack did not come from the bishops, most of whom were either ciphers of the King or genuine admirers of his cultural projects. The lower clergy were not the problem, either; most were ignorant of what had being going on at court. It was the middling sort – educated and inquisitive, but puritanical – who aimed their poisoned darts at Matthias. They had not been impressed by the cult of luxury, the crowds of chattering Italians, the marble and bronze statues, the observatory, or the beautiful, expensive books. The influential Franciscan preacher, Pelbart of Temesvar,[4] a theology professor at the Franciscan house in Buda in the 1480s and guardian of the house in Esztergom in the 1490s, was a persistent critic of the King's memory until his own death in 1504. Pelbart had frankly loathed the Renaissance court that Matthias had sustained in Buda, and he condemned the classics as 'pagan', their authors as 'heretics' and astronomy as 'sinful'. In his many sermons, which were widely printed and read, he flagellated what he saw as a wicked, spendthrift court, contrasting it not very favourably with the state of affairs that had prevailed under Hungary's pious and virtuous eleventh-century royal saint, Stephen I.[5]

The magnates and nobles, meanwhile, whose wilful behaviour Matthias had curbed for thirty years, chimed in with these complaints, keen to snatch at an opportunity to restore, as they saw it, the *status quo ante*. Keen also to be rid of the Hunyadis, they looked favourably on the candidacy of foreign princes whose divided loyalties would ensure they would not be around too much.

The Jagiellons of Poland waited hopefully in the wings. They had made one bid already for the Holy Crown in 1471, which had backfired with the ill-fated revolt of Vitez and Pannonius. Now the circumstances looked propitious and both Wladislas of Bohemia and his younger brother, John Albert, found parties rallying behind them in Hungary, though Wladislas was the more serious candidate of the two.

The Magyars had ancient and friendly ties with Poland, and the nobles looked forward to a monarch like Wladislas who had already gained the nickname *dobhze* (meaning 'good' or 'fine') on account of his relaxed and conciliatory manner. As one historian put it, his 'career as an amiable weakling on the Czech throne had amply demonstrated his qualifications'.[6]

The outcome of the parliament that assembled in Buda at the end of May, therefore, was almost a foregone conclusion. The delegates of Maximilian and John Albert were shunted aside. John Corvin was palmed off first with the empty title of King of Bosnia – soon rescinded – and later with the lowlier position of Ban of Croatia and Slavonia. Never the equal of his father, he accepted this pay-off after a brief and abortive attempt to resist.

Thus the Hunyadis disappeared from the centre stage of Europe and returned to provincial obscurity, this time in Croatia rather than Transylvania. Nothing more was now heard of John's marriage to Bianca Sforza of Milan. Such alliances meant little until they were consummated, as Beatrice was about to discover. There had never been any sign of Bianca actually packing her trunk for Buda, though both sides made various preparations for the great event. Bianca herself clearly thought she was destined to become a princess of Hungary: she gamely busied herself with learning Hungarian dances and her courtiers began trying out Hungarian 'long garments', Italian dress having become unpopular in Hungary (in itself another commentary on Beatrice's failure to win the hearts of the Hungarians).[7]

In Buda, Matthias had commissioned a beautifully illuminated manuscript for his library to celebrate the union of the Sforzas and Hunyadis, the *Marlianus*. The frontispiece of this eulogy to the marriage, now kept in Volterra, depicts the shields of Matthias and the Sforzas under an entrancing portrait of the King, attributed variously to Gherardo or the Lombard master, Ambrogio de Predis.[8] It is the most striking and lifelike of all the extant images of Matthias, showing him in profile wearing a crown of laurel leaves. What lifts it far above the common run of imperial portraits of Matthias from the late 1480s, however, is the ghostly, almost Mona Lisa-like, smile that plays around his lips.

But while Bianca tried out her new outfits and practised her Hungarian dances, nothing actually happened. At first, it was the Milanese court that stalled, still apparently worried that Beatrice might defy the odds and conceive a son, thus condemning Bianca to a more or less irrelevant life in Buda as a king's aunt as opposed to a king's wife. Then the Hungarians appeared to lose enthusiasm, as Matthias began dallying with the possibility of his son marrying the daughter of Maximilian of Habsburg instead. In 1489, the Milanese became anxious and Lodovico 'Il Moro' attempted to rekindle Matthias's interest in the project by ordering a valuable antique Greek statue of white marble, depicting Bacchus, or Pan, to be sent to Buda.[9] To Lodovico's great annoyance, the statue broke before it could be sent to Hungary, necessitating more delays for repairs. By the time it arrived in Buda, Matthias was already dead. Lodovico wrote to Beatrice, urging her to stick by her husband's son, but as it became clear that John Corvin was out of the running for the crown, the Milanese marriage was forgotten.

Instead, Bianca married Maximilian of Habsburg, whose fabulously wealthy first wife, Mary of Burgundy, had died young in a riding accident. John was lucky to be spared. Like his stepmother, Bianca turned out to be infertile and generally high maintenance and her marriage to Maximilian was an embarrassing disaster. In 1496, John, now Ban of Croatia, married Beatrice Frankopan, daughter of his father's old friend, the Croat magnate Bernardin Frankopan. She presented him with two children, Crysztof and Erzsebet. John died six years after his marriage, in 1502. He perished like his Hunyadi grandfather, fighting the Ottoman Turks. Matthias's two grandchildren did not outlive their father by long. They died between 1505 and 1508 and were buried in Gyula, in eastern Hungary. It was the end of the Hunyadis. Their mother married George of Brandenburg-Ansbach and died soon after.

It was not only the nobles who abandoned John in 1490. Rejecting the advice of Lodovico of Milan, Beatrice dealt John a crucial blow. She had never truly concealed her jealousy of his existence and after a brief, false embrace at Matthias's sickbed, soon reverted to her default position of hostility.

Matthias had always suspected that Beatrice suffered from delusions about her future prospects without him in Hungary, as he had indicated in his reproachful letter to her brother. His worst fears were realised as the ageing, portly Queen thrust her faded charms at Wladislas, deceiving herself into thinking he would be grateful to take her as his second wife. Whether because she felt physically excited by him, prompted by warm recollections of her dance with him as a teenager at Olomouc in 1479, or whether she was simply determined to remain politically important in Hungary, Beatrice pursued Wladislas with a determination that was to prove humiliating. The new King, who was called Ulaszlo in Hungarian, soon made it clear that in spite of his *dobzhe* nickname he was not a total pushover. He would not be rushed into marriage with an almost middle-aged, childless, ex-queen – especially not one with the kind of unflattering profile that Duknovic had recorded in the marble relief portrait.

After crossing the border into Hungary in the last days of July and reaching Buda on 9 August Wladislas deliberately took his time before paying Beatrice an obligatory visit on the 14th. To her fury, he offered the post of sister, not of wife. A few weeks later, he left for his coronation in Szekesfehervar without her, Beatrice having withdrawn in a sulk to her nephew's palace in Esztergom, which was to be her base for her final tragic years in Hungary.

Wladislas never had any intention of taking Beatrice to his marriage bed. But he was alarmed by her threats to switch sides to one of the rival candidates for the throne, especially his younger brother, and so resolved on a monumental act of deceit. He decided to go through a discreet marriage ceremony, as he informed his council, but only under protest. He would never consummate the union and would extricate himself from the arrangement at the first opportunity. 'She has raised a great army, contracted alliances with foreign sovereigns, has excited them in secret against me, and has threatened, if I do not marry her, to deliver my castles to my adversaries, chase me from the kingdom and treat my partisans as enemies', he told his council. 'I declare to you that I have never desired nor do I desire to marry Beatrice and that if I contract a marriage of form with her . . . I will always consider it as null.'[10]

Shortly after, the new King presented himself to the Queen and married her in a simple ceremony presided over by the flexible Tamas Bakocz, Bishop of Gyor. As soon as it was over, to Beatrice's disappointment and embarrassment, the King withdrew.

The new ruler got what he wanted from this charade. Beatrice was sufficiently impressed to lend her 'husband', as she now called him, money and soldiers. Altogether the Queen handed over about 100,000 florins, much of it borrowed from her aged father. Beatrice's aid enabled Wladislas to mop up his brother's remaining partisans and force him to abandon the fight. In February 1491, John Albert threw in the towel, mollified by a promise that he would receive the throne if his brother died without issue.

It was then that Beatrice's cup of humiliation began to overflow as she sat it out in Esztergom, waiting in vain for the husband who would never return, the farce of her marriage now the talk of Europe and the Queen herself the object of pitying glances and stifled giggles. 'The Queen is furious', a correspondent gossiped to the court of Milan on 18 October. 'She remains in Esztergom but no longer has any authority, poor woman, and while she puts on the address of her letters to the King "To my husband," he puts on his letters, "To the Queen" . . .'[11]

Fast becoming a tragicomic figure, Beatrice's last and most desperate throw of the dice was to stage an unexpected, dramatic return to Buda to confront her 'husband' face to face at the first parliament of the new reign in February 1491.

The attempted public relations coup failed completely. Indeed, it marked a new stage in the public collapse of her fortunes. Matthias had long warned Beatrice and her family about the price she would one day pay for her unpopularity. She had taken no more notice of her husband's warnings than she had of the sound advice of Diomede Carafa, given in his book *De institutione vivendi*, to cultivate the affection of her future subjects. Instead she had treated Hungary as a backdrop for herself and her all-Italian cast of fans and hangers-on. Now she was reminded that the Magyars remembered her insulting demeanour. As her humble cavalcade entered Buda on 14 March, the city greeted her in total silence. It made a ghastly contrast to the pageant that had marked her great entry into the city in 1476. The King observed her isolation and made sure a grand denouement never took place. Instead, a group of nobles and bishops arrived at her apartments and informed her that her position was hopeless. She would have to leave.

Beatrice withdrew to Esztergom, a broken force. It was the beginning of a series of such relentless tribulations as to resemble one of the classical tragedies the Queen enjoyed reading. Every indulgence and caprice, it seemed, was now to be paid for, many times over. Nothing was spared her as she undertook the long odyssey towards her ultimate destiny as one of the 'sad queens of Naples' of poetic memory, whose desperate plight caught the imagination of her romantic fellow countrymen.

She clung on in Hungary for a decade, despised and ignored, marooned in Esztergom in the company of her fretful and increasingly dissatisfied nephew. Even her 'reader', Bonfini, abandoned her, preferring to continue the work of writing up the *Rerum Ungaricarum decades* at the court in Buda. Back in Ferrara, Leonora and Ercole d'Este had taken note of this altered state of affairs and were busily soliciting alternative employment within the Church for their long-lost son. Beatrice, desperate to keep the child by her side, appealed to the new Borgia Pope, Alexander VI, one of her few sympathisers, who obliged by elevating Ippolito to the rank of cardinal. Beatrice wrote to her sister at the end of September 1493, glad to show she still had powers of patronage. She had no idea that Leonora, the great anchor of her life, had just died, aged 43. Her father followed a few weeks later, in January 1494.

Beatrice's loneliness increased. That summer, Ippolito left her for the first time; his excuse was that he needed to visit his widowed father, Ercole. While he was away, the parliament in Buda busied itself passing hostile decrees against foreigners. Pressure mounted for the unpopular Italian teenager to surrender the archbishopric of Esztergom or at least exchange it for a less prominent see. When Ippolito hurried back to Hungary in autumn 1495 a royal messenger met him at the frontier and forbade him to proceed until an exchange of dioceses had been completed. Ippolito was not especially bothered. When it came to money, there was not much to choose between the incomes of the five great sees. Esztergom, Pecs, Eger, Varad and Zagreb were all fairly similar in wealth, delivering an annual income at the start of the sixteenth century of between 18,000 and 25,000 florins.[12] It would have been another matter entirely had Ippolito been forced to exchange Esztergom's 25,000 florins for the humble 3,000 that went with the bishoprics of Vac or Csanad. As it was, Eger offered him a lower profile in Hungary and an equivalent income, while at the same time freeing him of any obligation to reside in the country alongside his tiresome aunt. By the end of 1497, when the Pope formally approved the transfer of the sees, and Ippolito was not only the absentee Bishop of Eger but the new Archbishop of Milan, Beatrice faced the threat of homelessness. Without Ippolito, her right to remain in the palace at Esztergom was uncertain.

She saw her abandonment by Ippolito as the last straw. 'You or your secretary write to us like a stranger,' she complained in a bitter letter of 6 March 1499, 'and not as to a mother, and moreover, we are the mother of Your Eminence and wish to remain so until our death ... We beg Your Eminence not to treat us so strangely ... for we do not deserve such treatment.'[13]

The letter had absolutely no effect. Indulged beyond redemption, Ippolito felt no need of a substitute mother in Hungary and was already embarking on a hedonistic existence back in Italy, collecting a long, profitable list of bishoprics and archbishoprics that would include Ferrara and Narbonne before his death in 1520 from a surfeit of crayfish. In 1505 he became the object of a great scandal when some of his minions in his presence virtually blinded his own half-brother – a result of the Cardinal's jealous rage over a woman in whom both men were then interested.

By then his greed for ecclesiastical benefices had made him fabulously rich, certainly more so than his brother, Alfonso, the new Duke of Ferrara. Beatrice's usefulness to him was over. She had also become dispensable by then in the eyes of Alexander VI who finally annulled her 'marriage' to Wladislas on 3 April 1500 in order to facilitate the latter's marriage to Anne of Candale, a princess of France, then the Pope's ally. Beatrice left Hungary at Christmas 1500, arriving in Venice at the end of January 1501 and heading for Ferrara. Here at least there was a friendly face and Ercole, rising 70, gave his doomed sister-in-law a gallant welcome. There was a last, faint echo of former, more glorious days in a sequence of balls and pageants but this upturn did not last long. Beatrice arrived 'home' to a Naples she had last seen a quarter of a century before, and just in time to witness the absolute ruin of her branch of the House of Aragon.

She had left Italy at the high noon of the Italian Renaissance and in the golden age of small independent city-states. She returned to an Italy that was changed utterly, over which the great powers of France and Spain were tussling as if it were a piece of meat. The troubles began in 1494, that 'most unhappy year for Italy', as the Florentine historian Francesco Guicciardini put it, 'truly the beginning of the years of wretchedness, because it opened the way for innumerable horrible calamities'.[14]

Beatrice's father was one of the catalysts of these events. In theory, Naples was a papal fiefdom and the relationship between the large and unwieldy kingdom in the south and its nominal overlord in Rome was often difficult. There had been a crisis at the start of Ferdinand's reign when Calixtus III had refused to accept him as king, probably because the Pope dreamed of giving the throne to one of his avaricious Catalan relatives. That crisis had passed when Calixtus died, and his successor, Pius II, had adopted a different course. But the tension between Naples and the papacy had returned in the 1480s under Innocent VIII. His visceral dislike of Ferdinand prompted him to encourage the impressionable young King of France to believe he might seize Naples on the basis of the old Angevin claim to the kingdom, and make Naples the headquarters of a new crusade against the Ottomans.

Charles VIII's decision to invade the peninsula was also encouraged by Lodovico of Milan. Two events accelerated matters. The first was the death of Lorenzo de Medici, aged only 43, in 1492. Without Lorenzo at the helm, Florence's golden age was over and the Florentines entered a new period of conflict and disruption marked by the overthrow of the Medicis and the brief triumph of religious puritanism and republicanism under the monk Girolamo Savonarola. Increasingly confused by events, the Florentines began to look on the French King as a divinely appointed strongman who had been sent to purge their country of corruption and restore order and virtue. The second was Ferdinand's own death on 28 January 1494, after which Charles felt able to assert his claim to the throne of Naples with even greater conviction. That spring, Charles dramatically proclaimed himself

King of both Jerusalem and Sicily. In September he crossed the border of Dauphiné and Piedmont with an army of 40,000. The French army swept down Italy, meeting no resistance. Indeed, wild enthusiasm for the French King gripped the land. When he entered Florence in the pouring rain on 17 November, it was to roars of 'Viva Francia!' and at the cathedral, Ficino himself, the high priest of the Medicis, delivered an oration that compared Charles to both Caesar and Charlemagne. In Naples, Beatrice's unpopular brother, Alfonso, realised he faced annihilation. Too late, he 'spent his time weeping, praying, and washing the feet of paupers'.[15] Charles formally entered the city on 22 February 1495, Alfonso having fled to the Sicilian monastery where he would die within a year.

The French invasion spelled disaster for the courts of Italy's petty princes, and for their art collections and libraries, many of which were now broken up and dispersed. At the same time, France did not profit from its action, for the very ease of the invasion inspired jealousy and fear. No sooner was Charles in Naples than a powerful anti-French coalition began to close around him, uniting the Pope, Ferdinand and Isabella of Spain, the Emperor Maximilian, Venice, Milan and Henry VII of England. After they hurriedly put together a 'Holy League' whose sole purpose was to counter French expansionism, Charles was soon forced to abandon Naples and return north.

The French had not given up on Naples, and returned in 1498. However, it was not France but the new great power of Spain that reaped the ultimate benefit of these seismic events. In the 1500s, Spain became the dominant power in Italy, including Naples.

By the time Beatrice returned, not only Alfonso but his heir and successor, Ferrandino, had also died and the throne had passed to Beatrice's more admirable younger brother, Federigo. But he was not able to rule for long. A Franco-Spanish agreement on division of the Italian spoils, the Treaty of Granada, signed in November 1500 and endorsed by the Pope, assigned the kingdom jointly to France and Spain. Beatrice had only a few weeks of peace following her arrival on 16 March 1501 before French troops invaded from the north and Spanish troops from Sicily, the Spanish entering Naples at the end of July. As they overran the city, Federigo and no fewer than four queens – Isabella, his own queen; Giovanna, the last wife of his father, Ferdinand; his brother Alfonso's widow, who was also named Giovanna; and Beatrice herself – fled to the nearby island of Ischia.

Beatrice's brother soon abandoned this gaggle of lost and disorientated queens. After France offered him the duchy of Anjou as a rather poor consolation prize for the loss of his kingdom, he left for France, dying in Tours in 1504. His widow, another of *Le tristi reyne di Napoli*,[16] joined him in 1502. There she was reduced to such poverty that she sold her books, jewels, embossed dog collars and even falcon hoods to survive.[17]

Beatrice remained in Naples. There was no danger of the new rulers of Naples throwing her out. She was, after all, *Diva Beatrix Aragonia*, a daughter of the House of Aragon, even if she had never displayed much interest in her Spanish antecedents. Of course, her heart remained Italian and her real feelings about the Spanish takeover of Naples can only be guessed at. She was now even more alone in the world. Ercole's death in 1505 snapped the last link with Ferrara and the House of Este. Beatrice barely knew the new Duke, Alfonso, his glamorous bride, Alexander VI's daughter, Lucrezia Borgia, or her two celebrated Este nieces, Isabella and Beatrice. Did she know – or care – that her former nemesis, John Corvin, had perished in far-off Croatia?

When she died at 1 p.m. on 13 September 1508, totally broke, after eighteen catastrophic years of widowhood, Celio Calcagnini, the humanist who composed her elegy in Ferrara, made her *via dolorosa* his keynote theme – as well as her civilising effect on the wild men of Hungary. 'She was raised by the soul above human vicissitudes', he said. 'Beatrice would have been the mother of kings if perfect happiness existed in this earth ... [but] she is happy now where there is neither adversity nor sadness, nor fear and where peace endures and happiness is eternal.'[18]

She was buried opposite the mother she never really knew in the little church of San Pietro Martire[19] in a simple marble tomb whose inscription claimed she had triumphed in the end. It was true in its way. Perhaps she had been misunderstood in Hungary, or had simply changed once back in Naples, warmed by the sun of her home city, her character tempered by the years of adversity. The city of her birth certainly rallied to her as she made her final exit from the stage. The ancient families of Naples vied with each other for the honour of bearing her coffin through streets that were crammed with mourners. Forgotten and even despised in Hungary, her memory lingered for generations in Naples, where it was remembered that during the last years of her life she had sustained several hundred of the poorest citizens out of her own pocket.

Typically, Beatrice went out as she lived – overspending wildly. In her will she ambitiously left thousands of ducats to various people and causes she believed in, including two of the other 'sad queens' of Naples, Giovannas one and two, and the new building of St Peter's in Rome. No one got a ducat because her treasury had long since been empty. Matthias would have smiled knowingly.

His empire had fallen apart as quickly and as totally as his carefully laid plans for the succession to the throne. The power of the Habsburgs had, it seemed, suffered only a temporary eclipse when Matthias and Beatrice made their splendid entry into Vienna and Wiener Neustadt. While the humiliated Emperor cut a pathetic figure in those his twilight years, his son, Maximilian, did not. His first marriage to his rich heiress in Burgundy had transformed his finances and given the Habsburgs an important power base in the Low Countries. His other great triumph had been to secure his election as King of the Romans at an Imperial Diet in Nuremberg in 1487. This ensured that the imperial title would remain with the Habsburgs after the death of Frederick.

Before his death, Matthias had resigned himself to the surrender of his Austrian conquests to Maximilian in order to ensure John's succession. But in the event Maximilian recovered his family's patrimony without lifting a finger on behalf of John, or paying any of the money Matthias had sought as compensation. Far from backing John's succession, on 19 April 1490, just days after Matthias died, Maximilian launched his own candidacy for the Hungarian throne from Innsbruck, based on the terms of the Treaty of Wiener Neustadt that had promised Frederick the Hungarian the crown if Matthias died without issue. Maximilian duly sent delegates to the parliament in Buda a few weeks later. This was mainly for show. Maximilian knew that the Hungarians felt a strong prejudice against all Germans and that a Hungarian diet would not choose him over the Polish candidates. The point was to expedite the recovery of the Habsburg lands in Austria, where popular sentiment favoured them.

The Hunyadi regime in Vienna vanished in days in the summer of 1490. Matthias had never established any kind of organic union between his conquests in Moravia, Silesia, Austria and Hungary. The reversion to the Habsburgs in Austria was thus smooth. The Hungarian governor of Vienna, Istvan Zapolya, and the newly appointed Hungarian bishop, Urban Docsi, simply packed up and left and the city opened its gates to the family that the Viennese had always seen as their legitimate lords. By 9 July, both Vienna and Wiener Neustadt were in Habsburg hands. 'In ten weeks he had won back everything that Matthias had conquered in ten years',[20] was the verdict of one historian. In early September, Maximilian took Klosterneuburg and by autumn he had driven the last Hungarian forces from Carinthia and Styria. For a few weeks the Habsburg army moved eastwards into western Hungary, briefly raising hopes – or fears – that a Habsburg might wear the Holy Crown after all. But Wladislas had ensconced himself in Buda, caution prevailed and the two sides recognised the new state of affairs at the Treaty of Pressburg signed in November 1491. The Hungarians lost most from this accord. They not only had to evacuate Matthias's conquests in Austria but pay a fine and hand over several border districts, including Eisenstadt, Guns and Bernstein.

The once devoted Silesian Germans also threw off Hungarian rule with alacrity. By 1490 they had forgotten any gratitude they had once felt and resented the autocratic rule of Matthias's provincial viceroy. The moment Matthias was dead they overthrew his government in Wroclaw and literally 'rolled [the viceroy] in front of the Wroclaw city hall'[21] to express their contempt. Matthias's empire was not only dead. It might never have existed.

The 'justice' that Matthias had represented suffered a slower, more lingering decline. Wladislaw turned out to be king *dobzhe* only as far as the nobility were concerned. The towns, and still more the peasants, suffered a relentless decline in status during the 16 years of his rule which so undermined their loyalty to the crown that when his heir, Louis, or Lajos in Hungarian, confronted an Ottoman invasion in 1526, they did not fight. The nobles' shortsighted rapacity helped condemn the country to defeat, division and permanent annihilation as a major power.

Anti-Semitism, that reliable bellwether of a society in decay, made its ugly appearance under Wladislaw in the 1490s, prompting outrages that would have been unthinkable had Matthias been alive. Perhaps it was fortunate that Matthias's old friend, Prefect Mendel, did not live to see them. The venerable head of Buda's Jews, who had welcomed Matthias and Beatrice to the city in 1476, died in 1495. A year later, a pogrom erupted in Buda and mobs ransacked the Jewish quarter, smashing windows and burning houses. Bonfini, still in Buda, had watched the proceedings with misgivings. 'The crowd grew from hour to hour,' he recorded. 'They smashed doors and windows, stole their [the Jews'] belongings, jumped on the pawned articles, and the gold and silver dishes [and] silk dresses . . . moreover the servants of the elegant Jews . . . started plundering themselves'.[22]

While the social order decayed from within, the country's external borders crumbled. The Croatian front collapsed first. The chain of fortresses that Matthias had erected across the south-west ceased to be manned. Only the city of Zagreb remained secure, thanks to the stout walls that Pannonius's old friend, Bishop Thuz, had built. Raiders from Bosnia scented that they could now attack Croatia with impunity. On 9 September 1493 an Ottoman army that had been raiding Carinthia further north was intercepted as it headed back south by a poorly armed and demoralised Croatian army of about 10,000 men at Krbavo Polje in the mountains of Lika. The result was a catastrophe: the Croats were practically wiped out. The news of the battle reached as far as England, prompting Henry VII to write to the Pope about its significance. Henry said he had been shocked to hear of 'the immense slaughter inflicted in Dalmatia and Croatia by the Turks and the great danger in which that country and every neighbouring province, especially Italy, is placed'. It was, he added, 'very distressing'.[23]

It was not all Wladislas's fault. Matthias had overspent in his last years on the library and other projects. He left his successor a huge debt of some 2 million florins, well over twice the annual revenue of the crown at its peak. 'Had he spent half as much against the heathen as he spent here, he would have driven the heathen back across the sea and had a great and glorious name from east to west',[24] one contemporary complained. Wladislas found himself a prisoner of the arrangements under which he had received the throne. A protégé of the nobles, as Matthias had never been, he was unable to resist their demands that he cut taxes and tighten feudal controls over the peasantry. Crown revenues duly shrank rapidly from around 700,000 florins to one-quarter of that level, as the King's right to levy taxes was limited or leased out, and as the royal mines were pawned to the Augsburg bankers, the Fuggers.

The infamous 'Black Army' vanished. At its height, it had been the terror of Europe. 'In no other nation can one find soldiers who bear heat and cold, work, labour and effort so lightly, carry out tasks so willingly and head into battle and death more joyfully', Bonfini wrote. 'They are braver and more persevering than Spartans.'[25] Now they dribbled away, leaving the country virtually undefended.

In Buda, the library wound down like a clock. For a while, the books that Matthias had commissioned continued to emerge from the Florentine workshops. But many others that were in various stages of production for the King in 1490 stayed in the custody of the Medicis, who kept them in lieu of the debts that they said the Hungarian crown owed them. Wladislas made feeble efforts to recover the missing stock. In February 1498, he wrote to the

Signoria in Florence, declaring that he was 'filled with the same desire to improve the library [as Matthias]' and suggesting he would complete whatever transactions were needed to have the books brought to Hungary. But as he had no spare money to back up his words, they mostly stayed where they were.[26] Whether there were ever 150 of them, as Wladislaw maintained in his letter, is open to conjecture. It seems a suspiciously round number as well as an exaggerated one. But there clearly were a good many. Half a millennium on, Angela Dillon Bussi, then vice-director of the Biblioteca Medicea Laurenziana, traced 19 in the library, after which they were exhibited in Budapest in 2002 at the bicentennial celebrations of Hungary's national Szechenyi Library.

For many authors, still at work on manuscripts intended for Matthias in the spring of 1490, his death posed a dilemma. What were they to do with works filled with laudatory accounts of Matthias's feats and with Matthias's future patronage in mind? Some hurriedly tried to repackage their works for other patrons. This was not always easy. Brandolini's comparison of republics to monarchies, *De comparatione reipublicae et regni*, took the form of a dialogue in which Matthias, John Corvin and a Florentine discuss the relative virtues of monarchies like Hungary and republics like Florence. But the writer is careful to give Matthias all the best lines and the trump cards. What was the writer to do with his dialogue once Matthias was dead? His solution was to dedicate it to Lorenzo de Medici. But then Lorenzo died in 1492, followed by Brandolini himself in 1497, and the book had yet to find a sponsor. As a result, Brandolini's brother tried to interest Lorenzo's son, Cardinal Giovanni de Medici, the future Pope Leo X, in the text.

There is no evidence that this strategy succeeded. Cardinal Medici's family had just been expelled from Florence, and it does not appear that he took even the slightest interest in a treatise that had clearly been designed to flatter the late King of Hungary. Brandolini's work survived but was neither printed nor mentioned in any contemporary political work. For centuries it lay forgotten in the Laurenziana – a casualty of Matthias's untimely demise – only to be rescued from obscurity in 1890, when the Hungarian historian Abel Jeno had it translated and printed in the journal of the Hungarian Academy.[27]

The *Epithoma rerum Hungararum* written by the Sicilian episcopal diplomat Ransano had a less obscure fate. Completed in the early 1490s, by which time Ransano was back in his diocese of Lucera in the kingdom of Naples, he dedicated the work nonetheless to the dead Matthias and to

Beatrice. However, the presence beneath the illustration of Ransano addressing the King and Queen of the arms of Tamas Bakocz, the rising star of the Hungarian Church and a cardinal after 1500, hints at the manuscript's fate. It would appear that after Ransano's death in 1492, one of his Dominican colleagues tried to find a sponsor for the work in Bakocz. Unlike Cardinal Medici, Cardinal Bakocz made this homeless Corvinian work his own. Perhaps this was why, unlike Brandolini's dialogue, the *Rerum Ungaricarum decades* did not disappear into obscurity. Maximilian II's indefatigable Hungarian librarian Janos Szambocky 'Sambucus' published it in Vienna in 1552.

The fate of a third work was equally illustrative of the dilemmas facing Matthias's writers in the early 1490s. The breviary illuminated by Attavante for Matthias was intended as a companion piece to the missal finished earlier. But Attavante did not get round to illuminating the breviary until 1492, by which time Matthias was dead. The breviary remained in Italy and later passed into the possession of Benedict XIV in Rome, who had his own arms placed on it. All three works are generally counted today as Corvinian works. Yet they were never actually part of the King's library in Buda and their story explains why it is hard to agree exactly what constitutes a Corvinian work.

As there could be no question of Wladislas spending a fortune each year on buying illuminated manuscripts in Florence, he made only a handful of fresh acquisitions. The new sovereign, as far as we know, did not spend hours on the royal couch under the stained-glass windows examining manuscripts. He may not have been conversant with Latin, let alone Greek. The vaulted halls echoed to the footfall of fewer and fewer people, as the foreign humanists who had been the library's mainstay packed their bags. The veteran Marzio stayed put until his death in 1497. So did Bonfini and the astronomer Bylica. But most of the Italians, like Ugoleto, Fonte, Brandolini, Ransano and many others, took their leave, feeling the magic had gone. With Matthias no longer around, the cultural bonds between Hungary and Italy had more or less snapped. Instead, Hungary began orientating itself towards the Habsburgs and Germany. After the departure of the Italians, the library was left virtually unguarded.

After Matthias's death, the first parliament of the new reign in 1491 had made a great show of concern about the library, proclaiming it an 'ornament of the realm'. The deputies forbade anyone except John Corvin to remove books without their permission. But the gesture was not followed through and books probably began to disappear from the library as soon as Matthias was dead. Both Beatrice and John Corvin helped themselves to some volumes. Beatrice had built up her own, smaller library in Buda of which only a couple of books remain, such as her breviary, Carafa's *De institutione vivendi*, Foresti's *De claris et selectis mulieribus* and the copy of *De bello Gothorum* illuminated in Naples and containing her portrait. But she may have removed some of Matthias's books, too, when she moved back to Italy. One possible candidate is the copy of Ambrose's sermons illuminated by Attavante, or his school, which is now in Paris. The clue is the shield of Matthias, which has been clearly overpainted with the shield of Aragon. As Csapodi said,[28] this means it was most likely returned to the royal library in Naples between Matthias's death in 1490 and the French invasion of 1501 which resulted in the library's dispersal. Since Beatrice reached 'home' just before the French got there, this work may have come with her from Buda to Naples. Another book she almost certainly took from Buda is Bonfini's *Symposion de virginitate*, which in any case was dedicated to her. The imperial librarian Sambucus found it and bought it in Naples in the sixteenth century.[29]

John Corvin was another who removed works from the library. With Ugoleto as his tutor, he was obviously well educated. This can also be deduced from the books dedicated to him, such as Marzio's *De egregie, sapienter, jocose dictis ac factis regis Mathiae*. We can assume he had more than a passing interest in the books of the library. He did, after all, feature in several texts and illuminations.

John Corvin's books would have drifted into Germany after his death in 1502, as a result of his widow's remarriage to George of Brandenburg-Ansbach,[30] who was then tutor to Wladislas's son, Louis. From 1515, by which time Beatrice was dead, George lived in Germany as Margrave of Ansbach. This explains why several Corvinian works are today in Germany, scattered among other Corvinas distributed between the libraries of Berlin, Dresden, Erlangen, Göttingen, Jena, Leipzig, Munich, Nuremberg, Stuttgart and Wolfenbüttel.[31]

Csapodi identified at least two of the nine Corvinas in Wolfenbüttel as having passed through George of Brandenburg-Ansbach's hands, for example. One was a eulogy to Matthias by the papal secretary Alexander Cortesius dating from the late 1480s, *De Mathiae Corvini*, and the other was the *Stellarium* of the court astronomer, Tolhopf, also from the late 1480s. Csapodi also believed the Hunyadi family's fourteenth-century bible, now in Erlangen, had passed from John to Beatrice Frankopan and from her to the Margrave of Ansbach.[32]

It is unlikely that John or Beatrice made major inroads into the library's stock. Much more seriously for the future of the 'august' library, Wladislas began giving away some of the most valuable books to ambassadors and to humanist allies of the Habsburgs. Miserably short of money, he gave several books to imperial delegates and to an English ambassador.[33] This apparently occurred in 1502, when there is a record of the arrival in Venice of an 'English ambassador who had been in Hungary'.[34]

Viennese humanists wheedled several works out of the King. The Yale University *Tacitus*, one of the four Corvinian manuscripts in the United States, left the library under the arm of the visiting German humanist, Jacob Spiegel, who in 1518 gave it to Erasmus's friend, Beatus Bild 'Rhenanus'. Bild was excited by the gift, writing the words: 'Hic liber sumptus est ex Biblioteca Budensi' inside. Acquired by the Teleki family of Transylvania in the early nineteenth century, it made its way to America in 1934.[35]

The Philostratus *Heroica* was another of Wladislas's gifts in the last years of his reign. 'Amidst appeals and tears',[36] Johann Gremper extracted this magnificent illuminated work from the King in 1513, not for himself but for the historian, rector of Vienna University and Habsburg diplomat, Johannes Cuspinian 'Cuspinianus'. Cuspinian had cast a covetous eye on Matthias's library while taking part in various diplomatic missions to Buda from 1510 onwards. After his death in 1529, the bibliophile Bishop of Vienna, Johann Fabri, bought the Philostratus and added it to his large collection. After the Bishop's death in 1541 the work passed into the Habsburg library, the Hofbibliothek.[37]

The Nuremberg humanist and Greek scholar Willibald Pirckheimer was said to have left Buda with several works from Matthias's library in 1514.

Another significant visitor to Buda who came away with a number of Matthias's books was Johannes Alexander Köll, 'Brassicanus'. This brilliant Professor of Greek and Rhetoric at Vienna University in the 1520s made several trips to Hungary on behalf of Maximilian during the months before the Ottoman invasion, which made him an important eyewitness concerning the state of the library before 1526. Among the books he removed were Plato's dialogues, Aeneas of Gaza's *Theophrastus* (another work that may well have started out in Pannonius's library), Athanasios of Alexandria's *Contra Apollinarem* and the letters of Thaselus Caecilius Cyprianus. These four he left, along with most of his books, to Bishop

Fabri,[38] who in turn left them to the college he had founded in Vienna as a students' lodging, and which was dedicated to St Nicholas. The college library eventually passed to the university and then in 1756 into the care of the Empress Maria Theresa, who instructed the Hofbibliothek to assume custody of the works.[39]

There was no librarian to stop the scholars from pilfering the collection after Marzio and Bonfini had died. Bonfini had not returned to Italy after Matthias's death, probably because he had already reached middle age by the time he reached Hungary and he no doubt balked at the prospect of abandoning work on his history book, the *Rerum Ungaricarum decades*, which he had barely started by 1490. Wladislas was delighted he had agreed to stay on, awarding him a peerage in 1492. He lived on for another decade, dying in 1503 in Buda.

As for Taddeo Ugoleto, he enjoyed a second career back in Parma, helping his brother Angelo run his printing business before dying between 1513 and 1515. Apparently, Ugoleto returned once to Hungary after Matthias's death in the early 1490s at the request of the new King but was so dismayed by the state of the library that he hurried back.[40] It is not hard to guess why he might have felt discouraged.

Ugoleto also returned from Buda with some of Matthias's books in his luggage, according to his biographer. 'If Taddeo did not return from Hungary with gold, he surely came back with plenty of codices', Affo said.[41] The works from Buda adorned an impressive library that was to be the cause of his death. His books attracted so much attention that the Farnese Pope Paul III insisted on 'borrowing' a great number. Predictably, he failed to return them and Affo said it was Ugoleto's fury at the Pope's behaviour that sent him to his grave.

Precious instruments from Matthias's observatory were sold off or given away in the same casual manner as the books. In 1501, the secretary to the papal nuncio told Matthias's brother-in-law, Ercole, that Wladislas had given away all of Matthias's astronomical instruments, including an astrolabe and a sundial.[42] Ercole wrote back, urging the nuncio to try and track down these items but nothing came of the attempt. There was a last record made in 1512 of the astrolabe that Regiomontanus had constructed for Matthias, when the University of Jena noted the existence of 'a large brass astrolabe with three insertible disks for different latitudes, exquisitely crafted and marked in Italian letters by Master Joh. De Monte Regio for the King of Hungary'.[43] It must somehow have come into the possession of

Frederick III 'the Wise', Elector of Saxony from 1486 to 1525, a man most famous now as the patron and protector of Martin Luther.

Again, it was Wladislas's poverty as much as his indifference that resulted in such losses. He needed every ducat. The threadbare court of the King contrasted oddly with the opulent state of his nobles. 'What pomp and elegance, not to say ostentation, then ruled in Hungary', the Habsburg diplomat Baron Sigismund von Heberstein recalled. 'The gigantic entourages of the bishops and nobles all appeared on the streets in mounted processions, gowns decorated with gold and silver, their mealtimes announced by the sound of trumpets . . . Meanwhile the King lives in such poverty that whenever he wants to make a present to a foreign delegation, he has to borrow money from usurers.'[44] The Venetian ambassador, Francesco Massaro, was equally unimpressed. 'Sometimes there is nothing to cook in his kitchens', he wrote contemptuously of the palace. 'Recently the court sent out a servant to borrow 14 ducats.'[45] When Hans Schweinpeck, a Habsburg courtier, visited Buda in the reign of Wladislas's son, Louis, the situation was the same, or worse. He wrote that the Hungarian nobles had 'handled all the King's revenues in such a manner that he has nothing to eat, had not even a good coat'.[46]

The shadows lengthened in Wladislas's last years. His French queen provided the King with an heir in July 1506 when she gave birth to Louis, but she died soon afterwards. Meanwhile, the worsening social tension in the country led to an explosion at the end of the reign in 1514. The trigger was a doomed attempt to revive the idea of a crusade, which Giovanni Medici, now Leo X, entrusted to Tamas Bakocz. The former Bishop of Gyor who had 'married' Beatrice to Wladislas had since scaled the giddy heights of the Hungarian Church, spending most of his revenues on attempts to awe the Romans with his splendour and thus win the Pontiff's crown. With this in mind, in 1512 he made an astonishing appearance at that year's carnival in Rome, 'with a magnificent retinue that amazed even the upper class citizens of the city').[47] Alas, he was trumped by the Medicis and Giovanni de Medici was elevated to the papacy in 1513 after the death of Julius II. Downcast by the failure of his project, Bakocz was consoled by Leo's suggestion that he manage a crusade in Hungary. He therefore returned from Rome in 1514, a year after Leo's election, to rally the country and at the same time to build the beautiful red marble quattrocento chapel in Esztergom that bears his name.

The papal bull announcing the crusade was duly read out in the churches of Hungary on Palm Sunday, 9 April, with disastrous results. While the gentry stayed at home, tens of thousands of their serfs rallied to the banner of an excitable Transylvanian nobleman, Gyorgy Dozsa, whom Bakocz entrusted with organising the military aspect of the campaign. Almost immediately, the peasant army escaped from the oversight of either Bakocz or the crown and began to settle accounts with the hated symbols of Hungarian feudalism rather than with the Turks. As the serfs made up more than 90 per cent of the population of some three-and-a-half million, vastly outnumbering the 40,000 nobles, the sight of them moving through the countryside in the summer of 1514 sent the nobles into a panic. Clamouring for the crusade to be disbanded immediately, a royal proclamation ordered the peasants to go home on pain of death. Most refused and under Dozsa's eccentric leadership went on to capture several towns, burn manor houses, kill nobles and torture to death the Bishop of Csanad, among others.

Within weeks, a more efficient, partly mercenary, force, led by Janos Zapolya, Voivode of Transylvania, crushed the rebel army near Timisoara. But the nobility remained dissatisfied and howled for retribution on a more spectacular scale. In consequence, Dozsa was subjected to a mock 'coronation', complete with a crown of molten iron and a red hot sceptre. To add a gruesome touch, his former companions in arms were forced to eat his charred flesh.

The contrast between these savage acts and the magnanimity with which Matthias suppressed the revolt against him in 1471–72 was striking and showed once again how far in a few short years the country had swerved from his legacy. After the sadistic suppression of the peasants' revolt, the nobles launched a ferocious legislative assault on the serfs' remaining liberties in the parliament held that October. Nobles were now exempted from all taxes, while peasants lost all their remaining rights. The rebellion, the parliament declared, 'has for all days to come put the stain of faithlessness on the peasants and they have thereby utterly forfeited their liberty and become subjects to their landlords in unconditional and perpetual servitude'.[48] By confirming that they saw 90 per cent of the population as hostile and defeated, the Hungarian nobles gained a Pyrrhic victory. The unprecedented oppression of the peasants and the blatant pursuit of a class war against them by the landlords made the peasants profoundly apathetic about their country's continuing independence.

Suleiman II, who had acceded to the throne of the Ottoman Empire in September 1520, four years after Wladislas's death, observed Hungary's enfeebled condition with interest. The new King of Hungary, Louis, was young and inexperienced. In 1521, aged 15, he confirmed Hungary's new German orientation by marrying the Emperor Maximilian's granddaughter, Mary, who had been born in Brussels in 1505 and raised in Malines, Innsbruck and Vienna.

The teenage King and Queen faced their first great foreign crisis the year they married. It had always been obvious to Janos Hunyadi that the fortress of Belgrade, lying on the confluence of the Sava and the Danube, held the key to Central Europe. Hunyadi had died in 1456 keeping the Ottomans out of the city and the Battle of Belgrade gave Hungary a valuable breathing space of three-quarters of a century. But Suleiman knew circumstances had changed. Setting out from Constantinople with a large army in January 1521, he toiled through southern Serbia in the spring, reaching the outskirts of Belgrade in early summer. This time there was neither a general of Hunyadi's calibre nor a rag-tag army of religious enthusiasts of the kind Capistrano had roused to meet him. The peasants remained at home, impassive, leaving the defence of the border to a small Hungarian force and some Serbian mercenaries who proved unreliable. Suleiman was before the walls by 31 July, his Grand Vizier, Ibrahim, a Greek convert to Islam, having been there for a month. The Ottomans overran the city on 8 August, leaving the Hungarians and Serbs holding only the citadel. The trapped Serbs then forced its surrender on 28 August, after which Suleiman staged his triumphal entry into Belgrade, using the occasion to convert the city's largest church into a mosque.

The collapse of Belgrade shocked Europe almost as much as the fall of Constantinople had done in 1453. 'This news is lamentable', the Venetian Doge wrote to Henry VIII's court in England, 'and of importance to all Christians.'[49] It also triggered the final collapse of the ring of forts that Matthias had constructed in the mid-1470s. This comprised an outer belt, running along the south of the country from Belgrade through Sabacs and Jajce to Knin in southern Croatia, and an inner belt running from Timisoara through Petrovaradin towards Bihacs and Senj in northern Croatia. The fall of Belgrade resulted in the domino-style collapse of several points in the chain, including the strategically important town of Knin in Dalmatia, most important because from hilly Knin you could practically see all the way to the Adriatic. As one historian noted, 'With the collapse of the southern chain of fortresses, the Hungarian military leadership lost the zone that was to have defended the whole kingdom.'[50]

For the moment, the Sultan withdrew from the kill, however. Instead, he turned back south to capture the island of Rhodes, a Christian outpost lying just a few miles from the Anatolian mainland. Five years passed before the Sultan returned to complete the Hungarian campaign but nothing had changed in the interval. Louis made some faint attempts to restore the crown's lost financial and military muscle by demanding the recovery of alienated lands, but he did not get far. He staged an even more foolish confrontation with the Fuggers, the German bankers who had taken over the lease and development of the mines in the north. Prodded by the xenophobes at court who did not like German bankers or their new Germanic Queen, Louis was tempted into seizing the Fuggers' assets in 1525. Again, the show of strength merely exposed his weakness. The old, dying patriarch of the House of Fugger, Jakob 'the Rich', roused himself, pulled every string he could in the Empire and the resulting storm of protests on behalf of the Fuggers forced Louis into a humiliating climbdown.

The row with the Fuggers had only just calmed down when Suleiman left Constantinople on 23 April 1526 with an army of about 100,000 behind him. Louis had no realistic chance of assembling an equivalent army. He could hardly go back to the Fuggers and beg for a loan. In any case, he was unimpressive as well as young, his feckless nature revealed by his dilatory response to the approach of the Turkish juggernaut. He did not leave Buda until 20 July, when he headed south with a small force of around 3,000. Intelligent outside observers already considered Hungary a lost cause, its independence having been gambled away by the selfish and short-sighted nobility. 'There is nothing here that is needed for the war', the clever papal nuncio, Antonio Burgio, observed. 'There is such hatred between the classes that one could fear that if the Turks would offer freedom to the serfs they would possibly rise against the nobles.'[51] Cardinal Campeggio, who was later sent to England to mediate between Henry VIII and his estranged wife, Catherine of Aragon, drew the same conclusion. 'There is no doubt that if the Turks push boldly ahead they will conquer the whole of Hungary', he wrote. 'Then the Hungarian nation will disappear without a trace.'[52]

Neighbouring states did not stir. The brother of Louis's Habsburg Queen was the Emperor Charles V. But he was far away in Spain. Their brother, Ferdinand, whom Charles had appointed as his vicar in his German lands, was distracted with the controversy over Luther and with the aftermath of the 'Peasants' War' that Luther's preaching had inadvertently triggered. France under Francis I offered no help. As the business over Prince Djem had

proved, France was inclined to ally with the Ottoman Turks. England under
Henry VIII at first promised 100,000 ducats,[53] but then lowered it to 25,000.
Neither sum arrived. Only Clement VII, Pope since 1523 and another
Medici, being Lorenzo the Magnificent's nephew, offered tangible help in
the form of 25,000 ducats, which a papal legate duly delivered.[54]

The Turks moved north at a leisurely pace, reaching Sofia in May, Nis in
Serbia in June and Petrovaradin, in Vojvodina, in mid-July. There the 1,000-
strong Hungarian garrison delayed matters. As a reprisal, the Grand Vizier
had 500 of them beheaded when they surrendered and another 300 sent off
to Constantinople as slaves.[55] The army moved into southern Hungary,
meeting scarcely any obstacle except foul weather. Passing Ilok and Osijek
in eastern Slavonia, they halted at Mohacs. There the armies, the Ottomans
outnumbering their foes by at least two to one,[56] confronted each other.

By then the Hungarian army had grown to about 25,000 and would have
been larger had Louis waited for reinforcements from Zapolya, the Voivode
of Transylvania, who was at the head of another 15,000. Instead, persuaded
that attack was the best form of defence, the Hungarians charged at around
3 p.m. on 29 August. The battle was over after scarcely an hour. Decimated
by a volley of cannonballs, they were routed. Louis drowned trying to
escape from the muddy battlefield on his horse. The Ottoman historian,
Ahmed Kemal Pashazade, wrote:

> The wretched king, having seen the compact mass of his troops cut into
> two by a blow of the sword and feeling his position was hopeless, fled
> from the battlefield, wounded . . . deceived of all hope, abandoned by all
> his men.
>   The rebel hurried with his horse and his armour into the river, so
> adding to the number of those who perished by water or by flame.[57]

Suleiman's terse war diary was less colourful. 'Massacre of two thousand
prisoners. Rain falls in torrents', the entry for 31 August read. 'Rest at
Mohacs; twenty thousand Hungarian infantry and four thousand of their
cavalry are buried',[58] read the entry for 2 September.

If Suleiman's count was accurate, almost the entire Hungarian army was
wiped out. The dead certainly included Archbishop Tomori, the army's
commander-in-chief, and six other bishops, whose heads were 'planted like
trophies'[59] the following day in front of the Sultan's tent. The only reason
why Miklos Olah, Archbishop of Esztergom since Bakocz's death in 1522,

was not among them was because Louis had sent him back to Buda before the battle started. Many soldiers appear to have drowned just like the King, for the inhabitants of Belgrade were astonished at the sight of their corpses floating downstream from Mohacs a few days after the battle.[60]

The road to Buda was open and Suleiman's army moved north on 3 September, reaching the half-deserted and undefended capital on the 8th. Mary had already fled by barge with her closest attendants to Bratislava. In the chaos that surrounded the Queen's departure, the overloaded barges carrying the state records sank in the Danube about 20 miles upstream. Most of the written documentation concerning Hungary's long history, including the records of the reign of King Matthias, disappeared.

Mary was still unsure whether her husband was alive or dead; on 31 August she wrote from Bratislava to the council in Vienna, saying: 'I am told that he got away. God grant that it be true for I have no certain information about him.'[61]

The Hungarians who remained in Buda still did not despair. They assumed Zapolya's army had stayed intact and would now deploy its defence of the city. When the news reached them that Zapolya's army had retreated east, the real panic began. Now everyone who could, packed and left. According to Pashazade, 'there remained only the people of low condition who wished to throw themselves under the protection of the Sultan'.[62]

There had been no time to move Matthias's library, which is why the Queen and Archbishop Olah took only a few prized works, such as the missal that Attavante had illuminated 40 years previously.

When the Sultan reached Buda, the pitiful remnant came out with the keys of the city and presented them to the conqueror, hoping to avoid further punishment. Suleiman duly moved into Matthias's palace to preserve it from attack but his hungry and battle-weary troops sacked and burned the rest of the city. The Sultan did not order this assault, as his war diary indicated. 'Fire breaks out in Buda, in spite of the measures taken by the Sultan', reads the entry for 14 September. 'The Grand Vizier hastens to check it; his efforts are useless.'[63]

For a week, the Sultan wandered the corridors of Matthias's palace, contemplating the statues, fountains and painted ceilings on which his Dalmatian craftsmen had lavished so much attention. It was for him now to ascend the great staircase after passing the two massive candelabra that stood at its feet, and ponder the Latin epigram Bonfini had composed over the bronze doorway with its panels of the Labours of Hercules. Perhaps he also sat on the couch that had once lain beneath the tall stained-glass windows of the library, leafing through what remained of the collection that Ugoleto had had lovingly bound, catalogued and embellished.

On 21 September, the Ottoman army began to evacuate the city. The soldiers took everything they could lift and tear off. The palace candelabra disappeared back to Constantinople to decorate the mosque that had once been the cathedral of Hagia Sophia. Two great cannons, which Hunyadi had captured from the Turks at Belgrade in 1456 and kept as trophies, went there as well. Pashazade wrote that the army stripped the city bare: 'The palace of the King, which with all its riches resembled a garden abounding in flowers and fruit, was stripped of all its valuables,' he recorded. 'Everything down to the smallest object was taken and loaded on to ships with the greatest care and dispatched to Belgrade.' He added: 'In front of the palace of the cursed king were also two monstrous cannons and three statues of marvellous work; the one and the other were taken as glorious trophies and loaded with the other baggage on the boats for transport.'[64]

It appears that the statues he referred to were not of Janos and Laszlo Hunyadi but images of Hercules, Apollo and Diana, because we know the Grand Vizier Ibrahim re-erected them on pedestals inside the Hippodrome in Constantinople.[65] The sight outraged pious Muslims for whom such images were idolatrous but the Sultan sided with his favourite. When the poet Sighani unwisely wrote some satirical verses on the subject,[66] the Sultan had him ride round the city on a donkey and then strangled.[67]

The Ottoman chroniclers made no direct mention of the fate of the library. Miklos Olah, on the other hand, writing a few years later in *Hungaria*, maintained the Ottomans took the books back to Constantinople, after tearing off the silver clasps on the bindings. From his place of exile in Brussels, where he had moved with Mary, he recalled the state of the library as he remembered it. He had seen

two vaulted rooms ... one of them was full of Greek scrolls, which the King [Matthias] collected together there with much care and exertion ... [while] in the other room were codexes in Latin. Each of them was bound in coloured and gold embroidered silk and they were allotted marks according to their type and branch of learning. The scrolls were mainly papyri covered in silk with studs and clasps of silver gilt.

Turning to the fate of the books, he continued: 'After the death of King Louis on the field of Mohacs on 29 August 1526, the Turks occupied Buda the following September . . . [They] tore up some of the books, while others they scattered far and wide, after stripping them of their silver and using it for other purposes.'[68]

Some historians have suggested Olah's version of events may have been inaccurate, reflecting his anti-Turkish bitterness. But there is no real reason to doubt the substance of the account. He was probably right about the clasps, too.

There is little doubt that most of the library books were included among the items of value 'down to the smallest object' that the Ottomans loaded on to ships in the Danube for transport to Constantinople. There were no further reports of the library's existence by western visitors to the city between 1526 and 1540, when Zapolya ruled Hungary as a vassal of the Sultan. Moreover, from now on, when stray books from Matthias's library reached collectors, it was because they had turned up either in Constantinople or in Venice, the city with the closest links to Constantinople.

While the barges drifted down the Danube through the Balkans the Ottoman army returned south on foot in a vindictive mood. They burned and looted their way home, razing the cathedral in Szekesfehervar that Matthias had embellished as a Hunyadi family chapel and where he himself was buried. The present cathedral, dating from the eighteenth century, is an almost entirely new structure. Further south, they burned down Pannonius's old bishopric of Pecs, as a result of which the tomb of Pannonius disappeared. They reached an ecstatic Constantinople on 23 November.

Suleiman had no immediate ambition to absorb Hungary into his empire and for years was content with a tributary state ruled by Zapolya, the opportunistic former Voivode of Transylvania. As Pashazade noted: 'The time for joining this province to the possessions of Islam had not yet arrived.'[69] When the Sultan returned to Hungary in summer 1529 on his way to besiege Vienna, Zapolya duly paid homage to Suleiman at Mohacs, kneeling to kiss his hand.

It was only after Zapolya's death in July 1540 that Suleiman resolved to wrap up matters. Apprised of Zapolya's double-dealings with the Habsburgs, he decided against entrusting the country to Zapolya's infant son or to his widow, Isabella. His janissaries quietly and bloodlessly occupied Buda on Thursday, 1 September, ordering Isabella to vacate the palace, surrender the keys of the arsenal and prepare for transport to

Transylvania, which Suleiman decided to leave as a vassal principality. Suleiman entered Buda that same Friday. Just as he had done in Belgrade, he symbolically ordered the city's largest church, which in Buda was the church of Our Lady, to be changed into a mosque. The Hungarian capital thus became 'le boulevard de l'Islam en Europe, la forteresse et le clef de l'empire Ottoman'.[70] From that Friday, for almost a century and a half, Buda was an Ottoman city, home to a new population of Muslims and mainly Orthodox Christians, most of whom were Greeks and Serbs. Jews resettled Buda and thrived but they had no direct connection to the community that had flourished under Prefect Mendel in King Matthias's reign; Suleiman had had them deported in 1526 to Constantinople.[71] To Buda's new inhabitants, distant memories of Matthias's reign meant nothing. Less and less remained to remind them of his 'invincible triumphs'. Stripped of its books, furniture, statues and ornaments, with only its bare walls and patches of paintwork on the ceiling, the palace was no longer a royal court but a barracks. Significantly, it was referred to not as a palace but as the castle.

At least it had some kind of function under the new order as the headquarters of the Sultan's pasha. The King's hunting lodges disappeared totally. Of the lodge near Buda, which Suleiman inspected in 1526, only the foundations remain. The palace at Visegrad, with its wine fountains, pleasure gardens and cages of wild beasts, was also deserted. Likewise, Vitez's palace in Esztergom. Less than forty years after Matthias's death, astonishingly little remained of his achievements. All had been erased, except for the library, or bits of the library: the precious books with their eye-catching raven motifs continued to drift like leaves around the Ottoman Empire and back to Europe – tantalising remnants of a vanished golden age.

CHAPTER TEN

'Who can restrain their tears?'

Lorenzo: *Where is this CORVINIAN LIBRARY to be seen?*
Philemon: *I will take post-horses ere sun-set, and borrow 'the wings of the*
         wind' when the fleetness of my coursers fails!
Lisardo: *You need do neither. List! The library of Corvinus has CEASED*
         TO EXIST.
Lysander: Oh horrible!

The Biographical Decameron, 1817[1]

Myths grew up around the King's library, fuelled by the popularity of
Pannonius's works and a romantic cult of 'lost' libraries that seized people's
imaginations following the Ottoman conquest of the Balkans and Hungary.
Inevitably, these myths led to gross exaggerations. After the Ottomans
captured Constantinople, for example, Lauro Quirini, writing in Crete,
claimed they had destroyed 120,000 Greek works, so many that the existence
of Greek literature was imperilled.[2] Other writers continued to put forward
fabulous claims concerning the library of the old emperors in Constantinople,
insisting a vast collection remained hidden in the secluded walls of the
palace of the Seraglio. The myth of the 'lost' imperial library was not
seriously deflated until 1687, when the French ambassador persuaded a
biddable Italian to obtain 16 volumes from the Seraglio, which were
dispatched to Paris for inspection. The disappointment was terrible when it
turned out that the books were of poor quality and not the amazing finds
everyone had expected. 'It was a myth in other words that the imperial
library had been preserved.'[3]

Lost behind the fault line dividing the Christian west from the Muslim east after the 1540s, Matthias's library in Buda became the object of similar speculation. The recovery of remnants of the collection in various parts of Europe only fuelled the passionate interest among collectors to find out what had happened to the rest.

Attavante's missal, as we have seen, made its way under the exiled Queen Mary's arm to Brussels. Following her flight from Buda in 1526, she never returned. After a few years of wandering, her brother, Charles V, sent her in 1531 to govern the Low Countries following the death of their aunt, Margaret. For the next quarter-century Mary held court in Brussels in company with the exiled Archbishop Olah whose *Hungaria,* published in 1536, was an elegiac recollection of Matthias's Hungary, a Garden of Eden of which a foolish and ungrateful people had been deprived.

The missal stayed with Mary and remained in Brussels after the Queen retired with her brother to Spain. Inside, the spidery signatures of several Habsburg governors of the Netherlands can still be seen.[4] 'On this gospel', one reads, 'the most serene Prince Charles of Lorraine, supreme governor of the Low Countries, vested with the supreme authority of her Majesty Maria Theresa, Queen of Hungary and Bohemia, solemnly took the oath on the day of his inauguration, 20 April 1744.'[5] The earliest signatures, dated 1599, are those of the Archduke Charles and Archduchess Isabella; the latest, belonging to Albert and Marie-Christine, are dated 1781. They are a reminder that Matthias's old missal had found a new role in the Netherlands as the book on which generations of Habsburg governors took their oath of office. It was only deprived of its role by the French Revolution, which ended the Habsburg regime in Brussels.

So it was that a book that had started out in Attavante's workshop in Florence in the mid-1480s, spent the next four decades in the palace in Buda and left with Mary for Bratislava after the Battle of Mohacs, served an entirely different function for the Habsburgs in what is now Belgium. Its travels were not over. Taken to Paris after Revolutionary France invaded the Low Countries, it was returned to Brussels after the Congress of 1815 and now lies in the Bibliothèque Royale de Belgique.

Other books from Matthias's collection accompanied the exiled Mary to Spain, though they cannot be named with any certainty. Although Mary remained healthy well into middle age, 'a virago', according to one English observer, and 'never so well as when flinging on horseback and hunting all the night long',[6] her tasks as her brother's deputy in Brussels eventually wore her down. A worsening struggle between Protestant and Catholic zealots in the 1530s, which would eventually tear the Low Countries in two, confused this sensible and pleasure-loving friend of Erasmus. Though never a Lutheran, hard-line Catholics constantly defamed her as a crypto-Protestant. Interestingly, one of her assailants was Bishop Fabri of Vienna, that keen collector of Corvinian manuscripts who had swept up most of Brassicanus's 'finds' in Buda. Fabri harshly compared her in a sermon to the leprous Mary who was the sister of Moses and Aaron in the Old Testament.[7]

Released from the burden of government when Charles V retired to Spain in 1556, she followed him with her amiable older sister Eleonora, ex-Queen both of Portugal and France. While Charles settled into rustic, pious retirement among the Jeromite friars at Yuste, the two ex-queens led a more worldly and peripatetic existence. Mary died on 28 October 1558 at the hamlet of Cigales, near Valladolid, five weeks after the death of her brother and several months after her sister. The heart attack that killed her may have been prompted by her fact that her nephew, Philip II, was demanding that she return and resume power in Brussels.

It is clear that Mary included literary works among the many treasures she packed for transport to Spain, for Philip later remarked that his aunt had bequeathed him precious books.[8] It is also likely that some were items from Matthias's collection, gathered up when she fled Buda in haste in 1526.

Significantly, three works from Matthias's collection remain in, or near, Madrid. A copy of Plato's letters is in the library of the Escorial. The *Compendium philosophiae,* a work of the twelfth-century French theologian and philosopher Guillaume de Conches, or Wilhelmus de Conchis, is in the Biblioteca Nacional, as is a copy of the *Historia Turcica* by Feliks Petancius 'Ragusinus'. According to Gabriel Halasz, writing in the 1930s, at least one of these works came from Mary, though he did not specify which. 'On lui doit la conservation de deux volumes de la Corvina, dont l'un passa en Espagne, tandis que l'autre, le Missel d'Attavante, est conservé aujourd'hui encore à la bibliothèque de Bruxelles', he wrote.[9] De Hevesy, meanwhile, claimed that all the books that Mary took to Spain were left to the Escorial.[10]

Lourdes Alonso de Viana, now head of manuscripts at the Biblioteca Nacional, believes Ragusinus's work reached Spain not thanks to Mary but as a result of the author visiting Spain in person in 1509 on behalf of Wladislas.[11] There is nothing written inside De Conchis's *Compendium philosophiae* to indicate its provenance, however it may have arrived in Mary's copious trunk.

Mary's brother showed no great taste for reading in retirement in Yuste, maintaining only a tiny library of about 30 books.[12] But Mary did not share his austere tastes or his religious devotion; to the end she retained her love of hunting, falcony and the arts. She certainly packed masses of stuff for Spain, much of which, including the bronze statue of herself, remains in the Prado museum. Her baggage included twenty-four Titians and a stack of old Flemish masters.[13]

Mary may have left Hungary with several Corvinian works in her possession as well as the missal but she did nothing to build up the growing cult of Matthias and of the library in the second half of the sixteenth century. That was the work of humanist scholars, mainly Germans, dwelling on Brassicanus's descriptions of his last visits to Buda in April, November and December 1525 and in January 1526. He had recorded his impressions of the last months of the library in dramatic terms in what was to become a widely cited work of 1530, the *De gubernatione dei* by Salvianus Massiliensis. 'I examined every book in the library', he wrote in his dedicatory preface. 'But shall I say books? So many pieces of treasure were there, I really felt as if I had not been in a library but as they say, in the bosom of Jupiter.'

He went on: 'I saw such a plenty of Greek and Hebrew volumes, which King Matthias had purchased with immeasurable money after the fall of Byzantium and many other Greek cities, releasing them from their shackles as if they had been slaves ... I saw such a plenty of old and new books in Latin as there can be found nowhere else according to my knowledge.'[14]

'We see Chrysostom, Athanasias, Cyril, [Gregory] Nazianzus,[15] Basil the Great, Gregory of Nyssa, Theophanus, infinite works of Dorotheus [of Gaza]', he continued. 'I have not mentioned the poets, orators, philosophers and historians ... we see innumerable Greek authors.'

He finished his preface with a dramatic 'keen' for what had now been lost to the world following the invasion of Hungary a few years before. 'I have heard like all Pannonia of the miserable way by which this truly golden library perished', he declaimed. 'Who on relating such events could restrain their tears? ... I am most inconsolably convinced that it has perished for all Christian people.'[16]

Brassicanus may have been laying it on rather thick, because other visitors to Buda in the 1520s had been more impressed by the air of decay. At much the same time that Brassicanus had been nosing around the stock, the Venetian ambassador, Lorenzo Orio, had described the library in different terms. 'As for the library, I have been inside and there are not many good books left', he told the Doge's secretary in 1520.[17] 'The good ones have all been stolen.'

The ambassador's words suggest Brassicanus exaggerated in hindsight, capitalising on the air of glamour and drama that already surrounded Matthias's most famous legacy. For one thing, he claimed he had spotted a copy of the complete works of the fifth-century BC orator Hyperides.[18] This would have been an extraordinary find, as only fragments of his orations have survived, and few recent historians have taken seriously Brassicanus's claim that he saw this lost treasure in Buda.

However, Brassicanus's words resonated powerfully with readers and collectors all over Europe. Soon, no one was able to argue with him in person about his description of the library in Buda, for in 1539 he died.

The Swiss scientist Conrad Gesner took up the matter of the library where Brassicanus had left off in the foreword to his *Bibliotheca universalis*, published in Zurich in 1545. The air of romanticism, already present in Brassicanus's description of the library, was still more evident in Gesner's description, which was not, of course, based on first-hand memories. Indeed, those with real memories of the library in Buda were now in short supply, apart from Olah who lived until 1568.

'In the time of our fathers, the monstrous attacks of the Turks caused the famous library of Buda, capital of the kingdom of Pannonia, to collapse, which the never sufficiently praised King Matthias had filled with works of all kinds and priceless Greek and Hebrew manuscripts', Gesner wrote. 'Some of these had been collected at immeasurable cost following the fall of Constantinople and the destruction of many towns in Greece.'[19]

The first, imperfect, publication in the 1540s of Bonfini's history, the *Rerum Ungaricarum decades*, which contained a wealth of detail about Matthias's court, added to the burgeoning mythology surrounding the late King's library. Although Bonfini had died back in 1503, the sheer size of his work had delayed its publication and it was not until 1543 that an incomplete first edition appeared in Basle and it was only in 1568 that Janos Szambocky, or Johannes Sambucus,[20] Maximilian II's librarian, prepared a first complete edition for publication, again in Basle. It quickly caught the attention of a general audience far wider than that composed only of Latin-speakers when a German translation followed in 1581.

If accounts of the library's magnificence kept its memory alive, the reappearance of a growing number of books in the markets of Constantinople or Venice whetted collectors' appetites still more. From the late 1530s onwards, enterprising agents of the Habsburgs and the kings of France, the Fuggers and individual humanists, often Hungarian or Croat bishops, were alert to their appearance.

Marcus Singkhnoser, secretary to the Emperor Charles, obtained Matthias's copy of the works of the fifth-century Byzantine historian, Dionysius Areopagita, in 1557 in Constantinople. Purchased by the Archbishop of Besançon in 1694, this volume remains in Besançon.

The Italian humanist, Antonio Brucioli, got hold of the copy of *Saturnalia* by Macrobius in Constantinople rather earlier, in 1544. Later, he presented this work to Cosimo I Medici's major-domo, Francesco Riccio, and it remains in Florence in the Medicea Laurenziana library.

Andras Dudith, a fascinating sixteenth-century bibliophile of mixed Croatian–Hungarian descent,[21] tracked down the *Ekklésiastiké historia* of Niképhoros Kallistos, a unique work, in Constantinople in the 1560s. Dudith was a Catholic bishop, though of a colourful kind. Presented in rapid succession to the bishoprics of Knin, Csanad, Pecs and Szeged thanks to the favour he enjoyed with Maximilian II, his attendance at the Council of Trent and his work as secretary to the devout and highly educated English Cardinal, Reginald Pole, failed to arrest his steady drift towards Protestantism. On an embassy to Cracow on behalf of the Emperor he jumped ship ecclesiastically, marrying a Polish Protestant and joining the Reformed faith. After spending his last years in the tolerant atmosphere of Wroclaw,[22] his library, including Matthias's copy of *Ekklésiastiké historia,* ended up in the Hofbibliothek in Vienna.

Another work that must have been bought in Constantinople was Aquinas's *Commentaria* on Aristotle – the only Corvinian work now in Prague. The clue is an inscription in Latin, reading 'one of the books of Nicolay Zaj'. As Zaj's (or Zay's) father, Ferenc, had been an imperial diplomat in Constantinople, and had taken part in an imperial diplomatic mission to Suleiman the Magnificent at his court north-east of Ankara in the spring of 1555, it is likely that Ferenc Zay obtained the *Commentaria* while passing through Constantinople.

As the story of these books makes clear, the bulk of the library in Buda was indeed brought back to Constantinople under Suleiman the Magnificent. But as Ottoman officials realised how much interest there was in these volumes, the books began to leak out from the Sultan's library. Lodovico Gritti, the bastard son of the Venetian Doge, Andrea Gritti,[23] may well have played a key role in this illicit trade. Earlier claims on the part of Hungarian historians that he robbed the library in Buda while working as the Sultan's agent in Hungary can be discounted; after the Battle of Mohacs there was no library in Buda to rob. However, Gritti may have 'eased' the passage of books from their new place of storage in Constantinople into the hands of collectors and book merchants. As Suleiman's man in Hungary during the years following the Battle of Mohacs until 1534, he would have been well apprised of what the library in Buda had once contained. And with his Venetian background, first-hand knowledge of Hungary, close contacts at Suleiman's court and notorious taste for bribes, his activities probably explain why some Corvinian manuscripts suddenly appeared in bookshops in Constantinople and Venice in the 1530s. Admittedly, Gritti's main business interests were in spices and jewels but his dealings were so multifarious that it is more than likely that they also included Matthias's books.[24]

The Venetians were assiduous hunters of Corvinian manuscripts in the mid-sixteenth century. With their intimate connections to Constantinople they were well placed to hear what was available. The Zenos, one of the grander old dynasties of the republic, who had long-standing ties with Constantinople and the Levant, obtained several, for example. Nicolò Zeno, a keen biographer of his seafaring ancestors,[25] sought out Corvinian manuscripts in Constantinople in the 1540s. One of his finds was an account of his famous ancestor, Carlo, which had been written in 1458 and dedicated to Pius II. After Nicolò brought this slice of his own family's history back to Venice, his son, Caterino, took the manuscript to Bergamo when he became governor there. An abbreviated Italian version was produced in Bergamo in 1591, which still survives. Sadly, the illuminated Latin original on which it was based now disappeared.[26]

Zeno not only obtained Corvinian works for his own library but sold others to interested agents working for buyers like the Duke of Ferrara. Alfonso II d'Este, a descendant of Beatrice's sister, Leonora, had a number of dealings with Zeno in the 1560s through his ambassador in Venice, Gerolamo Faletti. The latter reported back on his complicated negotiations with a Nicolò, or Niccolò, Zeni, or Zeno, who was presumably the same person. 'This man owns several books which were once the property of King Matthias, handwritten, both in Latin and Greek', Faletti told the Duke. 'He is not keen on selling them, this gentleman being quite wealthy and powerful.'[27]

Twenty days later Zeno had apparently relented: Faletti now sent the Duke a more promising letter. 'I am sending you four books, once the property of King Matthias so you can judge the quality of the rest, which number a hundred, all of them in the possession of Nicolò Zeni, though he does not want people to know he owns them or has agreed to sell them', he wrote.

'He recently told me he would like to sell 50; perhaps he does this only to add to the reputation of this collection. I would really like to buy them all, in accordance with Your Excellency's wishes, for even if most of these books have been printed since they were copied, nevertheless they are all on beautiful paper with miniatures and with old bindings.'[28] It is not certain exactly how many of Zeno's books reached Ferrara, and were later moved to Modena after the ducal court moved there in the sixteenth century. However, Faletti's letters explain why the Este library included 17 Corvinian works in the 1840s.

The Zenos kept some of the Corvinian finds for themselves, of course. Apart from the work referred to earlier, they also kept a copy of Hieronymus's letters, which Vitez had once owned. This remained in the family's possession until 1723, when it passed into the hands of the Habsburg Emperor Charles VI. Nor were the Zenos the only collectors of Corvinian works in Venice in the sixteenth century. The Dominicans in Venice also bought them.[29] Three of the four Corvinian manuscripts now in Venice, in the library of San Marco, were obtained by Gioacchino della Torre, the Dominican Prior: Averulino's work on architecture, which Bonfini had translated from Italian into Latin, Suetonius's lives of Roman emperors, illuminated by Cherico, and a copy of Martianus, illuminated by Attavante. Significantly, the Prior obtained these works for Venice in the early 1490s, long before the fall of Buda and during the time of Wladislas's notorious give-aways. They did not come from Constantinople.

In Germany, the Fuggers, the fabulously wealthy banking dynasty with important connections to both Hungary and Venice, were also on the lookout for stray Corvinian works in the 1540s. Jakob 'the Rich' had played a crucial role in Hungary's economic life in the 1520s until King Louis made his abortive attempt to drive the family out of the country. Jakob's older brother, Jörg, born in 1453, who was placed in charge of the family's operations in Central Europe, had been personally acquainted with Hungary while Matthias was alive. For that reason, it is possible that he saw the library in Buda for himself and so helped to plant an interest in its fate among his descendants. Either way, Jörg's grandson, Johann Jakob, became a passionate bibliophile and obtained a couple of Corvinian works for his enormous library. At least two of the King's books now remaining in

Munich passed through Johann Jakob's hands, one of which was Bede's *De natura rerum,* which he obtained in 1544.

For all his family's high Catholicism – they were great builders and restorers of churches – Johann Jakob was a keen collector of Jewish manuscripts, which explains his interest in 1564 in acquiring Matthias's copy of the works of the ancient Jewish scholar, Aristeas.[30] Johann Jakob did not keep hold of his treasures for long. With no head for business, he was forced to give up his stake in the family bank in the 1560s and in 1571 to sell his vast collection of books for a bargain 50,000 florins to Albrecht V, Duke of Bavaria.[31] As a result, the Fuggers' Corvinian manuscripts ended up not in Augsburg or Ingolstadt but in Munich.

While the Fuggers of Augsburg, the Zenos of Venice, the Venetian Dominicans, the wandering Bishop Dudith, Bishop Fabri of Vienna, and assorted agents of the Habsburgs hovered over Europe and the Near East, searching for remnants of the library of Buda, a little further to the west Francis I of France had picked up the scent and put his own men out on patrol. Several of his ambassadors to Venice had to combine ordinary diplomatic tasks with book-buying, scouring the shops of the city on behalf of their royal master in the hunt for relics of Matthias's collection and any other Latin and Greek manuscripts. It was fortunate that a number of them found this task very congenial.[32]

Francis's interest in classical manuscripts grew rapidly in the 1530s, after he had made his first acquisition of a collection of Greek manuscripts in 1521. Like Matthias, Francis was not much interested in printed books, greatly preferring works copied by hand.[33] Guillaume Pellicier, Bishop of Montpellier and his ambassador to Venice from 1439 to 1442, thus spent much of his time looking for them and sending them back to France. Pellicier collected on an industrial scale and did not restrict himself to Venice; after scouring the libraries of Provence for old manuscripts there were angry complaints in the 1570s that he had 'ravaged'[34] the region as far as other collectors were concerned.

Some of Matthias's books must have fallen into Pellicier's hands; in 1544 he sold two to Antonio Brucioli in Venice, who then sold them in 1564 to Cosimo I Medici's major-domo Francesco Riccio who,[35] as we have seen, also bought the *Saturnalia* from Brucioli. The activities of Pellicier and the other French ambassadors to Venice and Constantinople may account for the presence of some of the nine Corvinian works now in the National Library in Paris.[36]

Francis's interest in Greek manuscripts was not shared by his English rival, Henry VIII. This explains the paucity of Corvinian manuscripts in England today. English kings played no role in buying any of the six books now in English libraries.[37] This was the achievement of individual collectors. Sir Henry Lello, ambassador of Elizabeth I and then James I in Constantinople, for example, obtained the copy of Seneca's *Tragoediae* that is now in the Bodleian Library in Oxford during his stay in the Ottoman Empire.

The copy of Horace's *Opera*, now in the British Library, came via a more circuitous route. It, too, originally surfaced in Constantinople. As a note in the front of the book indicates, Antun Vrancic (in Hungarian Antal Verancsics), the learned Croat Bishop of Pecs and later Archbishop of Esztergom, hunted this work down in Constantinople in the mid-1550s. It would appear that Vrancic took part in the same diplomatic imperial mission to Suleiman's court as Ferenc Zaj in 1555, and while Zaj got hold of Aquinas's commentaries for himself, Vrancic obtained the Horace. He did not keep it, however, but passed the book on to Ogier Busbeq, the Habsburg ambassador in Constantinople, who in turn took it to Brussels. From there, it made its way to London at some point in the eighteenth century.

It is not clear how the copy of Gellius's *Noctes Atticae* now in Manchester passed into the hands of the eighteenth-century collector, John Byrom,[38] one of whose descendants later presented it to Chetham's Library. Some believe Byrom bought the work in a sale in Montpellier. If so, the *Noctes Atticae* was another Corvinian work that crisscrossed Europe over several generations, journeying first from Florence to Buda in the late 1480s, and then on to Constantinople in 1526, before escaping from the Seraglio at some point and floating around the book markets of Europe for a couple of centuries.

The copy of the gospels, the *Evangelistarium secundum*, now in Holkham Hall is another Corvinian work whose passage to England can only be guessed at. Nothing written inside the manuscript indicates its history, though Susan Reynolds, librarian to the Earl of Leicester, believes the 1st Earl, Thomas Coke, probably purchased this work in Venice as part of a job lot during his six-year Grand Tour from 1712 to 1718. At the time, the young Coke collected a mass of paintings, sculptures and books with the help of his companion, Thomas Hobart, and the *Evangelistarium* may have been among the 20 or so manuscripts that Coke bought from the well-known library of Bernardo Trevisani in May 1717. On 24 May, there is a record that Coke's valet 'gave to the Sacristy of Bernardo Trevisan for a present of books 2 crowns, 2 pauls and 5 bioux'.[39]

By the end of the 1560s, opportunities to pick up Corvinian works in the book markets of Venice or Constantinople were drying up. The mysterious merchant and politician Lodovico Gritti was long since dead, having been decapitated by some angry Romanians on one of his missions in the Balkans in 1534. Whoever was leaking books out of the Sultan's library had either died or been stopped. The collectors had to look elsewhere. Interest now switched back to Buda, where imaginative bibliophiles began claiming that Matthias's 'lost' library slept under Ottoman guard like the Sleeping Beauty, awaiting the arrival of a particularly enterprising prince.

One such would-be saviour, who really was a prince, was George, or Gyorgy, Rakoczi, the ruler of Transylvania from 1630 to 1648. As we have seen, Transylvania had not been incorporated into the Ottoman Empire along with the rest of Hungary in the 1540s but had been left to pursue an autonomous existence under vassal princes. While Hungary vanished as a state, Transylvania became the new centre of Hungarian culture and national aspirations under a succession of Protestant rulers. Naturally, they wanted to appropriate the mantle of the great Corvinus for themselves and appropriate whatever was left of the Buda library for their own capital in Alba Iulia, where the cathedral contained the Hunyadi tombs and where George's predecessor had established a university in the 1620s.

After a fruitless trip to Buda in the early years of his reign awakened his interest further, Rakoczi turned to his agent at the Sultan's court, Istvan Szalanczy, urging him to bring all his influence and money to bear on the more corruptible favourites at court. 'How many beautiful books are in Buda, just wasting away', the Prince lamented. 'If you could find a way, please offer 100 thalers to Zulfikar or 100 pieces of gold . . . for 50 [books]. If he could get them all, I would even give him 1,000 pieces of gold.' When the said Zulfikar merely recommended that he take his request to the Sultan, the Prince complied.

In February 1633, Rakoczi wrote directly to the Sultan, attempting to play on their shared dislike of the Catholic Church and the Catholic Habsburgs. If the Sultan were to help the Protestant men equip their university with a fine library, he said, young men would no longer have to go abroad to study and become infected with papist ideas. Rakoczi told the Sultan that his predecessor,

> seeing that the country is in great need of educated people, began to send youths of both noble and civil origin to study [abroad]. When they came

home, some of these youths with their extensive knowledge were most useful to their country, but quite a few became papists and instead of being useful are harmful both to their home and nation.

Therefore, in his lifetime, he founded a school here in Fehervar [Alba Iulia] based on our own [Reformed] religion ... and ... many potential scholars and professors have assembled around it. I hope in this way I won't have to send the sons of the country to the realm of the Pope, which would be a great disadvantage to Your Majesty's empire. However, my one great difficulty is that I have very few books in my school.

And I am aware that Your Majesty does have [books] for when the blessed Sultan Suleiman seized Buda he permitted us to obtain them ... [but] they are still there. As Your Majesty can derive no benefit from keeping them, nor be harmed by giving them away, I humbly urge you to deign to give them to us, so that the country need not have to spend a fortune on sending its citizens to be educated among the Germans.[40]

It was a good pitch. But it drew no response and in July 1633 Rakoczi complained that the Ottoman authorities in Buda did not even want to show the remaining books to one of his emissaries. He had heard that most of the books had been given away already to the Emperor. The dream of re-establishing Matthias's library in Transylvania faded.

In fact, although the Habsburgs had got hold of many of Matthias's books, they were equally convinced that others remained unclaimed in Buda. The imperial librarian, Peter Lambeck, yearned to find them.

Lambeck was a prodigy. Born in 1626 in Hamburg he had wandered around Europe in his twenties and thirties poring over libraries and book collections from Amsterdam to Paris, Toulouse, Leipzig, Dresden, Prague, Florence, Bologna and Rome before the Emperor Leopold named him vice-head of the Hofbibliothek in December 1662, Lambeck having abjured the Reformed religion and converted to Catholicism shortly before.

He promptly presented his sovereign with a wooden model of the new, grander, library building that he wanted to see built in Vienna. The entrance acknowledged Matthias as, in a sense, a co-founder. Alongside tributes in Latin to the Emperor Maximilian, to the humanists Conrad Celtis and Cuspinian and to Bishop Fabri, it referred to the 'Serenissimi Regis Hungariae Matthiae Corvini'.

As the inscription indicated, Lambeck cherished an enormous interest in Matthias and spent much of the 1660s trying to establish exactly what remained of the collection in Buda. For the first few years in Vienna, he was too busy supervising the construction of the new library and rounding up books from Habsburg collections dispersed around the provinces in Innsbruck and elsewhere to visit Ottoman Hungary. In any case, a visit was impossible outside the context of a diplomatic mission. However, in 1666 Lambeck got his chance. That year, an imperial embassy to Constantinople under Count Walter de Leslie was to pass through Buda in the first week of March and Lambeck was allowed to accompany the group. Most importantly, the Grand Vizier had ordered the Pasha of Buda to let the delegation tour the castle.

The visit was a crushing disappointment to Lambeck. Matthias's palace still stood, but only the faintest traces remained of the glorious halls, staircases and chambers that Matthias's contemporaries had described.

'In the palace at Buda are several courts and in one a fair fountain of marble with a Bason, or huge shell of Brass, with the Armes of the kings of Hungary, supported with Snails of that Metal',[41] an English account of the expedition read, continuing: 'On the right hand are the Stairs, the upper part of which have Rails and Ballestries of Porphyrie. The Dining-room is prodigiously great, and the Windows proportionable with the Jaumes of red Marble, as the chimney-piece is, which is curiously carved and rich and at the end of the said dining room is a noble square chamber.'[42]

The rest of the sights were dismal beyond belief, however. Buda, the same writer added, was

in so tatter'd a condition that could Suleiman the Magnificent return from the dead he would change and recant his opinion of thinking it the fairest City in the World. And as for the library, which the Visier permitted to be seen, and formerly was the glory of the World, for it had a thousand volumes of rare and choice Books, of excellent Authors, how poor a thing it is now and how much disagreeing with the fame and ancient lustre it had since the few books it hath are of little and no use, being almost consum'd by Moths, Dust and Rats.[43]

After perusing the 300 or 400 remaining books and deciding that most were fairly worthless, Lambeck took away only three, which returned with him to the Hofbibliothek: Pannonius's works and the sermons of St Augustine and St Gregory Nazianzenus. The men left Buda on 14 March and were back by the 23rd.[44]

That was that. The illusion had been punctured. But not quite, because the legend of Matthias's library was now so old and so vigorous that not all the book-hunters were ready to abandon their dream. For the better part of two centuries now, legends concerning the fabulous collection had been circulating around Europe and it was not possible to disabuse people of the myth all at once. A couple of adventurers still dreamed that they would be the ones to finally lift the veil on this great mystery.

The most important and interesting of these was an Italian by the name of Count Luigi Marsigli. Twenty years after Lambeck had found the moths and the rats nibbling the remains of Matthias's collection, this ambitious young man resolved to conduct his own search of the premises when the armies of the Emperor Leopold finally drove the Ottomans from Buda.

The end of Ottoman rule in Hungary was not the fruit of a dramatic military initiative on the part of the Habsburgs. It sprang from the vain resolve of Kara Mustafa, Grand Vizier to Mehmed IV, to emulate and if possible exceed Mehmed the Conqueror of Constantinople in 1453, and Suleiman the Magnificent, the conqueror of Buda in 1526. What prompted the Grand Vizier on this adventure remains a mystery because the Habsburg Empire at the time was submissive in its relations with the Sublime Porte. As recently as 1664, the Emperor Leopold had signed a treaty with the Ottomans, offering them more morsels of Hungarian and Croatian terri-tory. The terms had outraged the nobility in both lands but they confirmed that Vienna sought peace with the Turks at almost any price.

Possibly the only real reason for the war was that Kara Mustafa hoped through a spectacular military triumph to regain the prestige he was losing at court. Mehmed IV was a difficult, even repulsive, master. Addicted to his harem – a contemporary wrote that he was 'much inclined to carnality'[45] – his healthy sex life did not make him particularly easygoing. On the contrary, he was mercurial, an intriguer and ostentatiously cruel, with a mania for slaughtering both animals and Christians. He was also greedy. But then so, according to one historian, was the Grand Vizier: 'His aggressive avarice, his corruption and extreme jealousy of power made him capable of sacrificing anything and anyone to his own ambition.'[46]

The expedition began hopefully enough, with the Turkish behemoth setting out from Constantinople amid wild pomp in mid-October 1682 for Edirne. As an English merchant reported, it made a terrific impression. 'In this Sight was expos'd to view the greatest Riches of the Empire, consisting in Jewels of inestimable value, Horses, Clothes and Furniture, the

Magnificence whereof is not to be expressed in writing, unless it were possible to shew you Horses Furniture cover'd over with Diamonds, Rubies and Emeralds', he wrote. There were cavalry at the front with bows and lances, pashas and their retinues, judges wearing huge turbans 'at least a Yard Diameter', emirs in green, the Grand Vizier's secretary, 'with a vast and rich retinue' of his own, the Grand Treasurer and his retinue, the Vizier's Guard 'covered over with the Skins of Lyons, Bears, Tygers and Leopards', some 50 of the Vizier's pages, a procession of the Sultan's eunuchs, white and black, a procession of 'bauling [bawling] Holy men', two magnificent camels, one carrying the clothes of the Prophet Muhammad, the Master of the Horse and then the Sultan himself, 'on a Milk-white Horse covered over with jewels'.[47]

After a delay in Edirne, this circus advanced to Belgrade, into which Mehmed made his ceremonial entry in May the next year, before returning to Constantinople, leaving Kara Mustafa behind as commander-in-chief. The army then ploughed on, grinding through Mitrovica and Osijek in Slavonia towards Szekesfehervar. Leaving there on 28 June, the soldiers then crossed into the sliver of western and northern Hungary that the Habsburgs ruled.

As a small defensive Habsburg force scuttled back from Gyor in western Hungary towards Vienna, and as Kara Mustafa passed the spot where it was believed Suleiman had pitched camp in 1529, there seemed no reason why the Ottomans should not now grasp Vienna, especially as the garrison in the city was puny, numbering no more than about 2,000 men.

The city made ready to die with dignity. After the Archbishop of Esztergom celebrated an outdoor mass for the imperial army under the Duke of Lorraine, watched among others by young Marsigli, the old, the infirm and foreign residents began to slip away. The flight of the court to Passau in the first week of July, followed by about 60,000 of the city's wealthiest inhabitants, was not seen as a vote of confidence in the imperial army's ability to resist.

Vienna looked finished. However, the expected victory of the Ottoman army did not occur. The juggernaut had rolled in about a week too late, giving the capable organiser of Vienna's defences, Count Ernst Starhemberg, vital time. As July stretched into August and summer passed its zenith, dysentery ate away at Kara Mustafa's army and so, Starhemberg reported in mid-August, the mood in Vienna began to lift. 'They dare not thrust their heads out of their holes any longer', he boasted on 18 August. 'I will never deliver up the place, but with the last drop of my blood.'[48]

Moreover, outside help was now at hand. Urged on by the Pope, the armies of the German princes and Jan Sobieski, King of Poland, were rapidly converging on the besieged city. On 12 September, they came over the Kahlenberg hills outside Vienna and annihilated the besiegers. Had the Christian armies swept on, they might have liberated the whole of Hungary immediately. As it was, the Ottomans had lost all hope of taking Vienna and after beating a humiliating retreat to Belgrade in November, Kara Mustafa paid the familiar price. The Sultan's officials caught up with him in the last week of December in Belgrade. At his prayers when they arrived, 'he asked only for the rug on which he was praying to be moved, so that he might enter paradise at once by falling into the dust. After being throttled, his head was skinned, stuffed and sent to Constantinople.'[49]

The failure of the second siege of Vienna changed the balance of power in Europe. Austria had been revived – belated confirmation, it seemed, of Frederick III's predictions of Habsburg greatness. The ambitions of France – the ally of the Turks in the west – had been checked. Girding himself for war and prompted by the papal nuncio, Cardinal Buonvisi, Leopold resolved to drive the Ottomans far to the south and east and claim not only Hungary but Croatia, Serbia, Kosovo and even Constantinople.

The initial military results of the 'Holy League', compacted in 1684 between the Emperor, the Pope, Poland and Venice, were not impressive. In July 1684, the imperial army under the Duke of Lorraine advanced as far as Pest and surrounded the walls of Buda. On 9 September, the Elector of Bavaria brought reinforcements but the imperial army was soon as bogged down in Buda as the Turks had been a few years before in Vienna. The Sultan sent extra forces and the Habsburg armies encamped before Buda met stouter resistance than anticipated.

The siege dragged on. In November, the Bavarians stormed one of the towers of Matthias's palace but failed to breach the city's defences and as winter descended they retreated.

Austria did not relapse into its usual lethargy, however. The following year was consumed by frantic attempts to raise money and by small-scale campaigns in Hungary. The spring of 1686 saw the Duke of Lorraine back on the banks of the Danube within sight of Buda, the Duke attacking the city from the north and the Bavarians from the south.

This time the besiegers were more confident. As Jacob Richards related in his *Journal of the Siege of Buda*, a Pole who escaped from the city reported that the Ottoman garrison was now smaller than it had been, numbering no more than 7,000, down from around 15,000. About a thousand of these were Jews, who were amongst the most ardent supporters of the Muslim regime in Hungary. The Jewish chronicler, Izsak Schulhof, recorded that Buda's Jews were distraught on hearing that the Habsburgs had attacked the city.[50] 'Everyone was lamenting and weeping in despair, crying out for help and the weeping rose unto the skies', he wrote. 'Such distress as our souls suffered had not been heard before.'[51]

Throughout July 1686 the besiegers subjected what was left of Matthias's palace to non-stop battery from cannons. One of the last monuments to his reign was going down, brick by brick. On 2 July, according to Richards, 'the Bavarians play'd very furiously against the Castle ... and shot in several bombs, which occasion'd a new Conflagration'.[52] Four days later, 'a great number of Bombs were shot into the Town, which did great Execution ... [and] fire was seen to blaze out in several parts of the City ...'[53] On the night of the 9th, 'all night long there was nothing done but shooting of Bombs and Carcasses into the City'.[54]

On 23 July, Richards continued, the Duke sent the Ottoman governor of Buda a letter attached to the head of a pike in which he warned that 'he was ready to give a General Assault in which, if they succeeded, they would all be put to the sword, Man, Woman and Child'.[55] A final ultimatum followed on 31 July, delivered by the Duke's adjutant-general.

Richards noted: 'The Turks received him with great ceremony [and] ... he was presented with Rice, a roasted Pullet and little Pastries, with Coffee ... in a wooden lodging, adorned with carpets'.[56] The Ottoman garrison was determined to go down with the city, the governor saying he would willingly surrender any town in Hungary into Leopold's hands – but not Buda. When the Duke's emissary answered that he had not come to negotiate territory but only to surrender, 'the Basha made no other Answer but only shrugged up his shoulders remaining mute, like one that had been Thunder-struck'.

Still the end did not come immediately. The garrison hung on for a full month until at 3 p.m. on 2 September the Duke ordered a general assault. Even then, the imperial forces met 'obstinate resistance' at every stretch,[57] said Richards, and for around 45 minutes the Ottomans 'flung such an infinite Quantity of Stones, Arrows and Grenades'[58] that the offensive was slowed.

But with no relieving army in sight, the outcome was not in doubt. 'The Slaughter was very bloody', Richards recalled. 'Our Soldiers, having driven the Turks from the Defences, entered the City by main force, over-run the streets, put all to the Sword that encountered their fury, sparing neither age nor sex, so that there was nothing else to be seen but the dead bodies of the Slain.'[59]

Matthias's former palace finally collapsed, like Edgar Allan Poe's fictional House of Usher. The continual bombardment over the hot dry summer months had smashed much of it to pieces. Now the rest was set on fire.

But while from 5 p.m. that day the bulk of the imperial army busied themselves with the activities that normally followed an arduous siege, the 28-year-old Marsigli had a different objective. Born in Bologna, at an early age he had exhibited a talent for geometry and the sciences. Military matters fascinated him and as a teenager he had visited Constantinople to observe the flow of the currents in the Bosporus and the state of the Turkish fortifications, writing a treatise on the subject for Queen Christina of Sweden. In 1682, he resolved to put his many abilities to practical use, so he presented himself for service at the Habsburg court as an engineer and served his apprenticeship with the army at Gyor, where his skill at map-making brought him promotion. Strange things happened to Marsigli. As the Ottomans advanced into Hungary and towards Vienna the following year, for example, a band of Tartars captured the young Italian and transported him in fetters to Buda, from where he was sent to Sarajevo to work in an army tent, dispensing coffee to soldiers. The experience of being chained to a post and pouring the piping hot brew increased his loathing of the Ottomans though it made him a great fan of coffee, whose benefits he extolled in a book that he dedicated to Cardinal Buonvisi once he finally escaped in spring 1684 to Venetian-ruled Dalmatia.

Draughtsman, geographer, soldier, writer, historian and self-proclaimed expert on the Ottoman Empire, Marsigli was a dilettante intellectual, a seventeenth-century echo of the vagabond humanists of Matthias's era whose sense of adventure had led them to and fro across Europe, tacking from court to court like alien parasites, endlessly seeking patrons, dining with kings one minute and languishing in dungeons the next, their rollercoaster lives all too often ending calamitously.

'The book and the sword were both objects of his passionate love', wrote his eighteenth-century Italian biographer, Giovanni Fantuzzi, 'and so, having obtained information from other writers about the famous library once founded in Buda ... his soul was seized by worries concerning these treasures' depredation'.[60]

It might seem odd that Marsigli should still place any credence in the legends about the survival of the Corvinian library in the ruins of Buda but it is important to remember that many serious historians, Hungarians especially, well into the seventeenth century continued to dismiss any slighting remarks about the Corvinian library's disappearance as hostile and inaccurate 'German' propaganda.

Marsigli would have come across many people who had read the historical works of the Transylvanian chronicler Istvan Szamoskozy, who wrote also as Pal Enredy. Writing in the early seventeenth century, Szamoskozy said angrily: 'It is not true what the Germans wrote about the library ... and [how] all of it perished'. Against all the evidence he stoutly maintained that 'the library of King Matthias ... is still in Buda in its original place, having suffered no ravages'.[61]

Though weakened by wounds he had suffered during the siege, Marsigli asked permission of the Duke of Lorraine to go into Buda the day after it fell, 'and this being granted, amid the burning cinders and over enemy corpses lying in the streets he hurried to the main market that was still untouched by the flames'.

As Giovanni Fantuzzi related, 'he first reached a mosque that had served as the city's principal church, dedicated to St Stephen, when the castle was under Christian rule. On entering he found two interconnected chambers. In the centre of one, surrounded by manuscripts hurled around the place lay the body of the imam whose head had been not long ago cut off by the Emperor's soldiers'.[62]

In the church-turned-mosque he gathered up what he could of the books that the soldiers had strewn around, which turned out to be the Ottomans' local administrative records. After looking in on another mosque, he headed for the ransacked Jewish quarter whose residents had paid a heavy price for standing alongside the Ottoman defenders of the city. Again, Marsigli helped himself to more codices, this time with the help of the marauding soldiers who 'willingly gave Marsigli all the books, as they considered them useless loot and were ignorant of their true value'.[63]

This was only the hors-d'oeuvre, of course: Marsigli's real goal was Matthias's castle. Entering the smoking pile, Marsigli found himself standing in a room whose ceiling bore faded traces of astrological sequences. It sounds very much like the antechamber to the library, which was one of the rooms in the palace Matthias had had painted in this manner. Marsigli was among the last people to see the paintings. He was certainly the last man to both see them and understand their significance. Of course there was no sign now of the great globe that had once hung suspended from the ceiling. Nor was there any sign, once he had entered the adjoining chamber, of a couch or stained-glass windows. And naturally there was no sign of delicately illuminated manuscripts bound in leather and silk and held together with silver studs and clasps. There were in fact only torn old books scattered on the floor in the gloom among piles of shovels and pikes.

In the neighbouring chamber, presumably the second chamber of the library that had once housed the Greek manuscripts, Marsigli chanced on about ten large wooden chests. Each was five and a half feet long and one and a half feet wide and most of the lids were off, having taken a battering from the robbers who had prised them open, tearing off the heavy nails used to seal them shut. Evidently, thieves had hoped to find gold and silver inside and had been furiously disappointed to find moth-eaten books. These they had thrown around the floors of both chambers in disgust. The tattered volumes now lay at Marsigli's feet, mixed up with the tools that the robbers had used to rip open the chests.

Marsigli's expedition was a failure. It had, in fact, ended just like Lambeck's, 20 years earlier. For all the vagueness of the accounts of the library of Buda, Marsiglio knew that these miserable items were not the treasures that Bonfini, Naldi, Brassicanus, Olah and the others had described. As Marsigli recalled in a later essay on the library,

> I could not believe that what was lying in front of my eyes represented the remains of the once famous library.
>
> But although I looked carefully through all the other rooms in the palace, I found no traces of other books and thus came to the conclusion that what I had found were the library's [only] holdings at the start of the siege, when the books had been packed away to protect them from possible harm by fire, because they thought they would be safer in the vaulted chamber or, as I was told, because this was the hall of the old library and the books were put into chests there so that other parts of the hall could be used more conveniently.[64]

After about two hours of rifling around in the dust, Marsigli got some of the soldiers to help him pack up the books. He took a few for himself. The rest, numbering about 270, were loaded up for transport to the Hofbibliothek for inspection.

Lambeck was no longer there, having died in 1680. His successors confirmed what Marsigli already knew. Aside from the fact that none of the books was illuminated or bore the tell-tale emblem of the raven, the topics of these volumes did not match up with what was already known of the contents of Matthias's library. Naldi, among others, had insisted that Matthias's library had mainly comprised secular Greek and Roman classics, or as he put it, 'the proud Greek and the flourishing Latin'.[65] But most of Marsigli's finds were on religious topics. Altogether, about 147 of the 270 books were theological or ecclesiastical works, mainly treatises on canon law and on the Psalms. Only 117 were on secular topics. The librarians judged that Marsigli had chanced on the relics of the separate chapel library.

Naldi's poem had suggested that the chapel had been adjacent to the main library. 'Two sets of doors stand there [in the library], one of which lets everyone in and the other lets the King go out, whenever, placed in his private seat, he wishes to attend on his own to the sacred rites and the singing of hymns',[66] he wrote in De laudibus bibliothecae. Was this also the room where the Attavante missal had lain, into which Mary had rushed before hurriedly abandoning Buda in 1526, seizing the missal and a handful of other books before she went? Olah had also referred to the existence of other, smaller, libraries in the palace in Buda in his book Hungaria. He recalled: 'Apart from this [the main library], there were two other libraries in different parts of the citadel but they were inferior to it.'[67]

Francis Rensing, the imperial war commissary, said Marsigli's finds matched what was known of Matthias's collection 'neither in quality nor in quantity'. More recent historians have agreed. Csapodi suggested the books 'escaped the notice of looters and were left behind because Solyman [sic] and his retinue did not think it worthwhile to carry them off'.[68]

Marsigli was scantily rewarded for his noble intention. Shortly after he rescued the books from the burning castle, 'clouds of envy started to gather over [his] head', principally from the direction of the Duke of Baden, a general of Leopold's who had long nursed resentment of Marsigli. Charges against him reached the Emperor and were headed off only by the prompt action of the Duke of Lorraine. It was unfair. 'Least of all could he be called a grabber, or greedy', Beliczay wrote of Marsigli. 'No one could expect much else . . . than that he should help himself to a few volumes, taken more as a souvenir than for any other reason.'[69]

CHAPTER ELEVEN

The walls of the Seraglio

After centuries in which many people have yearned and searched in vain, we have seen them, held them.

Arnold Ipolyi, Constantinople, 1862[1]

In the entrance hall of the Hungarian National Museum in Budapest, a decorated frieze painted by Mor Than and Karoly Lotz between 1866 and 1875 runs round the ceiling, depicting the history of the Hungarians in a grand romantic sweep. Moving past the images of saints and scholars, the visitor's eye halts at panel number 34. Entitled 'Matthias and his scientists', it shows the great King seated and surrounded by books, instruments and a group of inventors.

The Magyar Nemzeti Muzeum is a temple to nineteenth-century nationalism. The brainchild of a benevolent aristocrat, Ferenc Szecheny, its foundation at the dawn of the nineteenth century both stimulated and reflected the awakening national consciousness of the Magyars, which was about to shake the Habsburg Empire to its foundations. When the present classical building was opened in 1847, it was only a year before Hungary slid into open warfare with the Emperor Francis Joseph. Months later, on 15 March 1848, Sandor Petofi, the youthful poet of the 1848 rebellion, proclaimed his newly composed 'national song' from the steps to an excited crowd. The refrain, 'Oh God of Hungarians, we swear unto thee, that slaves we will no longer be', was an open invitation to revolt.

Romantic nationalists were passionate about museums. They were all about history, and contemporary nationalists were convinced that 'the nation' could only assume its proper destiny once it had recovered its memory. The same preoccupation with collective memory fired the patriotic vogue for libraries, academies, historical societies, language movements and 'national' galleries. Unlike the private princely collections of the past, these were designed to be open to the public and to display educative, patriotic local works instead of the cosmopolitan collections of the elite. And whereas the princely collectors had cherished the small and the bijou, hence the fashion for miniatures, the nationalists tended towards ever more massive and monumental compositions – so useful for displays to crowds.

The vast artistic works of the era, with their simple pathos and raw emotion, remain the most popular exhibits in Budapest's National Gallery. A cluster of visitors is always to be found standing in a semicircle around Viktor Madarasz's 1859 composition, *The Bewailing of Laszlo Hunyadi*, which shows Matthias's mother, Erzsebet, mourning the death of her elder son, the victim of the spite of a young Habsburg king. The message of the painting was not lost on Hungarians in the 1850s, still mourning the Hungarian patriots shot at Arad in 1849 at the end of the lost war of independence on the orders of *their* young Habsburg King.

Madarasz executed his painting with its loaded theme at the end of a grim decade. With the aid of the proverbial Russian steamroller, the Hungarian revolt had been crushed and its leader, Lajos Kossuth, forced to flee abroad.

The 1850s were remembered as the decade of Alexander Bach, the middle-class bureaucrat who imposed an oppressive, centralised regime on the Empire, which relied a good deal on a busy and intrusive police force. This drive to restore absolutism put paid even to fairly innocent expressions of cultural activity. Until 1858, for example, the Hungarian Academy was not even able to hold plenary sessions, because no more than eight people were permitted to attend meetings.[2] Nationalism was not crushed, however: it was merely deprived of public expression. The policy of centralisation and absolutism identified with Bach had a provisional air to it. Everyone suspected the system would buckle as soon as the Empire experienced its next shock, which duly followed in 1859, when the restive northern Italian provinces revolted and a supportive French army massacred the Austrians at the Battle of Magenta.

By the time Madarasz won first prize in the Paris Exhibition of 1861 for his painting of the Hunyadis, therefore, Bach was already out of office and Franz Joseph was searching for a new accommodation with the restive Hungarians. Within a few years the Emperor had abandoned the policies of the 1850s altogether and granted Hungary its own responsible government. The old Austria disappeared, as the Empire was converted into a two-headed 'dual monarchy', the Austria-Hungary that was to last out the Emperor's life and which collapsed only under the strain of the First World War.

To many Hungarians the decades that followed the granting of home rule, from 1867 to 1918, were a golden age – 'the noon hour',[3] as John Lukacs put it, when the Hungarian capital rose like a phoenix, and at a pace and along lines that drew comparisons with Chicago. Buda and Pest disappeared into the new united city of Budapest in 1873. The year 1896 marked the zenith of this period, when the country was consumed with celebrations of the millennium of the Magyar conquest of the Danube basin. There was a great exhibition in Budapest, and the Emperor and Empress rode through the capital in a crystal-paned carriage.

If the age is suffused with golden memories it is because the descent was rapid. Dreams of national greatness collapsed with the outbreak of world war in 1914. From then on, for three-quarters of a century, one calamity followed another. With the end of the war came the defeat and collapse of Austria-Hungary and a savage territorial settlement. Curiously, although Hungary was the junior partner in the Empire, the victorious Entente powers treated the Hungarians even more brutally than the German Austrians. The Treaty of Trianon in 1920 left only one-third of the old Hungarian kingdom to the new independent Hungarian state and huge numbers of ethnic Magyars, including many living next to the new state, became unwilling citizens of Romania, Czechoslovakia and the Kingdom of Serbs, Croats and Slovenes, later renamed Yugoslavia. The whole of Transylvania, including Matthias's birthplace of Kolozsvar, now Cluj, went to Romania. So did a slice of eastern Hungary proper, including Vitez's former bishopric of Varad, which now became Oradea. Southern Hungary went to Serbia, with the border being placed well to the north of the ethnic boundary between the Serbs and Hungarians. The northern uplands of Hungary went to Czechoslovakia, as did Pozsony, which became Bratislava. A Faustian pact with Hitler in the 1930s succeeded in reversing some of those vast territorial losses, but only for a few uncertain years. After the Soviet Union invaded Hungary in 1944, it was clear the Romanians would recover the whole of Transylvania once more. Moreover, the Russian invasion was followed by the imposition of a particularly brutal form of communism in Hungary under Matyas Rakosi. A doomed uprising followed in 1956, after which Hungary passed several dreary, lobotomised decades under the Soviet Union's cynical placeman, Janos Kadar.

Even after Hungary recovered its own voice in 1990, the country's transition back to some kind of normality was hedged about with difficulties peculiar even by the standards of the former Soviet bloc. Real prosperity has eluded Hungary. The ghosts of 1956 and, further back, of the Trianon settlement, meanwhile, continue to rattle their chains. As the awkward atmosphere of the 50th anniversary commemoration of the 1956 uprising demonstrated, this was not a country totally at ease with itself.

The prolix nationalists of the 1830s might not have wailed so much about the horrors of Habsburg rule, therefore, had they had any premonition of the disasters that independence was to bring to Hungary. They had no idea that the great beneficiaries of the unravelling of the Empire would not be the Magyars but the Czechs, Slovaks, Romanians, Croats and Serbs.

That was not clear to Petofi's generation in the 1830s and 1840s. They saw only greatness ahead – a new Matthian age. Hence the sudden popularity of images and statues of the Hunyadis, Matthias having been recast in the public mind as a Magyar national hero.

Matthias had not been forgotten in the intervening years since Marsigli made his abortive attempt to discover the relics of the royal library. Throughout the eighteenth century, books on Hungary's history kept the memory and likeness of Matthias fresh in the minds of readers. The Augustinian historian Xystus Schier played a crucial role. His book, *De regiae Budensis bibliothecae Matthiae,* printed in Vienna in 1766 and reprinted in 1799, stimulated a new flowering of interest in the library.

But the level of interest in the eighteenth century was not what it had been a century before. Nor did it anticipate the degree of feeling on the subject after the national revival took off in Hungary, when demands began to be heard for the library to be returned and reassembled in Buda. From the time when this demand was first articulated in the 1800s to the 1870s, the resurrection of the library became something of a national obsession, so much so that when the Ottomans finally returned a number of books at the end of that decade, the city laid on a truly royal reception.

The irony of the whole affair was that Hungary was almost the only large or medium-sized country in Europe without a decent scattering of Corvinian works of its own. The more assertive parliaments of the 1830s and 1840s both recognised this problem and set out to remedy it. On 3 September 1844, the Hungarian parliament petitioned the Emperor in a filial but sly tone, reminding him that he had a substantial store of these treasures in Vienna and suggesting he might care to move some or all to the new National Museum. 'Amid the losses and misfortunes that have struck our homeland continuously over the course of the centuries, one of the most grievous is about the afore-mentioned library,' the parliamentary motion read, 'of which partly as a result of carelessness and extravagance after the memorable King's death, and partly on account of the savage rage of destructive enemies, who did not feel the value of the treasure they held in their hand, the nation now does not own a single item.'

The parliament went on:

> As it is known that some of the remains of King Matthias's glorious library, from different places and via different routes and at different times, made their way into the imperial library in Vienna and are being kept there . . . Your Majesty might deign on the one hand to mercifully order their extradition to the National Museum, and on the other, to recover the letters and records . . . concerning Hungary's affairs and history that for centuries have been locked away in the libraries and archives of the Vatican in Rome, of Berlin, Venice and Florence.

It was not quite true, as the parliament asserted, that none of Matthias's books remained in Hungary. Some great magnate families did possess a few works. Miklos Jankovich, a passionate antiquarian who delighted in 'plucking from the abyss of oblivion the heroic deeds of our ancestors',[4] donated two to the National Museum in the early 1840s, Quintus Curtius Rufus's *History of Alexander the Great,* which Cennini had copied in 1467, and Ransano's *Epithoma rerum Hungararum.* The Draskovics, one of the great magnate families of Croatia, also owned at least one, a work by the fourth-century bishop Hilarius on the Trinity, which is now the sole Corvinian manuscript in Croatia, in the National Library in Zagreb.

But most Hungarians thought this was insufficient compensation for the loss of a vast collection, which according to the prevalent legend had once contained 30,000 or even 50,000 volumes. It is easy to comprehend the indignation of the Hungarian patriots of the 1830s, therefore, at the paltry size of this remnant. Why did libraries in far-off Modena, Florence, Wolfenbüttel and, of course, Vienna possess whole portions of the famous Bibliotheca Corviniana, while the city that had once been its home had almost nothing?

Initially, Prince Metternich tried to help them. In spite of his reputation as the reactionary architect of the post-Napoleonic settlement, he was more conciliatory to the Empire's burgeoning national movements than he is sometimes given credit for. In the 1830s, Metternich encouraged the first faint stirrings of Croatian nationalism, if only to balance its Hungarian counterpart. At much the same time, he sought to appease Hungarian sensibilities by trying to recover some of the lost Corvinian works that Suleiman had hoarded away in Constantinople. The attempt ended in failure because the deputy head of the mission in Constantinople to whom Metternich entrusted the task in 1836 reported that he had found nothing.

Metternich returned to the fray in 1847. This time, instead of chasing shadows in Constantinople he concentrated on a more tangible target, the library of the Estes, which, as we have seen, held seventeen Corvinian works. After pressure was applied, the Duke, Francis V, agreed to return two of Matthias's books from his collection, the Attavante Chrysostom codex and the copy of Hieronymus's commentaries on St Paul, illustrated by the Di Giovanni brothers. They made their way to Vienna that autumn. Unfortunately for the fate of this initiative the books were soon forgotten, as a revolution broke out in Vienna in spring 1848. The imperial family fled to Tyrol and Metternich fled to England. The books, meanwhile, got to Vienna and remained there. It was only in 1891 that the Emperor finally handed them over to the Hungarian National Museum.

It was hardly surprising that progress in the business of recovering the Corvinas was slow. The Hungarians wanted *something* back but what they wanted and where it might be found they were not entirely sure. The mythology that had surrounded the library for so long confused people. Men continued to believe that the library had been gargantuan in size. They had read Naldi's 'praises of the august library' and cited it as an exact source of information. And Naldi had claimed that although the library of Asinius Pollio had 'once amassed ... thrice five thousand, if you counted them properly, yet Matthias has now followed them to no less an extent'.[5] That suggested 15,000 volumes. After Matthias's death, and especially after the fall of Buda to the Turks, the figure continued its remorseless ascent.

Writers in the seventeenth and eighteenth centuries had merely increased the scale. The Dutch writer Johann Lomeier's[6] much-admired – and frequently plagiarised – survey of European librarianship of 1669, *De bibliothecis liber singularis*, had boldly asserted that 'sparing no expense, [Matthias] established a great library where more than 50,000 printed books

and manuscripts were preserved'.[7] Julius Pflugk's account of the fate of
Matthias's library from 1688, *Epistola ad vitum Ludovicum a Seckendorff
... praeter fata bibliothecae Budensis*, had insisted that the library had
contained a *minimum* of 50,000 works.[8] Ugoleto's biographer, Ireneo Affo,
in 1781 had said Matthias exhibited 'so much fervour to accumulate rare
books in a library that it grew in a few years up to 50,000 volumes'.[9]
Likewise, Schier's *Dissertatio de regiae Budensis bibliothecae*. The British
writer Thomas Dibdin, who wrote about the library at length in the
Biographical Decameron of 1817, insisted that the number of volumes
contained in this 'wonderful collection' might be 'safely computed at thirty
thousand'.[10]

In the late 1830s, Henry Hallam sounded a more cautious note, stating
that the benchmark figure of 50,000 'must have been exaggerated'. Nevertheless, he, too, was reluctant to tackle the mystique of the library, and
described its dispersal as amongst the severest blows ever to have been
inflicted on European culture. 'It is possible that neither the burning of the
Alexandrian library ... nor any other single calamity recorded in history,
except the two captures of Constantinople itself, has been more fatally
injurious to literature', he wrote.[11] Other writers clung to the semi-magical
figure of 50,000 for decades, apparently unaware that few scholars now took
it seriously. Among them was Gertrude Rawlings, whose *Story of Books*,
published in 1901, regarded the old legend as gospel truth. The library of the
King of Hungary, she wrote with confidence, 'contained nearly fifty
thousand volumes, but only a comparatively small number survived the
barbarous attack of the Turks who stole the jewels from the bindings and
destroyed the books themselves'.[12]

Most writers on the Corvinian collection, whether from Hungary or
abroad, began from the same set of assumptions. They knew that Matthias
Corvinus had built a tremendous library. They knew the writings of Naldi,
Bonfini and Schier on the subject and were generally familiar with a handful
of famous works from the library, such as the Philostratus. But as to what
the rest of the library had contained, what was left of it and where those
relics might be found, they had little clue. Most of the cultured gentlemen
and prelates of the Hungarian parliament who now demanded the library's
return or restoration had never set eyes on a single Corvinian work.

As we have seen, the initial drive to recover the library ground to a halt in
the 1850s, until the disaster of Magenta embarrassed the policy of absolutism
and the need to reach a new arrangement with the nationalities again asserted

itself. The terms of the dualist compromise, which divided the Empire into two, had to wait until 1867, by which time Franz Joseph had suffered a second, shattering defeat at Sadowa, this time at the hands of Prussia.

But from 1861, the various diets and assemblies of the Empire had been restored and from that year on the campaign in Hungary to reconstitute Matthias's library recovered momentum. It was also the decade when interest revived in Constantinople as the probable location of much or even all of the lost library. This was the result of the efforts of a new generation of young middle-class historians, who were not satisfied with the outcome of Metternich's investigation of the Seraglio in the 1830s.

Floris Romer was an outstanding pioneer in this search. A Benedictine monk, he had ended up fighting in the revolutionary war of 1848–49 in which he gained the rank of captain. Jailed for several years in the Bach era, he emerged to become one of the country's greatest historians and archaeologists, before dying in 1889 in Oradea, where he held the rank of canon in Vitez's former see. By then he had countless provincial museums all over Hungary, many of an ethnographic character. In 1861, while living in Gyor, Romer also discovered a lost Corvinian work, a topographical description of Rome, the *Romae instauratae libri III,* of the fifteenth-century Italian historian Flavio Biondo, or Flavius Blondus, which Pietro Cennini had copied in July 1467.[13]

That was the start of a decade of discoveries. More sensationally, in 1862, three Hungarian scholars, Ferenc Kubinyi, the head of the National Museum, Arnold Ipolyi, a priest and art historian, and Imre Henszlmann, an art historian and archaeologist,[14] finally penetrated the inner recesses of the Seraglio. In contradiction to the report of the Austrian mission in 1836, they had also come across a treasure trove of indisputably Corvinian manuscripts.

The discovery was almost accidental. The initial aim of Kubinyi's visit to the Ottoman Empire was not to track down Matthias's books but to visit the burial places of various heroes from the war of independence who, like Kossuth, had taken refuge there. Ipolyi altered the purpose of the trip, persuading him that a conclusive search of the hidden recesses of the Seraglio might be more worthwhile. They set off without much of a clue as to what they might find there, however. As Ipolyi recalled in 1878, they felt 'like Columbus searching for the New World'.[15]

The mission was a daring one. In 1862, the authorities in Vienna were still nervous about Hungary. The repressive atmosphere of the Bach era had not entirely dissipated and many of its former lieutenants still saw seditious motives even in the most abstract scientific undertakings. They did not oppose attempts to recover the Corvinus library in Constantinople; they simply did not believe this was the true purpose of the visit. They suspected it was a cover for a mission to smuggle back the ashes of Ferenc Rakoczi, hero of an earlier revolt against the Habsburgs in the 1700s who had died in Rodosto – now Tekirdug – in Thrace, in 1735.

The Hungarians left Buda under a cloud of official suspicion, having packed gold chains as presents for the Sultan and some antique Hungarian robes for their hoped-for reception, and they were far from certain that the Turks would be at all friendly. As they reported to the Academy, they feared the Ottoman authorities in Constantinople in the 1860s would be just as reluctant to reveal their looted treasures to hostile or inquisitive European eyes as their counterparts in Buda had been generations earlier. They knew about the contemptuous way the Sultan had treated the Prince of Transylvania's request to obtain some of Matthias's books back in the seventeenth century.

But the Sultan was a far weaker figure now, and less inclined to deny the requests of foreign visitors. To their delight, the Corvina-hunters received a lavish welcome from the Foreign Minister, Fuad Pasha, who warned them that over the years many of the codices kept in Constantinople had perished in various fires, but also promised to open all the doors the visitors required.

'Finally, the great day arrived,' Ipolyi recalled, and on 21 May 1862 the three men were escorted into the Treasury with a good deal of pomp, strolling past piles of treasures collected over many centuries from various parts of the world and deposited there. However, the officials did not show them the library, and to their fury, in spite of the pledges of the Foreign Minister, they attempted to bring the visit to a close before the visitors had even set eyes on the room they had journeyed so far to see. 'Disappointed and tricked, we were forced to put decency aside', Ipolyi recalled. 'We warned him [the principal official] that this was not what we had come for.' There was one last evasive manoeuvre on the part of the palace guards, who now led the Hungarians off into a small library. Again, they knew this chamber was not the inner sanctum they sought. But then the veil was pulled aside at last. As Ipolyi recalled, 'Suddenly, the curtains of the door lifted and out in the foyer we caught sight of servants carrying codices covered in purple. Seeing them our hearts quivered; we wanted to scream . . . we had reached our goal!'[16]

The words were not out of place. For generations, men had dreamed of stumbling across the priceless library of the Raven King, though no one had been totally sure what it was or where it was to be found. Constantinople had been something of a last resort. For a second or two, Ipolyi was convinced that the joker had turned out to be the ace. But now, as the detectives bent over to inspect their discovery, they found the prize was smaller than they might have hoped. There were, in fact, no more than a handful of Corvinian works in the pile, six at the most. A little crestfallen, they begged the Ottoman officials to go back and search for a little longer. But this time the palace guards were adamant. They insisted there were no more books of the kind the three men sought. The visit was over.

Ipolyi hurried back to his lodgings, mingled feelings of frustration and elation battling it out in his soul. It was not the outcome he had dreamed of. And yet the day's discovery had put the efforts of most previous hunters well into the shade. The world needed to know. Ipolyi began scribbling frantically: to Archbishop Bartakovics, his ecclesiastical superior, to the *Pesti Naplo* newspaper and to his friend and colleague, Ferenc Toldy, director of the National Library.

'Hooray!' his letter to Toldy began. 'We have come upon King Matthias's library! . . . After many disappointments, by which time we wanted to give up altogether, today, finally, from the secret and hidden library of the Old Seraglio we discovered codices covered in purple with silver clasps, ornamented with miniature crests of Hungary and King Matthias.

'Only a few [have been found] so far', he conceded. 'But now it is enough that what no eye has seen and no hand has touched, after centuries in which many people have yearned and searched in vain, we have seen, and held.'[17]

Unsurprisingly, Ipolyi and his colleagues resolved not to leave Constantinople before paying another visit to the Seraglio, which took several days to organise. Again, to their frustration, they were not given free rein to rummage among the shelves of the main library themselves but were ushered into a room where the palace officials had laid out about 50 codices for them to inspect. To add to the unbearable tension, they gave them only a couple of hours to look at the books and take notes.

After the Ottomans had assured them that this second pile of books assuredly did not contain any works from the library of Matthias Corvinus, the Hungarians found at least nine that were clearly decorated with the familiar blue raven or with the arms of Hungary. The discovery strengthened them in the conviction that they had not yet cleared up the mystery.

Ipolyi and his two friends now began poring over the ground plans of the Seraglio, certain that there had to be another room, of whose existence they were unaware, where Matthias's treasures were stored. They sought to obtain clues in the condition of the books they had been allowed to see already. Some were damp and with mouldy covers. This suggested that they had been kept on the floor. Were the rest, then, in the palace basement? Perhaps the Ottoman officials had felt ashamed to show Europeans around such shoddy premises, the three men mused. Then again, perhaps the books were being stored in a room that contained some holy relics of the Prophet Muhammad into which no infidel could be permitted to enter.

At one point they hired a boat and bobbed around on the Bosporus, weaving between the fishermen's junks, trying to work out the precise layout of the palace from the water by counting the number of windows.

The theories multiplied, but to no purpose. The Ottomans had opened the doors of the Seraglio a mite only to teasingly close them once more. The three men were not allowed back for a third visit and left the city on the 31st.

After the publication of their findings, their subsequent correspondence with the German expert Andreas Mordtmann made them yet more certain that many other Corvinian works remained undiscovered in Constantinople. Mordtmann, who came from Hamburg, worked in Constantinople as the envoy of the Hanseatic League. A bibliophile, he had been exploring the same areas of the Seraglio as the Hungarians just before they showed up, looking for the remnants of the library of the former Byzantine emperors. Mordtmann was a perceptive man of wide tastes and during his searches for the imperial library his eye had alighted on several books that he had recognised as Corvinian manuscripts. Thoughtfully, he had noted down the titles.

When Mordtmann heard of the discoveries of the three Hungarians, he wrote to them, suggesting they swap lists. The results were revealing and exciting because the two lists of Corvinian manuscripts were very different. It was clear, in other words, that the palace officials had not shown the Hungarians everything after all.

The 1860s had seen a breakthrough in Constantinople. But there was no sign yet of the Sultan returning the relics of the Bibliotheca Corviniana to Hungary. There was also no sign that the other individuals or corporations in Europe then in possession of Matthias's books were minded to relinquish them. The British Museum had no intention of surrendering its copy of Horace, for example. Emperor Franz Joseph, who was King of Hungary, had also put no pressure on the Hofbibliothek in Vienna to transfer a single Corvinian manuscript to Hungary. The only hopeful sign of movement came in 1867, when the Sultan, harassed by the clamour of voices from all over Europe demanding to see the library as well, allowed the Hungarian Academy to send a second delegation.

This concession caused a great deal of excitement, as the Academy reported in its notes for 1867. They had 'received this piece of news with enthusiastic joy', they noted. 'At last, we can hope to clear up the history of the world famous library and also examine the remains believed to exist in Constantinople', they went on. 'How would posterity and the nation judge the Academy and the nation if this [opportunity] were to be missed?'[18]

What brought about the return of almost all remaining Corvinian manuscripts from Constantinople within only a few years of 1867 was the drama known as the 'Eastern Crisis'. The partial collapse of the Ottoman Empire did indeed 'clear up the history' of Matthias's books in the Seraglio and ensured that most were repatriated.

The position of the Ottomans in Europe had become less and less tenable throughout the first half of the nineteenth century. Stretching from Albania on the Adriatic through Bosnia and Herzegovina, Macedonia, southern Serbia and Bulgaria to Constantinople itself, the Sultan's domains still comprised a large but exposed portion of the south-east of the continent. The great powers were in the main indifferent to whether the Turks held on to the Balkans or not. But Tsarist Russia had a more interventionist agenda and its obvious ambitions to gain Constantinople and control the Straits had alerted Europe, Britain in particular, to the importance of 'managing' the decline of what was now called Europe's 'Sick Man'.

The Sultans, too, were aware of the fact that isolation was no longer an option, and that only playing one power off against another might preserve their empire in Europe from disintegration, or at least slow down the process. Initially the Ottoman authorities were quite successful in this. After the loss of some – but not much – territory to the new states of Greece and Serbia in the early decades of the nineteenth century, they clung on to the rest, playing on the fears of the great powers about each other and about Russian expansionism.

But by the 1860s the Ottomans confronted a new and unfavourable constellation in Europe. Democratic and nationalist ideas were spreading fast among the once docile Balkan peasantry, making the prospect of organised, large-scale revolts more likely. At the same time, opinion in

Europe had shifted strongly in favour of the rights of 'oppressed' nationalities, which made suppressing revolts more dangerous. There was always the likelihood of Russian intervention, given the Tsars' role as self-proclaimed protectors of the Ottomans' Orthodox Christians.

The Sultans, therefore, became increasingly conscious of the need to placate Austria, their other traditional enemy. Austria's position *vis-à-vis* the Ottomans was more nuanced than Russia's. Unlike Russia, whose appetite for territory remained boundless, the Habsburg monarchy's foreign policy after 1867 was complicated by the need to set Austro-German considerations against those of the newly assertive Magyars. Dualism meant sacrificing the interest of some nationalities to please others.

The Ottomans were aware that the condition of the Dual Monarchy was almost as delicate as their own. They were also aware that the Hungarians were viscerally hostile to Russia because of its role in crushing Hungary in 1849, and to Slav nationalism in general on account of the threat it posed to Hungary's territorial integrity. Abdulaziz, who became Sultan in 1861, observed the furore created in Hungary as a result of the academics' expedition to Constantinople in 1862. He had also noted the remarkable change in Hungarian attitudes towards 'the Turks' as a result of their concerns about Serbia.

The Sultan's first opportunity to capitalise on the growing pro-Turkish sentiment in the eastern half of the Dual Monarchy came in 1869, when the Suez Canal was ceremonially opened. A clutch of royal personages, headed by the Empress Eugénie of France, several Dutch and Prussian princes and the Emperor Franz Joseph, travelled to Ottoman Egypt for the great event. On his way to Egypt through Constantinople, the Sultan presented the Emperor with an unexpected gift: the four Corvinian works that the Hungarian academics had spotted in the Seraglio in 1862.

The gesture was a well-aimed one. Even if the somewhat philistine Emperor had no personal interest in the gift (his voluminous correspondence with the Empress during the visit, full of rhapsodies about the beauty of veiled women did not mention it) but he had the diplomatic sense to donate the books at once to the Hungarian National Museum on his return.

Their arrival created a tremendous stir, stimulating an appetite among the public for the rest of the books to be found, and bolstering the illusion that thousands of these books still lurked undetected. As the historian Ferenc Toldy declared at the time, the four recovered books were 'not the most precious' for countless others were surely 'still hidden behind the walls of the Seraglio. Everything must be there . . . the maiden is not dead; she is just asleep.'[19]

The first phase of the Eastern Crisis had produced a small crop of books for Hungary. The subsequent, more violent stage produced a bigger windfall. The immediate cause was a long-expected revolt against the Ottomans in the Balkans, which gave Russia the excuse to invade. The rebellion started in July 1875 in a remote corner of eastern Herzegovina. By the time it spread to Bulgaria the following spring it was clear the Ottoman Empire faced a serious crisis. It was a massive challenge to the new sultan, Murad V, who acceded to the throne in the chaotic summer months of 1876, following the deposition in May of Abdulaziz.

The new Sultan's dilemma was acute because the great powers were far less sympathetic than they had been. Even traditionally friendly England, the great rival of Russia's, felt alienated. Liberal English opinion was outraged by the violent methods the Turks used in Bulgaria, and William Gladstone, leader of the Liberal opposition, barnstormed the country – to the disgust of Queen Victoria – delivering harangues about the 'Bulgarian massacres' and calling for the expulsion of the Ottomans from Europe 'bag and baggage'.

Nor could Austria be counted on. Relations between Vienna and St Petersburg, unfortunately for the Sultan, were unusually cordial. In defiance of popular opinion among Hungarians and German liberals the Emperor had decided to use the Eastern Crisis to annex Bosnia and Herzegovina. Partly this was to shore up the Empire's profile as a great power; partly it was because he believed Austrian rule over Dalmatia was untenable without control of the Bosnian hinterland. He certainly did not want to see Bosnia and Herzegovina, with its large Serbian population, falling into the hands of restive, ambitious Serbia.

The Hungarians, however, felt as hostile as ever they had to Slavic agitation in the Ottoman Empire and to Russia. Magyars had no interest in helping to maintain Austria's prestige or 'mission'. The less prestigious and confident that Austria was the better, so far as Hungarians were concerned. History had taught them that only a humbled Austria allowed them to get their way. They were not touched by Austria's strategic concerns in Dalmatia. The Turks now enjoyed Hungarian sympathy. They were the great enemies of Russia and, *ipso facto*, Hungary's friend. Feelings of bitterness over the Battle of Mohacs and the century and a half of Ottoman rule had long since dissolved. In any case, Hungarians attributed the fall of the Hungarian kingdom mainly to the avarice of their own nobles and the indolence of the two kings who had followed Matthias on the throne. As the Hungarian statesman, Gyula Andrassy, put it in 1875, the Ottoman Empire 'possesses a utility almost providential for Austria-Hungary, for Turkey maintains the status quo of the small Balkan states and impedes their aspirations. If it was not for Turkey, all those aspirations would fall down on our heads'. He added: 'If Bosnia-Herzegovina should go to Serbia or Montenegro ... we should be ruined and should ourselves assume the role of the "Sick Man".'[20]

The summer of 1876 saw the Eastern Crisis enter a new, deadlier phase. On 2 July, Serbia and Montenegro declared war on the Sultan. The move aroused almost hysterical enthusiasm among the Pan-Slav party in Russia and equally spirited fury among Hungarians, who staged large pro-Turkish demonstrations. A crowd of about 12,000 took to the streets of the capital in the first week of October, presenting a ceremonial sword to the Ottoman commander Abdul Kerim. They even composed a popular song, 'Abdul Kerim has sent word', while the composer Ignac Szabadi Frank wrote a Turkish march and a delegation of students travelled to Constantinople in order to encourage their new allies to resist.

The Sultan faced an appalling strategic dilemma, for he was damned if he won *and* if he lost. If the Serbs and Bulgarians defeated him, the whole of Turkey-in-Europe would be lost. But if the Sultan humiliated the Serbs, outraged Russia stood ready to intervene on behalf of its Balkan protégé.

This latter scenario was the one that unfolded on 1 September 1876, after the Ottomans had crushed the Serbian army at Aleksinac. On 10 October, the Tsar wrote to Francis Joseph, treating war as inevitable and encouraging Austria-Hungary to join in the spoils. The English made a vain attempt to stop the slide to war by means of a conference held at Constantinople in December. But it broke up on 20 January 1877 without result. Russia had by now raised the stakes so high that to withdraw appeared inconceivable without a terrible loss of face. After the German Chancellor Bismarck assured Russia of German neutrality in a war between Turkey and Russia and of his determination not to lose 'one Pomeranian soldier'[21] over the Balkans – and after England had abandoned the fray, with Lord Salisbury admitting that continued defence of the Ottomans was 'impracticable'[22] – the die was cast.

War followed in April 1877 as expected, though it did not end in the complete annihilation of the Ottomans, as so many observers had predicted.

Instead, they held out against the Russians in the fortress of Plevna. By the time the Russians had forced Plevna to surrender in December 1877, had taken Edirne and were finally ready to advance on Constantinople, the English had moved battleships into the Straits to warn them off. Another messy compromise was then hammered out at the Berlin conference of 1878, where the powers approved Austria-Hungary's 'occupation' of Bosnia and Herzegovina and the creation of a new Bulgarian principality. At the same time, the Sultan preserved the balance of his European possessions and could breathe again.

But if Francis Joseph plucked Bosnia and Herzegovina out of the Eastern Crisis of 1878 – a dubious gain, as it turned out – the Hungarians made a rather more lasting gain with respect to the library of Matthias Corvinus.

After Abdulaziz's successor, Murad V, was hauled from the throne in September 1876 after only a few months, his successor, Abdul Hamid, restored Abdulaziz's policy of wooing the Hungarians with the promise of books. In April 1877 he ordered a new and more thorough search of the Seraglio for remnants of the library and, after finding 35 hopeful manuscripts, he ordered his adjutant, Tahir Bey, to escort them to Budapest and personally present them to the nation.

In the event, this was impossible. The authorities in Vienna, secretly in league with Russia, had no desire to see high Turkish officials receiving ovations in the second city of the Empire. Tahir Bey was not permitted to undertake his triumphal journey to Budapest and pressure was put on the Hungarian government to ensure the event was as low-key as humanly possible.

They did not succeed. Without Tahir Bey, the codices arrived by train at the end of April in a city that was determined to make the most of the affair. At the railway station, the codices were lifted on to a bier and escorted to the university, where a large crowd of civic and academic dignitaries was waiting to receive them. Moreover, while the crown's loyal ministers in Hungary felt obliged to abide by instructions to play down the Ottoman gesture, neither the opposition nor the general public felt remotely bound by this injunction. They hailed the arrival of the 35 codices (15 of which were positively identified as Corvinas) as enormously significant political as well as cultural symbols.

'They proclaim Hungary's former glory,' the opposition newspaper *Egyteres* declared, 'which even in its decline left behind books as former relics. They proclaim justice, which died out with the King . . . they proclaim the power of concerted national effort, when Hungary was the first nation in Europe and gave orders in Vienna.' The newspaper continued: 'What would Vienna be, compared to Budapest, if providence had given Hungary more Matthiases? We had only one Matthias who died in Vienna. With him, justice was lost. He died because of a rotten fig, providing us with an everlasting symbol that whatever originates from there is lethal poison for Hungarians.'[23]

The bitter tone, so evident in the pages of the opposition newspapers, was less obvious in the pages of the pro-government *A Hon*. Nevertheless, this, too, spoke of the returning Corvinian works in a fairly similar way, likening Matthias's rediscovered manuscripts to 'bright pieces of a meteor from an enormous body, scattered to the four winds'.[24]

The return of the books inspired the greatest demonstration of love for Turkey that a free European people had ever laid on. It took on its own peculiar quality precisely because it was unofficial and because Vienna disapproved. As the weekly *Vasarnapi Ujsag* reported on 6 May: 'A capital can only rarely, and on great occasions, boast of an event so huge as the reception of the Turkish guests. Even the Turks themselves never dreamed of such a welcoming, which the pen cannot describe.' It went on: 'Everyone has taken part with joy, great and small, young and old, men and women; it is only so called "official Hungary" that does not want to acknowledge it.' The newspaper continued: 'Wherever they go, people wave their shawls and raise their hats to salute them.'

It was not only the citizens of the capital who saluted the return of the remnants of the lost library, much as if it were the body of King Matthias himself. The provincial towns and cities scrambled to send delegates to Budapest to take part in the round of ceremonies and fired off telegrams serenading the virtues of the Ottoman Turks. Thousands of people lined the railway tracks as the books passed through Timisoara and Szeged, many overcome with the emotion of it all. At Timisoara, where the local authorities had forbidden people even to approach the railway station, they ignored the prohibition. According to the *Vasarnapi Ujsag*, 'by the time the train arrived, the public had already broken in'.

In Budapest, thousands streamed into the railway station on 29 April to see the train bearing Matthias's books pull in at 11.30 a.m. The station could not accommodate them and they spilled into the nearby Vaci Street and Deak Square. Another crowd massed around the entrance to the Hotel Hungaria, where the Turkish delegation was due to stay. Thousands lined the windows and balconies to observe the procession of carriages that took the Turkish visitors from the railway station to their hotel; here the first in a series of banquets was held on 30 April, to which more than 300 guests were invited and where the orchestra alternated between Turkish and Hungarian marches. Hungary and Turkey saluted one another in the florid toasts that followed, one of which came from a representative of the students of the university, who called for an Ottoman victory in the titanic struggle against unholy Russia.

That night there was another tremendous popular demonstration at the theatre, where the packed audience gave one ovation after another and the lead singer began incorporating into her song various *ad hoc* greetings to the Turks sitting in the audience. 'They clapped, cheered, waved their shawls for minutes and then Soldos had to repeat the song twice while the noisy ovation was also repeated twice', the newspapers reported. The head of the Turkish delegation attempted to respond adequately to the cheers by hurling his large diamond ring on to the stage, but was prevented from doing so by a polite warning that it might cause total pandemonium.

The ceremonies were far from over. The next day, Floris Romer officially welcomed the Ottoman delegation to the National Museum, after which they set off for parliament to hear the deputies propose a vote of thanks to Sultan Abdul Hamid for his benevolence; this was passed unanimously. Then they were off to the university, and back again to the Hotel Hungaria for another banquet, this time hosted by the city corporation under the mayor. Telegrams were read out from all over Hungary, poets recited their odes, a great many glasses were raised and the Ottomans offered a salute of their own to the Hungarians, those 'good friends to oppressed and threatened but valiant nations and who hate Russia with all their hearts, recognising it as the representative of barbarous tyranny'. The evening finished back at the theatre, where there were yet more ovations and cheering.

The remainder of the visit was something of an anticlimax. How could it not be? One member of the Ottoman delegation composed a poem on the theme of the rekindled love between Hungarians and Turks; they all did a little shopping in Budapest; they looked in on the zoo. The last night of the visit on 4 May was an occasion for a final, more modest, banquet at the Hungaria followed by a last visit to the theatre, this time by torchlight through the streets. The delegation left the next day, unable to accept any of the countless invitations they had received to honour the country's smaller towns and cities. The capital fairly glowed. Most of its residents had never seen anything like it; certainly not since the great days of 1848.

The Sultan got little in return for surrendering the books. When Russia declared war at the end of April, Austria-Hungary, having signed its secret protocol with the Tsar over Bosnia, stood aside. The passionate goodwill the Hungarians now felt towards Turkey made no appreciable difference to the outcome. All that can be said is that it partially righted a historical wrong and wiped away what remained of the former animosity between Hungarians and Turks. A significant part of the great king's patrimony had been recovered. It was 'home' at last.

It was not quite the end of the story. Books continued to be discovered and to move around. After the First World War, the terms of the peace settlement resulted in a number of Matthias's books moving from Austria to Hungary, and also from Hungary to Italy – and then back again – thanks to the Italian dictator Mussolini's decision to bring Hungary out of its post-war diplomatic isolation. The return of the two books from Italy in January 1927 – the same two illustrated by Attavante and Cherico that Metternich had prised away from the Prince of Modena in 1847 – caused a renewed flurry of excitement both at home and abroad. It was a last echo of the turbulence roused by the Sultan's return of the manuscripts of the Seraglio in 1877. *Time* magazine boldly declared, without much foundation, that the return of the two manuscripts, which it grandly described as 'the twin diadems of the library of the great Matthias Corvinus', was the first step towards the imminent restoration of the Habsburgs to the throne of Hungary.[25] It was no such thing. It merely paved the way for the signing of a pact between the two countries that April.

The return of the two works to Hungary delighted many Hungarians and inspired a burst of poetic prose from Jozsef Fogel, the Hungarian historian who had discovered 13 Corvinas lying hidden in the Nationalbibliothek in Vienna in the early 1920s. Warming to the theme of Matthias's celebrated raven, he wrote: 'Fly high, loyal bird, fly to the sky, fly over the Alps. You know your way. Take our thanks to all those who feel the aches of our dismembered country.'[26]

Notwithstanding Fogel's emotive language, there was no repeat of the public delirium that the return of the books from Constantinople had inspired half a century earlier. Nor was there in 1932, when Austria returned a further 16 Corvinian works. The mythology surrounding the Corvinian library had lost most of its power. No one now believed that the return of a set of ancient books was going to usher in a new age of greatness. The events of recent years had shown that. As Fogel remarked, Hungary had been dismembered, losing two-thirds of its territory under the Treaty of Trianon. The rump Hungary that remained was consumed by the desire for revenge but under no illusion that it was in a position to do much about it. National greatness was out of the question now – library or no library.

At the same time the Bibliotheca Corviniana shrank in its proportions in people's minds, thanks to modern scholarship. New professional historians like Fraknoi and Romer demolished the fantasy that Matthias's library could ever have held 50,000 or even 30,000 volumes. In the last quarter of the nineteenth century and the early years of the twentieth, the figure was revised remorselessly downwards. Romer put it at 5,000 in the 1870s, while Fraknoi lowered it further in the 1900s to between 1,000 and 3,000. Fogel put it still lower in 1927, at 'around five hundred'.[27] That was the low-water mark. Most recent historians have settled on Csapodi's preferred figure of about 2,500,[28] which he based in part on the maximum number of manuscripts that he thought could have been produced in Florence between 1485 and 1490.

It was not only the imagined dimensions of the library that were brutally exposed to harsh daylight. For generations, the illusion had also been maintained that the contents of the library were perfect translations. Men had invested the library books with almost superhuman qualities. The mystique surrounding the codices increased after they fell behind Ottoman lines in the sixteenth century, after which the collection became a sort of bibliographical El Dorado in western eyes. But after the 1870s, when Hungarian scholars first came into possession of a number of Corvinian works, it became obvious that the works were more flawed than anyone had imagined. Scholars like Jeno Abel in the late 1870s began to claim that the surviving books were, in fact, riddled with errors. Jeno described many of the Latin translations done for Matthias as 'worthless'.

After 1877 it was also no longer possible to believe that a great mass of Corvinian works remained undiscovered. It was simply incredible now to maintain 'the maiden slept' in Constantinople or anywhere else. The world had to accept that what remained was a few hundred books, scattered around Europe and America.

Only a few diehards cherished the conviction that another portion of the King's library in Buda remained inviolate elsewhere. The Ottoman Empire covered a vast area until the end of the First World War and it was just possible, in the minds of some scholars, that the books had been transported from Constantinople across the deserts to a more distant metropolis. Baghdad was the favourite option. As the French historian Hevesy wrote, 'An ancient tradition held that part of the deposit from Buda had been transported there.'[29] In 1877, the Austro-Hungarian ambassador to the Sultan, Count Ferenc Zichy, had asked a French consul in Baghdad, named Destrees, to look into the matter.[30]

If some of Matthias's books ever were stored there, they are not there now. The British have a history of inept interference in Mesopotamia. Several decades before George Bush and Tony Blair launched the 'war on terror' in the first decade of the twenty-first century, British troops were bumbling around these lands, claiming they were there to 'liberate' the Arabs from Ottoman rule. Then, as later, the results were mixed. Among the casualties of the fighting between British and Ottoman forces in Baghdad in 1917 was the university library, which is where some scholars believed – or rather hoped – it was just possible that some of Matthias's books were kept. As de Hevesy put it, 'The last hope of rediscovering a compact group of Corvinas disappeared.'[31]

'Matjaz will ride out'

The road to Crna, a village on the Slovene border with Austria, runs along the *vinska cesta*, an undulating highway that starts at the town of Maribor and is lined with vineyards, as its Slovene name suggests.

It's not all picturesque vines and farmhouses, though. Along the way the driver passes a good deal of rusting industrial clutter, debris from an era when this was an important centre for mining in former Yugoslavia. Deposits of zinc and lead were discovered at least as far back as the late Middle Ages and some mines date back to the fifteenth century – the age of Matthias.

Crna na Korosek is a sprawling village grouped around a small medieval core. Most of the older inhabitants once worked in nearby mines, and since the authorities closed them down because they were unprofitable in the years following Slovenia's independence from Yugoslavia in 1991, they have struggled to find new livelihoods. Much effort has been put into popularising the village as a base for mountain bikers and skiers, a logical step perhaps, because the villagers are passionate skiers and justly proud of their disproportionate contribution to Slovenia's national skiing team.

It was not the slopes that drew me to Crna, however, but its other claim to fame as an unlikely-sounding shrine to the memory of Matthias Corvinus. Half a millennium after his death, the village remains the centre of a cult of Matthias. Indeed, his memory is cherished more strongly here than anywhere outside Hungary, especially at the annual celebration in honour of 'Kralj [King] Matjaz', as the Slovenes call him, when the villagers gather each February to build elaborate white snow-castles in a nearby meadow.

Sadly, global warming intervened to prevent me seeing either the snow or the castles. As I drove along the *vinska cesta* – without a snowflake in sight

– I was alerted to the fact that Slovenia in early 2007 was destined to experience a 'green', that is, snow-free, winter.

'It's too warm even to make artificial snow,' Dusan, alias 'Dixie', the festival organiser, explained, regretfully. 'Would you like to see a video of last year's event?' I hunkered down in the foyer of the hotel where he worked as manager, flipped open my laptop and watched a bearded local man on the screen, galloping around in the snow among white castles, a Disney-style crown perched at a jaunty angle on his head.

I hadn't really missed an authentic survival of medieval Central European folklore. Crna na Korosek's Kralj Matjaz festival is not Slovenia's answer to Oberammergau. It is no older than the state of Slovenia itself, which hauled itself out of the ruins of the former Yugoslavia in 1991. My host, Dixie, was the man behind the whole idea, having observed the valley's slow decline from his vantage point as manager of the town hotel. As the mines ceased to work, one by one, Dixie spent his nights searching through books of Slovene legends for an appropriate local hero around whom to base a festival. 'Kralj Matjaz' was the answer he came up with. From a humble start in the early 1990s, when only a few villagers assembled to build half a dozen castles, the event had drawn more people each year and from further afield. The castles had become more ambitious and complex, too, especially once Slovene companies got in on the act, using especially artfully executed edifices of snow to advertise their wares and services. The local people were delighted by the festival's fame. 'It's our Loch Ness, our very own Nessie,' as one restaurateur put it.

But if the festival is modern, it is not in any sense a synthetic construction. It has roots, and rests on a solid foundation of folklore that has survived in the Mezana valley for centuries. In this popular history, which was mainly oral until the folklorists of the nineteenth century began writing it down, elements of real historical memory have naturally been mixed up with older mythological accounts.

When I asked Dixie what he knew of Kralj Matjaz, for example, the answer did not entirely match the sequence of events recorded by Bonfini in his chronicle. 'Matjaz won so many battles that in the end he thought he could fight even against God,' Dixie answered. 'Then, dark clouds came, so he said: "Oh, please mountain, help me". The mountain opened up and he goes in with his army.

'Now he is sleeping there but he will wake up when his beard has curled nine times round the table at which he sleeps.'

This was Matthias's life, the Slovene way. There are, in fact, many variations and endings to the Slovene legends of Matthias though, as Dixie indicated, they nearly all feature the King disappearing with his knights into the bowels of Mount Peca, the mountain that broods over Crna na Korosek and that now lies on the border between Austria and Slovenia. But there is no agreement concerning who or what he was escaping from. While some accounts say he had challenged God, others say he was escaping from the Turks, or even the Austrians.

Then there is the long beard that grows down to his feet and winds around the stone table against which his slumbering body rests. This is a scene depicted in countless Slovene fairytale books and recorded in the miniature plaster images of the King sold in Crna's tourist office. Of course, the Matthias of history would not have sprouted a beard: Beatrice would have scorned that as a barbaric touch. But Beatrice has found no place in the Slovene narratives in any case. Her role has been usurped by the beautiful Alencica, a woman occupying a somewhat ambivalent position in Matjaz's life, half sister, half wife and more goddess than queen.

It is not clear why memories of Matthias, however jumbled, have imprinted themselves so firmly on the memory of the Slovenes in Carinthia. It is far less curious that fuzzy memories of his reign should have lingered in parts of Croatia, Slovakia and Transylvania, which were all integral parts of the old pre-Trianon Hungary. But the Slovene lands of southern Carinthia and Carniola lay on the outer periphery of medieval Hungary, if not beyond it, apart from the eastern fringe. They came under Matthias's rule only briefly during the last years of the reign following the conquest of Vienna. Before that – and for centuries afterwards – the Austrian and German influence was paramount in these parts.

But the strength of the Matthias cult among rural Slovenes struck many visitors to Slovene Carinthia in the last century. 'King Matjaz is one of the many national heroes who end their earthly careers by withdrawing into a mountain where they sleep till the day of direst need', the British folklorist, F.S. Copeland, wrote in the 1930s. 'Then they shall awake and come forth and lead their people to victory, prelude to a golden age to come.'[1] Copeland noted one legend concerning a lime tree, which would blossom at the foot of Mount Peca for just one hour on the stroke of midnight at Christmas before it withered. Then, on St George's Day, 23 April, Matjaz would awaken, ride out and 'hang his shield on the withered lime tree and the tree will revive in token of the King's return and as an omen of better days. Matjaz will ride out with his black host and the battle will be fierce and swift.'[2]

Copeland elaborated in another essay on the Matthias cult in Slovenia. 'The legend of Kralj Matjaz is likewise the solar myth adapted to and transformed into historical tradition', he asserted.

Matjaz was elected by the people on Gosposvetska plain in Carinthia (where the historical dukes of Carinthia used to be installed with ancient rites); he ruled wisely and gloriously for many years and many are the tales told of his prowess and virtue.

Finally, he was overcome by a host that came out of the east, 'numerous as caterpillars in a turnip field'. At last, Kralj Matjaz and his few surviving followers were obliged to give way before the enemy. One of the mountains of the land opened and received them unto itself. In the hollow of that mountain King Matjaz sleeps amid his knights until the supreme need of his people shall rouse him to lead them to victory and freedom once more.[3]

Copeland noted that while Mount Peca was the usual setting for these stories, some legends identified different mountains in the chain of the Julian Alps as Matthias's resting place. Mount Triglav, which is now the symbol of Slovenia, was one. After scrambling around the foothills of Triglav, Copeland told of one encounter with an elderly woman who had urged him to look for the cave in which Matthias slept, as he ascended. It would be easy to recognise it, she said, on account of the number of ravens flapping around the entrance.

Lime trees, long beards, ravens, talismanic numbers and sleeping knights. It would be easy to dismiss altogether the connection between Kralj Matjaz, the mythical hero, and Matthias Corvinus, the historical figure. Some have done so, suggesting the Slovenes simply appropriated Matthias's name and grafted it on to different and unrelated memories of Slovene peasant heroes.

Not surprisingly, I prefer to believe the Slovenes preserved at least a fragment of the historical Matthias and that a continuous thread of memory links the bearded, sleeping figure in a cave in Mount Peca with Matthias Corvinus, conqueror and collector. It is not especially curious, after all, that the Slovenes should have remembered only what appeared relevant to them at the time, namely the epic battles, the invasions 'from the east' and the vaguer notion of a just king and liberator. It is not strange, either, that not a word about his scientific interests or his library found its way into their accounts. Why should they have cared about his illuminated manuscripts?

Matthias always gave off different lights, depending on the angle from which he was observed. Clearly this fooled and disconcerted his contemporaries, Pannonius and Vitez among them. Ever mercurial, changing shapes as it were, he adopted several different personas after beginning his reign as his father's son – a papal champion and a heroic defender of Europe against the Turks. During the middle years of his reign he stepped out from his father's shadow and became preoccupied with the messy, doomed conquest of Bohemia. He ended as his own man, a not-quite emperor who had gained fame the world over for his extraordinary liberality towards men of culture and for his love of precious books.

The scale of the calamities visited on his kingdom after his death encouraged men to recollect his reign in epic and mystical terms. It became an Eden from which man, or rather Hungary, had been banished on account of its sinfulness. As such, it was a constant source of longing and reproach. The library, which in his lifetime was only one of his grand passions, achieved fabulous dimensions as the pre-eminent symbol of this lost world.

The more sceptical and scientific spirit that dominated historiography in Hungary from at least the mid-nineteenth century inevitably shattered that myth and brought Matthias down to earth. He was no longer thought of purely as a new Hercules or Caesar, building his Temple of the Muses in the east. Instead, he has been re-evaluated as a rather canny upstart who found in the ideals of the Renaissance humanists a convenient basis for his rule. Modern historians of the Corvinian library no longer compare it to Ptolemy's legendary library in Alexandria, either. They prefer to deconstruct its 'function' in the context of Matthias's rule and struggle for legitimacy.

So we are left with a more man-sized Matthias – less like the Roman emperor portrayed on the Philostratus, and more like the 'brutta cera di uomo' – the ugly-looking fellow – that the Venetian ambassador described in the early days of his reign.[4] This life-size, warts-and-all Matthias still towers above the common run. His story, which started with a near-death experience, the achievements of his long reign and the traumatic, though ultimately unsuccessful, struggle to secure the continuity of his line, retain an awe-inspiring quality. His failures were on a heroic scale, too. No wonder they inspired legends of a great ruler who had suffered some kind of eclipse but who would nevertheless return in the hour of need, as Copeland wrote, and 'lead his people to victory and freedom'.

Those words seem appropriate to a man who, however arbitrary at times, can never be dismissed as a petty tyrant. Always a builder rather than a destroyer, the fact that the remnant of his library is his only real remaining monument would have surprised no one more than him. As it is, those white pages of vellum, covered in rich hues, offer a last glimpse – as if through a keyhole – of the noon hour of Matthias's reign, of the hopeful time when, as the Dubrovnik ambassador once wrote, 'all eyes turned to Matthias'.

Appendix

A list of extant manuscripts attributed to the Corvinian Library, and their dates and places of illumination where available.

Note: The figure of 216 works attributed to the library, including six incunabulae, is approximate, including works added to the royal library in Buda after Matthias's death and some books that Matthias undoubtedly possessed but gave away and that may never have formed part of his library. Of this figure, 53 are in Hungary and 41 in Austria, 39 in the Austrian National Library alone. Many of the rest are in Italy and Germany. Far smaller numbers are to be found in the libraries of Belgium, Britain, Croatia, the Czech Republic, France, Spain, Turkey and the United States.

AUSTRIA
Melk, Abbey Library
(Stiftsbibliothek)
Horae Beatae Mariae Virginis (illuminated Ferrara 15th century)

Salzburg University Library
(Universitatsbibliothek)
Herodian, *De Romanis imperatoribus, libri VIII*

Vienna, Austrian National Library
(Osterreichische Nazionalbibliothek)
Aeneas Gazaeus, *Theophrastus* (Florence or Buda[i])
Ali Ibn Ridvan, *Commentarius in Claudii Ptolemaei* (Bohemia *c.* 1400)
Appian, *De civilibus Romanorum bellis, liber II* (Florence 1460s)
Aquinas, Thomas, *Catena aurea in Lucae evangelium* (Bologna 1480s)
Aquinas, *De rege et regno* (Florence 1450–70)
Athanasius, *Contra Apollinarem*
Augustine, *Epistolae* (Florence 1485–90*)
Catullus, Caius Valerius, *Carmina* (Florence 1450–75)
Chrysostom, *Dialogus . . . Chrysostomi et Sancti Basilii* (Florence 1465)
Chrysostom, *Hypomnéma*
Chrysostom, *Hypomnémata*
[Pseudo-]Cyrillus, *Speculum sapientiae* (Florence or Lombardy 1443–70)

---

[i] The attributions to Buda following Csapodi are not universally accepted.

Diodoros, *Bibliothéké* (no illumination)
Elisabeth of Poland, *De institutione pueri regii*
Fonti, Bartolomeo, *Commentarium in Auli Persii* (Naples 1480–90)
Hésiodos, *Erga kai hémerai*
Hieronymus, *Epistolae* (Naples 1465–70)
Hieronymus, *Commentaria in Ezechielem* (Florence 1485–90*)
Hieronymus, *Expositio evangelii secundum Matthaeum* (Florence 1488**)
Livy, *Historiae Romanae, decas I* (Florence 1460s)
Livy, *Historiae Romanae, decas IV* (Florence 1460s)
Lucretius, *De rerum natura libri VI* (Florence *c.* 1481)
Marcellinus Comes Illyricus, *Chronicon* (Buda 1471–90)
Martinus Polonus, *Tabula Martiniani decreti* (Milan 1450–90)
Müller, Johannes 'Regiomontanus', *Epitome Almagesti* (Florence 1476–90***)
Niképhoros Kallistos, *Ekklésiastiké historia* (1320s)
Plato, *Phaedon* (Florence 1450–70)
Plutarch, *Vitae parallelae*
Ptolemy, *Magnae compositionis/Almagest* (Buda 1489)
Ptolemy, *Geógraphiké hyphégésis*
Salvianus Massiliensis, *De vero iudicio et providentia Dei* (Florence 1450–70)
Statius, *Silvarum libri V* (Buda 1470–90)
[Theophylactus,] *Commentarii Athanasii in epistolas Sancti Pauli* (Florence 1485–90*)
Trebizond, George of, 'Trapezuntius', In *perversionem problematum Aristotelis* (Rome late 15th century)
Trapezuntius, *Isagoge dialectica* (Buda and/or Florence 1470–90)
Virgil, *Opera cum commentariis* (Florence late 15th century)
Xenophon, *de institutione Cyri*
Xenophon, *Kyrupaideia* (no illumination)
Zónaras, *Epitomé Históríón* (little or no illumination)

BELGIUM
Brussels, Royal Library of Belgium
(Bibliothèque Royale de Belgique/
Koninklijke Bibliotheek van Belgie)
Missale Romanorum (Florence 1485–7*)

BRITAIN
Cambridge, Trinity College Library
Livy, *Historiarum libri* (Lombardy 1450–70)

Holkham Hall, Norfolk
Evangelistarium secundum ritum tramontanorum (Buda 1490)

London, British Library
Pliny, *Epistolae*
Horace, *Opera* (Florence 1450–70)

Manchester, Chetham's Library
Gellius, *Noctes Atticae* (Florence late 15th century)

Oxford, Bodleian Library
Seneca, *Tragoediae* (Northern Italy 15th century)

CROATIA
National and University Library
(Nacional i Sveucilisna Knjiznica)
Hilarius Pictaviensis, *De sancta trinitate* (Florence 1460s)

CZECH REPUBLIC
Olomouc, Cathedral Library
(Statni Archiv: Domski a Kapitolna Knihovna)
Alberti, Leon Battista, *De re aedificatoria* (Florence 1485–90*)

Prague, State Library
(Statni Knihovna)
Aquinas, *Commentarium in librum de coelo et mundo Aristotelis*
Nagonio, Giovanni 'Nagonius', *Ad divum Wladislaum regem pronostichon et panegyrichon* (Florence 1485–90* or **)

FRANCE
Besançon, Municipal Library
(Bibliothèque municipale de Besançon)
[Pseudo] Dionysius Areopagita, *Opera e Graeco in Latinum traducta per Ambrosium Traversarii* (Florence 1457)

Paris, French National Library
(Bibliothèque Nationale de France)
Ambrose, *Sermones* (Florence 1489*
Aristotle, *Opera* (Buda 1490–91)
Cassian, *De institutis coenobriorum* (Buda 1490–91)
Chrysostom, *Herméneia* (not illuminated)
Hieronymus, *Breviarium in psalmos David* (Florence 1488*)
Petrarch Francesco, *Le rime*
Ptolemy, *Geographiae libri VIII* (Florence 1485–90*)
[Pseudo-]Quintilianus, *Declamationes*
Seneca, *Varia opera philosophica* (Northern Italy 14th century)

Private
Martial, *Epigrammata*

GERMANY
Berlin State Library
(Staatsbibliothek zu Berlin)
Orationes ex historia Titi Livii, Sallustii, Curtii (Florence 1460s)

Dresden, Saxon 'Land' Library
(Dresda Sachsische Landesbibliotek)
Cicero, *Epistolae ad familiares* (Naples 1460s)
Valturio, Roberto, *De re militari* (Naples 1476–84)

Erlangen, University Library
(Universitatsbibliothek Erlangen)
Biblia (Bologna 15th century)
Xenophon, *Kyroupaideia*

Göttingen, Lower Saxony State and University Library
(Niedersachsische Staats- und Universitatsbibliothek)
Aristotle, *Physicorum libri VIII* (Florence 1460s)

Jena, University Library
(Universitatsbibliothek)
Guarino, Veronese, *Libellus* (Buda 1459–72)

Leipzig, University Library
(Universitatsbibliothek)
Konstantinos Porpyrogennetos, *Hypothesis* (not illuminated)

Munich, Bavarian State Library
(Bayerische Staatsbibliothek)
Agathias, *De bello Gothorum* (Naples 1483–4)
Aristeas, *Ad Philocratem* (Buda 1481)
Bede, Venerable, *De natura rerum* (Buda 1490)
Celsus, *De medicinis, libri VIII* (Florence 1460s)
Demosthenes, *Orationes contra Philippum regem Macedonom* ... (Florence 1460–70)
Polybius, *Historia* (not illuminated)
Porphyrios, *Bios Plótinu* (no, or few, illuminations)
Seneca, Thomas, *Historia Bononiensis* (Ferrara, or elsewhere in northern Italy 1460s)

Nuremberg, State Library
(Staatsbibliothek)
Petancic, Felix, 'Ragusinus', *Historia Turcica*

Stuttgart, Württemberg Land Library
(Wurttembergische landesbibliothek)
Augustine, *Expositio in psalmos David* (Florence 1485–90*)

Wolfenbüttel, Herzog August Library
(Herzog August Bibliothek)
Cortesius, *De Matthiae Corvini Ungariae regis laudibus bellicis carmen* (Rome or Umbria 1487–88)
Ficino, Marsilio, *Epistolarum ad amicos libri VIII* (Florence 1488–90***)
Ficino, Marsilio, *Epistolarum libri III et IV* (Florence 1482***)
Fonti, *Opera cum praefationem ad Mathiam* (Florence c. 1488*)
Priscianus Lydus, *In Theophrastum interpretatio de sensu et phantasia* (Florence (1484–90*)
Regiomontanus, *Tabulae directionum* (Bavaria c. 1472)
Synesius Platonicus, *Liber de Vaticinio somniorum psalterium Davidis* (Florence 1476–90***)
Tolhopf, Johannes, *Stellarium* (Buda 1488)

Würzburg, University Library
(Universitatsbibliothek)
Pamphilius, *Sermo apologeticus pro Origene* (Florence 1460s)

HUNGARY
National Szechenyi Library
(Orszagos Szechenyi Konyvtar)
Agathias, *De bello Gothorum* (Naples 1483–4)
Asconius Pedianus, *Commentaria in Ciceronis orationes* (Florence 1460s)

Augustine, *De civitate dei libri XXII* (Naples 1470s)
Baptista Mantuanus, *Parthenice* (Mantua or Lombardy 1480s)
Basil, *De Divinitate Filii et Spiritus Sancti* (Florence 1472)
Bernard of Clairvaux, *De consideratione* (Buda 1470–90)
Bessarion, *De ea parte evangelii* (Florence or Umbria 1450–70)
Boccaccio, *De casibus virorum illustrium* (Florence 15th century)
Bonfini, Antonio, *Rerum Hungaricarum Decades* (not illuminated)
Bonfini, Antonio, *Symposion* (Florence *c*. 1485)
[Chalcidius] US, Iohannes, *Altividi de immortalitate animae liber* (Florence 1450–70)
Chrysostom, *Homiliae in epistolas pauli* (Florence 1485–90*)
Curtius Rufus, *De gestis Alexandri Magni* (Florence 1467)
Cyprian, *Opera* (Florence 1450–70)
Cyril of Alexandria, *Thesaurus de sancta et consubstantiali trinitate* (not illuminated)
Damascus, John of, *Sententiae* (Florence 1485–90*)
Hieronymus, *Commentarii in epistolas S. Pauli* (Florence 1488**)
Iohanes Scholasticus, *Spiritualis gradatio* (Florence 1470)
Isocrates, *Oratio ad Demonicon* (Buda 1470s)
Petancius, *Genealogia Turcorum imperatorum* (Buda 1502)
Philostratus, *Heroica* (Florence 1485)
Plautus, Titus Maccius, *Comoediae* (Florence 1450s)
Poeta Christianus, *Genealogiae deorum* (not illuminated)
Polybius, *Historiarum libri I–V* (Florence 1450–70)
Quintilian, *Institutionum Oratoriarum libri XII* (Umbria, 1460–70)
Ransano, Pietro, *Epitoma rerum Hungaricarum* (Naples 1490)
Regiomontanus, *Canones LXIII* (Florence 1460s***)
Trapezuntius, *Compendium grammaticae* (Buda 1470–90)
Trapezuntius, *Rhetoricorum libri* (Buda 1480s)
Victorinus, *Commentarium in Ciceronis librum de inventione* (Hungary 1460s)
Xenophon, *De republica Lacedemoniorum* (Buda 1470–90)
Graduale (Buda 1480–90)

Incunabulae:
Nicolaus de Ausmo, *Supplementum* (Ferrara 1470s)
Thuroczi, Janos, *Chronica* (Augsburg 1488)

**Library of the Hungarian Academy of Science
(Magyar Tudomanyos Akademia – Konyvtar)**
Carbo, Ludovico, *Dialogus de Mathiae Regis laudibus* (Ferrara 1473–5)
Kyeser, Conradus, *Bellifortis* (1366–1405)

**Eotvos Lorand University Library, Budapest
(Eotvos Lorand Tudomanyegyetem Egyetemi Konyvtar)**
Caesar, *Opera . . . de bello Gallico* (Naples 1460s)
Cicero, *Orationes VII ad Verrem* (Florence 1460s)
Pseudo-Clemens Romanus, *Recognitionum libri X* (Florence 1472)
Curtius Rufus, *De gestis Alexandri Magni* (Naples 1470s)
Eusebius, *Chronica cum interpretatione S Hieronymi* (Florence 1460s)
Eusebius, *De evangelica preparatione* (Florence 1460s)
Panegyrici Latini XII (Florence 1450–70)
Scriptores historiae Augustae (Florence 1460s)
Silius Italicus, *De secundo bello Punico* (Florence 1460s)
Suetonius, *Vitae Caesarum*
Tacitus, *Annalium libri XI–XVII* (Naples 1467)

Terence, *Comoediae*
Tertullian, *Adversus Marcionem* (Florence 1468)
Theophrastos, *Historia plantarum* (Florence 1460s)

Gyor, Episcopal Treasury and Library
(Egyhazmegyei Kincstar es Konyvtar)
Biondo, Flavio, 'Blondus', *Romae instauratae libri III* (Florence 1467)

Esztergom, Cathedral Library
(Foszekesegyhazi Konyvtar)
Raynerus de Pisis, *Pantheologia*

ITALY
Florence, Medici Laurentian Library
(Biblioteca Medicea Laurenziana)
Abate, Gilberto
Ambrose, *Opera . . . de virginibus* (Ferrara 1489–90)
Ambrose, *Opera*
Ambrose, *De incarnationis Dominicae sacramento*
Appian, *Romanorum liber Libycus* (Florence 1490*)
Aquinas, *Quaestiones de Malo*
Athanasius
Augustine, *Quaestiones in bibliam* (Florence 1489–90*)
Augustine, *De trinitate*
Bernard, *Sermones super Cantica canticorum*
Calderinus, Domitius, *Commentaria in Iuvenalem* (Florence 1485–90*)
Cassiano, Giovanni
Cassiodorus, *Historia ecclesiastica tripartita*
Celsus, *De medicina libri VIII* (Florence 1470)
Ficino, *De triplici vita* (Florence 1490*)
Gregory, *Opera*
Gregory, *Moralia, Tom. I.*
Gregory, *Moralia, Tom. II.*
Hieronymus, *Commentaria in duodecim minores prophetas*
Hieronymus, *Opera*
Ioannes Duns Scotus, *Questiones*
Collectio Pseudoisidoriana
Leo, St
Peter Lombard, *Sententiarum libri IV* (Florence 1490s*)
Macrobius, Ambrosius, *Saturnaliorum libri V* (Florence 1450–70)
Martial
Martianus Capella, *De nuptiis philologiae et Mercurii libri IX*
Pontificalis
Remigio, S.
Romano, *Egidio*
Biblia Vol. I (Florence 1489–90*)
Biblia Vol. II (Florence, 1489–90)
Biblia Vol. III (Florence 1489–90**)

Milan, Trivulziana Library
(Biblioteca Trivulziana)
Miscellanea (Florence 1450–70***)
Porphyrio, *Commentaria et interpretationes in opera Horatii* (Florence 1485–90*)

Modena, Este Library
(Biblioteca Estense)
Alberti, Leon Battista, *De re aedificatoria* (Florence 1485–90)
Ambrose, *Opera, Hexamaeron* (Florence 1485–90*)
Ammianus, Marcellinus, *Rerum gestarum libri* (Florence 1488*)
Aquinas, *Commentarium in librum I Sententiarum* (Florence 1485–90*)
[Pseudo-]Areopagita, Dionysios, *Opera* (Florence 1460s)
Augustine, *Opus contra Faustum Manichaeum* (Florence 1485–90*)
Gregory, *Homiliae in Ezechielem* (Florence 1485–90*)
Gregory, *Dialogi de Vita* (Florence 1488–90**)
Halicarnassus, Dionysius, *Liber de originibus* (Florence 1485–90*)
Georgius Merula, *Opera* (Florence 1486–90*)
Origen, *Homiliae* (Florence 1476–90***)
Strabo, *Geographia* (Florence 1460–80***)
Valturio, *De re militari* (Lombardy, Venice or Romagna)
Miscellanea, Chrysostomus (Florence 1487*)
Miscellanea, Probus (Florence 1460–80**)

Naples, National Library
(Biblioteca Nazionale)
Chorale

Parma, Palatine Library
(Biblioteca Palatina)
Carafa, Diomede, *De institutione vivendi* (Naples, 1476)

Rome, Casanatense Library
(Biblioteca Casanatense)
Encyclopedia medica (Bohemia 14th century)

Vatican Apostolic Library
(Biblioteca Apostolica Vaticana)
Arrianus, Flavius, *De expeditione Alexandri Magni* (Naples 1480s)
Cyprian, *Opera et epistolae*
Livy, *Historiarum decas I* (1469–85)
Pannonius, Andreas, *Libellus de regiis virtutibus* (Ferrara 1467)
Pliny, *Historiae naturalis libri XXXVII* (Florence 1450–70)
[Pseudo-]Quintilianus, *Declamationes* (1469–85)
Sidonius, *Carmina*
Suetonius, *De XII Caesaribus*
Breviarium secundum consuetudinem Romanae curiae (Florence 1487–92*)
Missale fratrum minorum secundum consuetudinem Romanae curiae (Vienna 1460s)
Missale Romanum (Buda 1488–90)
Pontificale

Venice, Marciana Library
(Biblioteca Nazionale Marciana)
Averulino, *De architectura libri XXV* (Buda 1489)
Bunvenutus de Rambaldis de Imola, *Libellus Augustali* (Florence or northern Italy 1489–90*)
Martianus Capella, *De Nuptiis philologiae et Mercurii libri II* (Florence 1485–90*)
Suetonius, *De XII Caesaribus* (Florence 1450–70***)

Verona, Capitular Library
(Biblioteca Capitolare)
Livy, *Historiae Romanae decas I*
Livy, *Historiae Romanae decas III, de secundo bello Punico* (Florence 1450–70)
Livy, *Historiae Romanae decas IV, de bello Macedonico,* (Central Italy, 1450–70)

Volterra, Guarnacci Library
(Biblioteca Guarnacci)
Marlianus Mediolanensis, *Epithalamium* (Lombardy 1488)

POLAND
Krakow, Czartoryski Library
(Biblioteka Czartoryskich)
Frontinus, *Stratagemata* (Florence 1467)

Krakow, Jagiellonian Library
(Biblioteka Jagiellonska)
Orationale Wladislai II Regis

Torun, Copernicus University Library
(Biblioteka Kopernika)
Naldi, Naldo, *De laudibus augustae bibliothecae* (Florence 1485–90*)

Wroclaw, University Library
(Biblioteka Uniwersytecka)
Horológion (little or no illumination)

SPAIN
Madrid, Royal Library, El Escorial
(Real Biblioteca, El Escorial)
Plato, *Epistolae* (possibly Buda 1485–90)

Madrid, National Library
(Biblioteca Nazional)
de Conchis, Wilhelmus, *Philosophia* (Bohemia 1400s)

SWEDEN
Uppsala, University Library
(Universitetsbibliotek)
Miscellanea Graeca
Firmicius Maternus, *Astronimicorum libri VIII*

TURKEY
Istanbul, Topkapi
Ptolemy, *Geographiae libri VIII* (Florence 1450s)
Rannusius, *Sermo de ascensione* (Bohemia 1500s)

UNITED STATES
New Haven, Yale University
Tacitus, *Annalium libri XI–XVII* (Northern Italy 1450–70)

New York, Public Library
Livy, *Historiarum decas III* (Florence 1460s)

New York, Pierpont Morgan Library
Cicero, *Opera* (Florence 1450–70***)
Didymus, *De Spiritu Sancto* (Florence 1487**)
Iohannes Angeli, *Astrolabium*

* by, or in the style of, Attavante
** by Monte and/or Gherardo Di Giovanni
*** by, or in the style of, Cherico

Notes

Preface

1. The 'Pacta Conventa' between Coloman, or Kalman, of Hungary and the Croatian nobles is normally dated to 1102 and informed the relationship between Hungary and Croatia until 1918. Under its terms, Croatia remained a separate entity with its own parliament, the Sabor, and a viceroy, known as the Ban. Hungary's kings continued to be crowned separately in Croatia at Biograd na Moru for some time.
2. Georghe Funar, born 1949, mayor of Cluj, 1992–2004.
3. It was originally intended that the restored castle become a royal residence for Francis Joseph, in which spirit the autonomous Hungarian government invited the Gothic revivalist Friedrich Schmidt to restore it in the late 1860s. He declined, handing the commission to Ferenc Schulz, who died in 1870, after which Imre Steindl took over, resigning in 1874, after the budget was cut. See J. Sisa, 'Neo-Gothic Architecture and Restoration of Historic Buildings in Central Europe: Friedrich Schmidt and his School', *Journal of the Society of Architectural Historians*, 61, 2002, p. 181.
4. Matthias's reign from 1458 to 1490 overlapped with several English kings: Henry VI, 1422–61 and 1470–71, Edward IV, 1461–83, Richard III, 1483–85, Henry VII 1485–1509.
5. C. Csapodi, *Bibliotheca Corviniana: The Library of King Matthias Corvinus of Hungary*, Shannon, 1969, p. 78. The manuscript, *Chrysostom's Homilae XXIX in epistolam ad Corinthios*, perished along with the rest of the stock of the Biblioteka Narodowa, when the Germans rased Warsaw.

Chapter 1: 'Deep inside the palace'

1. See note XIV of *Letters of Marsilio Ficino*, II, p. 5, London, 1978.
2. Lodovico Sforza, 1452–1508, was not actually Duke of Milan until his nephew's death in 1494 but had held power since the death of his older brother, Galeazzo, Bianca Maria's father, in 1476.
3. N. Naldi, 'De laudibus augustae bibliothecae, ad Mathiam Corvinum Pannoniae regem serenissimum', Book II, in P. Jaenichen, *Meletemata Thorunensia, etc.*, III (of III), Torun, 1727–31, pp. 129–30.
4. Ibid., p. 130. Also, for this English version, see D. Keresztury, 'Bibliotheca

Corviniana', *New Hungarian Quarterly*, (Budapest), 10, 1969, p. 86.

5. N. Naldi, 'De laudibus angustae bibliothecae', II, *Meletemata Thorunensia*, III, p. 132.

6. Ibid.

7. S. Mitchell, 'The Image of Hungary and of Hungarians in Italy, 1437–1526', unpublished thesis, University of London, pp. 179–80. Carbone's book in praise of Matthias, 'Ad serenissimum principem et inclitum Pannoniae regem divum Mathiam Lodovico Carboni dialogues de ipsius regis laudibus rebusque gestis', seems not to have caught the King's fancy, for he was never invited to Buda. Carbone was born in Ferrara in 1435, died in 1435, and was a student alongside Pannonius in Guarino's academy. It appears that Pannonius despised him, if his biting epigram, 'Ad carbonam poetam', is any guide.

8. Mitchell, 'Image of Hungary', p. 131.

9. Ibid., p. 79.

10. L. Pastor, *The History of the Popes*, II, London, 1891, p. 403.

11. L. Pastor, *The History of the Popes*, IV, London, 1894, p. 439.

12. There are five extant letters from Ficino to Matthias, and three to Bishop Bathory of Vacs.

13. *The Letters of Marsilio Ficino*, translated from the Latin by members of the language department of the School for Economic Science, London, II, London, 1978, p. 4.

14. Ibid., p. 5.

15. Ptolemy, born *c.* AD 90, died *c.* AD 168.

16. Now in the Vienna National Library.

17. N. Ker, 'Oxford College Libraries before 1500', in *Books, Collectors and Libraries: Studies in the Medieval Heritage*, ed. A. Watson, London, 1985, p. 304.

18. Ibid., p. 310.

19. N. Ker, 'Patrick Young's Salisbury Cathedral Catalogue', *Books, Collectors and Libraries*, p. 178.

20. Pastor, *History of the Popes*, IV, p. 434.

21. A. Bonfini, *Rerum Ungaricarum decades quatuor cum dimidia*, Frankfurt, 1581, p. 583.

22. Mitchell, 'Image of Hungary', pp. 53–4.

23. A. Bonfini, *Rerum Ungaricarum*, 1581, p. 582.

24. Ibid., p. 593.

25. Ibid., p. 594.

26. E. Brown, *A Brief Account of some Travels in Divers Parts of Europe, viz, Hungaria, Servia, Bulgaria, Macedonia, Thessaly, Austria, Styira, Carinthia, Carniola and Friulia, through a Great Part of Germany and the Low Countries . . .*, London, 1685, p. 154.

27. Ibid., p. 155.

28. Also known as the *Nuremberg Chronicle*, after being published there in 1493, and, in German, as *Die Schedelsche Weltchronik*. It was published by Albrecht Dürer's godfather, Anton Koberger.

29. Miklos Olah, 'Hungaria', cited in *Old Hungarian Literary Reader*, ed. T. Klaniczay, Bekescsaba, 1988, p. 94.

30. Ibid., p. 94.

31. Bonfini, *Rerum Ungaricarum* , p. 649.

32. K. Gutkas, *Friedrich III und Mathias Corvinus*, St Polten, 1982, p. 29.

33. Ibid.

34. Ibid.

35. Johann Mailath, *Geschrichte der Magyaren*, Vienna, 1829, p. 161.

36. Bonfini, *Rerum Ungaricarum*, pp. 631–2.

37. Ibid., p. 632.

38. Ibid.
39. Ibid., p. 638.
40. C. Clough, 'Federigo da Montefeltro's Patronage', in *The Duchy of Urbino in the Renaissance*, London, 1981, pp. 132–3. The list of the Duke's 'familia' was compiled twenty-five years after the Duke's death by his former page, Susech de Castel Durante.
41. W. Coxe, *History of the House of Austria*, I (of III), London, 1847, p. 276.
42. Borso d'Este, 1413–71. Marquis of Ferrara from 1450. Confirmed as Duke by the Emperor Frederick in 1452, he received the ducal title from Pope Paul II just before his death in 1471.
43. Pius II, *Commentaries*, I, ed. M. Meserve and M. Simonetta, Cambridge, Mass., 2003, p. 226.
44. Ibid., p. 363.
45. E. Gardner, *Dukes and Poets in Ferrara*, London, 1904, p. 214.
46. E. Garin, *Astrology in the Renaissance*, London, 1982, p. 8.
47. C. Kaske and J. Clark, Marsilio Ficino, *Three Books on Life*, p. 267.
48. Ibid., p. 269.
49. Ibid., p. 237.
50. Olah, 'Hungaria', p. 96.
51. S. Andreescu, *Vlad the Impaler, Dracula*, Bucharest, 1999, pp. 235–6.
52. Ibid., p. 244, citing an edited version of Pius II's 'Commentaries' as they related to Vlad the Impaler contained in N. Iorga, *Studii si documente cu privire la istoria Romanilor*, III, Bucharest, 1901, p. lxxiv.
53. Hejj, *Royal Palace of Visegrad*, p. 10.
54. Ibid.
55. Bonfini, *Rerum Ungaricarum*, p. 632.

Chapter 2: Beyond the forest

1. W. Fraknoi, *Mathias Corvinus, König von Ungarn 1458–1490*, Freiburg, 1891, p. 14.
2. Walter Fitzwilliam Starkie, 1894–1976. Director of the Abbey Theatre in Dublin for seventeen years, he is chiefly famous for his 1957 translation of Cervantes's *Don Quixote*.
3. W. Starkie, *Raggle-Taggle: Adventures with a Fiddle in Hungary and Romania*, London, 1933, p. 213.
4. Ibid., pp. 216–21.
5. The exact year is not certain. Fraknoi insisted it was 1440, as both the Venetian ambassador and Enea Silvio Piccolomini, Pius II, said he was 18 in 1458.
6. E. Browne, *An Account of Several Travels through a Great Part of Germany*, London, 1677, p. 91.
7. L. Kurti, 'The Ungaresca and Heyduck Music and Dance Tradition of Renaissance Europe', *Sixteenth Century Journal*, 14, 1983, p. 71.
8. Fraknoi, *Mathias Corvinus*, p. 14. (The phrase in Latin was: 'Vos . . . Mathiam in medio vestri lasci, inter vestros lares educari primamque juventutem agere vidistis'.)
9. Ibid., p. 50.
10. G. Marzio, *De egregie, sapienter, jocose dictis ac factis regis Mathiae*, Chapter IV.
11. Bonfini, *Rerum Ungaricarum*, p. 654.
12. J. Szocs, 'The Peoples of Medieval Hungary', in A. Pok (ed.), *Ethnicity and Society in Hungary*, Budapest, 1990, p. 11.
13. H. Segel, *Renaissance Culture in Poland: The Rise of Humanism, 1470–1543*, New York, 1989, p. 34.

14. Fraknoi, *Mathias Corvinus*, p. 16.
15. Segel, *Renaissance Culture in Poland*, p. 23.
16. J. Huszti, 'Janus Pannonius', *Nouvelle Revue de Hongrie* (Budapest), April 1934, p. 364.

Chapter 3: 'I delight in everything that's new'

1. L. Domonkos, 'Janos Vitez, the Father of Hungarian Humanism (1408–1472)', *New Hungarian Quarterly* (Budapest), 20, 1979, p. 149.
2. *The Vespasiano Memoirs: Lives of Illustrious Men of the XVth Century*, trans. W.E. Waters, Toronto, 1997, p. 192. (First published 1926.)
3. Ibid., p. 193.
4. Ibid., p. 195.
5. Ibid.
6. C. Csapodi, *The Corvinian Library: History and Stock*, Budapest, 1973, p. 42.
7. M. and R. Rouse, *Cartolai, Illuminators and Printers in Fifteenth-Century Italy: The Evidence of the Ripoli Press*, Los Angeles, 1988, p. 20.
8. M. Evans, *The Sforza Hours*, London, 1992, p. 9.
9. C. Buhler, *The Fifteenth Century Book: The Scribes, the Printers, the Decorators*, Philadelphia, 1960, p. 19.
10. A. de la Mare, 'Vespasiano da Bisticci, Historian and Bookseller', Ph.D. thesis, University of London, 1966, p. 212.
11. C. Clough, 'Federigo da Montefeltro's Patronage', in *The Duchy of Urbino in the Renaissance*, London, 1981, p. 131.
12. Ibid., p. 136.
13. De la Mare, 'Vespasiano', p. 117.
14. J. Thompson (ed.), *The Medieval Library*, Chicago, 1959, p. 535.
15. De la Mare, 'Vespasiano', p. 156.
16. Now in the Budapest University library (Egyetemi Konyvtar, Budapest).
17. Now in the Biblioteka Czartoryskich, Cracow.
18. Seven known Corvinas copied by Petrus Cenninius were Curtius Rufus's *De gestis Alexandri*, Frontino's *Stratagemata*, Flavio Biondo's *Roma instaurata*, Appian of Alexandra's *De civilibus Romanorum bellis*, Asconius Pedianus's *Narrationes in Ciceronis Orationes*, Basil's *Homilia* and Suetonius's *De duodecim Caesaribus*. See K. Csapodi-Gardonyi, 'Les Scripteurs de la Bibliothèque du Roi Mathias', *Scriptorium*, 17, 1963, pp. 46–7.
19. De la Mare, 'Vespasiano', p. 186.
20. J. Alexander, *The Painted Page: Italian Renaissance Book Illumination 1450–1550*, London and New York, 1995, p. 18.
21. De la Mare, 'Vespasiano', p. 212.
22. T. Klaniczay (ed.), *Old Hungarian Literary Reader, 11th–18th Centuries*, Bekescsaba, 1985, p. 65.
23. D. Geanokoplos, *Constantinople and the West: Essays on Late Byzantine (Palaeologan) and Italian Renaissances and the Byzantine and Roman Churches*, Wisconsin, 1989, p. 61.
24. Ibid., p. 32.
25. N.G. Wilson, *From Byzantium to Italy: Greek Studies in the Renaissance*, Baltimore, 1992, p. 57.
26. Klaniczay (ed.), *Hungarian Literary Reader*, p. 67.
27. Wilson, *From Byzantium to Italy*, p. 43.
28. S. Torjai-Szabo, 'Das literarische Schaffen im Zeitalter des Humanismus und der

Renaissance' in *Ungarn-Jahrbuch, Zeitschrift für interdisziplinare Hungarologie*, Vol. 10, 1979, Munich, p. 140.

29. L. Thorndike, *Science and Thought in the Fifteenth Century*, New York, 1929, p. 146, citing G. Caraffa, *De gymnasio Romano*, Rome, 1751, p. 277.

30. J. Monfasani, *George of Trebizond*, Leiden, 1976, p. 26.

31. Ibid., p. 196.

32. Geanokoplos, *Constantinople*, pp. 45–6.

33. A. Grafton and L. Jardine, 'Humanism and the school of Guarino' in Grafton and Jardine, *From Humanism to the Humanities: Education and the Liberal Arts in Fifteenth- and Sixteenth-Century Europe*, London, Cambridge, Mass, 1986, pp. 67–8.

34. Klaniczay (ed.), *Hungarian Literary Reader*, p. 64.

35. L. Martines, *Power and Imagination: City States in Renaissance Italy*, London, 1979, pp. 312–13.

36. Ibid., p. 263.

37. *Vespasiano*, trans. Waters, p. 192.

38. C. Ady, *Pius II (Aeneas Silvio Piccolomini) the Humanist Pope*, London, 1913, p. 125.

39. E. Pallavicini, 'Elisabeth Szilagyi', *Nouvelle Revue de Hongrie*, Budapest, October 1940, p. 282.

40. J. Thuroczy, *Chronicle of the Hungarians*, trans. F. Mantello, Bloomington, Ind., 1991, p. 192.

41. W. Fraknoi, *Mathias Corvinus, Konig von Ungarn 1458–1490*, Freiburg, 1891, p. 31.

42. Ibid., pp. 32–3.

43. Ibid., p. 34. 'Regnum ex majori sua partie desolatum'.

44. 'a small house constructed beside the Istvanvar and looking out towards the lower hot springs', according to Thuroczy, *Chronicle of the Hungarians*, p. 202.

45. Mitchell, 'Image of Hungary', p. 185.

46. Ibid., p. 184.

47. W. Fraknoi, 'Cardinal Joannes Carjavals Legationen in Ungarn', *Ungarische Revue*, 1890, p. 400.

48. Fraknoi, *Mathias Corvinus*, p. 51.

49. I. Berkovits, *The Illuminated Manuscripts of Matthias Corvinus*, Budapest, 1964, p. 11.

50. The inscription reads 'Ego Mathias Rex Hungariae concessi hoc Missali fratri Thomae de Hungaria'.

51. Denes Szecsi, or Szechy, Bishop of Eger 1439–40, Archbishop of Esztergom 1440–65, Lord Chancellor 1453–65.

52. Thorndike, *Science and Thought*, pp. 147–8.

53. E. Zinner, *Leben und Werken des Joh. Müller von Königsberg, genannt Regiomontanus*, Osnabrück 1968, p. 146. (First published 1938.)

54. Mitchell, 'Image of Hungary', p. 192.

55. J. Bak (ed.), *Kings, Bishops, Nobles and Burghers in Medieval Hungary*, London, 1986, p. 175.

56. L. Pastor, *History of the Popes from the Close of the Middle Ages*, London, 1894, p. 65.

Chapter 4: 'Ceaselessly entangled in warfare'

1. W. George and E. Waters, transl., *The Vespasiano Memoirs: Lives of Illustrious Men of the XVth Century*, Toronto and Buffalo, NY, 1997, p. 196.

2. R. Betts, 'Social and Constitutional Development in Bohemia', *Past and Present*, 7, 1955, p. 40.
3. T. Izbicki, G. Christianson and P. Krey (eds), *Reject Aeneas, Accept Pius: Selected Letters of Aeneas Sylvio Piccolomini (Pope Pius II)*, Washington, 2006, p. 288.
4. F. Heymann, *George of Bohemia, King of Heretics*, Princeton, 1965, p. 438.
5. Ibid., p. 421.
6. K. Frojimovics, G. Komoroczy *et al.*, *Jewish Budapest: Monuments, Rites, History*, Budapest, 1999, p. 13.
7. These figures are taken from P. Engel, *The Realm of St Stephen: A History of Medieval Hungary 895–1526*, London and New York, 2001, p. 311. He writes that a Venetian source in 1476 put the King's income at about 650,000 florins, comprising 400,000 from the *porta*, 80,000 from monopolies, 60,000 from minting, 47,000 from the towns and 50,000 from a tax levied on a thirtieth of incomes.
8. Fraknoi, *Mathias Corvinus*, p. 123.
9. Ibid., p. 132.
10. Ibid.
11. Ibid., p. 133.
12. H. Brown, 'Venice', in *The Cambridge Modern History*, eds G. Ward, S. Prothero, and I. Leathes, *The Renaissance*, Cambridge, 1902, p. 278. Brown estimates Venice's income in 1500 at 1,145,580 ducats.
13. Heymann, *George of Bohemia*, p. 495.
14. O. Odlozilik, 'Problems in the Reign of George of Podebrady', *Slavonic and East European Review*, 20, 1941, p. 219.
15. Janus Pannonius, *The Epigrams*, ed. E. Barrett, Gyomaendrod, 1985, p. 42.
16. Ibid., p. 151.
17. M. Birnbaum, *Janus Pannonius, Poet and Politician*, Zagreb, 1981, p. 149.
18. Engel, *Realm of St Stephen*, p. 322.
19. Birnbaum, *Pannonius*, p. 182.
20. Heymann, *George of Bohemia*, p. 583.
21. The King summoned 15 Diets from 1458 to 1476 and only five after 1476: Engel, *Realm of St Stephen*, p. 311.
22. W. George and E. Waters (transl.), *The Vespasiano Memoirs: Lives of Illustrious Men of the XVth Century*, Toronto and Buffalo, NY, 1997, p. 196.
23. Regiomontanus left Buda between 15 March and 2 June 1471, according to his biographer, Ernst Zinner. E. Zinner, *Leben und Wirken des Joh. Müller von Königsberg, genannt Regiomontanus*, Osnabrück, 1968, p. 163. (First published 1938.)
24. R. Mett, 'Johannes Regiomontanus, ein Schuler des Georg von Peuerbach', in H. Grossing (ed.), *Der Die Sterne Liebte, Georg von Peuerbach und seine Zeit*, Vienna, 2002, p. 95.
25. Now in the Herzog August Bibliothek in Wolfenbüttel, one of the ten Corvinian manuscripts in the collection. The others are Alexander Cortesius's 'De Matthiae Corvini', *c.* 1485–90, Johannes Tolhopf's 'Stellarium', *c.* 1480, the Psalter of Queen Beatrice, *c.* 1476–84, Marsilio Ficino's 'Epistolarum ad amicos libri viii', 1489, 'Epistolarum libri iii et iv – de vita Platonis', 1482, 'Epistolarum libri iii et iv', 1484, Bartolommeo Fonte's 'Opera', Synesius Platonicus Cyreneus's 'Liber de vaticinio somniorum' and Priscianus Lydus's 'In Theophrastum Metaphrasis de sensu et de fantasia', 1487–89.
26. T. Kardos, 'Janus Pannonius: Poet of the Hungarian Renaissance', *New Hungarian Quarterly* (Budapest), 14, 1973, p. 80.
27. Carbone's work passed into the possession of a Brother Ambrose Cacic in Split in the eighteenth century before being purchased by Joszef Teleki on behalf of the

Hungarian Academy of Sciences in April 1840. There is one other copy, on paper, not parchment, in the Vatican.

28. Mitchell, 'Image of Hungary, p. 191.
29. K. Csapodi-Gardonyi, *Die Bibliothek des Johannes Vitez*, Budapest, 1984, p. 19.
30. Ibid., p. 73.
31. Ibid.
32. Ibid., p. 49.
33. Ibid., p. 46.
34. C. Csapodi, *Bibliotheca Corviniana: The Library of King Matthias Corvinus of Hungary*, Shannon, 1969, p. 15, citing V. Fraknoi, 'Miklos Modrusi puspok elete Munkaies Konyvtara', in *Magyar Konyvszemle*, Budapest, V, 1897, pp. 1–23.
35. According to Csapodi, at least six books returned from Constantinople in 1877 were Vitez's, including Albertus Magnus's *De mineralibus Libri V*, Socrates's *De regimen principatus ad Nicholaum Cypri regem*, Paladius Aemilianus's *De institutione* and Terentius's *Comaediae*. See Csapodi-Gardonyi, *Die Bibliothek des Johannes Vitez*, p. 49.

Chapter 5: Beatrice

1. A. Berzeviczy, *Béatrice d'Aragon, reine de Hongrie (1457–1508)*, Paris, 1911, I (of II), p. 126.
2. 'ut forma habituque Venerum, Dianam pudicitia et sapientia eloquentiatque Passadem ex omni parte referret'. From Bonfini's *Symposion trimeron sive De pudicitia coniugali et virginitati dialogi*, cited in C. Damianaki, *The Female Portrait Busts of Francesco Luarana*, Rome, 2000, p. 48.
3. Born between 1420 and 1425 at Vrana, near Zadar, once known as Lorena (hence the name Laurana) in 1420–25, died Provence 1502.
4. See 'The Bust of Beatrice d'Aragona', in Damianaki, *Female Portrait Busts*, pp. 76–83.
5. G. Hersey, *Alfonso II and the Artistic Renewal of Naples 1485–1495*, New Haven, Conn., and London, 1969, p. 33.
6. J. Roll, *Giovanni Dalmata*, Worms, 1994, plate no. 139. Dalmata was born in 1440 in Trogir and died in 1510. He worked widely in Rome, where his most famous work was on the tomb of Paul II. He also worked for Matyas in Hungary and Slavonia in the late 1480s, and he is mentioned in documents in 1488 and 1489 in connection with rebuilding the castle of 'Maykovez' (today, Majkovce) as 'Joannis Duknovich de Tragurio'. See Roll, *Dalmata*, pp. 170–2.
7. L. Kurti, 'The Ungaresca and Heyduck Music and Dance Tradition of Renaissance Europe', *Sixteenth Century Journal*, 14, 1983, p. 67.
8. Fraknoi, *Mathias Corvinus*, p. 150.
9. A. Ryder, *The Kingdom of Naples under Alfonso the Magnanimous: The Making of a Modern State*, Oxford, 1976, p. 55.
10. J. Bentley, *Politics and Culture in Renaissance Naples*, Princeton, NJ, 1987, p. 52.
11. Hersey, *Alfonso II*, p. 1, citing G. Gravier (ed.), *Raccolta di tutti i piu rinomati scrittori dell'istoria generale del regno di Napoli*, Naples, 1769–72, p. 2.
12. Bentley, *Renaissance Naples*, p. 65.
13. Ibid., p. 57.
14. Ibid., p. 58.
15. Ibid., p. 218.
16. R.W. Southern, *Western Society and the Church in the Middle Ages*, Harmondsworth, 1970, p. 102.

17. J. Symonds, *Renaissance in Italy: The Revival of Learning*, London, 1897, p. 198.
18. Ibid., p. 206.
19. M. de Cossart, *Antonio Beccadelli and the Hermaphrodite*, Liverpool, 1984, p. 9.
20. Ibid., p. 27.
21. Ibid., p. 30.
22. Ibid.
23. Ibid., p. 32.
24. Ibid., p. 9.
25. D. Rutherford, 'Philippic against Antonio Panormita', in *Early Renaissance Invective and the Controversies of Antonio da Rho*, Tempe, 2005, pp. 91–5.
26. Ibid., p. 181.
27. Ibid.
28. G. Hersey, *The Aragonese Arch at Naples 1443–1475*, New Haven, Conn., and London, 1973, p. 15.
29. Bentley, *Renaissance Naples*, p. 66.
30. Berzeviczy, *Béatrice d'Aragon*, I, p. 36.
31. Hersey, *Alfonso II*, p. 123, citing Paolo Giovio, *Historia Suis Temporis*, I, Florence, 1550, p. 11.
32. The works were Cicero's *Epistolae* and *De officiis*. See Damianaki, *Female Portrait Busts*, p. 160.
33. Bentley, *Renaissance Naples*, p. 75.
34. J. Jacquot (ed.), *La Musique instrumentale de la Renaissance*, Paris, 1955, p. 42, 'Il est donc sur que la Reine a joué de l'orgue.'
35. Ibid., p. 47.
36. Ibid. 'En 1483, l'évêque Bartholomée de Maraschi, responsable de la chapelle pontificale, célébra avec enthousiasme la chapelle de Mathias ("habet enim cantorum capellam qua nullam praestantiorem vidi") et la qualité des chants qui accompagnèrent la messe.'
37. J. Jacquot, 'Les Musiciens de Mathias Corvin', in *La Musique instrumentale de la Renaissance*, p. 38.
38. Berzeviczy, *Béatrice d'Aragon*, I, p. 69.
39. E. Gardner, *Dukes & Poets in Ferrara*, London, 1904, p. 134.
40. Ibid., p. 135.
41. E. Lee, *Sixtus IV and Men of Letters*, Rome, 1978, p. 36.
42. L. Pastor, *The History of the Popes*, IV, London, 1894, p. 243.
43. Mitchell, 'The Image of Hungarians in Italy, 1437–1526', p. 27, citing R. Wolkan, *Der Briefwechsel des Eneas Silvius Piccolomini*, I (of IV), Vienna, 1909–18, p. 548.
44. The fragment dating from the 1350s, and showing the head of a saint, was found in 1881 and is now in the Christian museum in Esztergom.
45. Berzeviczy, *Béatrice d'Aragon*, I, p. 108.
46. Ibid., p. 126.
47. Fraknoi, *Mathias Corvinus*, p. 9. He cites the papal legate as writing in 1463: 'Magnam ei adauget et aestimationem mater, quae, cum sit sanctimissime et sapientissime mulier, apud omnes est in reverentia et amore.'
48. E. Pallavicini, 'Elisabeth Szilagyi', *Nouvelle Revue de Hongrie* (Budapest), October 1940, p. 286. 'Elle quitta ce monde si tranquillement que nous n'en savons pas même la date exacte.'
49. E. Pallavicini, 'Béatrice d'Aragon, reine de Hongrie, 1457–1508', *Nouvelle Revue de Hongrie* (Budapest), January 1940, p. 40. According to Fugger, 'Er des Turkenkrieges ganz vergass und keine Stunde lang ohne ihr seine konnte.'
50. J. Mailath, *Geschichte der Magyaren*, Vienna, 1829, p. 72.
51. Jews were not normally allowed to bear arms in Europe but a German knight who

saw Mendel and his son mounted and bearing swords may not have been mistaken. At least two seventeenth-century ceremonial swords from Buda with Hebrew inscriptions survive, but the privilege of bearing swords accorded to leaders of the Buda Jewish community may have been far older. See T. Raj and P. Vasadi, *Jewish Life in Turkish Buda*, Budapest, 2003, p. 74.

52. K. Frojimovics and G. Komoroczy, *Jewish Budapest: Monuments, Rites, History*, Budapest, 1999, pp. 10–11.
53. Mailath, *Geschichte der Magyaren*, p. 73.
54. Berzeviczy, *Béatrice d'Aragon*, I, p. 153.
55. The *Apologeticum* was copied in 1455 by one Briccius de Polanka, presumably at Vitez's episcopal court in Varad/Oradea. The initials 'Jo E W' are thought to refer to 'Johannes Episcopus Waradensis'. It was clearly lent to Aeneas Sylvius Piccolomini: an extant note of his, dating from 1454, acknowledges return of the loan.
56. G. Razso, *Die Feldzüge des Königs Matthias Corvinus in Niederösterreich 1477–1490*, Vienna, 1993, p. 6.

Chapter 6: 'The Emperor has fled'

1. Mailath, *Geschichte der Magyaren*, p. 157.
2. V. Klaic, *Povijest Hrvata*, IV, Zagreb, 1980, p. 161.
3. Janos Thuroczy, born c. 1435. Died c. 1489. Notary at various times for the convent of Ipolysag and the Lord Chief Justice. In 1486 made protonotary for the court of appeals. His *Chronica Hungarorum* was published in Augsburg in 1488 as a successor to the earlier Hungarian chronicle produced in Buda by the printer Andras Hess. Quotation from Thuroczy, *Chronicle of the Hungarians*, pp. 224–5.
4. Berzeviczy, *Béatrice d'Aragon*, I, p. 181.
5. Andrew Wheatcroft, *The Habsburgs*, London, 1995, p. 73.
6. Z. Kosztolnyk, 'Some Hungarian Theologians in the Late Renaissance', *Church History*, 57, March 1988, p. 6.
7. G. Adrianyi, 'Die Kirchenpolitik des Matthias Corvinus (1458–1490)', in *Ungarn-Jahrbuch*, X, Munich, 1979, p. 84.
8. Polish astronomer, known also as Martinus Olkusz z Bylica, or Martin Bylica. Born 1433, died c. 1493.
9. A copper celestial globe, made for Martin Bylica by the Dominican instrument maker Hans Dorn in Buda in 1480, survives in Cracow, at the Jagiellonian University Museum. Bylica bequeathed his instruments to the university in 1492.
10. Hans Dorn. Born in Austria c. 1430, a Dominican, studied astronomy in Vienna under George Peurbach; moved to Buda in 1470s and returned to Vienna in 1491, dying in the Dominican monastery in 1509.
11. Z. Ameisenowa, *The Globe of Martin Bylica of Ilkusz and Celestial Maps in the East and in the West*, transl. A. Potocki, Wroclaw, Cracow and Warsaw, 1959, p. 46.
12. Ibid., p. 12.
13. Pietro Ransano, or Ranzano, alias Petrus Ransanus, born Palermo, Sicily, 1428, died 1492.
14. The issue is discussed by A. Miko in 'Divinus Hercules es Attila Secundus', Vol. 10, *Ars Hungarica*, Budapest, 1991, pp. 149–55 (in Hungarian).
15. E. Gardner, *Dukes and Poets in Ferrara*, London, 1904, p. 102.
16. Wheatcroft, *The Habsburgs*, p. 80.
17. Fraknoi, *Mathias Corvinus*, p. 207.
18. Ibid.
19. Mailath, *Geschichte der Magyaren*, p157.

20. Razso, *Feldzüge des Königs Matthias*, p. 15.
21. F. Opll and R. Perger, *Kaiser Friedrich III und die Wiener 1433–1485*, Vienna, 1993, p. 89.
22. Berzeviczy, *Béatrice d'Aragon*, I, p. 234.
23. Ibid., II, p. 289.
24. Jacobo, or Iacopo, Filippo Foresti, 1434–1520. An Augustinian prior, he spent most of his life in the monastery of St Augustine in Bergamo, where he also wrote *Supplementum Chronicarum* and *Confessionale*. See C. Damianaki, *The Female Portrait Busts of Francesco Laurana*, Rome, 2000, p. 45.
25. Brigata Ascolana dell'Arte, *Antonio Bonfini MCDXXVII–MCMXXVII*, Ascoli, 1928, p. 23.
26. See C. Csapodi, 'La Bibliothèque de la reine Béatrice', in *Beatrix Kiralyne Konyvtara*, Budapest, 1964, pp. 24–6.
27. J. Hale (ed.), *Encyclopaedia of the Italian Renaissance*, London, 1992, p. 122
28. 'Of 74 titles given in the inventory of Leonora's library, only six are not demonstrably religious'. W. Gundersheimer, *Ferrara, the Style of a Renaissance Despotism*, Princeton, NJ, 1973, p. 196.

Chapter 7: The librarian Ugoleto

1. Bonfini, *Rerum Ungaricarum decades*, IV, book VII, p. 631.
2. A. Berzeviczy, *Béatrice d'Aragon, Reine de Hongrie (1457–1508)*, Paris, 1912, Vol. II, p. 84.
3. Ibid., p. 56.
4. M. Birnbaum, 'Croatian Humanists at the Hungarian Court', *Journal of Croatian Studies* (New York), 1986, p. 11. Birnbaum names Matthias's Croatian barber as Stefanus de Ragusio, adding that he returned home, to Dubrovnik presumably, in 1506.
5. L. Gerevich, *The Art of Buda and Pest in the Middle Ages*, Budapest, 1971, p. 114.
6. J. Balogh, *A Muveszet Matyas Kiraly Udvaraban*, Budapest, 1966, p. 658.
7. Gerevich, *Art of Buda and Pest*, pp. 120–2.
8. V. Rees, 'Pre-Reformation Changes in Hungary', in K. Maag (ed.), *The Reformation in Eastern and Central Europe*, Aldershot, 1997, p. 31.
9. A. de Hevesy, 'Les Miniaturistes de Mathias Corvin', *Revue de l'Art Chrétien* (Paris), 61–4, 1911, p. 6.
10. I. Affo, *Memorie di Taddeo Ugoleto Parmigiano, Bibliotecario di Mattia Corvino, Re di Ungheria*, Parma, 1781, p. 19.
11. Ibid., p. 77.
12. Ibid., pp. 8–9.
13. Ibid., p. 15. Also A. de Hevesy, *La Bibliothèque du roi Mathias Corvin*, Paris, 1923, p. 17.
14. Affo, *Ugoleto*, p. 16.
15. According to Albinia de la Mare, it was 'choice rather than large'. Consisting entirely of Latin works, it was designed for practical use, not decoration. See A. de la Mare, 'The Library of Francesco Sassetti', in C. Clough (ed.), *Cultural Aspects of the Italian Renaissance, Essays in Honour of Paul Oskar Kristeller*, Manchester and New York, 1976, p. 171.
16. Ibid.
17. *The Letters of Marsilio Ficini*, transl. from the Latin by the Language Department for the School for Economic Science, London, 2003, III, p. 47.
18. Ibid.

19. Affo, *Ugoleto*, p. 21.
20. L. Labowsky, *Bessarion's Library and the Biblioteca Marciana*, Rome, 1979, p. 21; see M. Duhamel (ed.), *Catalogue général des manuscrits des bibliothèques publiques en France*, Départements, Vol. XXXIV, Paris, 1901, introduction, p. ix.
21. Labowsky, *Bessarion's Library*, p. 13.
22. W. Gundersheimer, *Ferrara: The Style of a Renaissance Despotism*, Princeton, NJ, 1973, p. 168.
23. Ibid., p. 169.
24. Ibid.
25. J.W. Thompson, *The Medieval Library*, Chicago, 1939, p. 532.
26. See J. Monfasani, *Byzantine Scholars in Renaissance Italy: Cardinal Bessarion and Other Émigrés*, Aldershot, 1995.
27. L. Cheles, *The Studiolo of Urbino, an Iconographic Investigation*, Wiesbaden, 1986, p. 17.
28. Clough, *The Library of the Dukes of Urbino: The Duchy of Urbino in the Renaissance*, p. 101.
29. J. Dennistoun, *Memoirs of the Duke of Urbino*, I, London and New York, 1909, p. 165.
30. Ibid., p. 166.
31. Ibid., p. 167.
32. Ibid., pp. 167–8.
33. R. Pasquale, *The Ducal Palace of Urbino, its Architecture and Decoration*, London, 1969, p. 102.
34. M. Jerrold, *Italy in the Renaissance*, London, 1927, p. 160.
35. Thompson, *The Medieval Library*, p. 551.
36. The books came back on 3 October 1491. Ibid., p. 552.
37. L. Labowsky, *Bessarion's Library at the Biblioteca Marciana*, Rome, 1979, p. 27.
38. Ibid., p. 562.
39. E. Lee, *Sixtus IV and Men of Letters*, Rome, 1978, pp. 114–15.
40. Ibid., photograph opposite p. 144.
41. Thompson, *The Medieval Library*, p. 564.
42. Lee, *Sixtus IV and Men of Letters*, p. 116
43. Ibid., citing M. Bertola, *Codici Latini di Niccolo V Perduti or Dispersi*, *Mélanges Eugène Tisserant*, VI, pt 1, Vatican City, 1964, pp. 129–40.
44. Pastor, *History of the Popes*, IV, p. 439.
45. K. Csapodi-Gardonyi, 'Les Scripteurs de la bibliothèque du roi Mathias', *Scriptorum*, 17, 1963, p. 27. The Latin translates as 'The writing is elegant, the copyists, themselves, I believe, not lacking knowledge.'
46. Hevesy, *Bibliothèque du roi Matthias Corvin*, p. 33. Also, Csapodi-Gardonyi, 'Scripteurs', p. 27; and J. Horemans, *Le Missel de Mathias Corvin & la Renaissance en Hongrie*, Brussels, 1993, p. 48.
47. Feliks Petancic, born *c.* 1455, died *c.* 1517. Wrote several works on the Turks, including 'Historia imperatorum regni Turcici', which was never published (the manuscript is in Nuremberg), *Genealogia Turcorum imperatorum* and *De itineribus in Turciam libellus*.
48. Based on a lecture by John Alexander of New York University, Institute of Fine Arts, entitled 'Francesco da Castello in Lombardy and in Hungary at the End of the Fifteenth Century', delivered at the conference Italy and Hungary: Humanism and Art in the Early Renaissance, Villa I Tatti, Florence, 7 June 2007.
49. D. Kniewald, *Feliks Petancic i Njegova Dela, Srpska Akademija Nauka I Umetnosti, Posebna Izdanja* (special edition), Belgrade, 1961, p. 8.
50. C. Csapodi, *The Corvinian Library: History and Stock*, Budapest, 1973, p. 63.

51. 'The bindery may have been contemporary with the foundation of the workshop.' A. Hobson, 'Two Renaissance Bindings', *Book Collector*, Autumn 1958, pp. 267–8.

52. L. Kajanto, *Poggio Bracciolini and Classicism: A Study in Early Italian Humanism*, Helsinki, p. 19.

53. E. Fryde, 'Lorenzo's Greek Manuscripts and in particular his own Commissions', in M. Mallet and N. Mann (eds), *Lorenzo the Magnificent: Culture and Politics*, London, 1996, p. 104.

54. Brandolini was one of the wave of Italians who came to Buda in the 1480s, returning to Italy after the King's death. His treatise on monarchy versus republic, *De comparatione reipublicae et regni*, apparently begun at Matthias's bidding, was then dedicated to Lorenzo de Medici instead. See L. Thorndike, 'Lippus Brandolini *De comparatione reipublicae et regni*: An Unpublished Treatise of the Late Fifteenth Century in Comparative Political Science', *Political Science Quarterly*, 41, New York, 1926, pp. 413–35.

Chapter 8: 'A glutton for books'

1. C. Csapodi, *The Corvinian Library: History and Stock*, Budapest 1973, p. 52. Also, Csapodi, *Bibliotheca Corviniana*, p. 21, here rendered in English as 'The king intends to outshine every other monarch with his library as he does in all other points and I think he will.'

2. J. Horemans, *Le Missel de Mathias Corvin et la Renaissance en Hongrie*, Brussels, 1993, p. 45.

3. 'Augustini Epistolae, et aliorum ad ipsum'. See J. Bradley, *A Dictionary of Miniaturists, Illuminators, Calligraphers and Copyists*, I (of 3), New York, 1973, p. 74.

4. S. Augustini, *Opus contra Faustum*, see Bradley, *Miniaturists*, I, p. 77.

5. S. Gregorii *Papae omiliae in Ezechielem prophetam*, see Bradley, *Miniaturists*, I, p. 77.

6. D. Hieronymus, *Commentaria in Ezechielem prophetam*, see Bradley, *Miniaturists*, I, p. 74.

7. Philostratus, *Heroica, icones, vita sophistarum et epistolae*, see Bradley, *Miniaturists*, I, p. 74.

8. S. Ambrosius, *Episcopi mediolalensis exameron: et alia*, see Bradley, *Miniaturists*, I, p. 76.

9. Titi Livii Patavini *Historia Romana*, see Bradley, *Miniaturists*, I, p. 78.

10. *De bello Gothorum*: now in the National Szechenyi Library, which purchased the Agathias from the collector Lajos Farkas in 1873. It is one of nine surviving manuscripts from Beatrice's library.

11. K. Csapodi-Gardonyi, 'Les scripteurs de la bibliothèque du Roi Mathias', *Scriptorum*, 17, 1963, p. 27.

12. Ibid., p. 33.

13. A. de la Mare, 'New Research on Humanistic Scribes in Florence', in A. Garzelli (ed.), *Miniatura Fiorentina del Rinascimento 1440–1525*, Florence, 1985, I, p. 467.

14. J. W. Thompson, *The Medieval Library*, Chicago, 1959, p. 543.

15. E. Goldschmidt, *Preserved for Posterity: The New Colophon*, II, 1950, p. 331, cited in C. Buhler, *The Fifteenth Century Book: The Scribes, the Printers, the Decorators*, Philadelphia, 1960, pp. 104–5.

16. Cited in L. Fischer, *Mathias Corvinus und seine Bibliothek*, Vienna, 1878, p. 6.

17. A. de Hevesy, 'Les Miniaturistes de Mathias Corvin', *Revue de l'Art Chrétien* (Paris and Brussels), 61–4, 1911, p. 109.

18. A. Berzeviczy, *Béatrice d'Aragon, reine de Hongrie (1457–1508)*, Paris, 1911, II, p. 21.

19. Ibid., p. 34.

20. L. Kurti, 'The Ungaresca and Heyduck Music and Dance Tradition in Renaissance Europe', *Sixteenth Century Journal*, 14, 1983, p. 78.

21. Berzeviczy, *Béatrice*, II, p. 49.

22. Ibid., p. 71.

23. W. Fraknoi, *Mathias Corvinus König von Ungarn 1458–1490*, Freiburg, 1891, p. 290.

24. A. Mallet, *The Borgias. The Rise and Fall of a Renaissance Dynasty*, London, 1969, p. 42.

25. C. Cherrier, *Histoire de Charles VIII roi de France*, I (of II), Paris, 1868, pp. 187–8.

26. V. Parry, 'The Ottoman Empire (1481–1520)', in *The New Cambridge Modern History, I, The Renaissance, 1493–1520*, Cambridge, 1957, p. 397.

27. L. Thuasne, *Djem-Sultan, Etude sur la question de l'Orient à la fin du XV siècle*, Paris, 1892, p. 148.

28. According to Csapodi, it is not John but Anne of Beaujeu. It is indeed difficult to tell the figure's sex. See Csapodi, *Bibliotheca Corviniana*, p. 116.

29. Thuasne, *Djem-Sultan*, p. 168.

30. R. Brown (ed.), *Calendar of State Papers and Manuscripts relating to English Affairs existing in the Archives and Collections of Venice*, Vol. I, *1202–1509*, London, 1894, p. 166.

31. Berzeviczy, *Béatrice d'Aragon*, II, p. 108.

32. Ibid., p. 88.

33. Ibid., pp. 111–12.

34. Ibid., p. 113.

35. Cherrier, *Charles VIII*, II, p. 334: 'a peine de vingt ans, [il] égalait son père en cruauté et en perfidie si'l ne le surpassait'.

36. Berzeviczy, *Béatrice d'Aragon*, II, p. 115.

37. Fraknoi, *Mathias Corvinus*, p. 263.

38. Tolhopf was born in Franconia, enrolled Leipzig in 1465, in 1473–74 made rector first of Ingolstadt and then Leipzig. Came to Buda 1480; died before 1503. His 1480 work 'Stellarium', once part of the Corvinian library, is now in Wolfenbüttel. See I. Thorndike, 'John Tolhopf Again', *Isis, Journal of the History of Science Society* (Chicago), 24, 1936, pp. 419–21.

39. Fraknoi, *Mathias Corvinus*, p. 268.

40. Never printed, as far as is known, the treatise is in the Biblioteca Laurenziana in Florence. For a discussion of the treatise's history and significance, see L. Thorndike, '"Lippus Brandolinus, *De Comparatione respublicae et regni*": An Unpublished Treatise of the Late Fifteenth Century in Comparative Political Science', *Political Science Quarterly*, 41, 1926, pp. 413–35.

Chapter 9: Collapse

1. H. Lamb, *Suleiman the Magnificent, Sultan of the East*, London, 1952, p. 90; also A. Bridge, *Suleiman the Magnificent, Scourge of Heaven*, London, 1983, p. 100.

2. Hevesy, *La Bibliothèque du roi Matthias Corvin*, p. 38.

3. R. Feuer-Toth, *Art and Humanism in Hungary in the Age of Matthias Corvinus*, Budapest, 1990, p. 68.

4. Pelbart of Temesvar: born Timisaora 1435, matriculated from Cracow, 1458, professor in the Franciscan House in Buda 1480–83; died Buda, 22 January 1504.

5. Z. Kosztolnyk, 'Some Hungarian Theologians in the Late Renaissance', *Church History: Studies in Christianity and Culture*, 57, March 1988, pp. 13–14.

6. R. Hoffman, *Land, Liberties and Lordship in a Late Medieval Countryside*, Philadelphia, 1985, p. 31.

7. Kurti, 'The Ungaresca and Heyduck Music and Dance Tradition', p. 76.

8. Csapodi, *Bibliotheca Corviniana*, p. 284.

9. I am indebted for this information to Daniel Pocs of the Accademia d'Ungheria, Rome, whose lecture, 'White Marble Sculptures from the Buda Castle', delivered at the conference Italy and Hungary: Humanism and Art in the Early Renaissance, Villa I Tatti, Florence, 8 June 2007, contained much fascinating material on relations between Milan and Buda in the last months of Matthias's reign. Pocs suggests that an antique marble fragment found in Buda may be a portion of the statue Lodovico sent to Buda after the King's death, most probably as a gift to his successor, Wladislas.

10. A. Berzeviczy, *Beatrice d'Aragon, reine de Hongrie (1457–1508)*, Paris, 1911, II, pp. 155–6.

11. Ibid., p. 170.

12. E. Fugedi, *Kings, Bishops, Nobles and Burghers in Medieval Hungary*, London, 1986, p. 390. The incomes of the richest five sees, based on a valuation of 1525, are listed as follows: Esztergom, 25,000 florins, Eger, 22,000, Pecs, 25,000, Varad, 26,000, Zagreb, 18,000.

13. Berzeviczy, *Béatrice d'Aragon*, II, p. 230.

14. D. Abulafia, 'Ferrante of Naples: The Statecraft of a Renaissance Prince', *History Today*, 45, February 1995, p. 19.

15. G. Hersey, *Alfonso II and the Artistic Renewal of Naples 1485–1495*, New Haven, Conn. and London, 1969, p. 6.

16. Ibid., p. 7.

17. W. McMurry, 'Ferdinand, Duke of Calabria and the Estensi', *Sixteenth Century Journal*, 8, October 1977, p. 21.

18. Berzeviczy, *Béatrice d'Aragon*, II, pp. 289–90.

19. The tomb was marked 'Beatrix Aragonea Pannoniae regina Ferdinandi primi Neap. Regis filia de sacro hoc collegio opt merita his sita est. Haec religione et munificientia se ipsam vincit'.

20. H. Wiesflecker, *Kaiser Maximilian I, das Reich, Osterreich und Europa an der Wande zur Neuzeit*, Munich, 1971, p. 288.

21. Hoffman, *Land, Liberties and Lordship*, p. 31.

22. K. Frojimovics, G. Komoróczy et al., *Jewish Budapest, Monuments, Rites, History*, Budapest, 1999, pp. 14–15, citing Bonfini, *Rerum Ungaricarum decades*, V, pp. 102–9.

23. *Calendar of State Papers and Manuscripts, relating to ... Venice*, I, 1202–1509, London, 1864, p. 216.

24. M. Birnbaum, *Humanists in a Shattered World, Croatian and Hungarian Latinity in the Sixteenth Century*, Budapest, 1986, p. 12, citing Konstantin Mihailovic.

25. Fraknoi, *Mathias Corvinus*, p. 278, citing Bonfini, *Rerum Hungaricum decades*, IV, p. 8.

26. According to Csapodi, some went to the Dominican friars in Venice while others passed into the hands of Georg Tanner of Vienna in 1555. See C. Csapodi, *Corvinian Library, History and Stock*, Budapest, 1973, p. 58.

27. L. Thorndike, 'Lippis Brandolinus *De comparatione respublicae et regni*, a Treatise in Comparative Political Science', in *Science and Thought in the Fifteenth Century*, New York, 1929, p. 233.

28. Csapodi, *Bibliotheca Corviniana*, p. 63.

29. Ibid., p. 47.

30. Georg (George) of Brandenburg-Ansbach: born 1484, Ansbach, died 1543. A

convinced Protestant, he promoted the spread of Lutheranism from 1528. Married three times: to Beatrice Frankopan in 1509 (who died in 1510), Hedwig of Münsterberg in 1525 and Aemilia of Saxony in 1533. His son and heir, George Frederick, was born in 1539.

31. Berlin Staatsbibliothek, *Orationes ex historia Titi Livii, Sallustii, Curtii*; Dresden, Sachsiche Landesbibliothek, Cicero: *Epistolae ad familiares*, Valturius: *De re militari*; Erlangen, Universitätsbibliothek, Xenophon: *Kyroupaideia, Biblia*; Göttingen, Niedersachsiche Staats- and Universitätsbibliothek, Aristoteles: *Libri physicorum VIII*; Jena, Universitätsbibliothek, Guarino: *Libellus*; Leipzig, Universitätsbibliothek, Konstantinos Porpyrogennetos: *Hypothesis*; Munich, Bayerische Staatsbibliothek, Celsus: *De medicina libri octo*, Beda Venerabilis: *De natura rerum*, Agathias: *De bello Gothorum*, Demosthenes: *Orationes*, Thomas Seneca: *Historia Bononiensis*, Aristeas: *Philocratem*, Polybios: *Historia*, Porphyrios: *Bios Plotinu*; Nuremberg, Staatsbibliothek, Petancius Ragusinus, Felix: *Historia Turcica*; Stuttgart, Wurttembergisches Landesbibliothek, Augustinus: *Expositio in psalmos David*; Wolfenbüttel, Herzog August Bibliothek, Fontius: *Opera*, Regiomontanus: *Tabulae directionum et profectionum*, Ficinus: *Epistolarum ad amicos libri VIII*, Tolhopf: *Stellarium*, Ficinus: *Epistolarum libri III et IV, psalterium Davidis*; Würzburg, Universitätsbibliothek, Pamphilius: *Sermo apologeticus*.
32. Csapodi, *Bibliotheca Corviniana*, p. 51.
33. Csapodi says this was Christoper Urswick, a roving Tudor clerical diplomat, though there may be some confusion here, for I can find no record of Urswick having ever gone to Hungary.
34. *Calendar of State Papers relating to . . . Venice*, I, 1202–1509, p. 295.
35. See W. Allen, *The Four Corvinus Manuscripts in the United States*, New York, 1938. The others are the Didymus *De Spiritu Sancto*, the Cicero omnibus in the Morgan Collection and the Livy in the Spencer Collection.
36. F. Foldesi, 'From Buda to Vienna', in O. Karsay, *Potentates and Corvinas, Anniversary Exhibition of the National Szechenyi Library*, Budapest, 2002, p. 100.
37. See H. Ankwicz-Kleehoven, *Der Wiener Humanist Johannes Cuspinian, Gelehrter und Diplomat zur Zeit Kaiser Maximilians I*, Graz and Cologne, 1959, p. 116.
38. Born 1478 in Swabia, Bishop of Vienna 1530–41. A friend of Erasmus, as bishop he became a strong opponent of the Reformation.
39. Foldesi, 'From Buda to Vienna', p. 101.
40. 'Maybe Taddeo never reached Buda, or if he did, he did not find the court the way it used to be, a place where studies were pursued with passion. He probably found the library spoiled and foresaw the inglorious ending the collection would suffer after King Ludovico's [sic] death when, under Soliman of Buda [sic], who took over Hungary in 1526, the library was scattered.' Uffo, pp. 30–1.
41. I. Affo, *Memorie di Taddeo Ugoleto Parmigiano, bibliotecario di Mattia Corvino, re di Ungheria*, Parma, 1781, p. 26.
42. Ameisenowa, *The Globe of Martin Bylica*, p. 46, citing Zinner, *Leben und Wirken des Johannes Müller*, p. 121.
43. E. Zinner, *Regiomontanus, his Life and Work*, Amsterdam, New York, Oxford and Tokyo, 1990, p. 100.
44. Birnbaum, *Humanists in a Shattered World*, p. 15.
45. J. de Iongh, *Mary of Hungary*, London, 1958, p. 67.
46. Ibid., p. 70, citing K. Stroegmann, 'Über die Briefe des Andrea da Burgo, Gesandten König Ferdinands . . . Sitzungsberichte der kaiserlichen Akademie der Wissenschaften', *Philos. Hist. Klasse*, 24 (2), 1857, p. 224.
47. L. Kurti, 'The Ungaresca and Heyduck Music and Dance Tradition of Renaissance Europe', *Sixteenth Century Journal*, 14, 1983, p. 74.
48. A. Vambery, *Hungary in Ancient, Medieval and Modern Times*, London, 1887, p.

275; also Bridge, *Suleiman the Magnificent*, p. 43.

49. *Calendar of State Papers . . . Venice*, III, *1520–1526*, London, 1869, p. 185.
50. G. David and P. Fodor, *Ottomans, Hungarians and Habsburgs in Central Europe, the Military Confines on the Era of Ottoman Conquest*, Leiden, Boston and Cologne, 2000, p. 14.
51. Birnbaum, *Humanists in a Shattered World*, p. 78.
52. Ibid., p. 79.
53. *Calendar of State Papers . . . Venice*, III, p. 591, also p. 617.
54. R. Merriman, *Suleiman the Magnificent 1520–1566*, Cambridge, Mass., 1944, p. 82.
55. M. de Hammer, *Histoire de l'Empire ottoman*, Paris, 1840, I (of III), p. 485. Bridge, *Suleiman the Magnificent*, p. 97.
56. Most military historians assume the '100,000' in Suleiman's army includes a vast number of camp followers and non-combatants and that the Sultan's actual fighting force cannot have numbered more than 40–45,000: see Merriman, *Suleiman the Magnificent*, p. 89.
57. *Histoire de la campagne de Mohacz par Kemal Pasha Zadeh*, trans. P. de Courteille, Paris, 1859, p. 103.
58. Lamb, *Suleiman the Magnificent*, p. 90; also Bridge, *Suleiman the Magnificent*, p. 100.
59. De Hammer, *Histoire de l'empire ottoman*, I, p. 487.
60. Ibid., p. 486.
61. De Iongh, *Mary of Hungary*, p. 105.
62. *Histoire de la campagne . . . par Kemal Pacha Zadeh*, trans. De Courteille, p. 109.
63. Lamb, *Suleiman the Magnificent*, p. 93.
64. *Histoire de la campagne . . . par Kemal Pacha Zadeh*, trans. De Courteille, p. 109.
65. De Hammer, *Histoire de l'empire ottoman*, Vol I, p. 489.
66. The poem ran: 'There lived two Ibrahims on the Earth, while one had all the idols crushed, the other brought new ones.' The first was the biblical Abraham. See J. von Hammer, *Geschichte des Osmanischen Reiches*, II, Pest, 1834, pp. 56–7, cited in F. Szakaly, *Lodovico Gritti in Hungary 1529–1534: A Historical Insight into the beginning of Turco-Habsburgian Rivalry*, Budapest, 1995, p. 118.
67. De Hammer, *Histoire de l'empire ottoman*, Vol I, p. 489.
68. M. Olah, *Hungaria*, cited in T. Klaniczay, *Old Hungarian Literary Reader 11th–18th Centuries*, Bekescsaba, 1985, p. 94.
69. Lamb, *Suleiman the Magnificent*, p. 94.
70. De Hammer, *Histoire de l'empire ottoman*, II, p. 214.
71. Frojimovics, Komoroczy *et al.*, *Jewish Budapest*, p. 25. The returnees from Belgrade, Sofia, Edirne and Constantinople after 1541 may have included some of the old deportees, of course.

Chapter 10: 'Who can restrain their tears?'

1. T. F. Dibdin, *The Biographical Decameron; or, Ten Days Pleasant Discourse upon Illuminated Manuscripts . . .* II (of III), London, 1817, p. 462.
2. J. Raby, 'Mehmed the Conqueror's Greek Scriptorium', *Dumbarton Oaks Papers*, 37, 1983, p. 15.
3. Ibid., p. 16.
4. The oldest is written thus: 'Super his evangeliis seu Missali Albertus et Isabelle Belgarum principes suum iuramentum solemniter fecerunt, 1599'. See *Le Missel de Mathias Corvin, & la Renaissance en Hongrie*, ed. J. Horemans, Brussels, 1993, p. 62.
5. Ibid., p. 62.

6. W. Stirling, *The Cloister Life of the Emperor Charles V*, London, 1852, p. 5.

7. B. Spruyt, '"En bruit d'estre bonne luteriene": Mary of Hungary (1505–58) and Religious Reform', *English Historical Review*, 109, 1994, p. 276.

8. J. Montgomery, *A Seventeenth-Century View of European Libraries, Lomeier's 'De Bibliothecis'*, Chapter X, Berkeley and Los Angeles, 1962, p. 59.

9. G. Halasz, 'La Reine Marie de Hongrie', *Nouvelle Revue de Hongrie* (Budapest), July 1937, p. 26.

10. Hevesy, *La Bibliothèque du Roi Mathias Corvin*, p. 41: 'Quant aux livres que Marie de Hongrie avait emportés en Espagne, ils passèrent dans la bibliothèque de L'Escorial.'

11. Author's conversation with Lourdes Alonso de Viana on 1 April 2007 in the Biblioteca Nacional in Madrid. The visit of Ragusinus to Spain she referred to comes from I. Berkovits, *Illustrated Manuscripts from the Library of Matthias Corvinus*, Budapest, p. 94.

12. Stirling, *Charles V*, p. 266.

13. H. Trevor Roper, *Princes and Artists: Patronage and Ideology at Four Habsburg Courts 1517–1633*, London, 1991, p. 40. (First published 1976.)

14. J. Raven (ed.), *Lost Libraries, the Destruction of Great Book Collections since Antiquity*, London, 2004, p. 95.

15. Gregory Nazianzenus, fourth-century Bishop of Nazianze in Cappadoccia; poet, orator and writer of many letters.

16. J. Brassicanus, 'De Bibliothecis cumprimis regia Budensis, as episcopum Augustensem Christophoruma Stadion', in J. Maderus (ed.), *De Bibliotheci atque archivis virorum clarissimorum*, Helmestadt, 1641, p. 140. Also Csapodi, *The Corvinian Library, History and Stock*, p. 82.

17. E. Milano, 'I codici corviniani conservati nelle biblioteche italiane', in *Nel Segno del Corvo, libri e miniature della biblioteca di Mattia Corvino re d'Ungheria (1443–1490)*, ed. A. Dillon Bussi *et al.*, Modena, 2002, p. 67.

18. 'Vidimus integrum Hyperiden cum locupletissimis scholis, librum multis etiam censibus redimendum'. Brassicanus, 'De Biblioth. Budensi'.

19. E. Gumillischeg, B. Mersich and O. Mazal, *Matthias Corvinus und die Bildung der Renaissance*, Vienna, 1944, p. 33.

20. Jano Szambocky, Joannes Sambucus: b. 1531, educated in Italy, court historiographer from 1564 to Maximilian II and Rudolf II. Devoted to Greek culture, he edited Pannonius's works as well as publishing Bonfini. On his death in 1584, his library was incorporated into the Hofbibliothek.

21. Andras, or Andreas, Dudith, 1533–89. A brief account of his life is included in J. Jankovics and I. Monik, *Andras Dudith's Library, a Partial Reconstruction*, Szeged, 1993.

22. For a short essay on Dudith as a humanist, see R. Lebegue, 'Un humaniste hongrois: André Dudith', *Nouvelle Revue de Hongrie* (Budapest), November 1935, pp. 407–11.

23. Andrea Gritti, Doge 1523–38.

24. According to Heinrich Kretschmayr, Gritti's nineteenth-century biographer, Gritti practically looted Hungary in the early 1530s. See F. Szakaly, *Ludovico Gritti in Hungary 1529–1534: A Historical Insight into the Beginning of Turco-Habsburgian Rivalry*, Budapest, 1995, p. 95.

25. Born 1515, best known for his 1558 work on the alleged voyages of his ancestors, Nicolo and Antonio, in the 1390s in the North Atlantic.

26. See Anon., *Catalogue of the William Loring Andrews Collection of Early Books in the Library of Yale University*, New Haven, Conn., 1913.

27. Milano, *Nel Segno del Corvo*, p. 68.

28. Ibid.

29. Csapodi, *The Corvinian Library*, p. 58.
30. Csapodi, *Bibliotheca Corviniana*, pp. 59–60. According to Csapodi, the Bede was a gift of Georgius Hermanus. It is not clear how Fugger obtained the Aristeas.
31. For a short description of the decline and fall of Johann Jakob Fugger, see R. Ehrenburg, *Capital & Finance in the Age of the Renaissance: A Study of the Fuggers and their Connections*, New York, 1963, pp. 119–23.
32. Pellicier's immediate predecessors as French ambassadors to Venice were Jean de Pins, Bishop of Rieux (1516–20), Georges de Selve, François Lerouse (1520–21), Jean de Langeal, Bishop of Avranches, Lazere de Baïf (1529–33), Bishop of Lavaur (1534–36) and Georges d'Armagnac, Bishop of Rodez (1536–39).
33. A. Tilley, 'Humanism under Francis I', *English Historical Review*, 15, 1900, pp. 469–70. According to Tilley, the King's library numbered 1,891 works by 1544, of which only 109 were printed volumes. About 190 were Greek manuscripts.
34. L. Delisle, *Le Cabinet des Manuscrits de la Bibliothèque Imperiale*, 3 vols., Paris, 1858–81, I, p. 162.
35. Hevesy, *Bibliothèque du roi Mathias Corvin*, p. 43.
36. Ambrose, *Sermones*; Cassianus, *De institutes coenobriorum*; Seneca, *Varia opera philosophica*; Quintilianus, *Declamationes*; Ptolemy, *Geographiae libri VIII*; Hieronymus, *Breviarium in psalmos David*; Petrarch: *Le rime*; Chrysostom, *Hermeneia*; Aristotle, *Opera*.
37. Two in the British Library (Pliny, *Epistolae de viris illustribus*; Horace, *Opera*). The other four are in Chetham's Library, Manchester (Gellius, *Noctes Atticae*), the Bodleian Library Oxford (Seneca, *Tragoediae*), Trinity College, Cambridge (Livy, *Historiarum decas I*) and Holkham Hall, Norfolk (*Evangelistarium secundum ritum tramontanorum*).
38. John Byrom, born 1692, died 1763. The suggestion that the books may have been purchased in Montpellier is contained in the file of notes on the book in Chetham's Library.
39. W. Hassall, *The Holkham Library: Illuminations and Illustrations in the Manuscript Library of the Earl of Leicester*, Oxford, 1970, p. 24.
40. Csapodi, *The Corvinian Library*, p. 73.
41. J. Burbury, *A Relation of a Journey ... from London to Vienna and thence to Constantinople in the Company of His Excellency Count Lesley ... Ambassador from Leopoldus Emperour of Germany to the Grand Signior ...* London, 1671, p. 90.
42. Ibid.
43. Ibid., p. 93.
44. For an account of the trip (in German), I. Von Mosel, *Geschichte der kaiserl. und konigl. Hofbibliothek zu Wien*, Vienna, 1835, pp. 81–3.
45. T. Barker, *Double Eagle and Crescent. Vienna's Second Turkish Siege and its Historical Setting*, New York, 1967, p. 64.
46. J. Spielman, *Leopold of Austria*, London, 1977, p. 96.
47. *A Letter from an Eminent Merchant in Constantinople to a Friend in London, giving an Exact Relation of the Great and Glorious Cavalcade of Sultan Mahomet the Fourth ... as he Marched out of Constantinople for ... the Siege of Vienna*, London, 1683.
48. *A True Copy of a Letter from Count Starembergh to the Duke of Lorraine concerning the present Condition of Vienna*, London, 1683.
49. Barker, *Double Eagle and Crescent*, p. 364.
50. T. Raj and P. Vasadi, *Jewish Life in Turkish Buda*, Budapest, 2003, p. 55.
51. Frojimovics, Komoroczy et al., *Jewish Budapest*, p. 39.
52. Anon., *An Historical Description of the Glorious Conquest of the City of Buda the*

Capital City of the Kingdom of Hungary, London, 1686, p. 19.
53. Ibid., p. 22.
54. Ibid., p. 23.
55. Ibid., p. 311.
56. Ibid., p. 41.
57. Ibid., p. 62.
58. Ibid., p.311.
59. Ibid., p. 62.
60. Fantuzzi quoted in J. Beliczay, *Marsigli, elete es munkai*, Budapest, 1881, p. 29.
61. Csapodi, *The Corvinian Library*, p. 72, citing M. Erdeli, *Tortenelmi adatok*, I, Buda, 1855, p. 204.
62. Beliczay, *Marsigli*, p. 29.
63. G. Fantuzzi, *Memorie della vita del Generale Co Luigi Ferdinando Marsigli*, Bologna, 1770, p. 54.
64. Beliczay, *Marsigli*, p. 31.
65. Naldi, *Concerning the Praises of the August Library*, Book IV, p. 252.
66. Naldi, 'De laudibus augustae bibliothecae', II, p. 130.
67. M. Olah, *Hungaria*, cited in T. Klaniczay (ed.), *Old Hungarian Literary Reader 11th–18th Centuries*, Bekescsaba, 1985, p. 94.
68. http://tertullian.org/articles/csapodi_corviniana.htm
69. Beliczay, *Marsigli*, p. 34.

Chapter 11: The walls of the Seraglio

1. Z. Jako, 'Ipolyi Arnold es a Konstantinapolyba kerult korvinak megtalalasa' (Arnold Ipolyi and the Discovery of the Corvinas in Constantinople), in I. Zombori (ed.), *Zsigmond Jako. Tarsadalom, Egyhaz, Muvelodes: Tanulmanyok Erdely tortenelmehez*, Budapest, 1997, p. 387.
2. L. Kosa, M. Szegedy-Maszak and T. Valuch (eds), *A Cultural History of Hungary (In the Nineteenth and Twentieth Centuries)*, Budapest, 2000, p. 135.
3. J. Lukacs, *Budapest 1900, A Historical Portrait of a City and its Culture*, London, 1988, p. 14.
4. L. Mravik, 'Plucked from the Abyss of Oblivion', *Hungarian Quarterly*, 44, 169, spring 2003.
5. Naldi, 'De laudibus augustae bibliothecae', III, p. 172.
6. Born Zutphen 1636, died Zutphen 1699.
7. C. Csapodi, *The Corvinian Library, History and Stock*, Budapest, 1973, p. 17.
8. L. Fischer, *König Mathias Corvinus und seine Bibliothek*, Vienna, 1878, p. 23.
9. I. Affo, *Memorie di Taddeo Ugoleto, Parmigiano, bibliotecario di Mattia Corvino*, Parma, 1781, p. 22.
10. T. Dibdin, *Biographical Decameron*, II, London, 1817, p. 460.
11. H. Hallam, *Introduction to the Literature of Europe in the Fifteenth, Sixteenth and Seventeenth Centuries*, I, London, 1843, p. 161. (First edition 1839.)
12. G. Rawlings, *The Story of Books*, London, 1901, p. 69.
13. Now kept in the episcopal seminary in Gyor.
14. Ipolyi: born 1823, died 1886, as Bishop of Oradea; Henszlmann, born 1813, died 1888; Kubinyi, 1796–1874.
15. A. Ipolyi, 'Matyas kiraly konyvtara maradvanyainak felfedezese 1862–ben', *Magyar Todomnyos Akadimia Ertesituje*, 1878, Budapest, p. 107.
16. A. Ipolyi, 'Matyas kiraly konyvtara maradvanyainak felfedezese 1862–ben' (The Discovery of the Remains of King Matthias's Library in 1862), memorial speech on

the death of Count Antal Porkesch-Osten, 25 February 1878, in *Magyar Konyvszemle* (Hungarian Literary Review), Budapest, 1878, p. 112.

17. Jako, 'Ipolyi Arnold es a Konstantinapolyba kerult korvinak megtalalasa', p. 387.
18. *Magyar Tudomanyos Akademia Ertesitoje* (Bulletin of the Hungarian Academy of Science), 1867, Budapest, pp. 238–9.
19. A. Miko, 'Stories of the Corvinian Library', in O. Karsay (ed.), *Potentates and Corvinas*, Budapest, 2002, p. 144.
20. G. Rupp, *A Wavering Friendship: Austria and Russia 1876–1878*, Cambridge, 1941, p. 39.
21. Ibid., p. 329.
22. Ibid., p. 335.
23. Miko, 'Stories of the Corvinian Library', p. 145.
24. Ibid.
25. 'Priceless Gift', *Time*, 24 January 1927. The two candidates were supposedly Archdukes Otto and Albrecht.
26. Miko, 'Stories of the Corvinian Library', p. 141.
27. Csapodi, *The Corvinian Library*, p. 19.
28. Ibid., p. 57. Csapodi's methodology was as follows: based on Vespasiano's claim that he had 200 manuscripts produced for Cosimo de Medici in 22 months, or just over 100 a year, he suggests that no more than 500 new codices can have been prepared for Matthias from 1485 to 1490. As one-third of the extant Corvinian books date from the last five years of Matthias's reign, that produces a total figure of 1,500. Adding in an estimated 500 acquired books, the figure is increased to 2,000. Including books still in preparation at the time of the King's death, a final figure of 2,500 is obtained.
29. Hevesy, *Bibliothèque du Roi Mathias Corvin*, p. 46.
30. Ibid.
31. Ibid.

Epilogue: 'Matjaz will ride out'

1. F.S. Copeland, 'Some Aspects of Slovene Folklore', *Folk-Lore, Transactions of the Folk-Lore Society*, 60, 2, 1949, p. 280.
2. Ibid., p. 281.
3. F.S. Copeland, 'Slovene Folklore', *Folk-Lore*, 42, 4, 1931, p. 44.
4. A. de Hevesy, 'Les miniaturistes de Mathias Corvin', *Revue de l'Art Chrétien*, Paris/Brussels, 1911, p. 1.

Select bibliography

Books

Affo, I., *Memorie di Taddeo Ugoleto Parmigiano, bibliotecario di Mattia Corvino, re di Ungheria*, Parma, 1781

Alexander, J., *The Painted Page, Italian Renaissance Book Illumination 1450–1550*, London, New York, 1995

Allen, W., *The Four Corvinus Manuscripts in the United States*, New York, 1938

Ameisenowa, Z., *The Globe of Martin Bylica of Ilkusz and Celestial Maps in the East and in the West*, transl. A Potocki, Wroclaw, Cracow, Warsaw, 1959

Andreescu, S., *Vlad the Impaler, Dracula*, Bucharest, 1999

Ankwicz-Kleehoven, H., *Der Wiener Humanist Johannes Cuspinian, Gelehrter und Diplomat zur Zeit Kaiser Maximilians I*, Graz, Cologne, 1959

Bak, J., ed., *Kings, Bishops, Nobles and Burghers in Medieval Hungary*, London, 1986

Balogh, J., *Die Anfange der Renaissance in Ungarn*, Graz, 1975

Barrett, E., ed., *Janus Pannonius, The Epigrams*, Gyomaendrod, 1985

Bentley, J., *Politics and Culture in Renaissance Naples*, Princeton, NJ, 1987

Berkovits, I., *The Illuminated Manuscripts of Matthias Corvinus*, transl. by S Horn, Budapest, 1964

Berzeviczy, A., *Béatrice d'Aragon, Reine de Hongrie (1457–1508)*, 2 vols, Paris, 1911

Birnbaum, M., *Janus Pannonius, Poet and Politician*, Zagreb, 1981

Birnbaum, M., *Humanists in a Shattered World, Croatian and Hungarian Latinity in the Sixteenth Century*, Budapest, 1986

Birnbaum, M., *The Orb and the Pen, Janus Pannonius, Matthias Corvinus and the Buda Court*, Budapest, 1996

Bonfini, A., *Rerum Ungaricarum decades quatuor cum dimidia*, Frankfurt, 1581.

Bradley, J., *A Dictionary of Miniaturists, Illuminators, Calligraphers and Copyists*, 3 vols, New York, 1973

Brown, E., *A Brief Account of Some Travels in Divers Parts of Europe, viz, Hungaria, Servia, Bulgaria, Macedonia, Thessaly, Austria, Styria, Carinthia, Carniola and Friulia, Through a Great Part of Germany, and the Low Countries . . .*, London, 1685

Buhler, C., *The Fifteenth Century Book: The Scribes, the Printers, the Decorators*, Philadelphia, 1960

Burbury, J., *A Relation of a Journey . . . from London to Vienna and Thence to Constantinople in the Company of His Excellency Count Lesley . . . Ambassador from Leopoldus Emperour of Germany to the Grand Signior . . .*, London, 1671

Clough, C., *Federigo da Montefeltro's Patronage in the Duchy of Urbino in the Renaissance*, London, 1981

Csapodi, C., *Bibliotheca Corviniana, The Library of King Matthias Corvinus of Hungary*, Shannon, 1969

Csapodi, C., *The Corvinian Library, History and Stock*, Budapest, 1973

Csapodi, C., 'La bibliothèque de la Reine Béatrice', in *Beatrix Kiralyne Konyvtara*, Budapest, 1964

Csapodi-Gardonyi, K., *Die Bibliothek des Johannes Vitez*, Budapest, 1984

Damianaki, C., *The Female Portrait Busts of Francesco Laurana*, Rome, 2000

David, G., Fodor, P., *The Ottoman Empire and its Heritage, Ottomans, Hungarians and Habsburgs in Central Europe; the Military Confines in the Era of Ottoman Conquest*, Leiden, Boston, Cologne, 2000

De Cossart, M., *Antonio Beccadelli and the Hermaphrodite*, Liverpool, 1984

De Courteille, P. (transl.), *Histoire de la Campagne de Mohacz par Kemal Pasha Zadeh*, Paris, 1859

De Hevesy, A., *La Bibliothèque du Roi Matthias Corvin*, Paris, 1923,

De Iongh, J., *Mary of Hungary*, London, 1958

De la Mare, A., 'Vespasiano da Bisticci, Historian and Bookseller', PhD Thesis, University of London, 1966

Dennistoun, J., *Memoirs of the Duke of Urbino*, 3 vols, London, New York, 1909

Dillon Bussi, A., and others, eds, *Nel Segno del Corvo, libri e miniature della biblioteca di Mattia Corvino re d'Ungheria (1443–1490)*, Modena, 2002

Engel, P., *The Realm of St Stephen, A History of Medieval Hungary 895–1526*, London, New York, 2001

Fantuzzi, G., *Memorie della Vita del Generale Co Luigi Ferdinando Marsigli*, Bologna, 1770

Feuer-Toth, R., *Art and Humanism in Hungary in the Age of Matthias Corvinus*, Budapest, 1990

Ficino, M., *The Letters of Marsilio Ficino, Translated from the Latin by Members of the Language Department of the School for Economic Science*, 2 vols, London, 1978

Fischer, L., *König Mathias Corvinus und seine Bibliothek*, Vienna, 1878

Fraknoi, W., *Mathias Corvinus, Konig von Ungarn 1458–1490*, Freiburg, 1891

Frojimovics, K., Komoroczy, G., *Jewish Budapest, Monuments, Rites, History*, Budapest, 1999

Fugedi, E., *Kings, Bishops, Nobles and Burghers in Medieval Hungary*, London, 1986

Gabriel, A., *The Medieval Universities of Pecs and Poszony*, Notre Dame, Indiana, Frankfurt, 1969

Gardner, E., *Dukes and Poets in Ferrara*, London, 1904

Garin, E., *Astrology in the Renaissance*, London, 1982

Gordon, P., *Two Renaissance Book Hunters. The Letters of Poggius Bracciolioni to Nicolaus de Nicoli*, New York, London, 1974

Grossing, H., ed., *Der Die Sterne Liebte, Georg von Peuerbach und Seine Zeit*, Vienna, 2002

Gundersheimer, W., *Ferrara, The Style of a Renaissance Despotism*, Princeton, NJ, 1973

Gutkas, K., *Friedrich III und Mathias Corvinus*, St Polten, 1982

Hassall, W., *The Holkham Library, Illuminations and Illustrations in the Manuscript Library of the Earl of Leicester*, Oxford, 1970

Held, J., *Hunyadi: Legend and Reality*, New York, 1985

Hersey, G., *Alfonso II and the Artistic Renewal of Naples 1485–1495*, New Haven, Conn., 1969

Hersey, G., *The Aragonese Arch at Naples 1443–1475*, New Haven, Conn., and London, 1973

Hoffman, R., *Land, Liberties and Lordship in a Late Medieval Countryside*, Philadelphia, 1985

Horemans, J., *Le Missel de Mathias Corvin et la Renaissance en Hongrie*, Brussels, 1993

Jacquot, J., ed., 'Les musiciens de Mathias Corvin', in *La Musique instrumentale de la Renaissance*, Paris, 1955

Karsay, O., ed., *Potentates and Corvinas, Anniversary Exhibition of the National Szechenyi Library*, Budapest, 2002

Kaufman, T., *Court, Cloister and City, The Art and Culture of Central Europe, 1450–1800*, London, 1995

Ker, N., *Books, Collectors and Libraries, Studies in the Medieval Heritage*, London, 1985

Klaic, V., *Povijest Hrvata od najstarijih vremena do svrsetka XIX stoljeca*, 5 vols, Zagreb, 1975

Klaniczay, T., ed., *Old Hungarian Literary Reader*, Budapest, 1985

Kniewald, D., *Feliks Petancic i Njegova Dela*, Srpska Akademija Nauka i Umetnosti, Posebna Izdanja (special edition), Belgrade, 1961

Kosztolnyk, Z., *Some Hungarian Theologians in the Late Renaissance*, Church History: Studies in Christianity and Culture, Vol. 57, March 1988

Labowsky, L., *Bessarion's Library and the Biblioteca Marciana*, Rome, 1979

Lee, E., *Sixtus IV and Men of Letters*, Rome, 1978

Maderus, J., ed., *De bibliotheci atque archivis virorum clarissimorum*, Helmestadt, 1641

Mailath, J., *Geschichte der Magyaren*, 5 vols, Vienna, 1829,

Martines, L., *Power and Imagination, City States in Renaissance Italy*, London, 1979

Mazal, O., *Königliche Bucherliebe, Die Bibliothek des Mathias Corvinus*, Graz, 1990

Mitchell, S., 'The Image of Hungary and of Hungarians in Italy, 1437–1526', unpublished thesis, University of London, 1994

Monfansani, J., *George of Trebizond, A Biography and a Study of his Rhetoric and Logic*, Leiden, 1976

Muresanu, C., *John Hunyadi, Defender of Christendom*, Iasi, Oxford, Portland, 2001

Naldi, N., 'De laudibus augustae bibliothecae, ad Mathiam Corvinum Pannoniae regem serenissimum, in P. Jaenichen', *Meletemata Thorunensia, etc.*, 3 vols, Torun, 1727–31

Neagu, C., *Servant of the Hungarian Renaissance, The Poetry and Prose of Nicolaus Olahus*, Bern, 2003

Opll, F., Perger, R., *Kaiser Friedrich III und die Wiener 1483–1485*, Vienna, 1993

Pasquale, R., *The Ducal Palace of Urbino, Its Architecture and Decoration*, London, 1969

Pius II, *Commentaries*, 2 vols, M. Meserve, M. Simonetta (eds) Cambridge, Mass., 2003

Pok, A., ed., *Ethnicity and Society in Hungary*, Budapest, 1990

Raj, T., Vasadi, P., *Jewish Life in Turkish Buda*, Budapest, 2003

Raven, J., ed., *Lost Libraries, The Destruction of Great Book Collections Since Antiquity*, London, 2004

Razso, G., *Die Feldzuge des Königs Matthias Corvinus in Niederosterreich 1477–1490*, Vienna, 1993

Richards, J., *A Journal of the Siege and Taking of Buda by the Imperial Army*, London, 1687

Roll, J., *Giovanni Dalmata*, Worms, 1994

Rouse, M. and R., *Cartolai, Illuminators and Printers in Fifteenth-Century Italy: The Evidence of the Ripoli Press*, Los Angeles, 1988

Rupp, G., *A Wavering Friendship: Austria and Russia 1876–1878*, Cambridge, 1941

Ryder, A., *The Kingdom of Naples under Alfonso the Magnanimous, The Making of a Modern State*, Oxford, 1976

Sakcinsky, I., *Kroatisch-Dalmatische Kunstler am Hofe des ungarischen Königs Mathias Corvinus*, Zagreb, 1860

Segel, H., *Renaissance Culture in Poland: The Rise of Humanism, 1470–1543*, London, 1989

Sop, N., *Ianus Pannonius, pjesme i epigrami*, Zagreb, 1951

Stangler, G., Csaky, M., Perger, R., Junger, A, eds, *Matthias Corvinus und die Renaissance in Ungarn 1458–1541*, Schallaburg, 1982

Stirling, W., *The Cloister Life of the Emperor Charles V*, London, 1852

Stoye, J., *Marsigli's Europe, 1680–1730, The Life and Times of Luigi Ferdinando Marsigli, Soldier and Virtuoso*, New Haven, Yale University Press, 1994

Szakaly, F., *Lodovico Gritti in Hungary 1529–1534, A Historical Insight into the Beginning of Turco-Habsburgian Rivalry*, Budapest, 1995

Szekely, G., Fugedi, E, eds, *La Renaissance et la Réformation en Pologne et en Hongrie*, Budapest, 1963

Thompson, J., ed., *The Medieval Library*, Chicago, 1959

Thorndike, L., *Science and Thought in the Fifteenth Century*, New York, 1929

Thuasne, L., *Djem-Sultan, étude sur la question de l'Orient à la fin du XV siècle*, Paris, 1892

Thuroczy, J., *Chronicle of the Hungarians*, transl. by F. Mantello, Bloomington, 1991

Von Mosel, I., *Geschichte der kaiserliche und königliche Hofbibliothek zu Wien*, Vienna, 1835

Waters, W. E., transl., *The Vespasiano Memoirs. Lives of Illustrious Men of the XVth Century*, Toronto 1997

Wiesflecker, H., *Kaiser Maximilian I. Das Reich, Österreich und Europa an der Wende zur Neuzeit*, Munich, 1971

Wilson, N. G., *From Byzantium to Italy, Greek Studies in the Renaissance*, Baltimore, 1992

Zinner, E., *Leben und Werken des Joh. Muller von Königsberg, genannt Regiomontanus*, Osnabruck 1968

Zombori, I., ed., *Zsigmond Jako. Tarsadalom, Egyhaz, Muvelodes: Tanulmanyok Erdely Tortenelmehez*, Budapest, 1997

Journals and Essays

Abulafia, D., 'Ferrante of Naples, the Statecraft of a Renaissance Prince', *History Today*, 45, February 1995

Adrianyi, G., 'Die kirchenpolitik des Matthias Corvinus (1458–1490)', *Ungarn-Jahrbuch*, 10, 1979

Betts, R., 'Social and Constitutional Development in Bohemia', *Past and Present*, 7, 1955

Birnbaum, M., 'Croatian Humanists at the Hungarian Court', *Journal of Croatian Studies*, 27, 1986

Csapodi-Gardonyi, K., 'Les Scripteurs de la Bibliothèque du Roi Mathias', Scriptorium, 17, 1963

Csontosi, J., 'Bildnisse des König's Mathias Corvinus under der Königin Beatrix in den Corvin codexen', *Ungarische Revue*, 1890

De Hevesy, A., 'Les Miniaturistes de Mathias Corvin', *Revue de l'Art Chrétien*, 1911

De la Mare, A., 'New Research on Humanistic Scribes in Florence', in A Garzelli, ed., Miniatura Fiorentina del Rinascimento 1440–1525, Florence, 1985

Domonkos, L., 'Janos Vitez, the Father of Hungarian Humanism, (1408–1472)', *The New Hungarian Quarterly*, 20, 1979

Fraknoi, W., 'Cardinal Joannes Carjavals legationen in Ungarn 1458–1461', *Ungarische Revue*, 1890,

Fraknoi, W., 'Miklos Modrusi, puspok elete, Munkai es Konyvtara', *Magyar Konyvszemle*, 5, 1897

Fryde, E., 'Lorenzo's Greek Manuscripts and in Particular his own Commissions', in M. Mallett, N. Mann, *Lorenzo the Magnificent, Culture and Politics*, London, 1996

Fugedi, E., 'A King for his Season', *The New Hungarian Quarterly*, 34, 1990

Gatto, K., 'Images of Women and Love in the Poetry of Janus Pannonius 1434–1472', in S. Vardy, A. Vardy, eds, *Triumph in Adversity. Studies in Hungarian Civilisation in Honor of Professor Ference Somogyi* . . . New York, Boulder, 1988

Goldschmidt, E., 'Preserved for Posterity, Some Remarks on Medieval Manuscripts', *The New Colophon: A Book Collector's Quarterly*, 2, 1950

Halasz, G., 'La Reine Marie de Hongrie', *Nouvelle Revue de Hongrie*, July 1937

Held, J., 'The Defense of Nandorfehervar in 1456, A Discussion of Controversial Issues', in S. Vardy, A Vardy, eds, *Society in Change. Studies in Honor of Bela K. Kiraly*, Boulder, Colo., New York, 1983

Hobson, A., 'Two Renaissance Bindings', *The Book Collector*, Autumn 1958

Huszti, J., 'Janus Pannonius', *Nouvelle Revue de Hongrie*, April 1934

Kardos, T., 'Janus Pannonius; Poet of the Hungarian Renaissance', *The New Hungarian Quarterly*, 14, 1973

Keresztury, D., 'Bibliotheca Corviniana', *The New Hungarian Quarterly*, 10, 1969

Kosztolnyk, Z., 'Some Hungarian theologians in the Late Renaissance', *Church History*, 57, March 1988

Kurti, L., 'The Ungaresca and Heyduck Music and Dance Tradition of Renaissance Europe', *The Sixteenth Century Journal*, 14, 1983

Lebegue, R., 'Un Humaniste Hongrois: André Dudith', *Nouvelle Revue de Hongrie*, November 1935

Miko, A., 'Divinus Hercules and Attila Secundus. King Matthias as Patron of Art', *The New Hungarian Quarterly*, 34, 1990

Odlozilik, O., 'Problems in the Reign of George of Podebrady', *The Slavonic and East European Review*, 20, 1941

Pallavicini, E., 'Elisabeth Szilagyi', *Nouvelle Revue de Hongrie*, October 1940

Razso, G., 'The Mercenary Army of King Matthias Corvinus', in J. Bak, B. Kiraly, eds, *War and Society in Eastern Central Europe*, Colombia, 1982

Raby, R., 'Mehmed the Conqueror's Greek Scriptorium', *Dumbarton Oaks Papers*, 37, 1983

Spruyt, B., '"En bruit d'estre bonne luteriene": Mary of Hungary (1505–58) and Religious Reform', *English Historical Review*, 109, 1994

Tilley, A., 'Humanism under Francis I', *English Historical Review*, 15, 1900

Thorndike, L., 'Lippus Brandolini de comparatione reipublicae et regni: An Unpublished Treatise of the Late Fifteenth Century in Comparative Political Science', *Political Science Quarterly*, 41, 1926

Index